Spying for the Peo

Since the end of the cold war, the operations of secret police informers have come under the media spotlight, and it is now common knowledge that vast internal networks of spies in the Soviet Union and East Germany were directed by the Communist Party. By contrast, very little historical information has been available on the covert operations of the security services in Mao Zedong's China. However, as Michael Schoenhals reveals in this intriguing and sometimes sinister account, public security was a top priority for the founders of the People's Republic, and agents were recruited from all levels of society to provide intelligence and ferret out "counterrevolutionaries." On the basis of hitherto classified archival records, the book tells the story of a vast surveillance and control apparatus through a detailed examination of the cultivation and recruitment of agents, their training, and their operational activities across an eighteen-year period from 1949 to 1967. These revelations add an entirely new dimension to modern China's troubled social and political history. Although the story may be safely set in the past, the development of human sources to sustain an oppressive domestic order is nothing if not eerily relevant to students of the present.

Professor Michael Schoenhals has researched the politics and history of the People's Republic of China for more than twenty-five years. Now at Lund University, his publications on the subject include *Doing Things with Words in Chinese Politics: Five Studies* (1992) and, with Roderick MacFarquhar, *Mao's Last Revolution* (2006). In 2003, the Swedish Research Council awarded him the prestigious "researcher of excellence" title.

Spying for the People

Mao's Secret Agents, 1949–1967

MICHAEL SCHOENHALS

Lund University

CAMBRIDGE
UNIVERSITY PRESS

CAMBRIDGE UNIVERSITY PRESS
Cambridge, New York, Melbourne, Madrid, Cape Town,
Singapore, São Paulo, Delhi, Mexico City

Cambridge University Press
32 Avenue of the Americas, New York, NY 10013-2473, USA

www.cambridge.org
Information on this title: www.cambridge.org/9781107603448

First published 2013

Printed in the United States of America

A catalog record for this publication is available from the British Library.

Library of Congress Cataloging in Publication Data
Schoenhals, Michael.
Spying for the people: Mao's secret agents, 1949–1967 / Michael Schoenhals.
pages cm
Includes bibliographical references and index.
1. Intelligence service – China – History – 20th century. 2. Secret service – China –
History – 20th century. 3. Spies – China – History – 20th century. 4. Domestic
intelligence – China – History – 20th century. 5. Internal security – China – History –
20th century. I. Title
JQ1509.5.I6S36 2012
327.1251009'045–dc23   2012013901

ISBN 978-1-107-01787-0 Hardback
ISBN 978-1-107-60344-8 Paperback

Contents

Illustrations follow page 14.

Acknowledgments

I had not meant to write *this* book. When I first approached the Swedish Research Council for funding nearly a decade ago, I had a different book in mind – one that had been gestated on the basis of dossiers on members of the general public maintained by China's Communist Party in the 1950s and 1960s. My plan was to perform an archaeological salvage operation, to fashion accounts of lives on file in an evolving – as I had come to think of it – dossier dictatorship. Much as I already knew what was in the dossiers, however, it quickly dawned on me that my understanding of their context of creation was woefully inadequate. Somehow, before I could confidently tell my stories, I needed to develop a grasp of the Maoist surveillance state – the system that had generated so much of my raw data. Credit for allowing me to begin to develop just such a grasp must go to the anonymous flea marketeer who sold me a tattered copy of the 1957 *Lectures on the Subject of Agent Work*. From its title in Chinese I was, at the time, not able to tell what this nondescript Ministry of Public Security booklet was about, but it would play a seminal role in the conception of the research on which my findings would come to rest. For accepting my Christopher Columbus–inspired defense ("Admittedly, Your Majesties, I have failed to present you with a new route to India. However, I am able to offer you instead an entirely new continent") of a line of inquiry resulting in a book very different from the one they had agreed to fund, I owe the board of directors of the Swedish Research Council a big debt of gratitude.

For help in locating obscure titles already in the public domain, a special thanks to Ann-Sofi Green and the helpful staff of our library here at Lund University, and to the librarians at the Universities Service Centre for China Studies at the Chinese University of Hong Kong. For critical comments on selected chapter drafts, a big thanks goes to Jeremy Brown, David Chambers, and Timothy Cheek. Thanks also to Christopher P. Atwood, Hans van de Veen, and Claire Conceison for answering my questions and to Ingalill Björk and Carlos Tuesta Soldevilla for managing my research funds and helping me with institutional contacts. For his invaluable close reading of my manuscript, his helpful querying, and his meticulous editing, a big and very special thanks to Alec Forss. For their professionalism and immensely appreciated editorial support, a heartfelt thanks to Marigold Acland, Sarika Narula, Helen Greenberg, and Camilla Knapp at Cambridge University Press.

Work on this book was supported by research grants from the Swedish Research Council, Lund University's Joint Faculties of Humanities and Theology, Carl Fredrik Lyngby's Bequest in Support of Scientific Research in the Field of Sinology, the Elisabeth Rausing Memorial Fund, Gyllenstiernska Krapperupsstiftelsen, and the Société Royale des Lettres de Lund. Its first chapter drafts were written in the congenial atmosphere of St. John's College, Vancouver, where for six months in the winter of 2004–5 it was my pleasure to be hosted by St. John's College and the Center for Chinese Research at the Institute of Asian Research, University of British Columbia. Research on instruments of social control and everyday life more broadly continued during my six months in the winter of 2005–6 as a visiting scholar at the Contemporary China Research Institute, Chinese Academy of Social Sciences, Beijing. The final chapter revisions were carried out in August 2011 – as an affiliate of the Centro d'Ateneo per la Promozione della Lingua e Cultura Italiana G. e C. Feltrinelli – under the giant magnolia tree at Villa Giulia, Gargnano, Italy.

Abbreviations

CCP	Chinese Communist Party
CMPS	Central Ministry of Public Security
CPSU	Communist Party of the Soviet Union
CSAD	Central Social Affairs Department
KGB	*Komitet Gosudarstvennoi Bezopastnosti* (Soviet security and intelligence service 1954–91)
NEMPS	Northeast Ministry of Public Security
NEPSC	Northeast Public Security Conference
NPSC	National Public Security Conference
PLA	People's Liberation Army
PRC	People's Republic of China

Introduction

On December 1, 1967, a meeting called by PRC Vice-Premier and Minister of Public Security Xie Fuzhi ordered the indefinite suspension of all operational use of agents (*teqing renyuan*), as well as the decommissioning of safe houses nationwide, and the launch of a general inquiry into whether the men and women who for the past eighteen years had been in China what *inoffizielle Mitarbeiter* were in East Germany had, in Xie's words, "done any bad stuff" (*zuole shenme huaishi*).[1] Four and a half decades later, historians still struggle to understand what triggered this drastic course of action. Was it simply how Xie chose to respond to Mao Zedong's Cultural Revolutionary wish to see the "public security, procuratory, and legal sectors beaten to a pulp"?[2] A few months earlier,

---

[1] *Jianguo yilai gongan gongzuo dashi yaolan* (*Survey of Major Events in Public Security Work Since the Founding of the Nation*) (Beijing: Qunzhong chubanshe, 2003), p. 319. A Google search for translations of the East German Ministry of State Security term *inoffizielle Mitarbeiter* in English-language texts quickly yields well over two dozen alternatives, including "unofficial informant," "confidential informant," "citizen informant," "part-time informer," "unofficial informer," "Political Police informer," "volunteer spy," "undercover collaborator," "unofficial collaborator," "informal collaborator," and "agent." In this book, the term "officer" (as in "public security officer," "operational officer," "field officer," or "desk officer") refers to a man or woman working for the public security organs of the PRC, while the term "agent" is used exclusively to refer to a person who is not him- or herself an employee of those same organs but has been recruited by an officer in support of an operation. The agent may serve as a passive provider of information or play a more proactive role, depending on the nature and particulars of the operation (see Chapter 2).

[2] The context in which an exasperated Mao had spoken on the subject is discussed in Michael Schoenhals, "'Why Don't We Arm the Left?': Mao's Culpability for the Cultural Revolution's 'Great Chaos' of 1967," *The China Quarterly*, No. 182, June 2005, pp. 277–300.

in July 1967, Xie had specifically tasked his deputies with exploring ways of meeting this stated desire on the part of the CCP Chairman.[3] Or was it prompted – in part or in full – by something completely different, such as a fatal loss of faith, perhaps, in the political integrity of lower-level public security officers and hence in the utility of the agent operations they ran? Or was the reason more simply cold war paranoia?

The ripple effects of the order were in any case profoundly disruptive, and an official ministry chronicle from 2003 surveying operational work in this period speaks of how it suffered nationwide.[4] Shanghai was one of the cities most affected. The municipal director of public security and his deputy holding the counterintelligence portfolio had already come under fire from Cultural Revolutionary rivals, who charged them with using secret agents to pursue highly dubious "revisionist" security ends.[5] Now it was implied that everything they and their predecessors had achieved on the covert front in China's largest metropolis needed to be reassessed.[6] Farther to the south, in the coastal province of Zhejiang, operational work came to an almost complete standstill. Here an inquiry outsourced to the armed forces targeted not just individuals but the very institution of the agent, as the political/semantic distinction was dropped between what until only recently had been the good agents of the PRC and the dreaded *tewu* of its enemies.[7] In an official inquiry report entitled "Views on the Thorough Beating to a Pulp of So-Called 'Domestic Agents'," the PLA in Zhejiang claimed to have unearthed evidence of a vast underground network of agents that had infiltrated the entire provincial public security apparatus. The report further asserted that since the founding of the

---

[3] Shi Yizhi, *Wo zai gonganbu shi nian* (*My Ten Years in the Ministry of Public Security*) ([Beijing]: privately printed, 2002), p. 18.

[4] *Jianguo yilai gongan*, p. 319.

[5] Shanghai shi gonganju bangongshi zhengzhibu nongbaochu geming zaofandui, ed., *Dadao litong waiguode fangeming xiuzhengzhuyi fenzi Wang Jian* (*Down with Counter-revolutionary Revisionist Element Wang Jian Who Maintains Illicit Links with Foreign Countries*) (Shanghai, 1967), pp. 12–13.

[6] "Zhou zongli jiejian di shiwu ci quanguo gongan gongzuo [*sic*] huiyi quanti tongzhi de jianghua" (Premier Zhou's Address to All Comrades Attending the 15th National Public Security Conference) [5.30–7.30 p.m. on February 8, 1971], p. 19.

[7] The negatively charged term *tewu* does not have a good equivalent in the English language. As employed by public security officers in Mao Zedong's China, it was meant to refer, often with reasonable precision, to operatives or assets of hostile intelligence services, but in popular discourse and the CCP media it tended to become simply a term of abuse thrown indiscriminately at just about anyone suspected of maintaining links with perceived external enemies of the PRC. Where references to *tewu* are made or quoted in this book, because of the term's inherently fuzzy meaning, it has been mostly left untranslated.

PRC, the people of the province had in reality been at the mercy of a "dictatorship of agents"![8] In colluding with their so-called revisionist controllers, these men and women had done far more than just "bad stuff," if the report was to be believed. By the end of 1969, the green light had been given for agents in Zhejiang to be "handed over to the masses." According to one account, there were widespread cases of outed agents being denounced, beaten, and subjected to public humiliation.[9] In the rest of China, including where agents had been dispatched overseas, the situation was not very different. The English-speaking actor Ying Ruocheng, who since 1952 had served the Beijing municipal Bureau of Public Security as an agent reporting on the activities of members of the foreign expatriate community in the capital, and who would one day become vice-minister of culture, was arrested together with his wife in 1968 and imprisoned for three years.[10] One highly placed CMPS officer recalled in 2001 that "No small number of secret operational assets – people who had managed to penetrate the enemy's innermost – were summoned to be, as it was called, investigated, or disposed of in secret, or publicly exposed."[11]

The events of 1967–69 all but closed the chapter on the use of agents by public security organs in Mao's China. Only cautiously, at first, did a policy reversal get underway in 1971, when Premier Zhou Enlai (credited by historians with building up the CCP's intelligence and security services half a century earlier) insisted that "In the past, although some bad people did manage to worm their way in among them, our agents and 'eyes and ears' did on the whole play no small number of positive roles."[12] At the 15th NPSC, which convened in early 1971 and marked the first such national gathering of senior public security officers in over five years, Zhou ordered provincial and municipal leaders to "embark on a level-headed summary [of work in this field]."[13] By 1973, a new CMPS leadership was reaffirming that secret agents constituted legitimate

---

[8] Cheng Chao and Wei Haoben, eds., *Zhejiang "wenge" jishi (1966.5–1976.10)* (*Record of Events in Zhejiang's "Cultural Revolution"* [*May 1966–October 1976*]) ([Hangzhou]: Zhejiang fangzhi bianjibu, 1989), pp. 117–18, 133.

[9] Ibid., pp. 117–18, 133, 165.

[10] Ying Ruocheng and Claire Conceison, *Voices Carry: Behind Bars and Backstage during China's Cultural Revolution and Reform* (Lanham, MD: Rowman & Littlefield, 2009), p. 3.

[11] Sun Mingshan, ed., *Lishi shunjian II* (*Moments in History II*) (Beijing: Qunzhong chubanshe, 2001), p. 552.

[12] "Zhou zongli jiejian," p. 19.

[13] Ibid.

and important instruments of operational activity.[14] China's most senior active military officer, Marshal Ye Jianying, who addressed the 16th NPSC in the spring of 1973, spoke positively of public security work being in the midst of a crucial "turnaround."[15] In practice, this turnaround included a drive to recruit new agents, their deployment now viewed as "urgently called for in the present situation."[16] Even though it would be another three years before Mao's death in the autumn of 1976, the U-turn heralded, in terms of its historical significance, the beginning of the post-Mao era. As such, however, it falls outside the temporal scope of this study.

Attempted here is a historical examination and analysis of agent work in the first eighteen years of the PRC – as an aspect of *domestic* politics, the operation of the state, and what in the Western press at the time was called "life under communism."[17] (Readers expecting to read the story of Mao's secret agents on intelligence and espionage missions abroad will be disappointed: the battle of wits here takes place on the home turf, by and large, even when it pits the unsung heroes of the CMPS against the operatives of the American and British "imperialists."[18]) It seeks to cover agent activity, historical context, operational doctrine, and realities on the ground. What were agents in the early PRC and what were they supposed to achieve? What qualities and qualifications were they meant to possess? More fundamentally, *who* were they? How were they recruited and run? How were they rewarded? How were their services discontinued? By providing empirically grounded answers to questions like these, their story illustrates just how domestic agent operations mixed uniquely Chinese characteristics with those generic to the work processes

---

[14] *Jianguo yilai gongan*, pp. 335, 348–49.

[15] Ibid., p. 350; Ye Jianying, "Zai di shiliu ci quanguo gongan huiyi shang de jianghua" (Speech at the 16th National Public Security Conference) [afternoon of May 5, 1973], p. 4.

[16] Zhongguo renmin jiefangjun Beijing tielu fenju gongan fenchu junguanzu, "Guanyu ermu jianshe gongzuo de shixing yijian" (Tentative Views on How to Develop Eyes and Ears) [February 26, 1973], p. 1. The "present situation" refers to the post-1971 thaw, described in Roderick MacFarquhar and Michael Schoenhals, *Mao's Last Revolution* (Cambridge, MA: Belknap Press of Harvard University Press, 2006), pp. 345–54, 373–78.

[17] *Time* magazine, October 8, 1956.

[18] On the subject of CCP intelligence operations overseas in the Mao era, see Michael Schoenhals, "Zhongguo gongchandang zhongyang diaochabu jianshi" (Brief History of the Central Investigation Department of the Chinese Communist Party), in Zhu Jiamu, ed., *Dangdai zhongguo yu tade fazhan daolu* (*Contemporary China and Its Development Road*) (Beijing: Dangdai Zhongguo chubanshe, 2010), pp. 252–72.

of all state agencies employing covert means to maintain and defend state power.

Bone of Contention

Agents had been a bone of contention in Mao's China well before the decision in 1967 to suspend their use. Critics had initially argued that their covert deployment in a People's Republic was morally reprehensible; they later argued that it violated the spirit of the Maoist "mass line" before finally insisting that it bore all the hallmarks of revisionism. Advocates, on the other hand, consistently maintained that the use of agents was indispensable – that they were uniquely effective instruments for combating enemies of the socialist new order.[19] Past experience, they pointed out, had proven their value as providers of all-important human intelligence. Hence, when the power and influence of the advocates peaked, in the mid-1950s, China's national railroad network alone saw more than 10,000 public security agents serving in a variety of capacities.[20]

At the time of the founding of the PRC, some senior public security officers had favored the recruitment and deployment of secret agents in both rural and urban society.[21] Others were skeptical, claiming that there was no clear operational purpose for them to serve in the countryside. Agent running, they added, was in any case simply too sophisticated a praxis for the average rural public security officer to competently manage. Had the skeptics reasoned in terms of modernity, they might have pronounced it incompatible with "widespread rural illiteracy, technological backwardness, bureaucratic inefficiency and incompetence of alarming proportions," which was what the political scientist Vivienne Shue in *The Reach of the State* identified as ubiquitous to so much of Mao's China.[22] Not least, the *absolute* clandestinity that running agents necessitated would have clashed head on with rural social realities and been

---

[19] *"Teqing gongzuo" jiangyi* (*Lectures on the Subject of Agent Work*) (Beijing: Zhongyang renmin gongan xueyuan, 1957), pp. 1–2.

[20] Wang Jinxiang, "Zai di qi ci quanguo tielu gongan baowei gongzuo huiyi shang de baogao" (Report to the 7th National Conference on Railroad Public Security and Protection Work) [March 18, 1955], p. 25.

[21] Wang Jinxiang, "Dongbei gongan baowei gongzuo qingkuang yu jinhou renwu" (The Situation and Future Tasks of Public Security and Protection Work in the Northeast), *Gongan baowei gongzuo* (*Public Security and Protection Work*), No. 17, February 15, 1950, p. 12.

[22] Vivienne Shue, *The Reach of the State: Sketches of the Chinese Body Politic* (Stanford, CA: Stanford University Press, 1988), p. 47.

practically impossible to achieve. The skeptics among the decision makers eventually prevailed: in due course the fielding of agents by rural bureaus of public security was curbed. At the Central People's Public Security Academy in Beijing in 1957, officer cadets were told that "in ordinary rural village areas, work is to be carried out by relying on the masses, without any further deployment of agents."[23] For most of the eighteen years covered by this book (with a handful of exceptions, to be noted in due course), agents served only as instruments of *urban* operational activity.

Other limitations imposed on the fielding of agents also found their way into CMPS doctrine. In urban China, below the national and provincial levels, only duly empowered officers in municipal bureaus of public security and their branches (*not* local police officers working out of ordinary police stations) had the right to recruit and run agents. Here a practical problem presented itself in the form of the occasional need to recruit as agents those who Mao called the "running dogs of imperialism . . . the Guomindang reactionaries and their accomplices."[24] Given how the CCP constantly exhorted ordinary citizens to inform on anyone acting in the least bit suspicious, clandestine work under these conditions proved none too easy; hence, proponents of agent operations quietly encouraged public security officers to, when necessary, tactically misrepresent their actions to "the masses." In 1954, CCP Politburo member Peng Zhen suggested to more than 800 public security officers from all over China attending the 6th NPSC that "if you are afraid the masses will alert the enemy [to your operation], then you may tell them there's nothing problematic about [the person they suspect] and the masses will back off. The masses will take our word for it, they will not be overly suspicious."[25] But remarks like this had a way of backfiring, given the ease with which they could be construed ex post facto as "shielding bad people." In 1968, those

---

[23] "*Teqing gongzuo*," pp. 14–15. For a brief summary of general problems plaguing operational work in China's rural villages at the time, see Gonganbu erju bangongshi, "Nongcun zhencha poan zhong de yixie wenti" (Some Problems Affecting the Operational Cracking of Cases in Rural Villages), *Renmin gongan* (*People's Public Security*), No. 13, December 8, 1952, November 20, 1956, p. 7.

[24] *Selected Works of Mao Tsetung*, 5 vols. (Beijing: Foreign Languages Press, 1965, 1977), Vol. 4, pp. 417–18.

[25] *Guanyu Mao Zedong tongzhi wuchanjieji zhuanzheng xueshuo he sufan gongzuo fangzhen luxian de xuexi cailiao* (*Materials for the Study of Comrade Mao Zedong's Doctrine on the Dictatorship of the Proletariat and Policy and Line in the Elimination of Counterrevolutionaries*) (Beijing: Zhongyang zhengfa ganbu xuexiao zhengce falü jiaoyanshi, 1960), p. 380.

who had ousted Peng from power went so far as to claim that during his fifteen-year tenure as mayor of Beijing, the capital's Bureau of Public Security had effectively served as an undeclared "station" running *tewu* and spies "for the United States and Chiang Kai-shek"![26] Arrested agents such as Ying Ruocheng, who had associated with countless foreigners and whose father, Sir Ignatius Ying, lived on Taiwan, supposed that they had been thrown into prison not simply as "suspected spies of this or that foreign power" but, more importantly, because they were political pawns tied to the fate of their masters.[27]

In addition to the difficulties posed by their covert deployment in urban society at large, the recruitment and running of agents inside the ubiquitous socialist "work units" (*danwei*) after 1949 was another cause for concern.[28] In the absence of effective conflict resolution mechanisms, the legitimate intra-*danwei* compartmentalization of information concerning agents and resident operational officers working as agent handlers under the cover of another occupation developed into a latent source of friction. Inquiries conducted by the CMPS in the mid-1950s found that quite a few agent handlers behaved arrogantly, with an exaggerated sense of their own importance. Not surprisingly, when their covers or the covers of their agents were blown, they were routinely accused by their ordinary work unit colleagues – rightly or wrongly, in public or in private – of the twin sins of "isolationism" (*gulizhuyi*) and "mysticism" (*shenmizhuyi*). While in theory these deplorable -isms signified a serious failure to keep those with a *legitimate* need to know in the loop (and public security officers had it impressed upon them to not trust unconditionally even "comrades who've been around for many years"[29]), inside many *danwei* bitter complaints were also voiced by those who, from a purely operational point of view, did *not* have such a "need" but felt politically entitled to one. During the CCP's "free airing of views" and rectification campaign in the spring of 1957, some agents – to the fury of not just operational officers but also members of the party's higher echelon – turned whistle-blower

[26] "Beijing shi 'wenhua dageming' dashiji" (Record of Major Events in the "Great Cultural Revolution" in Beijing), *Beijing dangshi ziliao tongxun* (*Beijing Party History Materials Newsletter*), supplement No. 18, June 1987, pp. 9–10.

[27] Ying and Conceison, *Voices Carry*, pp. 3, 54–55.

[28] On "work units" (i.e., places of employment), see Xiaobo Lü and Elizabeth J. Perry, eds., *Danwei: The Changing Chinese Workplace in Historical and Comparative Perspective* (Armonk, NY: M. E. Sharpe, 1997).

[29] Zhang Youyu, "Zai huiyi shang de jianghua" (Speech at the Conference), *Renmin gongan zengkan* (*People's Public Security: Supplement*), No. 20, December 25, 1950, p. 14.

and exposed the system of which they were or had been part, believing it to be partially responsible for what Mao Zedong himself in a recent speech had called "defects and mistakes in our work."[30] Needless to say, accused of leaking state secrets and endangering national security, they found themselves front-line targets of the ensuing anti-Rightist campaign.

Finally, making agent work even more of a contentious issue was the corrupting influence of the power, vested in the office of the handler with his or her stable of agents, to bend the rules of proper proletarian conduct in order to prevail on the covert front. During the early years of regime consolidation, senior CCP leaders contended that the occasional mismanagement of this power was due in part to the fact that "a majority of our cadres lack experience and knowledge of how to utilize [agents]."[31] But serious problems soon arose with alarming frequency in the course of operations where agents were used to monitor domestic dissent or target the activities of hostile intelligence services on Chinese soil. Initially, the CMPS was prepared to frame its criticism in more comradely terms: officers had allowed themselves to be "*confused* by the 'achievements' of agents" and "*deceived* by their tricks of the trade: 'boasting, flattering, and cheating.'"[32] This softer tone was to change, however, as increasingly higher professional demands were placed on officers. By the early 1960s, corruption had been identified internally as endemic to many parts of urban China's public security sector. A National Conference on Political Protection Work held in 1964 lambasted the misuse of operational funds, misappropriation of confiscated property, and other examples of what was referred to as the influence on operational officers of a "bourgeois *tewu* work style."[33]

None of the charges that accompanied the nationwide suspension of the use of agents by public security organs in December 1967 were, in other words, entirely new. New was only the position of the CMPS leadership – one that represented a significant departure from Minister of

---

[30] *Selected Works of Mao Tsetung*, Vol. 5, p. 410.

[31] Wang Jinxiang, "Zai dongbei zhengzhi jingji baowei chuzhang yewu gongzuo huiyi shang de baogao" (Report to Vocational Work Meeting of Political and Economic Protection Office Chiefs from the Northeast), *Gongan baowei gongzuo*, No. 19, September 15, 1950, p. 24.

[32] Guofang daxue dangshi dangjianshi, ed., *Zhonggong dangshi jiaoxue cankao ziliao* (*Reference Material for Teaching CCP History*), 27 vols. (Beijing: Guofang daxue, 1986), Vol. 19, p. 256. Emphasis added.

[33] *Jianguo yilai gongan*, p. 280.

Public Security Luo Ruiqing's appraisal from 1958 concerning the first nine years of PRC public security work:

[There are those who want to] make out operational work to be something bad, applying a kind of logic that results in a formula like this one: operational work equals cases involving agents, cases involving agents equal isolationism and mysticism, isolationism and mysticism equal an ideological line that is bourgeois, which makes operational work bourgeois stuff [*dongxi*]. That public security and protection organs engage in operational work is due to the influence of the bourgeoisie, which points at the existence of a two-line struggle – and so on and so forth. *This kind of logic is incorrect.*[34]

A decade later, Luo's successors were to maintain that the logic of the detractors had in fact been entirely correct.[35] Significant elements and modus operandi of operational work, they argued, had simply not delivered against changing policy objectives.

Missing Dimension

In the introduction to their seminal 1984 study *The Missing Dimension: Governments and Intelligence Communities in the Twentieth Century*, Christopher Andrew and David Dilks lamented the fact that academic historians frequently tended to either ignore intelligence altogether or treat it as of little importance.[36] While after 9/11 this general observation may no longer hold true, the fact that not one of the seventy book titles reviewed in *The Journal of Intelligence History* since its first issue in 2001 deals with Chinese intelligence or intelligence in China forces one to conclude that academic historians *of China* are, a quarter of a century

---

[34] Luo Ruiqing, "Guanyu jiunian douzheng zongjie de jige wenti" (On How to Summarize Nine Years of Struggle), *Gongan jianshe* (*Public Security Construction*), No. 277, December 1, 1958, p. 25. Emphasis added.

[35] Cf. *Jianguo yilai gongan*, p. 324.

[36] Christopher Andrew and David Dilks, eds., *The Missing Dimension: Governments and Intelligence Communities in the Twentieth Century* (London: Macmillan, 1984), p. 1. In a paper given in 2002, Andrew declared, "I stand by my claim" that "intelligence 'is still denied its proper place in studies of the Cold War.'" He went on to suggest that part of the reason "is the relative inaccessibility of the intelligence archive by comparison with other primary sources. *The root of the problem, however, is cognitive dissonance* – the difficulty of adapting traditional notions of international relations and political history to take account of the information now available about the role of intelligence agencies" (emphasis added); Christopher Andrew, "Intelligence, International Relations and 'Under-theorization,'" in L. V. Scott and Peter Jackson, eds., *Understanding Intelligence in the Twenty-First Century: Journeys in Shadows* (London: Routledge, 2004), p. 32.

later, still not taking much of a professional interest in (or contributing significantly to the literature on) intelligence.[37]

Does this really matter? Yes it does, but for reasons that are not immediately evident. The biggest problem is not that insufficient attention has been paid by historians to, for example, operational work or agents per se, but rather that the absence of the intelligence dimension from history does "distort our understanding of [history's] other, accessible dimensions."[38] Work on the present book has been driven by a conviction that our understanding of the Maoist system of governance, for instance, as well as our appreciation of the history of everyday life (*Alltagsgeschichte*) in China after 1949, urgently need to be enriched by drawing on what Wesley K. Wark calls intelligence's "under-exploited and unrealized...usable past."[39] To begin with, we need to illuminate the role of agents – the men and women whom the CCP's first public security director in Beijing referred to, tongue in cheek, as the "people's *tewu*" – and add it to the list of what a best-selling U.S. textbook calls the "techniques for making

---

[37] The exceptions that deserve to be mentioned are Frederic Wakeman, Jr.'s magisterial *Spymaster: Dai Li and the Chinese Secret Service* (Berkeley: University of California Press, 2003), which deals with Republican China, and political scientist Michael Dutton's prize-winning *Policing Chinese Politics: A History* (Durham, NC: Duke University Press, 2005), marketed as a "history of public security in China" from the 1920s to the present. Some of the key data on which Dutton's discussion of public security in the PRC rests cannot be independently verified: in his preface he asks his readers to "simply...take their own leap of faith about the veracity of [the highly classified] material" used. Needless to say, readers of a work of serious historical scholarship must *never* take such a "leap of faith," since how can one assess a historian's interpretation of his or her "material" and "documents" if one is not told what they are? Also, how can one judge whether a particular analysis of a source is right or wrong, perceptive or muddle-headed, unless one knows what that source is? In spite of this, Dutton excels in the realm of sophisticated postcolonial theorizing, and his analysis is interesting and readable in its own right. Both Wakeman's and Dutton's studies are, it deserves to be further pointed out, fundamentally different from books such as Roger Faligot and Remi Kauffer's *Kang Sheng et les services secrets chinois* (Paris: Robert Laffont, 1987) or John Byron and Robert Pack's *The Claws of the Dragon: Kang Sheng – The Evil Genius Behind Mao – and His Legacy of Terror in People's China* (New York: Simon & Schuster, 1992). These two nonacademic best-sellers were based on what their authors claimed was sensational "inside information," but once its provenance could be independently verified, much of it proved to be highly inaccurate, derived from secondary or tertiary sources, inadequately analyzed, and often simply misunderstood.

[38] Andrew and Dilks, *Missing Dimension*, p. 1.

[39] Christopher Andrew, Richard J. Aldrich, and Wesley K. Wark, eds., *Secret Intelligence: A Reader* (London: Routledge, 2009), p. 530. On the subject of *Alltagsgeschichte*, see Alf Lüdtke, ed., *The History of Everyday Life: Reconstructing Historical Experiences and Ways of Life* (Princeton, NJ: Princeton University Press, 1995).

the system work."[40] Those of us who "study China for a living" (to borrow Elizabeth Perry's turn of phrase[41]) must find room in our analyses of Maoism as a way of life for the informers, collaborators, and secret police assets – to name but three of the kinds of social movement participants that our studies of *guanxi* still shun and our analyses of *danwei* prior to the advent of reform largely ignore.[42]

Admittedly, the obstacles standing in the way of an independent scholarly endeavor in this direction are formidable. In December 1981, the CCP issued a blanket ban on the publication of historical writing deemed to be potentially "detrimental to the normal conduct of our present and future intelligence and protection work."[43] The new century has seen the controlled release by the CCP of the occasional declassified document from the covert front, but requests from Chinese academic historians for permission to conduct rigorous research on the topic are quietly rebuffed by the powerful custodians of the relevant archives. Quasi-official memoirs and biographies of a handful of early CCP spymasters have appeared in print in China, but anyone making use of them is well advised to bear in mind the words of the CIA analyst Olivia Halebian, who, in a 1965 review of Soviet intelligence revelations, wrote: "We must assume that all memoirs, biographies, and historical studies of the . . . intelligence services are prepared with the aid of disinformation experts."[44]

---

[40] Kenneth Lieberthal, *Governing China: From Revolution Through Reform* (New York: W. W. Norton, 1995), pp. 170–82.

[41] In Jeffrey N. Wasserstrom and Elizabeth J. Perry, eds., *Popular Protest & Political Culture in Modern China*, 2nd ed. (Boulder, CO: Westview Press, 1994), p. 3.

[42] On this topic in general, see the classic study by Gary T. Marx, "Thoughts on a Neglected Category of Social Movement Participant: The Agent Provocateur and the Informant," *American Journal of Sociology*, Vol. 80, No. 2 (1974), pp. 402–42. Collaboration in Republican China – between ordinary (and some far from ordinary) Chinese and their Japanese occupiers, rather than between selected participants in social or political movements and the institutions those very movements sought to destroy, undermine, or otherwise resist – has already been the subject of some unsettling research, most notably by historian Timothy Brook. See his groundbreaking study *Collaboration: Japanese Agents and Local Elites in Wartime China* (Cambridge, MA: Harvard University Press, 2005).

[43] Zhonggong zhongyang xuanchuanbu bangongting, ed., *Dang de xuanchuan gongzuo wenjian xuanbian* (*Selected Documents on the Party's Propaganda Work*), 4 vols. (Beijing: Zhonggong zhongyang danxiao chubanshe, 1994), Vol. 2, p. 984.

[44] Olivia Halebian, "New Light on Old Spies: A Review of Recent Soviet Intelligence Revelations," Center for the Study of Intelligence, https://www.cia.gov/library/center-for-the-study-of-intelligence/kent-csi/vol9no4/html/v09i4a09p_0001.htm (accessed February 2, 2012).

Serendipity, then, is what in the end has made academic research on the subject possible. Were it not for chance discoveries in flea markets and the back rooms of antiquarian bookshops in urban China of archival material that has *not* been subject to positive information management, this book would – to borrow an expression coined by Richard J. Aldrich – be little more than that of "an official historian, albeit once removed."[45] Only by augmenting the information that has ended up in the public domain courtesy of the CCP's official declassification regime with uncensored primary data (including what the syllabi of cutting-edge courses on Chinese social history at North American and European universities now, for want of a better term, refer to as "garbage materials"[46]) has the quasi-independent constitution and prefiguration of a documentary record become possible.[47] This has involved systematically contrasting the norm (spelled out in textbooks and policy directives) against the reality on the ground as documented in operational postmortems and similar texts once intended exclusively for in-house consumption by officers with a need to know. A mere fraction of the many texts actually consulted in this process are listed in the bibliography at the end of this book.

What the underexploited past of the intelligence dimension of Mao's China brings to light is *not* a sensational, hitherto secret history: it is not argued here that operational work played a role behind the scenes so decisive as to necessitate a reassessment of everything previously presumed known. But what an understanding, for example, of the work performed

---

[45] Richard J. Aldrich, *The Hidden Hand: Britain, America and Cold War Secret Intelligence* (London: John Murray, 2001), p. 5.

[46] The relevant branch of the human sciences devoted to the study of such materials is sometimes called "garbology" by its practitioners, most of whom are younger historians and graduate students of PRC history. Sinological garbology, a rigorous but undertheorized field still in its infancy, is not to be confused with the general academic discipline by the same name (see en.wikipedia.org/wiki/Garbology) or with what spies and journalists do as they rummage through other people's waste in search of information. In "Finding and Using Grassroots Historical Sources from the Mao Era," social historian Jeremy Brown rightly cautions against fetishizing the Chinese urban flea market as "an unconventional source for historical materials," but suggests that when duly *"supplemented and corroborated by other sources"* (emphasis added), flea market garbage materials do "have the potential to fundamentally shift the way we view the period [of Mao's China]"; http://dissertationreviews.wordpress.com/2010/12/15/finding-and-using-grassroots-historical-sources-from-the-mao-era-by-jeremy-brown/ (accessed February 2, 2012).

[47] Where these data include the actual *names* of agents or operational targets, I have in quoted passages replaced these names with letters in the English alphabet (e.g., "agent A," "suspect M") or, in a handful of instances, simply left them out altogether.

by informers (and it has to be stressed that far from all agents served this particular "enabling" intelligence function) permits is, at the very least, a significant refinement of existing narratives of relations between the authorities and domestic dissent, between the two competing centers of political power in Beijing and Taipei, between the ruling Communist Party and the PRC's small so-called democratic parties, and between the central government in Beijing and the (ethnic minority) communities along the national perimeter. It is one thing to surmise or appreciate in the broadest of terms that intelligence on "persons of operational interest" was systematically developed using covert human sources, but it is quite another to acquire a detailed picture of just *how* this was done. Once it is better understood, the role of penetration agents alone holds the key to far more accurate and fuller academic accounts of Chinese politics and society between 1949 and 1967. A suitable analogy can be drawn with historical writing about World War II: prior to the 1973 revelation of the contributions to the Allied war effort made by code breakers and intelligence services, historians had tended to describe and explain the progress of the war in a one-dimensional way. This account had to be drastically revised when it transpired that many of the assumed causal relationships were nothing of the kind, and that what had really triggered and precipitated some events had been aspects related to the conduct of covert operations hitherto altogether unknown. Mao's social and political revolution may have been more modest in scale than the violent conflict of global magnitude, but its intelligence dimension – today no longer a known unknown – in many respects exerted no less of an influence on its tortured progress.

Perhaps the most intriguing finding to tentatively emerge from a study of agents in Mao's China does not relate to their utilization as providers of information, nor does it derive from how their – no doubt suspected – presence in this passive role may have affected the behavior of the communities in which they moved.[48] Rather, it derives from the aggressive (and in due course increasingly prioritized) deployment of agents provocateurs as a proactive response to any number of real and imagined political threats. In *Anatomy of a Dictatorship*, historian Mary Fulbrook suggested that *inoffizielle Mitarbeiter* in East Germany may at times have pushed target groups or networks to more extreme positions with the intent of creating the "conditions for the arrest of dissidents which might

---

[48] Steve Hewitt, *Snitch! A History of the Modern Intelligence Informer* (New York: Continuum, 2010), p. 6.

otherwise have been avoidable."[49] In Mao's China, active measures of a
similar kind were tacitly endorsed by the CMPS. Regulations on paper
may have strictly banned "letting agents incite people to commit a crime
and [in the process] fabricating bogus cases wronging the innocent" and
cautioned officers against tasking agents with "luring the enemy to commit crimes or playing a key role in this context."[50] But as part of their
basic training, operational officer cadets had it impressed upon them that
"we need to put in place agents or penetration agents in order to be able
to *actively promote the unfolding of a case*, in a timely fashion expose the
political scheming of the enemy, and thus effectively attack the enemy."[51]
And provocation no doubt served a particularly useful role in "promoting
the unfolding of a case" where a senior CCP figure had decided a priori
that the crime was one of counterrevolution but the evidence needed to
prove this was nonexistent. A *Red Flag* editorialist and Central Committee ghostwriter – the son-in-law of Wang Chaobei, a legendary figure in
pre-1949 CCP intelligence operations in Northwest China – famously formulated what his detractors in 1967 would refer to as the "three sinister
fundamental principles of survival in PRC politics," the most important
of which was to be tactically "adept at leading the other side to commit
mistakes."[52] For those bold enough, there would have been few better
ways of doing just that than by instructing their agents to provoke, con-
spire, deceive, and feed false information to those who stood in their way.
As historians, we neglect the profound implications of this at our peril.

[49] Cf. Mary Fulbrook, *Anatomy of a Dictatorship: Inside the GDR 1949–1989* (Oxford: Oxford University Press, 1995), p. 51.
[50] Liaoning sheng gonganting dangzu, "Guanyu '1956 nian quansheng gongan gongzuo jiben zongjie he 1957 nian gongzuo renwu' de baogao" (Report on "Basic Summary of Province-Wide Public Security Work in 1956 and Tasks for 1957"), *Gongan jianshe*, No. 186, April 15, 1957, p. 9; Hunan sheng Xiangxi tujiazu miaozu zizhizhou gonganju, "Guanyu Yongshun, Longshan, Jishou deng di pohuo 'Zhongguo minzhudang ren-min geming weiyuanhui' fangeming anjian de zongjie baogao" (Summing Up Report on Cracking the Case of the Counterrevolutionary "China Democratic Party People's Revolutionary Committee" in Yongshun, Longshan, and Jishou), *Gongan jianshe*, No. 220, March 10, 1958, p. 20.
[51] "Teqing gongzuo," p. 12.
[52] Tang Shaojie, personal communication (based on a conversation with Red Guard leader Kuai Dafu), Tsinghua University, December 2010; *Changcheng (The Great Wall)*, No. 2, December 3, 1967. The two other fundamental principles were "there is no honesty to speak of in political struggles" and the imperative of "organizing in accord-ance with the principle of absolute loyalty."

FIGURE 1. Luo Ruiqing, minister of public security, addressing a session of the Chinese Peoples Political Consultative Conference in 1951

FIGURE 2. Xie Fuzhi, minister of public security from 1959 to 1972

FIGURE 3. The Central Ministry of Public Security in the early 1950s

FIGURE 4. Beijing police officers

瀋陽市公安局
關於建立特情工作的方法

茲將瀋陽市公安局關於建立特情工作的方法，發給你們參考。
東北人民政府公安部
一九五〇年十月五日

工廠企業中的特情工作是怎樣開始的？

一、開始遇到了那些問題：

1、思想上認為特情工作是比較難的工作，這方面情況了解的不多，又無經驗，也缺辦法。不知從何着手才好。有的認為着手偵察對象，才來建立特情人員；有的認為建立特情應該是內綫，有的認為建立特情是為了破案。經過研究討論，認識上才逐漸一致了。

2、對工廠企業員工的情況了解了那不多，認為工廠企業中建立特情困難較多，第一種特情力量短時間內建立不起來，經過實踐，有困難，也有辦法，可以作。

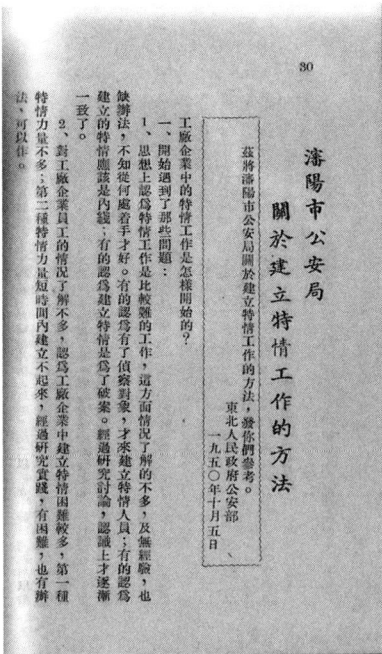

FIGURE 5. "Agent Work Initiation Procedures," as drawn up by the Shenyang Bureau of Public Security

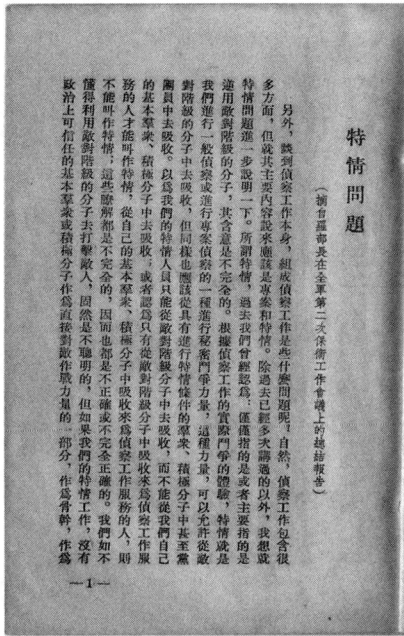

特情問題
（摘自羅瑞卿在全軍第二次保衛工作會議上的總結報告）

另外，幾個偵察工作本身、組織偵察工作是些什麼問題呢？自然，偵察工作包含很多方面，但說其主要內容說就是專案和特情。我想就特情問題進一步說明一下。所謂特情，過去我們曾認為，僅僅指的是或者主要指的是我們敵對階級的分子，其含意是不完全的。根據偵察工作的當前鬥爭的體驗，特情就是我們進行一般偵察或進行專案偵察的一種進行秘密鬥爭力量。這種力量，可以允許從敵對階級的分子中去吸收，但同樣也應該由我們自己的基本羣衆或積極分子中去吸收。以過去的特情採用從敵對階級分子中去吸收，而不能從我們自己的基本羣衆、積極分子中去吸收，或者認為只有從敵對階級中去吸收為偵察工作服務的人才叫做特情，從自己的基本羣衆、積極分子中吸收為偵察工作服務，這些部份，就不能叫做特情，這種說法，因而也都是不正確或不完全正確的。我們如不能利用我們的基本羣衆或積極分子去打擊敵人，固然是不聰明的；但如果我們的特情工作，沒有懂得利用敵對階級的分子作為直接對敵作戰力量的部分，作為骨幹，作為政治上可信任的基本羣衆或積極分子作為

—1—

FIGURE 6. A ministerial report on agent work (1952)

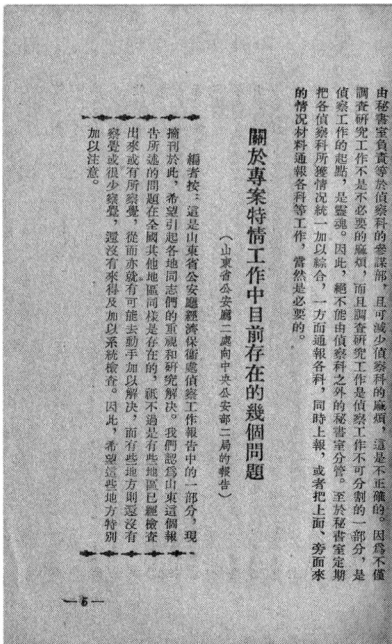

關於專案特情工作中目前存在的幾個問題
（山東省公安廳第二處向中央公安部二局的報告）

由秘書室負責等於偵察科的麻煩，且可減少偵察科的麻煩，這是不正確的。因為不僅調查研究工作不是不必要的麻煩，而且調查研究工作是偵察工作不可分割的一部分，是偵察工作的起點，是靈魂。因此，絕不能由偵察科之外的秘書室分管。至於秘書室定期把各偵察科所獲情況統一加以綜合，一方面通報各科，同時上報，或者把上面、旁面來的情況材料通報各科等工作，當然是必要的。

編者按：這是山東省公安廳縣鎮游保衛處偵察工作報告中的一部分，現摘刊於此，希望引起各地同志們的重視和研究解決。我們認為山東這個報告所述的問題在全國其他地區同樣是存在的，這不過是地區已經檢查出來或有所覺察，從而亦就有可能去動手加以解決，而有些地方則還沒有覺察或很少覺察，還沒有來得及加以系統檢查。因此，希望這些地方特別加以注意。

—5—

FIGURE 7. "Some Problems in Case Agent Work at Present," a report to the CMPS 2nd Bureau

FIGURE 8. Yang Qiqing, director of the CMPS 1st Bureau prior to 1950

FIGURE 9. Chen Long, director of the CMPS 1st Bureau from 1950 to 1953

FIGURE 10. Ling Yun, director of the CMPS 1st Bureau from 1953 to 1964

FIGURE 11. Perception management: the crimes of *tewu* on exhibit in Shanghai's Nanyang Model High School in 1950

FIGURE 12. Shanghai student charged with being a member of the Democratic Republican Party (DRP), an allegedly counterrevolutionary organization

FIGURE 13. Critical infrastructure: the first Wuhan Yangzi River Bridge, completed in 1957

Baotou Nuclear Fuel Plant, China   KH-7 Mission 4038 5 June 1967

FIGURE 14. "Agent cover": Baotou Nuclear Fuel Plant photographed by an American KH-7 reconnaissance satellite on June 5, 1967

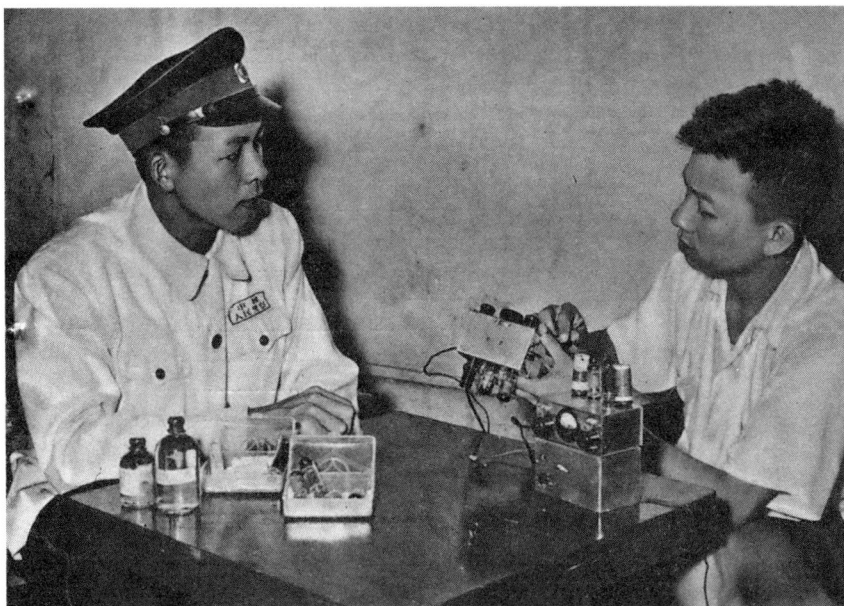

FIGURE 15. A surrendered Guomindang operative explains his communications equipment to public security officers in Guangdong

FIGURE 16. Lei Rongtian, director of the CMPS 2nd Bureau in the early 1950s

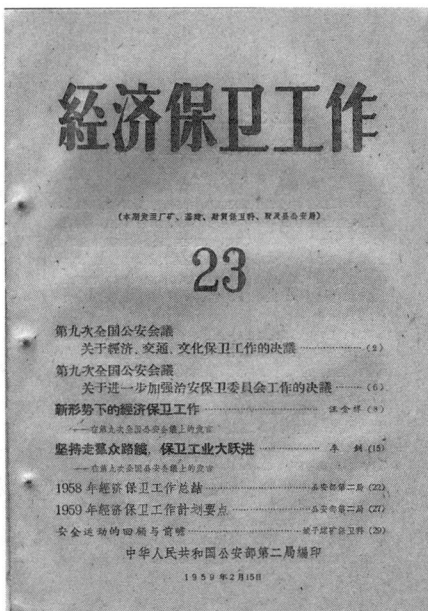

FIGURE 17. *Economic Protection Work*, a serial produced by the CMPS 2nd Bureau

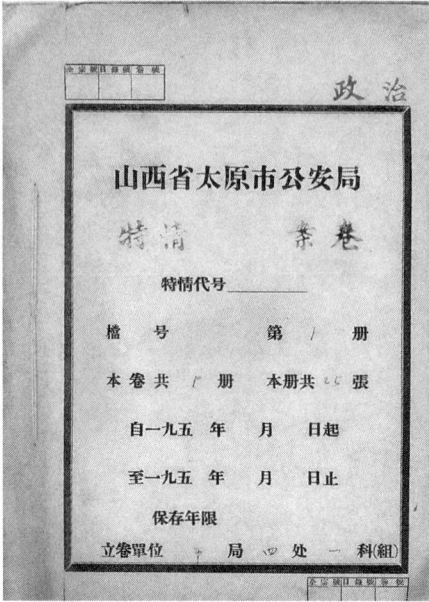

FIGURE 18. Cover of an agent's Personal File

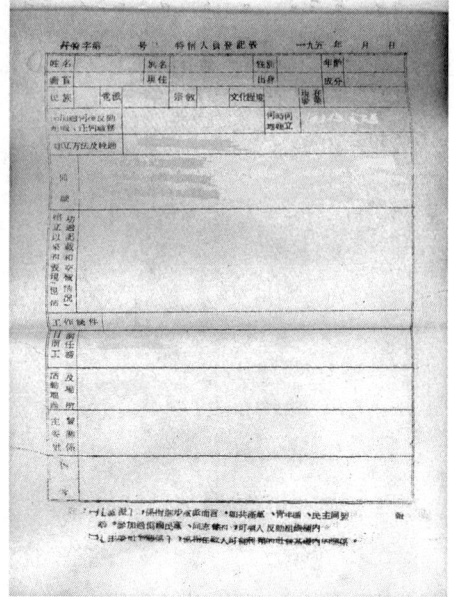

FIGURE 19. An agent's Registration Form

FIGURE 20. "*Tewu* No. 08" (middle) at a public sentencing rally organized by PLA-controlled public security organs in Guangxi, 1968

I

Public Security

The Institutional Framework

In Mao's China, the power to recruit and deploy agents for domestic operational purposes was vested exclusively in the public security organs. These organs formed a hierachy of organizations stretching – in the urban civilian sphere – from the branches of municipal bureaus of public security at the bottom to the CMPS at the very top. Agents were but one of their choice instruments of operational activity: a 1957 inventory also mentioned physical surveillance, interception of postal communications, and technical operations.[1]

Their contrasting formal designations notwithstanding, these *public* security organs were the functional equivalent of the then Soviet Union's domestic agencies of *state* security – the KGB. In the period when Sino–Soviet relations could be described as those of "fraternal socialist allies," this was duly acknowledged by Chinese leaders: "Our ministry safeguards the security of the state," Minister of Public Security Luo Ruiqing remarked in April 1958, "and what the Soviet Union calls the Committee for State Security also safeguards the security of the state."[2] When bilateral relations started to turn sour, CCP leaders began to claim that the public–state terminological distinction was significant, but it is doubtful whether they ever succeeded in convincing anyone of this. In May 1962, Party Vice-Chairman Liu Shaoqi made the following assertion in front

[1] "*Teqing gongzuo*," pp. 1, 4.
[2] Luo Ruiqing, "Zai liang sheng yi shi huibao huiyi shang de zhishi" (Instructions at Report-Back Meeting for Two Provinces and One Municipality), *Gongan jianshe*, No. 245, June 16, 1958, p. 2.

of an audience of provincial and municipal public security officers in Beijing:

> Yours are called bureaus of public security, right? The term "public security" – what does it mean? It means you're in charge of the public's tranquility [*guan gonggong anning*]. Who, then, are the public? They're the people. In the Soviet Union, they speak of the Committee for Security. It stands for the security of the rulers, in addition to involving the people's security and state security.[3]

In actuality, as Liu himself would have been only too well aware of, the CMPS devoted the full resources of an entire directorate or bureau exclusively to "the security of the rulers." To the extent that significant differences did indeed exist between public security in the PRC and state security in the Soviet Union, those differences had little to do with the distinction implied by Liu.

In the English language, the term "public security" is used loosely to refer to the function of a government that ensures the protection of institutions, organizations, and citizens against threats to their well-being and the prosperity of their communities. The question of whether from 1949 to 1967 the public security organs of the PRC actually served this aim – and if so, to what degree – has no simple answer. While the KGB is regarded by many historians as embodying the very negation of that function of government, the verdict in the PRC case has been more accommodating. Half a century later, the opinions of ordinary Chinese at the time can only be guesstimated; few records exist to gauge public opinion at the time. In 1957, when Shanghai residents were asked by the CCP to freely "air their views" on what they viewed as positive and negative about the new socialist order, three out of ten expressed resentment toward the police.[4] In Beijing, public opinion was no less critical and – interestingly enough – more than 95 percent of the negative comments made were admitted by the police themselves as being essentially accurate.[5] For the purposes of the present narrative, the terms "public security" and its adjunct "public security organs" are employed in

---

[3] *Pipan ziliao: Zhongguo Heluxiaofu Liu Shaoqi fangeming xiuzhengzhuyi yanlun ji* (Denunciation Materials: Counterrevolutionary Revisionist Utterances by China's Khrushchev Liu Shaoqi), 3 vols. (Beijing: Renmin chubanshe ziliaoshi, 1968), Vol. 3, p. 267.

[4] Luo Ruiqing, "Zai liang sheng yi shi huibao huiyi shang de zhishi," p. 7.

[5] Beijing shi gonganju, "Guanyu jiedao mingfang zhong qunzhong dui wo gongan bumen suo tide yijian de zhenggai qingkuang baogao" (Situation Report on Responses to Critique Directed at Our Public Security Organs by the Urban Masses During the Airing of Views), *Gongan jianshe*, No. 238, May 20, 1958, p. 4.

conformity with convention rather than in any firm belief in their ultimate moral appropriateness or semantic felicity.[6]

Throughout the 1950s and 1960s, much of the institutional framework of Chinese public security remained in a state of flux. Like revolution, it was a work in progress, manifest in the evolution and devolution of bureaucracies, successive long-, medium-, short-term, and contingency plans, shifting assignments, and competing missions. Operational departments were no exception, as this chapter – the aim of which is to allow the reader to connect the narrow agent-related subject matter of the rest of the book to its institutional context – seeks to show.

A Central Party Ministry

Its creation formally ratified on October 19, 1949, the Ministry of Public Security of the Central People's Government (which by then had already existed de facto for over three months as the Ministry of Public Security of the CCP Central Revolutionary Military Affairs Commission) began functioning on November 1, 1949, at the end of a two-week-long constituting conference of senior public security officers convened by Mao Zedong's CCP Center and Premier Zhou Enlai's Government Administration Council. At the national level, the creation of this new ministry signaled the dissolution of the CSAD, the CCP's integrated intelligence and counterintelligence/security body, which had been created a decade earlier.[7]

Despite losing its "central" designation at the time of the abolition of the PRC's regional governments in 1954 (and being given the name it has officially had ever since, the Ministry of Public Security of the People's Republic of China), the CMPS continued, well into the second half of the 1970s, to be referred to in-house – including in print – as the Central Ministry of Public Security (*Zhongyang gonganbu*), or CMPS (*Zhonggongbu*) for short. One possible reason for this anomaly (for which there

---

6 Compare civil liberties attorney Frank J. Donner's comment on his own use of the terms "national security" and "subversive" in *The Age of Surveillance: The Aims and Methods of America's Political Intelligence System* (New York: Vintage Books, 1981), p. xxii: "They have become so deeply rooted in our political culture, in intelligence documents, in court decisions, in legislation, and in scholarly studies that it would be impossible, if not misleading, to offer substitutes. They are used throughout this book in an intelligence context and are therefore to be read as though in quotation marks."

7 Zhu Chunlin, ed., *Lishi shunjian I* (*Moments in History I*) (Beijing: Qunzhong chubanshe, 1999), pp. 4–6.

is no equivalent in any other PRC government ministry) may have been a strong desire on the part of the institution and its staff to maintain a link in symbolic/linguistic terms to the organs directly subordinate to the Communist Party Central Committee, all of which have continued to this day to have designations that begin with "Central" (e.g., the CCP Central Organization Department). Certainly, in real terms, leadership of the CMPS was firmly in the hands of the Communist Party. As Liu Shaoqi remarked on October 18, 1950, the "Ministry of Public Security is led by the Communist Party, and there is to be nothing furtive about this."[8]

Beginning in 1949, the CMPS would be charged with codifying public security doctrine and shaping the PRC's domestic public security order in line with CCP principles and priorities. According to the rough division of labor among members of the Central Committee Secretariat informally agreed upon on the eve of the founding of the PRC, Liu Shaoqi was to be the point person for matters in the political-legal sphere, while Zhou Enlai was to oversee intelligence and public security.[9] Chinese historians maintain that the actual modus operandi of the CCP leadership after the PRC's founding, however, was significantly less rigid than the existence of a list of "who does what" suggests.[10] That Mao Zedong, for example, always sought to make sure that he was kept well informed of the work of the CMPS in particular, and that his influence over it was keenly felt, was recalled decades later by Zhou Enlai. At the 15th NPSC in 1971, in an attempt to show that, at the highest level, Mao's "proletarian revolutionary line" had all along guided PRC public security work, Zhou declared:

On numerous occasions, Chairman Mao personally revised and ratified the documents produced by the National Public Security Conferences. Some of those documents were written by Chairman Mao himself.... In those seventeen years [1949–1966], Liu Shaoqi was only able in a few rare instances to meddle in the affairs of the public security organs. For example, he might write a letter to Luo Ruiqing asking him to do this or that. Such things did happen. But as far as the instructions that were publicly known were concerned, it was Chairman Mao

---

[8] *Suqing "Liu" du* (*Eradicate "Residual" [Liu] Poison*), 2 vols. (Shanghai: Shanghai shi gonganju bangongshi nongbaochu geming zaofandui, 1967), Vol. 2, p. 19. See also Dutton, *Policing Chinese Politics*, p. 139.

[9] Zhonggong zhongyang wenxian yanjiushi and Zhongyang dang'anguan, eds., *Jianguo yilai Zhou Enlai wengao* (*Zhou Enlai's Manuscripts Since the Founding of the Nation*), 3 vols. (Beijing: Zhongyang wenxian chubanshe, 2008), Vol. 1, pp. 740–41.

[10] Author's conversation with a senior researcher at the Contemporary China Research Institute, Beijing, September 16, 2009.

who dominated. Peng [Zhen] and Luo still had to convey and implement Chairman Mao's instructions, since the broad ranks of police officers obeyed Chairman Mao.[11]

Zhou added that public security had, since 1949, been one of two (foreign affairs was the other) crucial "fronts" in which Mao had always taken a close personal interest.[12]

What Zhou failed to divulge was the degree of friction that had initially existed between himself and Mao over who was to be the ultimate arbiter in PRC matters of state and security. Mao had grumbled in private to regional strongman and fellow Politburo member Gao Gang about feeling sidelined, and in 1950 he clearly resented the degree to which Zhou Enlai's cabinet appeared poised to become a crucial center of gravity in the still evolving PRC political structure.[13] Specifically, with respect to the CMPS, Mao is reported to have become incensed when, very shortly after the ministry had been created, he discovered that he was not being routinely updated on what it was doing. "I am the Chairman of the Center," Mao – according to the recollections of a secretary present – barked at Luo Ruiqing, "so why is your Ministry of Public Security keeping me in the dark and not sending me reports?" Luo, self-critically, explained to Mao that since the ministry was a government and not a party organ, its work reports were being sent to Zhou Enlai's cabinet and not directly to Party Central. In a fit of anger, Mao took Luo to task, telling him, "From now on, Ministry of Public Security reports [also] come directly to me. When you burn incense, you want to make sure you do it in front of the right shrine!"[14]

How CCP leadership was to be maintained in institutional terms inside the CMPS and at lower levels of the PRC public security system took almost a year to iron out. In Northeast China, Gao Gang's regional minister of public security, Wang Jinxiang, explained that the "abolition of the Social Affairs Department will be followed by the creation of party groups within each bureau of public security, and the function of these groups is to implement the short- and long-term policies of the party through the [institutional] *form* of the government, hereby guaranteeing

---

[11] "Zhou zongli jiejian," pp. 8–9.
[12] Ibid., p. 9.
[13] Zhao Jialiang and Zhang Xiaoji, *Banjie mubei xia de wangshi: Gao Gang zai Beijing* (*The Past Beneath a Broken Tombstone: Gao Gang in Beijing*) (Hong Kong: Dafeng chubanshe, 2008), p. 74.
[14] Sun Mingshan, ed., *Lishi shunjian III* (*Moments in History III*) (Beijing: Qunzhong chubanshe, 2004), p. 333.

party leadership."[15] This, in the end, became the formula adopted at the 2nd NPSC in the autumn of 1950; that is, public security organs constituted "organs of state power [*guojia zhengquan de bumen*] as well as implementers of the party's traitor elimination and protection policies. They are working organs under party branch leadership."[16]

A thorny issue also grappled with at this time was how to exercise CCP leadership and oversight where "protection" interfaced with other functions of government in institutions that in themselves were not public security organs.[17] Here the respective positions of the senior leaders concerned seem also to have initially been some distance apart. In the autumn of 1950, when Li Weihan, Zhou Enlai's cabinet secretary-general, received the transcript of a report delivered by the CMPS Party Group to the 1st National Conference on Economic Protection Work held earlier in the year, he revised those passages stipulating that protection work had to obey the "leadership of the CCP and the senior administrator" to instead read that it should simply obey the "leadership of the senior official." Li's revision had been slated for distribution to public security officers nationwide, but when Mao perused the final preprint of it on September 27, 1950, he annulled Li's revisions before writing in the margin, "In protection work, it is imperative that particular stress be put on the leadership role of the party and that [this work] be subject to the *actual* direct leadership of party committees, since anything else would be very dangerous."[18] In the years to come, this statement of Mao's would be repeatedly quoted by CMPS leaders in key policy pronouncements. When ordinary public security officers had to take refresher courses on the so-called political imperative of relying on the masses and relying on the party, it was Mao's words that they were told to remember above all.

Under CMPS auspices, the initial formulation of public security doctrine and the drawing up and revision of long-term policy were typically conducted at, or in direct conjunction with, major gatherings of senior public security officers from all over China. Fundamental matters relating to operational work were, according to one participant, initially resolved

[15] Wang Jinxiang, "Dongbei gongan baowei," p. 16.

[16] Luo Ruiqing, "Zai di er ci quanguo gongan huiyi shang de baogao" (Report to the 2nd National Public Security Conference) [October 16, 1950], p. 3. The term "traitor elimination" (*chujian*) fell into disuse and ceased to be part of the official lexicon after 1949.

[17] "Protection" was how the CCP normally referred to what in the English language is better known as "security." At times, the term also referred to "public security" in general.

[18] Liu Xingyi, *Yang Qiqing zhuan* (*Biography of Yang Qiqing*) (Beijing: Qunzhong chubanshe, 2006), p. 249.

at the 1st and 2nd National Conferences on Operational Work, held in Beijing in 1950 and 1952.[19] That national gatherings like these witnessed serious policy debate at times was recalled half a century later by a secretary involved in producing the minutes from the first conference:

A very lively debate unfolded at the Ministry of Public Security's 1st Conference on Operational Work about how best to define our long-term policy for operational work. My role was to draft a conference summary for Luo Ruiqing and I attempted to reconcile the views of the two sides. When he saw my draft, Luo became furious. He called me aside and gave me a real dressing down, insisting that in matters of principle there was no room for compromise [*tiaohe*]. He then told me to right away begin drafting a new summary. Because time was very tight, as soon as I had finished a page Luo would get down to reading and revising the text. At the end, the moment we were done finalizing the summary, Luo rushed off to the conference [venue] to deliver it. The conference was a great success, but I myself was rather badly bruised from the whole affair.[20]

Little is known in detail about the views of those participants who lost out, but the position of those who came out on top on this occasion is well documented. Often referred to metaphorically as "using a long line to catch a big fish" and associated with the operational work of the CCP Northeast Social Affairs Department (the civil war predecessor of the NEMPS), this policy had already been quietly endorsed by Mao in late 1949. After briefing the CCP Chairman on the strengths and weaknesses of his operational resources, regional NEMPS Vice-Minister Chen Long had been encouraged specifically by the CCP Chairman to "introduce to other parts of China, as quickly as possible, the Northeast's operational work experiences."[21] An early metaphorical summary of what those experiences amounted to was that enemies should *not* be rashly eliminated the moment they were identified, but that instead "one should probe the roots to the end, and then net them all in one swoop. One should proceed as if pulling out a nail, which means pulling the whole thing out. One should not proceed as if picking apples, picking them off one by one."[22]

[19] Ling Yun, "Zai di liu ci quanguo gongan huiyi shang de fayan" (Statement at the 6th National Public Security Conference), *Gongan jianshe*, No. 102, October 12, 1954, p. 11.

[20] Wang Zhongfang, *Lianyu (Purgatory)* (Beijing: Qunzhong chubanshe, 2004), pp. 69–70.

[21] Xiu Lairong, *Chen Long zhuan (Biography of Chen Long)* (Beijing: Qunzhong chubanshe, 1995), p. 351.

[22] Gao Gang, "Zai dongbei di si jie gongan huiyi shang de jianghua" (Speech at the 4th Northeast Public Security Conference), *Tianjin gongan*, Vol. 1, No. 2, August 15, 1950, p. 25.

On October 15, 1950, Luo Ruiqing presented Mao and the CCP Center with a report from the 1st National Conference on Operational Work that described the long-term policy it had adopted as "taking a long-term view and making operational use of penetration agents."[23] Explaining what this meant, Luo said that it entailed "taking into consideration the long-term nature of the covert struggle, and setting out to develop operational work in terms of ideology, organization, and tradecraft, with the aim of meeting the long-term needs of an extended struggle." When an actual specific case was to be cracked, he added, "consideration should be given to other cases that tie in with it. Myopia as well as impetuosity are to be resisted in operational work."[24] No doubt because its members would have been fully preoccupied with the war on the Korean Peninsula (this was the month that the first units of the PRC's armed forces crossed the Yalu River into North Korea), it would take until November 24 before the CCP Center had ratified the policy and called on "party committees at all levels to supervise and urge its implementation."[25]

Well before the end of the decade, the policy had generated enough feedback to warrant its partial revision. At the 9th NPSC (which met for fifty-five days in the summer of 1958 and was attended by an unprecedented 920 delegates), it was revised to read "take a long-term view and make operational use of penetration agents; rely on the masses, and crack cases at just the right moment." A 9th NPSC Resolution on Operational Work explained the change by saying that the new amended formulation "more accurately reflects the praxis of our struggle and experiences gained in these past nine years." "As previously laid down," the resolution claimed, the old long-term policy had been "correct in the past, and is still correct [*jinhou haishi zhengquede*], when dealing with certain [*yidingde*] large cases and crucially important cases."[26]

At the 1st National Conference on Operational Work in 1950, the CMPS produced a national threat assessment and identified priority targets against which operational resources were henceforth to be directed.[27]

[23] *Jianguo yilai gongan*, p. 14.
[24] Tao Siju, ed., *Xin Zhongguo di yi ren gongan buzhang Luo Ruiqing* (*New China's First Minister of Public Security Luo Ruiqing*) (Beijing: Qunzhong chubanshe, 2002), p. 68.
[25] Zhonggong zhongyang wenxian yanjiushi and Zhongyang dang'anguan, eds., *Jianguo yilai Liu Shaoqi wengao* (*Liu Shaoqi's Manuscripts Since the Founding of the Nation*), 7 vols. (Beijing: Zhongyang wenxian chubanshe, 2005–8), Vol. 2, p. 557.
[26] *Di jiu ci quanguo gongan huiyi shiwuge jueyi* (*The Fifteen Resolutions of the 9th National Public Security Conference*) (Guangzhou: Guangzhou sheng gonganting, 1958), p. 3.
[27] *Zhongguo renmin gongan shigao* (*Draft History of the Chinese People's Public Security*) (Beijing: Jingguan jiaoyu chubanshe, 1997), p. 251.

The conference furthermore defined the methods in accordance with which agent work and anti-*tewu* operations were to be developed.[28] Nonetheless, much remained to be done in the wake of the conference with respect to operational work. In the summer of 1952, a 2nd National Conference on Operational Work discussed specifically the use of agents. The documents from that conference as submitted by the CMPS to the CCP Center argued for the extensive "cultivation of agents in accordance with the principles of necessity and capability, in a steady, planned, targeted, bold, and all-out way."[29]

Regular indicators of where this "necessity" was most pronounced would henceforth be given by the CMPS in quarterly – later annual – planning documents submitted for ratification to the Center. The CMPS annual plan for 1957, for example, advocated significantly strengthening operational work "in the struggle against the enemy in coastal and border areas, and in particular in large and medium-sized cities, in critical industrial and mining regions, as well as in other regions and sectors where the threat level is elevated [*diqing fuza*]."[30] The plan for 1964 encouraged officers as a matter of policy to attempt the mobilization of mainland relatives of known ethnic Chinese members of hostile intelligence services abroad and, when possible, to secure their commitment to the anti-*tewu* struggle.[31]

How to give additional substance to operational capability on the subnational level, however, was not the task of the CMPS, but rather of regional, provincial, and municipal bureaus of public security. The Guangdong provincial Bureau of Public Security, for example, informed the ministry in Beijing in February 1957 that it had no plans, "generally speaking, to recruit any more agents this year."[32] A little more than a year later, the Qinghai provincial Bureau of Public Security, on the other hand, told the CMPS of how in 1958, "in accordance with the principles of necessity and capability, we plan to deploy 610 new agents (political protection 260, economic protection 50, and crime 300)."[33] Provincial

---

[28] *Jianguo yilai Liu Shaoqi wengao*, Vol. 2, p. 557.
[29] Ibid., Vol. 4, pp. 324–27.
[30] "Di ba ci quanguo gongan huiyi guanyu 1956 nian gongan gongzuo zhuyao qingkuang he 1957 nian gongzuo de yijian" (Opinion of the 8th National Public Security Conference on the Major Circumstances of Public Security Work in 1956 and Work in 1957), *Gongan jianshe*, No. 184, March 5, 1957, p. 9.
[31] "1964 nian gongan," p. 4.
[32] Guangdong sheng gonganting, "1957 nian gongan gongzuo jihua" (Plan for Public Security Work in 1957), *Gongan jianshe*, No. 186, April 15, 1957, p. 18.
[33] Qinghai sheng gonganting, "1958 nian gongan gongzuo guihua (chugao)" (Plan for Public Security Work in 1958 [Draft]), *Gongan jianshe*, No. 266, August 5, 1958, p. 2.

planning documents may have shared many of the same formal qualities and a common language, but they varied significantly with respect to substance. To confidently speculate on the basis of only a handful of such documents about broader general trends is simply impossible.

Soviet Expertise: Unwelcome Guidance

The CMPS, like all other PRC ministries, hosted a number of Soviet advisors in the 1950s, the first two having been invited in a letter to Stalin written by Liu Shaoqi on October 10, 1949.[34] The relationship between the advisors and their Chinese hosts was never an easy one. The language barrier created problems, and proud Chinese public security officers with years of operational experience often resented being lectured to or having their own opinions in operational matters summarily dismissed by the socialist elder brother. One of the senior interpreters on the Chinese side later admitted that the Soviet advisors to the CMPS "worked very conscientiously and enthusiastically" but that they "did not understand the Chinese situation, were unfamiliar with their Chinese surroundings, and suffered from a lack of basic knowledge of the history of Chinese communism. Hence much of the time their proposals were inappropriate, at times even laughable."[35]

By April 1957, the relationship between the KGB advisors and the CMPS had become so strained that the ministry informed the State Council and CCP Center that it did not advocate inviting a new group of advisors (save for those with very specific expertise in purely technical matters) when the contracts of those already in Beijing were due to expire.[36] The issue was broached by Nikita Khrushchev in conversation with Mao Zedong during the CPSU leader's brief visit to Beijing at the end of July 1958; the details of what actually transpired are murky, but the departure of the advisors en bloc in September 1958 (a departure that the Chinese side is said to have requested) clearly occurred as a result of serious friction between the two sides. Chinese historians cite both Mao and Zhou Enlai as voicing irritation with the KGB advisors "coming and

---

[34] *Jianguo yilai Liu Shaoqi wengao*, Vol. 1, pp. 100–1.

[35] Zhao Ming, quoted in Shen Zhihua, *Sulian zhuanjia zai Zhongguo (1948–1960)* (Soviet Experts in China [1948–1960]) (Beijing: Zhongguo guoji guangbo chubanshe, 2003), p. 250.

[36] Zhonggong zhongyang wenxian yanjiushi, ed., *Deng Xiaoping nianpu 1904–1974* (*Deng Xiaoping Chronicle 1904–1974*), 3 vols. (Beijing: Zhongyang wenxian chubanshe, 2009), Vol. 3, p. 1358.

going as they like" and with their allegedly "problematic work style."[37] In addition, there may well have been fundamental disagreements in matters of operational policy and praxis: the Resolution on Operational Work, passed by the 9th NPSC on August 16, 1958, devoted a paragraph specifically to the "problem of learning from foreign countries" and in this context cited specifically a divergence of views concerning "the role of agents" as a problem.[38] A month later, on September 16, 1958, Luo Ruiqing shared with the departing head of the advisors "our Party Center's views on the withdrawal of the Soviet experts."[39]

CMPS–KGB relations continued to deteriorate in the years that followed as the rift between the Soviet and Chinese Communist Parties grew. By 1962, Chinese public security officers had become alarmed by the growing threat posed to national security by the increased activity of what were now, unlike in the early 1950s, explicitly referred to as Soviet *tewu* operating on PRC soil. To help them develop a generally more critical informed view of the KGB, the CMPS began sponsoring the translation into Chinese of "American imperialist researchers' writings" on Soviet state security. In 1964, a selection of essays from Simon Wolin and Robert Slusser's *The Soviet Secret Police* from 1957 appeared "for official use only," and the following year a full translation of David Dallin's massive study entitled *Soviet Espionage* was published by the CMPS.[40]

So highly sensitive were all aspects of CMPS–KGB relations that they were only discussed behind closed doors at the very apex of the public security system, including at the meeting of senior public security officers in the last ten days of August 1962, which set the agenda for the 12th NPSC.[41] Once a CCP response of sorts had finally been formulated, the Party Center attached an unusual instruction to two interrelated Top Secret documents (highlighting the threat of Soviet *tewu* activity) communicated inter alia to CCP committees in PRC embassies abroad, explaining that they were to be discussed and reacted to immediately upon receipt and then promptly destroyed.[42] In an effort to further minimize the likelihood of leaks, when the CMPS in April 1964 disseminated the year's

[37] Shen Zhihua, *Sulian zhuanjia*, pp. 298, 305.
[38] *Di jiu ci quanguo gongan huiyi*, p. 2.
[39] Tao Siju, *Xin Zhongguo di yi ren*, p. 256.
[40] Dai Wendian, ed., *Zhongguo gongan tushu zongmu* (*General Index of Chinese Books on Public Security*) (Beijing: Zhongguo renmin gongan daxue chubanshe, 2007), p. 289.
[41] *Zhongguo renmin gongan shigao*, p. 319; *Jianguo yilai gongan*, pp. 234–35.
[42] Zhonggong zhongyang zuzhibu bangongting, ed., *Zuzhi gongzuo wenjian xuanbian 1963 nian* (*Selected Organization Work Documents: 1963*) (Beijing, 1980), p. 242.

public security work plan as adopted by the 13th NPSC, it redacted in full the section on how to respond to the "subversive sabotage activities of the modern revisionists" from the text of the plan made available in writing to county-level public security officers.[43] The counterintelligence and security measures adopted appear, on the whole, to have been very effective: the files seen by the senior KGB archivist Vasili Mitrokhin, who defected to Great Britain after the end of the cold war, "do not identify a single KGB agent in Beijing with access to classified Chinese documents."[44]

Problems notwithstanding, KGB doctrine influenced much of what was done and developed within the CMPS after 1949. In a roundabout way, this was admitted to in a CCP Central Committee circular issued on May 16, 1966, which denounced Luo Ruiqing for the allegedly "grievous errors" he had committed in the past seventeen years. One of the circular's attachments dealt exclusively with the "bourgeois poison" he was said to have spread during his tenure as minister of public security, claiming that Luo "in very many respects . . . allowed himself to be influenced by the mysticist stuff [*shenmizhuyi de dongxi*] from the Soviet Union, so much that he would adopt it lock stock and barrel." In the attachment, just about the only thing that Luo was still given credit for was that he had (albeit for the wrong reason!) resisted KGB attempts to exert even greater dominance. It was admitted that Luo, for all his faults, had "stood up to the great-nation chauvinism of the Soviet experts because it offended his personal honor."[45]

A Tale of Two Ministers

Two long-serving ministers were at the helm of the CMPS during the first two decades of its existence. The first was Luo Ruiqing, from 1949 to 1959, and the second was Xie Fuzhi, from 1959 until his death from stomach cancer on March 26, 1972. Both were decorated Red Army veterans who had taken part in the Long March – Luo as a senior security officer, Xie as a political commissar. During the War of Resistance against Japan, Luo had been in Yan'an, serving first as the dean of studies and

[43] "1964 nian gongan gongzuo yaodian" (Main Points of Public Security Work in 1964), *Gongan jianshe*, No. 562, April 24, 1964, p. 4.

[44] Christopher Andrew and Vasili Mitrokhin, *The Mitrokhin Archive II: The KGB and the World* (London: Penguin Books, 2006), p. 285.

[45] Quoted in *Chedi qingsuan Luo Ruiqing zai zhengfa gongzuo fangmian de taotian zuixing* (*Thoroughly Eradicate the Heinous Crimes of Luo Ruiqing in the Politics and Law Sector*) (Shanghai: Shanghai shi zhengfajie doupigai lianluozhan, 1967), p. 7.

vice-president of the Kangda ("Anti-Japanese Resistance Military and Political University"), later as director of the 8th Route Army's Political Department.[46] Elected an alternate member of the CCP Central Committee at the 7th National Congress in April 1945, he was a senior PLA political commissar in the North China Theater during the 1947–49 Civil War. Xie Fuzhi, three years Luo's junior, had advanced steadily through the ranks during the War of Resistance, which he spent mostly in the Shanxi-Hebei-Shandong-Henan border region. For many years he served as political commissar next to Chen Geng – a senior field army commander who, prior to joining the Red Army, had earned a reputation among the CCP leadership as a skilled operative in the Shanghai underground in 1928–31 – and it was together with Chen that Xie had led PLA units to chase armies of the Guomindang across the country, all the way to the Burmese border, thus himself ending up in Southwest China at the end of the Civil War. Here he served throughout the 1950s in positions of power in the Sichuan and Yunnan provincial CCP and regional military establishments.[47]

If the recollections of members of his personal staff are to be believed, Luo Ruiqing would in 1949 have preferred to remain in the PLA rather than become a government minister. His political secretary recalls how Mao Zedong himself had to talk Luo into accepting his new civilian posting during a dinner in June 1949. "I hear you don't want to do the work of a minister of public security but want to go on fighting?" Mao is supposed to have begun, before proceeding to explain why Luo would simply have to change his plans: "We're now about to create a new state machinery: how are we going to be able to do that if everybody refuses and insists on staying in the military?" While Luo reluctantly agreed to take up his new post, it would appear that his own preference was for it to have been given instead to someone with a strong professional background in intelligence or counterintelligence. Both Mao and Zhou Enlai disagreed, however, for they wanted a military officer with the right mix of leadership, networking, and organizational skills – qualities they deemed Luo to possess – to oversee the creation and work of New China's public security apparatus.[48]

---

[46] Wang Dinglie and Wen Xianmei, eds., *Bashu jiangshuai zhuan* (*Biographies of Generals and Commanders from Sichuan*) (Chengdu: Bashu shushe, 1989), pp. 73–86.

[47] Wang Zhongxing and Liu Liqin, *Di er yezhanjun – Liu Bocheng huixia de 10 ge jun 247 wei jiangjun* (*The 2nd Field Army – The 10 Corps and 247 Generals under Liu Bocheng's Command*) (Beijing: Guofang daxue chubanshe, 1996), p. 90.

[48] Zhu Chunlin, *Lishi shunjian I*, p. 4; Sun Mingshan, *Lishi shunjian III*, p. 299.

What kind of minister was Luo? At the time, foreign foes and friends alike insisted on comparing him to his Soviet counterpart(s). In March 1956, his face appeared on the cover of *Time* magazine in the United States, and in an accompanying article it was said that Luo "has modeled his machine on the Soviet MVD [Ministry of Internal Affairs] and become the nearest Chinese equivalent to a Beria."[49] In the United States, of course, this comparison implied the strongest possible criticism, not praise. Some six years earlier, a similar comparison – this time extolling praise – had been made by the senior Soviet advisor to the CMPS, who told his Chinese interpreter that "Minister Luo is your Dzerzhinsky! The two are both fair-minded, honest, frank, approachable, and capable of understanding people, not to mention able to take in the divergent views of the masses."[50] The Soviet advisor's impression can be contrasted with the recollections of some of the children of Luo's Chinese subordinates. The son of a three-star general who had at one point served under Luo remembers how the latter would order his father to stand to attention while speaking to him over the telephone. While in no way implying that he could not at times be fair-minded and honest, he and a number of his friends (who had known each other since they were toddlers in the Yan'an kindergarten during the War of Resistance) all stressed that Luo also had an unreasonable streak to his personality.[51]

Members of Luo's own family while he was still alive (and friends and colleagues since his death in 1978) paint a picture of a man whose personal concern was not so much with what *Time* saw as modeling a public security machine on Soviet/Leninist patterns as with learning the *dao* of statecraft from Chinese history. They had rarely seen Luo studying the classics of Marxism-Leninism or the works of Mao Zedong, his children admitted in 1967, "but on the other hand we often see him diligently studying books like *Sun Zi – The Art of War*."[52] Luo's secretary recalled that he used to read extensively, taking his cue from the CCP Chairman, from *Records of the Grand Historian* by Sima Qian

---

[49] *Time* magazine, March 5, 1956. Lavrentiy Pavlovich Beria (1899–1953) was head of Stalin's security apparatus and the Soviet secret police during World War II.

[50] Sun Mingshan, ed., *Lishi shunjian IV* (*Moments in History IV*) (Beijing: Qunzhong chubanshe, 2006), p. 86. Felix Edmundovich Dzerzhinsky (1877–1926), together with Lenin, had founded the Bolshevik secret police and security apparatus, the All-Russia Extraordinary Commission for Combating Counterrevolution and Sabotage (the Cheka), in 1917.

[51] Author's conversation with Qiu Luguang and others, Beijing, December 29, 2006.

[52] *Da pipan ziliao* (*Great Criticism Materials*) (Beijing: Shoudu dazhuan yuanxiao hong-daihui zhengfa gongshe ziliaozu, 1967), Vol. 3, p. 1.

(ca. 145–86 BC), *Records of the Three Kingdoms* by Chen Shou (233–97 BC), *Comprehensive Mirror to Aid in Government* by Sima Guang (1019–86), and *A Concise and Readable General History* by Wu Chengquan (1695–1711).[53]

Promoted to PLA chief of staff on September 18, 1959, Luo Ruiqing was succeeded as minister by Xie Fuzhi. At a big rally six days later, at which the entire staff of the CMPS bid farewell to Luo, the outgoing minister had this to say about his successor:

> Many of our comrades already know him. He's done military work, been a provincial 1st party secretary, done mass work, has broader experience than I have, has lots of grassroots experience.... The arrival of a new minister will create a new working atmosphere. I've been around for too long and often fail to see some of our flaws and errors, but with a new leading comrade in place, perhaps it will become possible to overcome [our] flaws and errors more quickly.[54]

Notwithstanding the accolades he received from Luo, Xie was widely perceived as a weak minister. Institutional resistance to his leadership was pronounced, and in matters involving operational activity he often chose, prior to the Cultural Revolution, to acquiesce to his deputies even when it appeared that he strongly disagreed with them.[55] One colleague remembered Xie complaining at a meeting of the CMPS Party Group in 1969 about how "during these past ten years that I have spent in the Ministry of Public Security, I have not really been a minister – only a political commissar."[56]

Xie's biography has yet to be written. The biographer of one of his deputies, however, provides a damning and not necessarily fair characterization of the minister. He was – presumably behind his back – nicknamed "Xie the flip-flop" because of his "mastery of the art of currying favors with people, of changing his position at a moment's notice, and of climbing to higher office by hook or by crook." (Worth noting is that while a minister, Xie, unlike Luo Ruiqing, actually made it into the CCP Politburo in 1966.) The same biographer claims that Xie also had an annoying habit, strongly resented by his colleagues, of regularly interrupting them in public with comments like "Now this won't do! That's not right!" or

---

53 Sun Mingshan, *Lishi shunjian III*, p. 309.
54 Luo Ruiqing, "Zai gonganbu quanti ganbu dahui shang de jianghua" (Speech at a Gathering of All Cadres in the Ministry of Public Security), *Renmin gongan*, No. 78, October 26, 1959, p. 7.
55 Cf. Dutton, *Policing Chinese Politics*, p. 212.
56 Shi Yizhi, *Wo zai gonganbu*, p. 19.

"Not necessarily! Don't be so sure!" without justifying his opinions or coming up with solutions.[57]

History would not be kind to Xie. His obituary in the *People's Daily* highlighted his loyal service to "Chairman Mao's revolutionary line" in the Cultural Revolution.[58] But it was precisely this controversial role as Mao's enabler in some of the darkest episodes in that movement that made him countless enemies among those who outlived him. Xie was posthumously expelled from the CCP as a counterrevolutionary on October 16, 1980, and to this day there have been no known attempts by surviving colleagues, former subordinates, or even family members to petition the authorities to reverse the verdict.

The CMPS 1st Bureau: Preempting Subversion

A need for effective high-level coordination might, in the eyes of some, have motivated the concentration of all operational work at the ministerial level in one single "chief" directorate, but this was not the structure favored at the time of the CMPS's creation. "Our country is so large and so complex," Chen Long explained, that "it is not possible to concentrate altogether the operational work in the struggle against the enemy in a single functional department."[59] Instead, responsibility for operational work was from the outset divided and shared among a number of functional bureaus (*ju*) at the highest level, and among separate corresponding (albeit not always with the same mandates, which were contingent on circumstances on the ground) offices (*chu*) in provincial and municipal bureaus of public security.

As one of the six "original" CMPS bureaus, the 1st (Political Protection) Bureau was the most powerful CMPS operational unit, the mission areas of which had been determined at the same meeting of senior public security cadres in October 1949 that had created the ministry itself. It was the only bureau headed concurrently for its first year in existence by a CMPS vice-minister, Yang Qiqing, with all the high-level access and swift decision-making routines that this entailed. It was tasked specifically with

---

[57] Tao Siju, ed., *Gongan baowei gongzuo de zhuoyue lingdaoren Xu Zirong zhuan* (*Biography of the Outstanding Leader of Public Security and Protection Work Xu Zirong*) (Beijing: Qunzhong chubanshe, 2002), pp. 198, 203.

[58] *Renmin ribao (People's Daily)*, March 30, 1972.

[59] Quoted in Yan Youmin, *Gongan zhanxian wushi nian: yiwei fubuzhang de zishu* (*Fifty Years on the Public Security Front: A Vice-Minister's Own Account*) (Beijing: Qunzhong chubanshe, 2005), p. 132.

leading and coordinating on a national level the exposure, prevention, and disruption of activities deemed to pose a direct threat to China's domestic *political* order, including – most significantly in terms of its resources – the activities of hostile intelligence services on Chinese soil. Its lower-level equivalents also functioned as a domestic intelligence agency more broadly, routinely collecting information on local communities and persons of operational interest. The 1st Bureau was large – so large, in fact, that in the final months of 1955, the CMPS split it into two separate bureau-level entities: the Bureau for Operations Against Imperialist *Tewu*, which retained the designation 1st Bureau, and the Bureau for Operations Against Guomindang *Tewu*, henceforth called the (new) 2nd Bureau. But the trial separation failed, and on March 18, 1957, the two bureaus were reunited, with their name and designation reverting back to what it had been originally – that is, the 1st (Political Protection) Bureau.[60]

Long-term policies for political protection designed to guide the work of the 1st Bureau had been drawn up in the summers of 1950 and 1952 at the 1st and 2nd National Conferences on Operational Work. Later, at moments of political uncertainty, CMPS vice-ministers would reaffirm the continued validity of these policies in front of the officers concerned. For example, on April 12, 1958, Wang Jinxiang (who had been appointed CMPS vice-minister when the NEMPS was abolished in 1954) explained to public security officers from Southwest China that although the Great Leap Forward, which was getting underway as he was speaking, was certain to have an impact on their work, "political protection departments will, as in the past, continue to handle cases involving *tewu* sent here from overseas, because they [the political protection departments] maintain unified control over our overseas sources of intelligence and have additional operational means at their disposal."[61]

Long-term policies were augmented by annual and/or biannual work plans. These were, apart from the first couple of years after 1949, drawn up within the 1st Bureau itself and approved by the CMPS. A detailed summary of the 1st Bureau's work plan for 1959–60, which appeared in the CMPS Top Secret *Public Security Work Bulletin* in October 1959, listed the following tasks: (1) "Make active arrangements for operational and case-cracking work, resolutely attack the *tewu* of the Chiang

[60] *Jianguo yilai gongan*, pp. 95, 124.
[61] Wang Jinxiang, "Zai Sichuan, Yunnan, Guizhou sansheng gongan gongzuo zuotanhui shang de zonghe fayan" (Comprehensive Statement at Informal Meeting on Public Security Work in Sichuan, Yunnan, and Guizhou), *Gongan jianshe*, No. 260, July 1, 1958, p. 15.

Kai-shek gang's Central Committee [Group Two]"; (2) "On a major scale, embark on investigation and research work"; (3) "In a planned way, aggressively marshal the use of turned assets"; (4) "Thoroughly clear up residual leads"; and (5) "Strengthen the fight in frontier and ethnic minority regions."[62]

Indicative of public security being a work in progress, policies and work plans of specific duration aside, lesser regulatory texts often remained in effect only briefly as circumstances changed. A handful of texts did have a significantly longer shelf life, however. In practical terms, the 1st Bureau stressed, agent work was the "most powerful and most important weapon of the operational departments of the People's Public Security organs in their covert struggle against enemy *tewu* and spies, and against assassins and saboteurs."[63] One text produced by the bureau that came to illustrate this and have a lasting, profound impact was the Top Secret *Agent Work Manual*, first distributed in draft form to delegates attending the 6th NPSC in 1954.[64] The resolution passed by the conference described it, and the operational *Case Work Manual* with which it was paired, as encapsulating existing experiences, regulations, and routines and ordered all officers to study the two texts carefully.[65] Luo Ruiqing, in his report to the conference, added that they were still open to revision and invited delegates to come up with suggestions for improvement "for the sake of strengthening and improving operational work."[66] Subsequent editions of the *Agent Work Manual* came to function as the agent-running officer's bible, its contents to be consulted regularly and, when practical problems arose, to serve as a guide to action. Commenting in 1956 on operational work in Jiexiu county, Shanxi province, the short-lived CMPS Bureau for Operations Against Guomindang *Tewu*

---

[62] "Gonganbu yiju tichu jinnian he mingnian dui Jiangbang de zhencha gongzuo guihua" (Ministry of Public Security 1st Bureau Puts Forth Plan for Operational Work Targeting Chiang Kai-shek Gang These Two Years), *Gongan gongzuo jianbao* (*Public Security Work Bulletin*), No. 77, October 20, 1959, pp. 2–5.

[63] *Dadao litong waiguode*, pp. 11–12.

[64] No copy of the *Agent Work Manual* has so far come to light, and all references to it in this study are based on secondary sources, e.g., quotes from or descriptions of it in other CMPS texts.

[65] "Di liu ci quanguo gongan huiyi jueyi" (Resolution of the 6th National Public Security Conference), *Gongan jianshe*, No. 98, September 28, 1954, p. 12.

[66] Luo Ruiqing, "Zai di liu ci quanguo gongan huiyi shang de baogao" (Report to the 6th National Public Security Conference), *Gongan jianshe*, No. 98, September 28, 1954, p. 42.

described how county officers "embarked on a conscientious overhaul of agent work in accordance with the principles outlined in the *Agent Work Manual*... while taking into account the actual circumstances of their own agents."[67]

As one might have expected in what prided itself on being a system of scientific planning, the performance of the 1st Bureau and the performance of the political protection sector nationwide were subject to regular assessment and evaluation. Quantifiable information in particular was collected, aggregated, and analyzed as part of an elaborate management system that had been set up on the orders of the CMPS in January 1950.[68] The guiding principle was that evaluation of past performance was supposed to inject an element of realism into future planning; this was not always the case, however, especially where racking up impressive short-term statistics was difficult, or impossible even, to combine with a "long-term view" and guarding against "impetuosity." The 8th NPSC set the 1957 "crack rate" (*poanlü*) target for "cases involving imperialist and Guomindang *tewu*" at 50–70 percent; in September 1957, the CMPS noted with disappointment that during the first half of 1957, the actual rate had barely approached 30 percent.[69] This did not prevent the ministry from demanding a national average rate of 60 percent for political operations in its work plan for 1958.[70] The 1st Bureau's director claimed in 1959 that the national average crack rate for cases involving espionage, *tewu*, and counterrevolution was well over 90 percent, but the reliability of this figure (attributed to interagency cooperation and a correct implementation of the mass line) is anybody's guess.[71]

---

[67] Gonganbu erju sichu, "Jiexiu xian zhengdun teqing gongzuo jingyan" (Experiences from Overhaul and Consolidation of Agent Work in Jiexiu County), *Renmin gongan*, No. 9, August 10, 1956, p. 21.

[68] *Jianguo yilai gongan*, pp. 6–7.

[69] "Lizheng wancheng 1957 nian gexiang yewu gongzuo de zhibiao" (Strive to Meet the Targets for Vocational Work in 1957), *Renmin gongan*, No. 16, February 15, 1957, p. 12; Gonganbu dangzu, "Guanyu quanguo gongan tingjuzhang zuotanhui de qingkuang baogao" (Situation Report from a National Informal Conference of Directors of Bureaus of Public Security), *Gongan jianshe*, No. 204, November 17, 1957, p. 8.

[70] Zhongyang gonganbu, "1958 nian quanguo gongan gongzuo jihua yaodian" (Key Points of Plan for Public Security Work in 1958), *Gongan jianshe*, No. 212, January 13, 1958, p. 3. On the unrealistic targets set in this and similar provincial plans from 1958, see Dutton, *Policing Chinese Politics*, pp. 206–7.

[71] Ling Yun, "Jinyibu tigao douzheng yishu zhansheng yinbi diren" (Further Improve the Art of Struggle and Defeat the Hidden Enemies), *Renmin gongan*, No. 84, April 8, 1960, p. 18.

Directors of Operations: *Primus Inter Pares*

For the first twelve months of its existence, the 1st Bureau was headed concurrently by the CMPS vice-minister (there was, at the time, only one), Yang Qiqing. Like Luo Ruiqing, Yang was an ex-military man, experienced in matters pertaining to security in the armed forces. Born in Pingjiang county, Hunan, in the year of the Republican Revolution, 1911, Yang got his start in covert operations as a boy, serving as an underground messenger and guard during a local Communist-led peasant insurrection of the kind immortalized by Mao Zedong in his "Report on the Peasant Movement in Hunan." Already an experienced guerrilla operative, at the age of eighteen he was welcomed into the ranks of the CCP and soon joined the Red Army. On the Long March he served close to the central leadership in a security capacity, and in recognition of his services, he was in 1937 appointed to lead the 8th Route Army's powerful Traitor Elimination Bureau. In this capacity, he served out the War of Resistance against Japan in Yan'an. At the start of 1947, he was made director of the CCP Social Affairs Department of the Shanxi-Hebei-Shandong-Henan Base Area; a year later, at the time of the creation of the Party Center's regional North China Bureau, he was made vice-director of its Social Affairs Department. When that department wound up operations at the time of the founding of the PRC, he became the most senior of its officers to join the CMPS.[72]

As director of the 1st Bureau during the first twelve months of its existence, Yang devoted much of his energy to straightforward institution building. His biographer writes that this included everything "from systematically investigating and mounting case operations targeting the *tewu* of the enemy and the state of their organization, to fielding agents, launching physical surveillance operations, putting technical means to use, and setting about creating and managing vocational archives and card indexes."[73] Little is known about how he personally judged the relative merits of different instruments of operational activity, but he appears to have shared with many of his colleagues a fondness for penetration agents, something he humorously conveyed in the following remark made in 1949: "By attaching our eyes to the enemy's own body, we'll know what kind of shit's coming out the moment he lifts his arse. That way we

[72] Liu Xingyi, *Yang Qiqing zhuan*, passim.
[73] Ibid., p. 183.

can take preventive measures. This has to be viewed as an indispensable component of our protection plan."[74] Whether or not this is how Yang regularly conveyed his views, the crude language actually belies a sophisticated communication strategy. Indeed, a long-serving CIA analyst, proposing remedies for breakdowns in communication between intelligence departments and policy makers, once called for analysis to be presented "in a more aphoristic, conversational manner. If colorful, anecdotal language gets a better reception, it should be used to help convey analytical information and judgments."[75] As many of their speeches illustrate, not just Yang but other senior CMPS officers, too, delighted in discussing agent work in metaphorical terms, regularly comparing a lack of operational resources to "dancing in the nude" and Guomindang double agents to radishes ("red on the outside, white on the inside").

In the autumn of 1950, a professionally overburdened Yang Qiqing was able to hand over the directorship of the 1st Bureau to a forty-year-old colleague whose exploits on the covert front had already earned him a meritorious citation from the CCP Center and the personal attention of the Party Chairman. Hailing from the Manchurian port city of Fushun, Chen Long came from a background distinctly different from that of Yang. He had been sent as a student by the CCP to the University of the Toilers of the East in Moscow in 1936. By the time he returned to China in 1938, after having seen Stalin's Great Terror firsthand, he was said to have been ambivalent about how the Soviet Union managed its state security work.[76]

After spending the War of Resistance with the CSAD in Yan'an, Chen was transferred in late 1945 to his native Northeast China, where he worked as a senior operational officer in Harbin and later in Shenyang. Having evidently performed his duties successfully, he rose quickly through the ranks to the post of regional public security vice-minister. After the founding of the PRC, he was briefly transferred to Nanjing, where, as municipal director of public security, he oversaw and led operational work in the former republican capital. His departure, and that of other public security officers like him, from the Northeast provoked local resistance, with complaints voiced in early 1950, at the 4th NEPSC, about the large number of experienced officers being transferred to other

[74] Ibid., p. 189.
[75] Andrew, Aldrich, and Wark, *Secret Intelligence*, p. 137.
[76] Xiu Lairong, *Chen Long zhuan*, p. 79.

parts of China.[77] After serving in Nanjing for less than a year and playing a critical role at the 1st National Conference on Operational Work (where he delivered a keynote address), he moved to Beijing, where he was formally appointed director of the CMPS 1st Bureau on November 24, 1950.[78]

As director, Chen aggressively pursued what he called a policy of "maintaining a firm domestic foothold, while keeping our eyes open to all that goes on overseas."[79] His priority was apparently to focus the resources of the 1st Bureau on major external threats to the PRC (represented principally by the United States and Chiang Kai-shek's Guomindang) while delegating the handling of lesser homegrown threats to regional, provincial, and municipal public security organs. On April 19, 1952, Zhou Enlai's Government Administration Council formally appointed Chen CMPS vice-minister while permitting him to simultaneously hold on to the directorship of the 1st Bureau.

After having been diagnosed with a serious heart condition, Chen began in 1952 to entrust more and more of the leadership of the 1st Bureau to his ranking deputy, Ling Yun. (Chen's official biographer estimates that more than half of the leading cadres on the PRC's operational front lines of political protection were long-standing colleagues or subordinates of Chen's by this time.[80]) Seven years his junior, Ling had been a protégé of Chen Long in Yan'an and, after the founding of the PRC, had served as director of the municipal Bureau of Public Security in Ji'nan, Shandong. From there he was transferred to Beijing in the spring of 1952 to become deputy director of the 1st Bureau at the same time that Chen was promoted to concurrent CMPS vice-minister.[81] On June 5, 1953, Ling formally succeeded Chen as director of the 1st Bureau.[82]

When the CMPS, at the end of 1955, saw it expedient to split the 1st Bureau in two, Ling became director of the new Bureau for Operations Against Imperialist *Tewu*, while his ranking deputy, Li Guangxiang, was appointed to lead operations against Guomindang *tewu* and homegrown

---

[77] Dongbei renmin zhengfu gonganbu, "Guanyu jiaqiang zhencha gongzuo de zhishi" (Instructions on Strengthening Operational Work), *Gongan baowei gongzuo*, No. 17, February 15, 1950, p. 19. See also Dutton, *Policing Chinese Politics*, p. 145.

[78] Zhongyang renmin zhengfu renshibu, ed., *Zhongyang renmin zhengfu renminglu* (*List of Appointments by the Central People's Government*) (Beijing, 1952), p. 47.

[79] Xiu Lairong, *Chen Long zhuan*, p. 385.

[80] Ibid., p. 403.

[81] Ibid., pp. 402–3.

[82] Zhongyang renmin zhengfu renshibu, ed., *Zhongyang renmin zhengfu renminglu* (*List of Appointments by the Central People's Government*) (Beijing, 1954), p. 48.

threats. Born in Shanxi, Li was in his late thirties and had spent the War of Resistance as a political commissar holding down intelligence and security-related posts as an officer with various "traitor elimination" units in Northern China. After the war, he served first under Yang Qiqing in the North China Social Affairs Department's 2nd (Surveillance, Interrogation, Public Order, and Intelligence) Office and then in the Beiping municipal Bureau of Public Security's 2nd (Surveillance and Interrogation) Office.[83] Together with Yang, Li joined the CMPS 1st Bureau at the time of its creation, and prior to becoming its deputy director in 1953 had served for some time as the head of its 1st Office. When the original CMPS 1st Bureau was reconstituted, he was sent to Guangzhou to lead and beef up the capacity of that city's public security bureau.[84]

By the time Ling Yun was promoted to vice-minister of public security on February 12, 1964, he was already the longest-serving CMPS bureau director. He also continued to lead the 1st Bureau until September 9, 1964, when the CCP Center approved a number of personnel changes in the CMPS leadership, including Ling's handover of the bureau to his highest-ranking deputy, forty-five-year-old Mu Fengyun.[85] Mu had joined the 8th Route Army and CCP in 1938 and spent the War of Resistance with the CSAD in Yan'an.[86] Like Ling Yun, Mu had been a protégé of Chen Long and had advanced steadily through the ranks. By the time the CCP was forced to abandon Yan'an in 1947, he had become a section chief in the central party leadership's security detail. He participated in the CCP's peaceful takeover of Beiping, and in August 1949 he was put in charge of organizing and training the 400-plus-strong contingent of plainclothes officers in charge of the security of delegates attending the 1st Plenary Session of the Chinese People's Political Consultative Conference, which brought the PRC into being.[87] He then joined the CMPS 1st Bureau, where his promotion to a deputy directorship was possibly related to his successful running of a number of turned Guomindang *tewu*.[88] Ling Yun evidently had a high opinion of him in 1954: it was with Mu by his side that Ling had briefed Chen Long on the work of

---

[83] Zhu Chunlin, *Lishi shunjian I*, p. 372.
[84] Sun Mingshan, *Lishi shunjian IV*, pp. 315–53.
[85] *Jianguo yilai gongan*, p. 279; Zhonghua renmin gongheguo neiwubu, ed., *Renminglu (List of Appointments)* (Beijing, 1964), p. 26.
[86] Sun Mingshan, *Lishi shunjian IV*, pp. 744–53; Zhu Chunlin, *Lishi shunjian I*, pp. 387–97.
[87] Sun Mingshan, *Lishi shunjian II*, pp. 41–50.
[88] Ibid., pp. 541–63.

the 1st Bureau when Chen had returned from two months of medical treatment in Moscow for his heart condition.[89]

Mu was stripped of his duties in August 1966. Both he and his predecessor, Ling Yun, were now accused of the generic Cultural Revolutionary crime of being "party persons in power taking the capitalist road." One reason for the purging of both men may well have been the fact that their political protection work had given them unique insights into many of the *real* domestic challenges to CCP power, and as such allowed them to discern fatal flaws in the threat scenario presented as justification for the Cultural Revolution. Any director of the CMPS 1st Bureau worth his salt would have been able to instantly assess whether the picture painted by CCP Vice-Chairman Lin Biao in May 1966 made any sense, and there is no reason to believe that they would have backed Lin's infamous claim that "Recently a number of weird things and weird signs have drawn our attention to the possibility of a counterrevolutionary coup, one in which people will be killed, political power will be usurped, capitalism will be restored, and the whole of socialism will be done away with."[90]

The CMPS 2nd Bureau: Preventing Sabotage

The CMPS 2nd (Economic Protection) Bureau led and coordinated operations against forces who might attempt, as an editorial in the *People's Daily* on July 9, 1950, put it, "to stand in the way of the economic construction embarked upon by the Chinese people, and forever keep the Chinese people in a state of poverty and backwardness."[91] Like the 1st Bureau, it had already existed in embryonic form for a couple of months before it formally came into being in October 1949.[92] Initially lacking a charter and a national structure – including counterparts at lower levels, dedicated channels of communication, personnel, funding, and a clear division of responsibilities – it became truly operational only in the summer of 1950, after Zhou Enlai's Government Administration Council on March 24, 1950, passed the Decision to Institute Protection Work in State Financial and Economic Departments.[93] The decision led to a concerted effort, for which the role of functional coordinator was assigned to the

---

[89] Xiu Lairong, *Chen Long zhuan*, p. 428.
[90] Quoted in MacFarquhar and Schoenhals, *Mao's Last Revolution*, p. 38.
[91] *Renmin ribao*, July 9, 1950.
[92] Zhu Chunlin, *Lishi shunjian I*, pp. 7–9.
[93] Zhongyang renmin zhengfu zhengwuyuan, "Guanyu zai guojia caizheng jingji bumen zhong jianli baowei gongzuo de jueding" (Decision to Launch Protection Work in State

2nd Bureau, to do whatever was needed to ensure security against sabotage of the young People's Republic's vital infrastructure, which included banking and finance, industry, trade, transportation, power systems, public works, telecommunications, and essential services.[94]

As acknowledged by Luo Ruiqing at the 1st National Conference on Economic Protection Work held in the spring of 1950, Northeast China – where a majority of the country's heavy industry was concentrated – led the way in strategic planning, capacity building, and the setting of priorities in economic protection.[95] At the 4th NEPSC, Gao Gang had predicted that "the main target that our enemies will seek to attack is economic construction; second are the heads of leadership organs and Soviet experts."[96] In response, in addition to public and semipublic economic protection work, the 2nd Bureau initiated various clandestine forms of work. As one deputy director of public security in the capital told delegates attending the 1st Beijing municipal Conference on Economic Protection Work in October 1950, "If we want to get at the hidden enemies, mere administrative management will not be sufficient. We need to institute agent and operational work, grasp the enemy's circumstances, trends, and activities, and become good at analysis and research. This is the only way we can defeat the hidden enemies."[97] The 3rd National Conference on Economic Protection Work, held in August 1952, affirmed that the problem of deeply ensconced enemy operatives and *tewu* was one that in no way could be "solved altogether solely by relying on mass movements, ideological education, run-of-the-mill investigations, and simply staying on guard."[98]

Financial and Economic Departments), *Tielu gongan tongxun* (Railroad Public Security Bulletin), No. 3, December 15, 1950, p. 1.

94 Some statistics from 1950 illustrating what the 2nd Bureau was up against in terms of enemy sabotage may be found in Michael Schoenhals, "Recruiting Agents in Industry and Trade: Lifting the Veil on Early People's Republic of China Operational Work," *Modern Asian Studies, FirstView* Article, pp. 1–25, published online November 25, 2011 http://dx.doi.org/10.1017/S0026749X11000734 (accessed December 13, 2011).

95 Luo Ruiqing, "Zai quanguo jingji baowei gongzuo huiyi shang de zongjie baogao" (Summing Up Report at the National Conference on Economic Protection Work), *Gongan baowei gongzuo*, No. 18, June 1, 1950, p. 10.

96 Gao Gang, "Zai dongbei di si jie," p. 25.

97 Feng Jiping, "Zhi kaimuci" (Opening Remarks), *Renmin gongan zengkan*, No. 20, December 25, 1950, p. 11.

98 "Di san ci quanguo jingji baowei gongzuo huiyi jueyi" (Resolution of the 3rd National Conference on Economic Protection Work), *Tielu gongan tongxun*, No. 13, December 8, 1952, p. 6.

A problem that would plague the 2nd Bureau for years was that it did not receive, in terms of resources, the same kind of priority treatment accorded to the 1st Bureau and the sector of political protection. Not until after the launch of the PRC's 1st Five Year Plan in 1953 was priority given to the protection of engineering projects (that formed a critical part of the plan).[99] An editorial entitled "Strongly Reinforce Economic Protection Work" in the *People's Daily* highlighted the threat posed by saboteurs operating deep undercover.[100] The editorial became a centerpiece of study campaigns in factories and enterprises across China during the final quarter of 1954, alerting workers to the possible presence of enemies in their midst.[101] But change was slow in coming, and speaking in October 1954, Beijing's director of public security, Feng Jiping, offered a highly critical analysis of the situation:

> If next we proceed to examine our economic protection departments, then we find that here the inability to hit the enemy on target and the weakness of operational work is even more pronounced. Already for quite some time, chaos has prevailed in operational work managed by economic protection departments. Since 1953, despite a major attempt at rectification and basic clarification of the roots of the chaos, and even though work has improved in many respects, operational work as the key to any fundamental transformation has remained extremely weak.[102]

In China's largest industrial city, Shanghai, the situation was equally worrisome. With respect to more or less the entire sector covered by the CMPS 2nd Bureau, the city in 1960 still lacked a "powerful contingent of agents capable of battling hidden enemies and had only feeble intelligence resources." Local officers were often poorly skilled in their trade and were no match for wily enemies.[103]

---

[99] Zhonggong zhongyang zuzhibu bangongting, ed., *Zuzhi gongzuo wenjian xuanbian (1953–1954)* (*Selected Organization Work Documents [1953–1954]*) (Beijing, 1980), p. 343.

[100] *Renmin ribao*, August 21, 1954.

[101] "Gedi gongan xuanchuan gongzuo dongtai" (Trends in Public Security Propaganda Work), *Gongan jianshe*, No. 111, December 20, 1954, pp. 26–27.

[102] Feng Jiping, "Jianjue guanche di liu ci quanguo gongan huiyi jueyi wei jinyibu jiaqiang shoudu gongan gongzuo er fendou" (Resolutely Implement the Resolution of the 6th National Public Security Conference and Struggle to Further Strengthen Public Security Work in the Capital), *Shoudu gongan zengkan*, Vol. 6, No. 1, February 21, 1955, p. 11.

[103] Gonganbu Shanghai gongzuozu, "Shanghai shi duidi douzheng zhong de yixie wenti" (Some Problems in the Struggle Against the Enemy in Shanghai), *Gongan gongzuo jianbao*, No. 166, November 26, 1960, pp. 6–8.

The situation in Southern China hints at how relative freedom to adapt CMPS and 2nd Bureau policies to local conditions shaped much of what happened on the ground. Although the 6th NPSC in 1954 had *expressly* linked prioritization of operational work to the strengthening of economic rather than political protection departments, the Guangdong provincial head of public security reasoned as follows: "That was with reference to the situation in the country as a whole. Given the concrete situation prevailing in Guangdong, when determining where to place the priority in operational work, it is political protection that has to come first, while economic protection comes second. Everybody agrees unanimously that we should set our priorities in this way."[104] In southern front-line provinces like Guangdong, Fujian, and Yunnan (with their porous borders across which Guomindang *tewu* and operatives of hostile intelligence services often sought to enter the PRC and travel farther inland[105]), economic protection therefore remained a secondary priority compared to political protection.

A radical remedy that may have been an attempt to overcome some of the institutional obstacles impeding effective economic protection was enacted in the final months of 1955, when the CMPS executed a major internal restructuring plan. While little is known about who was the driving force behind this controversial plan, Bai Jun, deputy director of the 2nd Bureau in late 1959, implied that CMPS Vice-Minister Wang Jinxiang was among those who favored the reform as a means of resolving the problems with the way the bureau had operated prior to 1955.[106] As part of his plan, the original 2nd (Economic Protection) Bureau was split into three: the Capital Construction Protection Bureau (13th Bureau), the Industry Protection Bureau (14th Bureau), and the Finance and Trade Protection Bureau (15th Bureau). The restructuring was to prove

---

[104] Wen Minsheng, "Dali jiaqiang yinbi douzheng zhong de zhencha gongzuo" (Strongly Reinforce Operational Work on the Covert Front), *Gongan jianshe*, No. 113, January 10, 1955, p. 7.

[105] An important source through which senior public security officers were briefed on these penetration activities consisted of the special so-called Hong Kong and Taiwan news editions (*Gang-Tai xiaoxi ban*) of the Top Secret CMPS serial *Public Security Intelligence*. A comprehensive institutional survey of hostile intelligence services active on the borders of the PRC at the end of the 1950s may be found in "Diguozhuyi, Jiang feibang he minzuzhuyi guojia zai woguo zhouwei jiaqiang tewu jigou" (Imperialist, Chiang Kai-shek Bandit Gang and Nationalist States Reinforcing *Tewu* Organs Around Our Country), *Gongan qingbao*, No. 6, January 26, 1960, pp. 3–5.

[106] Bai Jun, "Xiang dang qingzui" (Asking for Punishment from the Party for My Crimes), *Gongan jianshe*, No. 326, December 30, 1959, pp. 48–54.

almost as short-lived as the (simultaneous) division of the 1st Bureau. On March 18, 1957, the 13th and 14th Bureaus were merged and redesignated the 2nd (Industry Protection) Bureau. Meanwhile, the director of the 15th Bureau held the "original" Economic Protection Bureau very much responsible for the many problems he himself continued to confront. These were, he said, due "first and foremost [to the fact that] the vocational bureau – the original Economic Protection Bureau – managing this field of work within the Central Ministry of Public Security did not, at the same time as it stressed the work of protecting factories, mines, and capital construction, pay the same kind of attention to Finance and Trade Protection Work."[107] On December 2, 1958, the 15th (Finance and Trade Protection) Bureau was absorbed by the 2nd Bureau, which now reverted back to its original designation as the 2nd (Economic Protection) Bureau.[108]

The statistics illustrating the performance of the economic protection sector as a whole are opaque and, as in the case of the 1st Bureau, difficult to evaluate. On the ground, the contextualizing information that sometimes accompanied them does nevertheless give something akin to a well-rounded local picture. In the following report from a CMPS 2nd Bureau task force surveying the "extremely complex political situation" in Shanghai's foreign trade sector in early 1962, it is important to note that in line with a policy of "using a long line to catch a big fish," the cases mentioned were intentionally *not* cracked. As excerpted in the CMPS *Public Security Work Bulletin*, the task force report stated:

Forty-seven of the [altogether 4,914] trading firms surveyed either serve as enemy operative premises or are run by persons who are themselves spies or *tewu* elements. Nineteen of these trading firms are imperialist and Chiang Kai-shek *tewu* premises. For example, the [offices of the] Hong Kong merchant firm C. Cordon & Co. [located in the Hong Kong and Shanghai Bank Building on the Shanghai Bund] serve as premises for communication and the transfer of funds for the bandit Investigation Bureau of the Interior Ministry [*Neidiaoju*]. The head of the firm has maintained close links to Chen Guofu, Pan Gongzhan, and other *tewu* elements, and has teamed up with his own younger brother, who is employed by the Shanghai Minerals Import and Export Corporation, to steal intelligence and sabotage our export trade. The remaining twenty-eight trading firms have *tewu* elements serving as their managers, assistant managers, directors, shareholders, or holding other critical positions. These *tewu* elements use import-export business

---

[107] Yan Dingchu, "Zai di yi ci quanguo caizheng maoyi baowei gongzuo huiyi shang de baogao" (Report to the 1st National Conference on Finance and Trade Protection Work), *Gongan jianshe*, No. 166, July 6, 1956, p. 14.
[108] *Jianguo yilai gongan*, p. 95.

as their cover and in the course of sightseeing, tourism, calling on relatives and friends, and technical exchanges exploit their contacts to gather intelligence and engage in *tewu* activities.[109]

At the macro level, on the other hand, the invariably large decontextualized figures mentioned convey only a bare minimum of useful information. Wang Jinxiang, at the 9th NPSC in the summer of 1958, for example, announced that "according to highly incomplete statistics, we have since 1951 already...cracked 35,000 cases of [attempted or actual] sabotage and all kinds of political cases inside organs and enterprises in the industry and mining, capital construction, finance and trade, and transport sectors."[110] Without a similar statistic for the cases *not* cracked, this figure by itself does not say much about the effectiveness of economic protection work at the time.

Economic Protection: "We're *All* Amateurs at This!"

The early directors of the CMPS 2nd Bureau were anonymous figures during their tenure and, even today, half a century later, only scant biographical information about them is available. The bureau's first director was one Lei Rongtian from Xiaoyi county, Shanxi, who had joined the CCP as a twenty-year-old student in 1935. During the War of Resistance, he served initially in the forces of the Shanxi warlord Yan Xishan before rising steadily through the ranks as a political commissar in the 8th Route Army units commanded by Chen Geng. When Zhou Enlai's cabinet formally confirmed his appointment on December 16, 1949, Lei was still with Chen, serving as the political commissar of the 2nd Field Army's 14th Corps, which at the time was advancing on Guangdong province.[111] Lei led the 2nd Bureau during its critical launch phase, but neither contemporary sources nor recent historical literature make any mention of this or, indeed, with only a handful of exceptions, of him.

---

[109] "Shaoshu yu wo you maoyi wanglai de waishang Huashang de zhengzhi qingkuang jiwei fuza" (The Political Circumstances of a Small Number of Foreign and Overseas Chinese Firms That Trade with Us Are Extremely Complex), *Gongan gongzuo jianbao*, No. 236, March 21, 1962, p. 3.

[110] Wang Jinxiang, "Xin xingshi xia de jingji baowei gongzuo: zai di jiu ci quanguo gongan huiyi shang de fayan" (Economic Protection Work Under New Circumstances: Statement at the 9th National Public Security Conference), *Jingji baowei gongzuo* (*Economic Protection Work*), No. 23, February 15, 1959, p. 8.

[111] *Zhongyang renmin zhengfu renminglu* (1952), p. 48; Wang Zhongxing and Liu Liqin, *Di er yezhanjun*, pp. 52–58.

There is reason to believe that Lei may well have felt out of his depth in his role as CMPS director tasked with economic protection. He was inexperienced in operational matters and unable to claim for himself anything like the kind of expertise that the former "traitor elimination" officers serving with Yang Qiqing in the 1st Bureau possessed. An officer from Northeast China promoted to a deputy directorship in the CMPS in the winter of 1952 recalled decades later an early briefing he requested and received from Lei:

> I then returned once more to the 2nd Bureau, [now] to look up its director, Lei Rongtian. I hoped he would tell me what I ought to pay attention to when working in the Ministry of Public Security. After having talked a little about this and that, when he got to talking about operational work, he shook his head as if to indicate that here we're all amateurs at this, we don't have the necessary competence. It was work that had to be managed by people who knew what they were doing. He added, now that you've come, things may improve a little, since you're a professional. I promptly said that, like him, I too was an amateur and did not know the first thing about operational work. He replied saying once you begin working here, you will slowly discover what I mean.[112]

By early 1955, Lei had been transferred out of the CMPS to head the secret bureau (nominally part of the Ministry of Geology) in charge of locating and mining uranium deposits for use in the Soviet and Chinese nuclear bomb programs. One of the last major events involving the CMPS 2nd Bureau during his tenure as director was the completion of a nationwide security investigation of China's geology sector workforce – from its engineers to ordinary miners. According to an interim assessment by the CMPS and the Ministry of Geology in August 1954, the investigation resulted in the identification of activists, the recruitment of a number of agents, increased security overall, and the better professionalization of protection as a whole.[113] Security investigations of this kind had a number of important operational components, and by the mid-1950s, the practice of utilizing background checks on staff to profile for agent material and recruit agents was becoming routine.

After Lei had left the 2nd Bureau, as noted previously, the CMPS briefly divided the task of overseeing economic protection among a number of new lesser bureaus. Which one of their directors served as the de facto

[112] Yan Youmin, *Gongan zhanxian*, pp. 87–88.
[113] Zhongyang gonganbu and Dizhibu, "Guanyu zai dizhi xitong jixu guanche qingli duiwu gongzuo de zhishi" (Instructions on Continuing Purification of Workforce in Geological Sector), *Gongan jianshe*, No. 103, October 15, 1954, p. 10.

head(s) of economic protection work in the CMPS between late 1955 and the end of 1958 is not known. But by January 1959, the status of the CMPS 2nd Bureau had more or less reverted back to what it had been upon Lei Rongtian's departure from office. Li Zhao – about whom there is almost no biographical information – was appointed the new director of the bureau. In his memoirs, a one-time colleague refers to Li in passing as a junior member (in charge of radio communications) of an advance party of CSAD cadres dispatched from Yan'an to the city of Zhangjiakou within days of the Japanese surrender on August 15, 1945.[114] Li is also referred to in passing in the memoirs of a different former colleague as leading, together with Chen Long, a small advance party of CCP Northeast Social Affairs Department cadres that entered the city of Shenyang in 1948 in order to prepare its takeover ahead of the arrival of the main PLA units.[115] After the founding of the PRC, he initially remained in Northeast China, and it was as a NEMPS delegate that he attended the 1st National Conference on Economic Protection Work. After the conference, he is known to have transmitted the "spirit" of what it had decided to a regional gathering of senior public security officers.[116]

The paucity of biographical material on Li is to some extent made up for by the far greater number of texts written by him – compared to his predecessor(s) – during the time when he actually held office in the 2nd Bureau. Hence, from his speeches published in the 2nd Bureau serial *Economic Protection Work* (classified "Secret"), we know that in May 1958, when he was already director of the lesser Economic Protection Bureau, he cautioned against "trusting exclusively in a few operational officers and agents while neglecting the capacity of the masses to discover, keep a watchful eye over, and control the enemy," and he sharply criticized those who "go so far as to have blind faith in technology while not recognizing the value of human [assets]."[117] When the propaganda of the Great Leap Forward reached a climax in the summer of 1958, Li held up as an ideal a Beijing cement plant where, he claimed, "everyone

---

[114] Zhu Chunlin, *Lishi shunjian I*, pp. 364–66.
[115] Ibid., p. 229.
[116] Wang Jinxiang, "Zai dongbei zhengzhi jingji," p. 19.
[117] Li Zhao, "Jin yi bu guanche qunzhong luxian geng haode baowei gongye dayuejin" (Implement the Mass Line One Step Further and Do an Even Better Job of Protecting the Industrial Great Leap Forward), *Jingji baowei gongzuo*, No. 17, November 12, 1958, p. 5.

everywhere, from inside the plant to outside the plant, from staff to family dependents, from the workshop to the canteen, from adults to little children, is taking action to block loopholes, check up on bad people, and solve long-pending cases; and where everyone is doing protective work and where it is safe everywhere."[118] Li survived the Leap and the years leading up to the Cultural Revolution unscathed. At the start of it, he was transferred from the CMPS to Beijing municipality and the post of director of public security in the capital.

Cooperation: An Elusive Goal

In theory, operational departments, their leaders and staff, were engaged in a single concerted public security effort. Responsibility for ensuring that this was the case fell ultimately upon the CMPS Party Group. Lesser party bodies and party members in lower-level organs were reminded of their own obligations toward the same end in rectification rituals and political study. To instill in officers the right unity of purpose and esprit de corps was a rationale behind regularly studying and discussing in groups the works of the CCP Chairman. In 1950, the Beijing municipal Bureau of Public Security had included in its very first set of *Political Teaching Materials* Mao's "Combat Liberalism," an essay that denounced the "liberal tendency shown by certain people among us," a tendency that "eats away at unity, undermines cohesion, causes apathy, and . . . prevents policies from being carried through"; on the eve of the Cultural Revolution seventeen years later, the CMPS called on officers across China to spend the Spring Festival rereading "Serve the People," the classic 1944 eulogy to one of their fallen comrades, in which Mao told members of the CCP Center's security detail how "we . . . have joined together for a common revolutionary objective."[119]

There were arguably times when this cooperation and partnership proceeded smoothly and as intended. Otherwise, a huge operation like the Class A Case No. 12 – which for more than a decade pooled operational resources from the CMPS, fourteen provinces, and three municipalities,

---

[118] Li Zhao, "Rang anquan hongqi chabian quanguo" (Plant Red Banners of Security Nationwide), *Jingji baowei gongzuo*, No. 12, September 1958, p. 5.

[119] Beijing shi gonganju, ed., *Zhengzhi jiaocai (Political Teaching Materials)* (Beijing, 1950), pp. 49–53; "Gonganbu fachu 1966 nian chunjie qijian kaizhan aiminyue huodong de tongzhi" (Ministry of Public Security Issues Notification Launching a Cherish-the-People Campaign during the Spring Festival), *Renmin gongan*, No. 216, December 4, 1965, p. 3.

in addition to Soviet technical expertise, to thwart the efforts of saboteurs fielded by the Guomindang Central Committee Group Two (*Zhongwei-hui erzu*) Mainland Railroad Work Group out of Hong Kong – would never have gotten off the ground, much less met with success.[120] When the work to be carried out warranted it, the heads of the public security organs involved would designate one particular party the mission manager. In 1958, Wang Jinxiang explained how in the economic protection sector, depending on the exact nature of the threat to a specific asset, the task of protecting it might justify the mobilization of operational resources from other sectors. If, for example, Wang observed, it involved an enemy operative physically inside a factory or corporation, the lead agency should come from within the economic protection sector, with the political protection sector providing assistance. Conversely, if the threat was external, then the political protection sector was to take operational responsibility, with other agencies providing backup. If they considered it appropriate, superior bodies could override this standard procedure and insist on a different pooling of resources, depending on the circumstances.[121]

However, in the routine circumstances that usually prevailed, and particularly in the absence of a politically mandated campaign with superior organs *ordering* cooperation toward a specific and clearly circumscribed goal, there were widespread and serious problems. Among the operational departments and officers engaged in political protection work in Southwest China in the mid-1950s, for example, there was only a bare minimum of lateral information sharing, which prompted serious complaints from regional leaderships. Only by themselves initiating joint research, coordinating deployment of resources, and "fighting shoulder to shoulder" would they ultimately be successful in their work, the regional Bureau of Public Security observed in a 1954 work report to the CMPS.[122] In Hebei, the provincial deputy public security director complained to his officers about their apparent unwillingness to devote resources to following up intelligence "coming down from the top or shared by other localities." (Since most of it was substantial, he said, it should be given

---

[120] "Shier hao zhuan'an huibao tigang" (Report Outline on Case No. 12) [October 20, 1963].

[121] Wang Jinxiang, "Xin xingshi xia," pp. 12–13.

[122] "Xi'nan ge shengshi zhengbao bumen diaocha yanjiu gongzuo de jidian jingyan" (Some Experiences Gained from Investigation and Research Work by Political Protection Departments in Southwest China), *Gongan jianshe*, No. 113, January 10, 1955, p. 20.

a higher priority, and someone should be appointed specifically to deal with it.[123])

Across civilian–military institutional boundaries, the problem of poor cooperation was, if anything, even more pronounced. At the 6th NPSC, the provincial public security director in Fujian illustrated the resulting disarray as follows:

In the city of Xiamen, for example, there are the Bureau of Public Security operational departments as well as the operational units belonging to border defense units. When it comes to case surveillance and agent work, they sometimes cancel each other out: that is to say, the same case may be subject to operational work by both parties, or the agent of party A is the operational target of party B. The two are completely independent, and there have as a consequence been damaging cases of the enemy being able to benefit from this, gain legal cover, and steal our intelligence.[124]

The same public security officer who had remembered Lei Rongtian in 1952 stating that in the CMPS 2nd Bureau "we're all amateurs" further recalled how, upon joining the ministry, an old-timer had told him how it felt to be working in the 2nd Bureau, mentioning that "with respect to operational work, there was some conflict between the 1st and 2nd bureaus. He shared with me some criticism directed at the 1st Bureau."[125] Part of the problem would seem to have been the professional pride (if not blustering self-importance) of officers working in political protection: in the Beijing municipal Bureau of Public Security, according to the findings of a CMPS task force concerned specifically with questions of morale, the staff employed in the office tasked with political protection regarded their own operational work as superior to all other work and could be very condescending toward "comrades employed in the other vocational departments." In turn, the staff employed in the 1st Section of the office in question regarded themselves as the most important of all, because their operational work targeted the "imperialists," which they deemed more important than the work of officers who targeted other enemies. What is more, within any given section, an officer involved in secret case

---

[123] Wang Dongning, "Zai Hebei quansheng zhencha gongzuo huiyi shang de zongjie baogao" (Summing Up Report at the Hebei Province-Wide Conference on Operational Work), *Gongan jianshe*, No. 132, July 16, 1955, pp. 10–11.

[124] Ye Song, "Zai di liu ci quanguo gongan huiyi shang de fayan" (Statement at the 6th National Public Security Conference), *Gongan jianshe*, No. 102, October 12, 1954, p. 22.

[125] Yan Youmin, *Gongan zhanxian*, p. 87.

operations invariably regarded himself as superior to officers preoccupied with more ordinary forms of investigation and research.[126]

Conversely, in some places, officers employed in the economic protection sector clearly suffered from low self-esteem, and not always without reason. A survey conducted in Jiangsu by the provincial Bureau of Public Security discovered in 1954 that grassroots economic protection officers did not really think of operational tasks as being their responsibility; rather, they believed that such work belonged solely to political protection units. The survey found that factory leaders and workers alike sometimes held economic protection units in barely disguised contempt, speaking of them as the "garbage section" (*lajike*).[127] But even where they did see themselves, and were in a sense viewed, as equals, this did not necessarily solve the problem. In the Tianjin municipal Bureau of Public Security, among the rank and file, the prevailing attitude toward officers from other operational offices was one of suspicion: when asked to join forces to solve an operational task, it was not uncommon for them to insist that "Either we do it or you do it!" or to argue that instead of attempting to coordinate, they might as well try to compete: "It's hard for you to accommodate me, and it's no less difficult for me to accommodate you, so why don't we each give it our best and see who solves it?"[128] Indeed, a CMPS notification on investigatory work noted that "it happens a lot that the very material that the political protection office has just investigated will shortly thereupon be investigated once more by the economic protection office, which is a waste [of] human and material resources."[129]

If, like *Time* magazine in its 1956 feature on Luo Ruiqing, one were to compare the institutional framework of public security discussed in this chapter to a machine, it would resemble a giant contraption that ran less than smoothly, but that ran all the same. Not all of its cogs, wheels, and

[126] Gonganbu Beijing shichazu, "Guanyu Beijing shi gonganju chuanda guanche di liu ci quanguo gongan huiyi jueyi kaizhan piping yu ziwo piping qingkuang de kaocha baogao" (Investigation Report on the Beijing Bureau of Public Security's Implementation of the Resolution of the 6th National Public Security Conference and the Unfolding of Criticism and Self-Criticism), *Gongan jianshe*, No. 112, December 31, 1954, p. 2.

[127] Jiangsu sheng gonganting, "Guanyu jingji baowei gongzuo de jiancha" (Examination of Economic Protection Work), *Gongan jianshe*, No. 111, December 20, 1954, p. 9.

[128] Gonganbu Tianjin shichazu, "Guanyu Tianjin shi gonganju zhencha gongzuo de kaocha baogao" (Investigation Report on the Tianjin Bureau of Public Security's Operational Work), *Gongan jianshe*, No. 118, March 7, 1955, p. 5.

[129] Gonganbu, "Guanyu gaijin diaocha cailiao gongzuo de tongzhi" (Notification on Improving Documentary Investigation), *Gongan jianshe*, No. 121, March 26, 1955, p. 26.

levers were closely interconnected, and a breakdown in one part did not necessarily lead to a slowdown in another area. Redundancy was built in: one set of wheels momentarily grinding to a halt rarely translated into a cessation of motion altogether, as a different set began to spin in their stead. It was a machine capable of running on crude unprocessed *information*, converting it to political power with reasonable efficiency, according to the circumstances. And it is to agents as one key source of such information – and therefore power – that the next chapter will turn.

2

Agents by Category

Informers, Enablers, and Guardians

If all one had to go by were contemporary foreign visitors' reports, one could be excused for believing that the operational activities of public security organs in Mao's China were entirely a matter of mobilizing the revolutionary masses. "I still have to meet someone," a resident Belgian correspondent for Agence France Presse wrote in the early 1960s, "who has actually discovered a microphone in his Peking home or office."[1] A Canadian journalist working for the *Globe and Mail* described at some length the housewife "with the knitting needles" residing on the ground floor, who kept an eye on the activities and habits of her neighbors. "To maintain the security and interests of the state," he wrote in 1958, was one of her "unspoken duties."[2]

Yet the neighborhood watch that casual observers might catch a glimpse of did not convey the whole picture. Yes, urban police stations were aided on a voluntary basis by a sizable local contingent of so-called social eyes and ears (*shehui ermu*), who kept an eye on people deemed of interest.[3] But in addition, well out of sight, public security organs

---

[1] Jacques Marcuse, *The Peking Papers: Leaves from the Notebook of a China Correspondent* (New York: E. P. Dutton, 1967), p. 34.

[2] Gerald Clark, *Impatient Giant: Red China Today* (New York: David McKay, 1959), pp. 42–43.

[3] Michael Dutton refers to these people as "local activist-informants." See Dutton, *Policing Chinese Politics*, pp. 288–89. An early (1952) discussion of their backgrounds and uses in the context of gathering "social intelligence" (*sheqing*) and assessing the mood in society at large is translated in Michael Schoenhals, ed. and trans., *Public Security in the People's Republic of China: A Selection of Mood Assessment Reports (1951–1962)*, published as *Contemporary Chinese Thought: Translations and Studies*, Vol. 38, No. 3, Spring 2007, pp. 48–53.

employed assets of an altogether different sort. On the final day of the 1st National Conference on Economic Protection Work in 1950, Luo Ruiqing had explained to officers from all over China why "history" would punish them unless they developed specialized and entirely covert operational resources "as a basic means whereby we can vanquish our enemies." In the short run, any officer dragging his feet in regard to developing covert resources, he added, in what sounded like a veiled threat, would also be committing "a major political error."[4] Given the highest ministerial seal of approval, public security organs set about aggressively recruiting and secretly deploying large numbers of agents.[5] Looking back in 1957, it was possible for the CMPS to assert that "the agent contingent of the public security organs, having been built up over a number of years, is already of a definite size and has played a major role in operational work."[6]

So sensitive was the matter that official silence was complete. The CMPS would on occasion permit writers of fiction or movie scripts to *hint* at the existence of covert operational resources, but only as long as they did not provide any clue as to precisely what they were and exactly how they functioned.[7] Prior to December 1967 and the beginning of the "Thorough Beating to a Pulp of So-Called 'Domestic Agents,'" the very existence of domestic agents had yet to become widely known. In the summer of 1967, public security officers in Shanghai charging the leadership of the CMPS 1st Bureau with revisionism had still dutifully self-censored their accusations in print (which were otherwise full of details of alleged "heinous crimes") by substituting "xx work" for "agent work," "xx networks" for "agent networks," "cultivation and recruitment of xx" for "cultivation and recruitment of agents," and so on.[8] The degree to which the topic has remained taboo in the post-Mao era is illustrated by the fact that in 1997, a *Draft History of the People's Public Security* published in Beijing "for official use only," but on sale in ordinary bookshops, suggested that on the covert front no small number of successes had been scored since 1949, thanks to the strategic deployment of various operational resources. Significantly, however, it did not allude – much less explicitly refer – to agents.[9]

[4] Luo Ruiqing, "Zai quanguo jingji baowei," p. 11.
[5] *Jianguo yilai Liu Shaoqi wengao*, Vol. 4, pp. 324–27.
[6] "Teqing gongzuo," p. 14.
[7] Zhu Chunlin, *Lishi shunjian I*, pp. 571–86.
[8] *Dadao litong waiguode*, pp. 10–13.
[9] *Zhongguo renmin gongan shigao*, pp. 251–52, 270–73.

"Is It Moral, Then? It Is Highly Moral"

Not one but two, ultimately conflicting, definitions of what constituted an agent enjoyed currency among public security officers at the time of the founding of the PRC. The first, older definition – dating back to the War of Resistance against Japan, possibly even earlier – made an important political distinction: in the words of Luo Ruiqing, "we used, in the past, to maintain that the term 'agent' referred exclusively, or mainly, to hostile class elements that we had turned." Adherents of this definition would, therefore, not speak of assets that belonged to what they saw as the natural class or activist constituency of the CCP as agents. As Luo put it, "there are some comrades who don't like the sound of the word 'agent.'"[10]

A second, alternative definition came to supersede and replace the first one in due course, but in 1949–50 its proponents had still to make their case. In its regional serial *Public Security and Protection Work* (classified "Top Secret"), the NEMPS explained on August 22, 1950, that the correct way of assessing a person's status had to be on the basis of the *function* he or she performed. How to understand and employ the word agent was to be determined by what the agent *did* – or had the capacity to do – and not by notions of where he or she, as an individual, might reside on the political spectrum from left to right.[11] Regardless of what kind of person the agent was, the regional ministry argued, he or she "should be in a position to identify, establish contact with, obtain intelligence on, and fight the enemy. That should be our standard."[12]

During Chen Long's two-and-a-half-year tenure as director of the CMPS 1st Bureau, the functionalist definition of the term agent, lobbied for by the NEMPS, came to gain increasing acceptance.[13] How long it took for older public security officers to become comfortable with it is impossible to say, but by 1957 officer cadets entering the Central People's Public Security Academy in Beijing were told of how "historically, by habit... the political referent of the word agent had excluded

---

[10] Luo Ruiqing, "Zai quanjun di er ci baowei gongzuo huiyi shang de zongjie baogao" (Summing Up Report at the 2nd All-PLA Conference on Protection Work), *Jingji baowei gongzuo huiji* (*Collected Economic Protection Work*), No. 5, July 1953, pp. 1–2.

[11] Dongbei renmin zhengfu ganganbu, "Gei Liaodong sheng gongganting de xin: guanyu teqing gongzuo de jige sixiang renshi wenti" (Letter to the Liaodong Provincial Bureau of Public Security: On Certain Matters of Ideology and Understanding Relating to Agent Work), *Gongan baowei gongzuo*, No. 19, September 15, 1950, pp. 55–58.

[12] Ibid., p. 57.

[13] "*Teqing gongzuo*," pp. 2–3.

party and Youth League members and activists, and comprised mainly backward elements, hostile class elements, and *tewu* elements. This distinction later proved in our actual work not to be entirely appropriate and indeed too inflexible, so a decision was made to dispense with [it and] . . . refer only to agents."[14] In what was clearly an attempt to establish a uniform authoritative definition, the CMPS in the textbook *Lectures on the Subject of Agent Work* asserted, "Agents are secret operational resources, working under the direction of the public security organs, who have been recruited from various social strata by those same organs to serve the struggle against the destructive activities carried out by spies and *tewu* of the imperialists and the Chiang Kai-shek clique and by other counterrevolutionary elements."[15]

Coinciding with the process whereby the CMPS assigned a neutral in-house meaning to the term agent was an ethical dispute among the public security rank and file about the appropriateness of the covert use of agents in the first place (pragmatic resolution of this dispute was only gradually achieved after 1950 through the personal interventions of senior CMPS leaders). The dispute centered on whether the CCP's claim to being truly revolutionary in effect compelled it to dispense with the covert deployment of agents in the "new society." To put it differently: was there really a difference between the secret agents of the new regime and the dreaded *tewu* of the ancien regime? Most importantly, how was one to reconcile a genuine postrevolutionary order with the occasional recruitment of agents from the very classes that a *People's Daily* editorial had identified as the "remnant forces of counterrevolution over which dictatorship will be exercised"?[16]

At the start of 1950, 15,845 people, of whom roughly two-thirds were new in their positions – that is, they were not holdovers from the Republican police – were employed by the municipal Bureau of Public Security in Beijing.[17] In the capital and in cities elsewhere, new and inexperienced lower-level officers, many of them demobilized PLA soldiers uncomfortable in their new role, were concerned that the "masters of New China" – which they took to mean the ordinary working-class men and women with whom they interacted on a daily basis – would become disenchanted with

[14] Ibid., p. 3.
[15] Ibid.
[16] *Renmin ribao*, September 22, 1949.
[17] Mu Yumin, *Beijing jingcha bainian* (*One Hundred Years of the Beijing Police*) (Beijing: Zhongguo renmin gongan daxue chubanshe, 2004), p. 451. See also Dutton, *Policing Chinese Politics*, p. 144.

them, or that they would befall an even worse fate if they were found to be operating covert agent networks that for an outsider might be hard to distinguish from those that had been run by the Guomindang and the Japanese in the past.[18] It would have been anathema for any member of the People's Police to see his own name (and, by extension, that of the CCP) linked to the dreaded *tewu*. The significance of this issue is highlighted by a chief security officer's report to the 1st Beijing municipal Conference on Economic Protection Work in October 1950. Employed at Beijing's Shijingshan Power Plant, he revealed that one of the most pressing tasks he faced was to "rectify the erroneous view of some of our power plant's employees, who maintain that what we protection officers do amounts to *tewu* work."[19]

The problem was, of course, that the difference between the old and the new society was not always easy to distinguish when it came to operational activity. In fact, and quite significantly, among agents themselves, there would occasionally be those who sensed a continuity in practice, if not in name. In the autumn of 1950, the municipal Bureau of Public Security in Shenyang complained as follows:

Some [agents] speak about our agent work and the counterrevolutionary *tewu* in the same breath, as if they were one and the same. These are the people who in the past served as *tewu* but got nothing out of it and grew to resent it. Today, when we tell them to act as agents for us (when we haven't yet explained to them that this is something completely different from serving as the *tewu* of the enemy), they're still inclined to turn us down. In some cases they need to be educated numerous times before they begin to change their stance.[20]

Complaining in a speech in May 1950 about how some of his men had yet to fully grasp the continued need for covert forms of operational activity such as the use of agents, Xu Jianguo, public security director in the city of Tianjin, even indicated that ordinary police officers were themselves in need of "education" along similar lines.[21]

---

[18] Wang Jinxiang, "Zai Dongbei zhengzhi jingji," p. 20.
[19] Guo Yumin, "Zai huiyi shang guanyu Shijingshan fadianchang jianli anquan xiaozu gongzuo de dianxing baogao" (Pilot Conference Report on the Creation of Security Groups in the Shijingshan Power Plant), *Renmin gongan zengkan*, No. 20, December 25, 1950, p. 19.
[20] Shenyang shi renmin zhengfu gonganju jingji baoweichu, "Guanyu jianli teqing gongzuo de fangfa" (Agent Work Initiation Procedures), *Gongan baowei gongzuo*, No. 20, November 25, 1950, p. 38.
[21] Xu Jianguo, "Zhengdun duiwu gaijin lingdao tigao zuzhi zhandouli" (Rectify Our Contingents, Improve Leadership, and Raise the Combat Power of Our Organization), *Tianjin gongan*, Vol. 1, No. 2, August 15, 1950, p. 13.

It was left to Luo Ruiqing to persuade those who remained uncon-
vinced that "under today's new circumstances, in the needs of the new
struggle," it was simply not an option to rely *solely* on "the masses."
In practical terms, he insisted at the end of the 1st National Conference on Economic Protection Work, successful operational work would
always mean recruiting the occasional unsavory "alien-class element" or
"hostile element" to "render services to us": "Is this moral, then? It is
highly moral. As I said earlier, it is the idea of giving somebody a taste
of his own medicine. . . . One of our moral standards is the protection
of the people's interests. We absolutely do not want any abstract moral
standards unrelated to the interests of a concrete class."[22] The fact that
Luo was to repeat this very same line at another conference more than
two years later may indicate that it took time for his message to be
accepted.[23]

Morals aside, operational departments clearly also needed to confront
in more substantial terms the issue of what made "our" agents better
than "their" *tewu*. In the *Lectures*, the relevant page-long discussion
of the matter began with the following reminder: "When we speak of
agents, we need to point out that there are differences in principle between
our agents and the *tewu* elements of the *tewu* agencies of the capitalist
countries."[24] The first difference had to do with the nature of the state: in
the PRC it was said to be a "people's democratic dictatorship led by the
proletariat and based on the worker–peasant alliance." Lifted verbatim
from the preamble to the 1954 PRC Constitution, this formulation was –
one assumes – entirely familiar to the intended audience of the *Lectures*.[25]
Equally familiar, albeit emanating from a very different kind of source
(V. I. Lenin's *The State and Revolution*), would have been the *Lectures'*
sweeping characterization of the state in capitalist countries as "political
power in the hands of the bourgeoisie, employed to oppress and exploit
the broad laboring masses." The public security organs of the PRC, in
short, were fundamentally different from "*tewu* agencies" because the
latter were but "evil tools protecting the interests of the oppressive ruling
classes."[26]

A further difference had to do with the putative purpose of agent work
per se. In the PRC, according to the *Lectures*, it was to "curb, guard

[22] Luo Ruiqing, "Zai quanguo jingji baowei," pp. 14–15.
[23] Luo Ruiqing, "Zai quanjun di er ci baowei," p. 2.
[24] "*Teqing gongzuo*," pp. 4–5.
[25] *1955 Renmin shouce (1955 People's Handbook)* (Tianjin: Dagongbao she, 1955), p. 2.
[26] "*Teqing gongzuo*," p. 5.

against, and strike [back] at" the destructive acts of hostile forces.[27] In contrast, *tewu* operations conducted by foreign adversaries and domestic enemies of New China were characterized as aggressive and as serving an inherently reactionary purpose. It was claimed that the latter aimed at globally "suppressing the revolutionary movement of the working class and broad popular masses" and specifically at "subversion and sabotage against socialist and enemy states."[28] Under these circumstances, the public security organs of the PRC were essentially assuming a defensive stance; this was asserted whenever the opportunity arose. In the first week of November 1963, coinciding with an announcement from the CMPS that nine groups of armed *tewu* totaling ninety men had been "wiped out" along the South and East China coast since the month of June, the *People's Daily* published an article in which it asked whether, "according to the principles of peaceful coexistence put forward by Lenin, one is only permitted to suffer blows, while not being allowed to hit back? No, absolutely not. To claim as much is to insult the great Lenin."[29]

A final difference between what the *Lectures* carefully qualified as *"an absolute majority of* our agents" (emphasis added) and all of the various "elements" serving the *"tewu* agencies of the capitalist countries" centered on methods of recruitment, running, and rewarding:

An absolute majority of our agents consist of patriotic elements who have been recruited on the basis of their socialist and patriotic ideological awareness and who therefore are able to work self-consciously [*zijuede*] for us. We always train our agents to work loyally and objectively for the sake of striking at the enemy and protecting good people, to reflect circumstances truthfully, without exaggerating or understating, not to frame people, and not to use means such as instigation. The *tewu* contingent of the *tewu* agencies of the capitalist countries, on the other hand, is made up of reactionary, selfish and self-serving, decadent and degenerate elements and criminal elements. They serve as *tewu* to obtain money and status, although some of them also pledge loyalty to the capitalist system and uphold the interests of the bourgeoisie. They are trained by the *tewu* agencies to make use of instigation, trumped-up charges, and framing people.[30]

The context in which these points were made was a discussion of the need to maintain secrecy. It should be remembered that the argumentation was

[27] Ibid., pp. 2, 5.
[28] Ibid., p. 5.
[29] *Zhongguo gongchandang lun guoji xingshi he shehuizhuyi guojia duiwai zhengce* (*The Chinese Communist Party on the International Situation and the Foreign Policy of Socialist States*) (Beijing: Renmin chubanshe, 1964), p. 155.
[30] "*Teqing gongzuo*," p. 5.

in no way meant to convince the public, but was directed solely at public security officers. Nobody else was, after all, meant to know that agents even existed.

Secret Investigation Agents

The CMPS distinguished, including for internal statistical purposes, between three major categories of domestic agents.[31] The three were regularly listed together (albeit with the hard numbers redacted) in the transcripts of senior officers' speeches. For example, the then director of one of the lesser bureaus into which the CMPS 2nd Bureau had temporarily been broken up explained in a survey of achievements and problems in 1955 that "we put in place *nn* case agents [*zhuan'an zhencha teqing*], *nnn* secret investigation agents [*mimi diaocha teqing*], and *nnn* agents tasked with guarding critical assets [*yaohai baowei teqing*]."[32]

In terms of absolute numbers and distribution, the so-called secret investigation agents represented arguably the most common type of agent. Essentially long-term providers of human intelligence, such agents were developed extensively in the first half of the 1950s. They were positioned in work units as well as in what was simply called urban "society" – a term broad enough to cover almost any public space but normally understood to encompass the world outside the archetypal PRC *danwei*.[33] As stipulated by the CMPS, secret investigation agents had as their operational task to (a) "gather information and report on the activities of the enemy" and (b) "collect other data that the public security organs need in the struggle against the enemy." With the consent of their handlers, some moved regularly in the "complex strata [*fuza jieceng*] of society," where as participant-observers they surreptitiously engaged in "social investigation" (*shehui diaocha*).[34] Others moved in very ordinary circles and had little or nothing of interest to report to their handlers. Indeed, provincial bureaus of public security regularly hinted, in their annual work plans

---

[31] The agent categories employed in the fight against ordinary as opposed to "political" crimes, counterespionage, and so on, were slightly different and bore different designations. See Zhou Xing, "Zai quanguo xingshi zhencha gongzuo huiyi zongjie" (Summary at National Conference on Crime Surveillance), *Gongan jianshe*, No. 130, June 18, 1955, p. 13.

[32] Yan Dingchu, "Zai di yi ci quanguo," p. 14.

[33] Agents were a hidden component of what Victor N. Shaw calls the institutional mechanism of intra-*danwei* "control through para-security." See his *Social Control in China: A Study of Chinese Work Units* (Westport, CT: Praeger, 1996), pp. 117–40.

[34] "*Teqing gongzuo*," p. 12.

submitted to the CMPS, at a steady turnover in secret investigation agents "who serve no purpose."[35] Locations where no secret investigation agents were active were sometimes referred to in public security jargon as "blank spaces" (*kongbai*).[36]

Secret investigation agents played a particularly significant role immediately after 1949, when the CCP's hold on power in many parts of China was still tenuous. How senior party leaders viewed the relationship between undercover investigation and effective social and political control may be gleaned from their speeches. Speaking at a regional gathering of public security officers in the spring of 1950, Xi Zhongxun, the second secretary of the CCP Center's Northwest Bureau (located in Xi'an), argued that

[p]ublic spaces must be properly controlled. The way to go about it is to think in more proactive terms, to send in plainclothes [officers], to reinforce surveillance, and in the process discover leads on *tewu*. Pay attention to observing those telltale little signs of something not quite normal: once you add them up and proceed to investigate, you will be able to figure out the patterns of *tewu* activity. To merely position more guards and restrict people's movements, that is to take a passive attitude and is of limited use.[37]

Xi's words echoed what, in a completely different setting, a British officer leading a counterinsurgency mission in Northern Ireland might have told his men a quarter of a century later. In the latter context, the use of informers was intended to assist the creation of "a knowledge base of the . . . community" and identify people in order to "build up a profile of allegiances and familial and political associations, as well as to identify who the 'visitors' were and who was out of place."[38] In the PRC, early on, the deployment of secret investigation agents often served a similar purpose.

Just how big a role secret investigation agents were meant to play in the new order was at first unclear. One public security officer, writing in

---

[35] Gonganbu erju, "Zhencha gongzuo qingkuang ji xiabannian de gongzuo jihua yaodian" (Operational Work Situation and Main Points of Work Plan for Second Half of [1956]), *Gongan jianshe*, No. 175, October 15, 1956, p. 19.

[36] Cf. Zhongyang gonganbu, "Guanyu quanguo youdian xitong qingli yaohai renyuan de qingkuang tongbao" (Situation General Circular on the Weeding Out of Critically Positioned Persons in the National Post and Telecommunications Sector) [1954], *Gongan jianshe hedingben (Collected Public Security Construction)*, p. 29.

[37] Xi Zhongxun, "Wei jiaqiang renmin de gongan gongzuo er douzheng" (Fight to Strengthen the People's Public Security Work), *Gongan baowei gongzuo*, No. 18, June 1, 1950, pp. 70–71.

[38] Andrew, Aldrich, and Wark, *Secret Intelligence*, p. 263.

Changchun Public Security at the beginning of 1950, argued that "in every corner, every site, we ought to have our own 'eyes and ears' and assets." The fact that his article was reprinted in June of the same year by the Beijing Bureau of Public Security in *People's Public Security: Supplements*, a journal "for official use only," would seem to indicate that his views also resonated with those of other officers.[39] However, the saturation of public spaces with agents would soon come to be seen as problematic: the resources it called for in terms of agent quality simply didn't exist. As a realistic alternative to indiscriminate deployment, a number of priority urban areas were identified, namely, those locations and trades that were deemed to be "complex," a catchall label meaning home to a larger than usual number of suspicious characters of one kind or another.[40] Writing from Hong Kong in 1953, A. Doak Barnett – an American who had a few years previously lived and worked in Shanghai – observed that "a nationwide system of police informers has been organized," but went on to add that "secret police organizations... do not appear to be as omnipresent as their counterparts in the Soviet Union."[41]

Complex locations and trades – the latter also often identified as "special" trades (*teye*) – were those that public security organs categorized as likely to attract persons of operational interest, either as proprietors or as patrons. In its postmortem of an operation against a ring of Guomindang saboteurs in 1950, the Office of Public Security in Shangqiu, Henan province, noted that for liaison purposes, hostile forces preferred the use of "trading posts, inns, restaurants, cinemas, Anglican churches, Protestant churches, hospitals, and other sites where the composition of the staff is complex."[42] According to an in-depth survey conducted by the Tianjin municipal Bureau of Public Security in 1950, the "most complex of all the special trades" were establishments providing accommodation – hotels, inns, boarding houses, and guest houses. Because they

---

[39] Lu Qian, "Zemyang faxian he peiyang jijifenzi" (How to Identify and Foster Activists), *Renmin gongan zengkan*, No. 9, June 25, 1950, p. 96.

[40] "Tehu guanli yu teye guanli" (Management of Special Households and Special Trades), *Tianjin gongan*, Vol. 1, No. 4, September 30, 1950, p. 18.

[41] A. Doak Barnett, "Social Controls in Communist China," *Far Eastern Survey*, Vol. 22, No. 5, April 22, 1953, p. 48.

[42] Shangqiu xingzhengqu gonganchu, "Guanyu pohuo fei 'Dixiajun Xuzhou di san fangmianjun Su-Lu-Yu-Wan jiaofei zongsilingbu' an de chubu zongjie" (Tentative Summary of Cracking the Case of the Bandit "Underground Army Xuzhou 3rd Front Army Jiangsu-Shandong-Henan-Anhui Bandit Extermination General Command), *Tielu gongan tongxun*, No. 3, December 15, 1950, p. 14.

were difficult to control, they often served as bases for criminal activity by "reactionary elements."[43] A second Tianjin assessment a little over a decade later painted an equally sober picture, prompting the CMPS to observe that this was a "universal problem," not just in Tianjin, but in all of China's cities.[44]

An entirely different trade in which public security organs took an interest and sought to develop secret investigation agents was that of seal carving and stamp making. Seals in general had always played an important role in China, where the imprint of one's name seal served as a means of personal identification similar to a written signature in a European or North American cultural context. In the early 1950s, when the situation in many parts of China still remained chaotic and the new authorities struggled to maintain basic law and order, some establishments did a brisk trade in the fabrication of false official seals and bogus identity papers.[45] Similar circumstances prevailed in places that offered document-copying services to the public and that had access to typewriters and mimeograph machines. The latter establishments were of two kinds: those operated legally and those illegally. Licensed operations were few to begin with, and over the years became fewer still. In the whole of Shanghai in the summer of 1960 there were only a dozen altogether, employing a total of 508 staff, the political backgrounds of which, a survey initiated by the municipal Bureau of Public Security found, were highly diverse. Security lapses and the leaking of contents of documents were fairly common. Those establishments that provided copying services illegally (there were an impressive eighty-six such enterprises, the survey found, typically one-man operations, in Shanghai's Hongkou, Nanshi, and Luwan districts alone) made up, by comparison, an even more "complex" community.[46]

In addition to monitoring the trades just described, operational officers sought to position secret investigation agents in places (besides hotels) regularly frequented by foreigners and inside their respective communities, the latter almost by default regarded as highly suspect. A Chinese

---

[43] "Tehu guanli," p. 18.

[44] "Tianjin deng shi zai lüdian zhong chahuo dapi weifa fanzui fenzi" (Large Numbers of Law-Breaking Elements Found in Hotels in Tianjin and Other Cities), *Gongan gongzuo jianbao*, No. 226, December 11, 1961, pp. 4–5.

[45] "Tehu guanli," p. 18.

[46] "Shanghai cong dazi tengxieshe zhong chachu yi pi wulei fenzi" (Shanghai Discovers a Number of Five-Category Elements in Typing and Copying Shops), *Gongan gongzuo jianbao*, No. 138, July 27, 1960, pp. 7–8.

historian working for the Beijing Bureau of Public Security writes of how already in 1949

the Surveillance and Interrogation Office [*Zhenxunchu*] of the municipal Bureau took the opportunity [of foreigners having to register with the police in order to obtain legal residence permits] to develop a number of covert assets among the foreign trading firms and original expatriate organizations, and in this way embark on secret investigation for the sake of improving our understanding of their circumstances at an even higher level. In this way, no small number of additional leads on suspected espionage activities were investigated. As operational work against imperialist spies gradually got underway, motivated by the needs of the struggle, the Surveillance and Interrogation Office was expanded. What had begun as an Investigation and Research Group [*Diaoyanzu*] became an Intelligence Section [*Qingbaoke*] tasked specifically with investigating and controlling the circumstances of foreigners. Its resources were used primarily to target imperialist spies.[47]

The same historian wrote that by the summer of 1950, the municipal Intelligence Section in Beijing was running agents whose secret investigation work targeting resident foreigners was sometimes conducted under the cover of "itinerant traders."[48]

The relative priority attached by operational departments to the positioning of secret investigation agents in society at large was linked to local as well as national-level factors, including the progress of major political campaigns. As one of the first such campaigns, the Suppression of Counterrevolutionaries, began to wind down in the national capital in the autumn of 1951, the Beijing Bureau of Public Security announced its intention to henceforth shift its primary operational focus away from the "complex" locations and trades previously discussed. It now specifically mentioned factories, public institutions, and schools as the places where it planned to develop new operational assets.[49]

Universities had not been on the early CMPS lists of complex locations, but by April 1953, if not earlier, they too were drawing increasingly on the operational resources of public security organs.[50] One reason for

---

[47] Zhu Zhencai, *Jianguo chuqi Beijing fan jiandie daan jishi* (*True Record of Big Counterespionage Cases in Beijing Shortly After Liberation*) (Beijing: Zhongguo shehui kexue chubanshe, 2006), p. 347.

[48] Ibid.

[49] Beijing shi gonganju, "Zhixing di si ci quanguo gongan huiyi jueyi jihua" (Plan for the Implementation of the Resolution of the 4th National Public Security Conference), *Renmin gongan zengkan*, No. 30, November 20, 1951, p. 46. For a provocative analysis of the Suppression of Counterrevolutionaries campaign, see Dutton, *Policing Chinese Politics*, pp. 161–79.

[50] *Jianguo yilai gongan*, p. 59,

this, the CMPS explained the following year, was that universities were home to thousands of unrepentant critics of the new order, something that made campuses part of the "social foundation of enemy activity."[51] (In 1957, CCP Secretary General Deng Xiaoping would speak of "places where there are loads of intellectuals" as "principal sites where Rightist elements are active."[52]) One early lesson learned in trying to optimize the efficiency of secret investigation agents in universities was the imperative of positioning agent handlers in just the right places and in close proximity, which in this case often meant under the cover of another occupation within the same *danwei*. It was this concern that partially motivated a reorganization of the existing security system in Chinese universities undertaken in the second half of 1953, shortly after the nationalization of all institutions of higher education. In accordance with a policy drawn up by the CMPS and ratified by the CCP Center in August 1953, university administrations across the country abolished their originally public and highly visible security organizations, which had been created immediately after 1949. The officers hitherto employed in these organizations were rotated away to other universities where their connection with the security organs was not public knowledge. There, it was meant, they would continue "with a posting in the personnel section serving as their cover, to engage in security work." While this operation may have appeared simple enough on paper, it immediately ran into difficulties caused by friction between genuine personnel cadres and the undercover operational officers meant to be working next to them. Other issues to be ironed out included how many officers personnel sections were supposed to have – and, even more fundamentally, what exactly their tasks were to include (and not include).[53]

In March 1954, some of the difficulties were resolved in principle by the superordinate organs concerned and were spelled out in a joint notification that, among other things, set the ratio of personnel to security cadres: in a small university with a personnel section employing six cadres, two were to be security officers; in a large university employing twenty-five cadres, ten were to be security officers.[54] The notification also

---

[51] Zhonggong zhongyang zuzhibu bangongting, *Zuzhi gongzuo wenjian xuanbian 1953 nian–1954 nian*, p. 175.

[52] Guofang daxue dangshi dangjianshi, *Zhonggong dangshi jiaoxue*, Vol. 22, p. 295.

[53] Zhonggong zhongyang zuzhibu bangongting, *Zuzhi gongzuo wenjian xuanbian 1953 nian–1954 nian*, pp. 175–77.

[54] Ibid., p. 178.

spelled out the security-related tasks that agent-running officers posted in personnel sections would henceforth have:

[To] carry out in-depth surveys and research into – and gradually understand the political mien of – teachers and staff and their family members residing on campus, elements among the student population who have serious political problems, persons who have returned from overseas and who maintain complex [substantive personal] relationships, and elements belonging to one of the five counterrevolutionary categories who have wormed their way into the schools. Establish control over these people's words, deeds, and movements with the aid of on-campus resources such as activist elements in our party, Youth League, Public Order Committees, and unions, and in this way aid and complement the operational work of the public security organs and strike at the covert enemy.[55]

Feedback to the CMPS from below described the agents secretly recruited by campus-based officers as "indispensable resources." The utilization of such agents in the course of operations targeting "senior intellectuals," one provincial Bureau of Public Security reported, "turns out to be of very special significance as far as safeguarding [classroom] teaching [content] is concerned."[56] One suspects that this entailed students serving as agents reporting on anything deemed to be politically incorrect in the lectures of their professors.

"Building Up Resources Over Time": Operating in Ethnic Minority Regions

An important exception to the CMPS rule that operational departments were not, on the whole, meant to field agents in rural China applied to the vast swaths of territory (in the 1950s almost entirely rural) inhabited by ethnic minorities – Tibetans, Yi, Uighur, Hui, Kawa, and others. The ministry considered these areas to be "special and complex" and, in view of this, called for exceptional practices, not least with respect to operational work. This was duly noted shortly after the 6th NPSC in

---

55 Ibid., p. 179. The five categories of counterrevolutionary elements were "bandit chieftains, professional brigands, local tyrants, *tewu*, and leaders of reactionary sects." See Michael Schoenhals, "Demonizing Discourse in Mao Zedong's China: People vs. Non-People," *Totalitarian Movements and Political Religions*, Vol. 8, Nos. 3–4, September–December 2007, p. 470.

56 Jiangsu sheng gonganting di si chu, "Guanyu Nanjing shi ge dazhuan xuexiao guanche Zhongyang gonganbu wenhua baowei gongzuo zhishi de jiancha baogao" (Examination Report Concerning the Implementation of the Central Ministry of Public Security's Instructions on Cultural Protection Work in Institutions of Higher Learning in Nanjing) [February 1954], *Gongan jianshe hedingben*, p. 14.

a fairly detailed set of instructions drawn up by the CMPS 1st Bureau (in consultation with the State Nationalities Affairs Commission), at the request of Luo Ruiqing, that stipulated that in ethnic minority areas "with respect to the development of agent work, in accordance with our needs in the struggle against the enemy, the emphasis for now is on cultivating and recruiting secret investigation agents."[57] The list of specific targets to be investigated was unique to each region. In Xinjiang, for example, it included communities home to "elements who on the eve of and after Liberation returned to China from India, Pakistan, and Afghanistan."[58] Public security officers suspected, and not always unjustifiably, that some recent returnees worked for hostile intelligence services.

In 1954, the CMPS spoke of how "on the whole, in these areas enemy activities present a very serious threat," one that for officers entering them was, for many years, significantly higher than elsewhere in China. In Tibet and the Qamdo region of what was then Xikang province, the overriding priority of officers was often simply force protection – referred to by the CMPS as to "first and foremost make sure to protect the safety of our own party and military."[59] Some of the few informative (albeit still far from truly substantial) accounts of operational work at the time available to historians are eulogies published in memory of officers who died in the course of duty. That agents were being run by public security officers in Tibet is confirmed by the story of an operational officer who arrived in Lhasa with one of the earliest contingents of the PLA 18th Corps in 1951. The officer, who was murdered in Lhasa in April 1958, had at the time of his death (according to a posthumous account by a colleague) overseen "investigation and research and operational work targeting Tibetan elite and religious circles."[60]

Meanwhile, public security officers surmised that members of the ethnic minority ancien regime who had escaped to Taiwan and Hong Kong were (in the words of an officer from Inner Mongolia) "very obviously by

[57] Zhongyang gonganbu, "Guanyu zai shaoshu minzu diqu guanche di liu ci quanguo gongan huiyi jueyi de zhishi" (Instructions on the Implementation of the Resolution of the 6th National Public Security Conference in National Minority Areas), *Gongan jianshe*, No. 97, September 18, 1954, p. 5; Luo Ruiqing, "Di liu ci quanguo gongan huiyi de zongjie" (Concluding Summary at the 6th National Public Security Conference), *Gongan jianshe*, No. 98, September 28, 1954, p. 67.

[58] Abliz, "Zai di liu ci quanguo gongan huiyi shang de fayan" (Statement at the 6th National Public Security Conference), *Gongan jianshe*, No. 102, October 12, 1954, pp. 18–21.

[59] Zhongyang gonganbu, "Guanyu zai shaoshu minzu," p. 2.

[60] Sun Mingshan, *Lishi shunjian II*, p. 621.

no means asleep over there."[61] But it was also appreciated that the threat to local representatives of the new order did not necessarily come from the ethnic minorities themselves. Along the Stilwell Road to Burma (a transport artery traversing a section of the Yunnan border populated mainly by the Dai and Jingbo), as the regional public security director made it known in his address to the 6th NPSC, "all of the eateries and tire repair shops have been taken over and are run by reactionary former [Guomindang] military officers."[62] Illustrative of the balance of forces between the CCP and the Guomindang in the early 1950s were the undercover intelligence operations mounted by the public security organs along the border between Tibet and China proper, where the new authorities' hold on power remained shaky for a long time. The biggest such operation, "Station 208," was for three years run out of the Political Protection Office in Chengdu and led by a young public security officer who had no less than seventeen successfully "turned" former Guomindang police officers and *tewu* working directly under him. In the course of their work, they managed to recruit well over 100 agents and informal contacts among the local ethnic minority population. Preparing the ground for the subsequent military offensive that would wipe out the Guomindang "bandits" still hiding in the area, the activities of Station 208 proved indispensable to the success of the military operation.[63]

The use of secret investigation agents in ethnic minority and frontier regions was rarely off the agenda in the high-level meetings on operational matters convened by the CMPS. It was one of the three topics on the agenda of the 2nd National Conference on Operational Work, which sought inter alia to formulate a response to "the activities of enemy *tewu* in our frontier regions, in particular their attempts to exploit the national minorities and similar schemes." The conference proposed "concretely tasking and reinforcing our operational resources along those sections of our national border, where our armed forces are deployed, and among

---

[61] Wu Tong, "Zai di liu ci quanguo gongan huiyi shang de fayan" (Statement at the 6th National Public Security Conference), *Gongan jianshe*, No. 102, October 12, 1954, p. 16.

[62] Zhou Xing, "Zai di liu ci quanguo gongan huiyi shang de fayan" (Statement at the 6th National Public Security Conference), *Gongan jianshe*, No. 97, September 18, 1954, p. 14.

[63] "Jiemi mimi qingbaozhan '208': jiejue Chuanxi 'lushang Taiwan'" (Uncovering the Secrets of Secret Intelligence Station No. 208: Resolving Western Sichuan's "Taiwan on Land"), Xinhua News Agency, http://news.xinhuanet.com/mil/2010--01/26/content_12875155.htm (accessed February 2, 2012).

the national minorities living there."[64] The subject came up again at the 6th NPSC two years later, this time resulting in the previously mentioned instructions that favored "cultivating and recruiting secret investigation agents." The instructions stated that in ethnic minority areas

> every effort must be made to build up a crack contingent of agents. We should primarily recruit politically reliable patriotic elements to work for us, but also to the extent that it is possible seek to utilize the elements from the middle and upper strata who have drawn closer to us. In terms of methods, we should abide by the principles of "associating widely and fostering priority targets; rigorous control and prudent tasking" and in our areas of public activity – such as united front and trade work – strive by means of making friends to prompt them to share some information with us. We should avoid making casual acquaintances for no purpose: after prolonged trials, and for the sake of a specific operational objective, they should be utilized with caution. Experiences gained from agent work in the interior may *not* be rigidly applied: henceforth, the recruitment of agents in national minority areas should normally *not* be done in the name of the public security organs; incriminating evidence or coercive recruitment methods should not be employed; agents should not be given any titles and recruitment formalities not compatible with local customs should not be used; tasks should not be narrowly specific, but rather the main thing should be to win them over politically and intensify their patriotic education. They should be given the necessary economic assistance insofar as their day-to-day life is concerned, and there should be a long-term commitment to uniting with them so as to make them work for us.[65]

The instructions obviously drew upon the results of accumulated operational experience. Short-term security-related tasks aside, they constituted the clandestine component of the CCP's implementation of social reforms in ethnic minority and frontier regions. Such reforms took time since, as one of China's preeminent anthropologists observed in the late 1970s, "if no proper ground has been prepared with the utmost patience for a voluntary transformation, then despite the fact that a social reform is truly beneficial to the people of all nationalities, it will turn into a deplorable mess."[66] In 1958, however, not all members of the CCP leadership were prepared to give them time, choosing instead as part of the Great Leap Forward to push through by brute force a number of changes that did anything *but* consider local customs and instead provoked unrest in virtually all of China's ethnic minority and frontier regions. In many parts

---

[64] *Jianguo yilai Liu Shaoqi wengao*, Vol. 4, p. 325.
[65] Zhongyang gonganbu, "Guanyu zai shaoshu minzu," p. 5.
[66] Fei Hsiao Tung, *Toward a People's Anthropology* (Beijing: New World Press, 1981), p. 42.

of Qinghai, Ningxia, and Xinjiang, the security situation swiftly deteriorated, something Guomindang and foreign intelligence services, in turn,
sought to exploit. By the spring of 1960, the CMPS in its Top Secret
serial *Public Security Intelligence* noted a marked increase in activities by
Indian operatives in Tibet, including in Lhasa, where "one of the [ethnic]
Tibetan officers in our urban work team was turned by the Indian consulate and made to provide intelligence on our operational work targeting
their Lhasa consulate."[67]

By July 1961, the CMPS was calling for an all-around reassessment
of operational work and the use of agents in ethnic minority regions.
An executive six-point summary of the findings of its specially appointed
task force was released to provincial-level public security officers. One
of the points made was that *"Insofar as the struggle against the enemy
in the national minority areas is concerned, we need to think in terms
of building up our resources over a long period of time.* We need to
strengthen secret work among the middle and upper strata of the nationalities and inside religious [circles] and monasteries, strengthen operational work, and build up capacity in the form of agents."[68] What the
summary described was tantamount to a strategic reset, an operational
policy framework that sought to end the counterproductive engagement
that had characterized the situation in ethnic minority and frontier regions
since 1958. In thus doing, it sought to restore the quantity and quality
of agent work to a level commensurate with the requirements of gradual
and less confrontational social reform.

Case Agents

As Luo Ruiqing metaphorically once put it, ordinary secret investigation
agents were the net you laid and then waited for fish to get caught in. Case
agents, on the other hand, were a net you threw when and where you
could see fish waiting to be caught.[69] Case agents thus differed from agents

[67] "Yindu tewu jiajin zai Xizang diqu de huodong" (Indian *Tewu* Intensify Activities in
Tibetan Region), *Gongan qingbao*, No. 35, April 11, 1960, p. 3.
[68] Gonganbu xibei gongzuozu, "Dui jiaqiang shaoshu minzu diqu gongan gongzuo de jige
zhengce wenti de yijian" (Opinion on Certain Policy Matters Relating to the Strengthening of Public Security Work in National Minority Areas), *Gongan gongzuo jianbao*,
No. 211, September 5, 1961, p. 5. Emphasis in the original.
[69] Luo Ruiqing, "Zai di ba ci quanguo gongan huiyi shang de zongjie" (Concluding
Summary at the 8th National Public Security Conference), *Gongan jianshe*, No. 184,
p. 17.

used for general information-gathering purposes. As a major category, they were further divided into subcategories, of which the first and by far the most important was the penetration agent (*neixian*), referring to men or women who were actually inside the operational target. "With respect to case agents," the 1957 *Lectures* emphasized, "*very particular emphasis should be put on the fostering of penetration agents.*"[70] A second subcategory consisted of case agents who, despite not actually being on the inside, were in positions allowing them to report on a target's activities and monitor its movements.[71]

Case agents, the CMPS argued, were operational instruments that could be used to "identify the enemy, close in on the enemy, and in the process discover what the enemy is up to." Once they had "penetrated the enemy," they were in a position to investigate and "gather information on the enemy's secret sinister designs and planned destructive activities, as well as obtain other important intelligence." In an ideal scenario, case agents could be used productively to "control the enemy's movements" and (in a CMPS pet phrase) "curb, guard against, and strike at the criminal activities of the enemy." They could also be used to "facilitate the use of other operational tools and the exposure of the criminal evil acts of the enemy." And, assuming he or she was in the right place at the right time, the consummate case agent might even be able to confuse, provoke, and "entrap [the enemy] and manipulate him by fomenting enemy discord and disunity from the inside."[72] In April 1958, a brief account appeared in the CMPS 2nd Bureau serial *Economic Protection Work* citing eleven cases of "counterrevolutionary networking organizations" (*jiuhexing fangeming jituan*) that had been successfully "cracked" in the provincial finance and trade sector the previous year. The account noted the following:

These counterrevolutionary organizations operated under an extreme profusion of names such as the "People's Party," "China Peasants' and Workers' Party," "All the Common People's Party," "Peasant Party," "Democratic Party," "Liberal Party," "Chinese Eradicate Communism and Resist Russia National Salvation Army," "United Army of the Chinese Nation," "Anti-Communist National Salvation Army of the Chinese Nation," "China Peasants' Alliance," "Chaling Subcommittee of the China Revolutionary Committee," "Xi'an Subcommittee of the Mainland Work Committee," "Interplanetary World," etc. They had action programs as well as long-term expansion policies, and some also put out publications. . . . Many good experiences were accumulated in the course of cracking

---

[70] *"Teqing gongzuo,"* p. 11.
[71] Ibid.
[72] Ibid., p. 2.

these cases. They showed the importance of the leadership prioritizing and taking part in the struggle in person, relying on and mobilizing the broad masses of staff and workers, actively selecting agents, obtaining evidence, speedily determining the state of cases, and cracking them in a timely fashion, in this way delivering a major blow to active counterrevolutionary activities. In some instances, the cases were cracked within a month of being discovered, and *one very important reason for the speed with which these cases could be cracked was the identification of capable penetration agents.*[73]

It is clear from the speeches of senior officers and the reports that came to the CMPS that the utilization of case agents (and penetration agents in particular) was a source of some frustration at the operational level. To put it simply, their successful utilization was very difficult and often met with failure. A survey conducted in Tianjin by the CMPS in early 1955 found that "operational offices have by now all managed to field a number of agents, but have very few that have actually managed to penetrate the enemy (some offices do not have a single such agent)."[74] In his address to the 6th NPSC, Luo Ruiqing revealed that while the political protection sector in Beijing – the municipal equivalent of the CMPS 1st Bureau – employed a very significant number of agents, not even 1.5 percent of the total had "actually managed to penetrate the enemy." An absolute majority of case agents were merely able to "move around in the periphery of the enemy" or "report very ordinary things," and a fair number were "of no use whatsoever." Luo noted that the situation in Beijing was by no means the worst: "There are cases," he added, "that are far worse."[75] While Guangzhou appears to have performed better than Tianjin and Beijing, the city's public security director readily admitted that, most of the time, he was forced to rely on operational instruments other than agents. Of the total number of cases (*zhuan'an*) handled by the Guangzhou Bureau of Public Security, only 17.8 percent were able to use penetration agents. In 42 percent of cases, agents were only able to "move around the periphery." The remaining 40.2 percent of cases employed no agents at all, and most of the time, "we are only able to rely on postal interception and physical surveillance to resolve matters."[76]

---

73 "Jianxun" (News in Brief), *Jingji baowei gongzuo*, No. 9, April 1958, p. 21. Emphasis added.

74 Gonganbu Tianjin shichazu, "Guanyu Tianjin shi," p. 4.

75 Luo Ruiqing, "Zai di liu ci quanguo gongan huiyi shang de baogao," pp. 27–28.

76 Guangzhou shi gonganju, "Guanyu zhencha gongzuo de jiancha" (Investigation into Operational Work), *Gongan jianshe*, No. 113, January 10, 1955, p. 10.

Case agents were linked to so-called Case Groups (*zhuan'anzu*) – ad hoc operational task forces set up by public security operational departments. An authoritative directive issued by the CCP Center in October 1955 contained a concise description of what these were supposed to be and do. It stated that Case Groups (adding that they were known in some places as "nuclei" [*hexin xiaozu*] or "crack groups" [*jinggan xiaozu*]) should be "made up of a small number of capable individuals who meticulously examine and study intelligence, investigate bad elements, [and] develop tactics and interrogation methods with the aim of clarifying and determining the rights and wrongs and seriousness of a case, as well as set forth proposals for how it should be dealt with."[77] Overall, the work engaged in by Case Groups was, again, acknowledged to be very difficult. CMPS Vice-Minister Yang Qiqing, talking to a number of Case Group heads on November 26, 1955, pointedly criticized those who thought it could be otherwise:

Some comrades naively believe that the public security organs have a set of mysterious and special ways of going about their work of dealing with hidden counterrevolutionary elements. These comrades believe that after having acquired the necessary knowledge, they will be able to find "shortcuts" that allow them to solve all problems. In actuality, assumptions like this are unrealistic.... Other than painstaking and detailed investigation and research, there is no other smart way or magical solution.[78]

In the first years of the PRC, the setting up of Case Groups proceeded in an only partially regulated manner. In the absence of a set of uniform guidelines, the flimsiest of grounds sometimes sufficed. This is illustrated in the case of a Shandong factory where an ad hoc Case Group to investigate foreign espionage was created merely – and needlessly, as it turned out – on the basis of one man's recollection of a fellow employee having visited Chongqing prior to 1949 and, while there, having acted as a translator for the U.S. Army.[79] In an attempt to remedy the situation, the CMPS issued the first (draft) edition of a Top Secret *Case Work Manual* at the 6th NPSC in 1954. Like the *Agent Work Manual*, it was produced

---

[77] Zhongguo renmin jiefangjun zongzhengzhibu baoweibu, ed., *Sufan yundong wenjian xuanbian* (*Selected Documents from the Campaign to Eliminate Counterrevolutionaries*) (Beijing, 1959), pp. 31–32.

[78] Yang Qiqing, "Zhuan'an xiaozu zemyang jinxing gongzuo" (How Case Groups Carry Out Their Work), *Gongan jianshe*, No. 147, December 20, 1955, p. 18.

[79] Shandong sheng gonganting erchu, "Xiang Zhongyang gonganbu erju de baogao" (Report to the 2nd Bureau of the Central Ministry of Public Security), *Jingji baowei gongzuo huiji*, No. 5, July 1953, p. 6.

for the CMPS by the 1st Bureau.[80] No copies of the conference version, or possibly later revised editions of it, have yet come to light; in the 1950s, numbered copies were kept in the secure archives of public security bureaus. When copies went missing, as they inevitably did, their loss was viewed as serious enough to warrant mention in reports to the CMPS.[81]

In the *Case Work Manual*, the CMPS spelled out under what circumstances and what conditions Case Groups were to be launched and operated.[82] Officers are likely on the whole to have welcomed this regulation of the conditions under which they worked, although they may have disagreed about details. Regulation was complicated, however, by the fact that criteria for setting up groups still remained subject to momentary change in mass campaigns, such as the Elimination of Counterrevolutionaries launched in 1955. While the *Case Work Manual* had laid down three fairly strict criteria that had to be satisfied if and when a Case Group was to be created and a case opened, the high-powered Central Group of Ten (of which Luo Ruiqing was ranking deputy head) at the head of the aforementioned campaign temporarily modified the criteria, expanding them by adding a further seven.[83] Ensuing complaints from operational officers – the new criteria entailed a heavier workload and necessitated the reopening of some old cases – were met with a disappointingly unsubstantial response on the part of the CMPS leadership:

> The spirit of the criteria for the latter kind of cases is basically consistent with that of the criteria spelled out in the *Case Work Manual*. Some comrades are of the opinion that there has been a considerable lowering of standards applied to cases in the Elimination of Counterrevolutionaries campaign, and they feel as if they have been wasting their time, but this is not correct.[84]

The launch of the Cultural Revolution in 1966 saw a further "lowering of standards" and the adoption of criteria even less stringent than those

---

[80] "Di liu ci quanguo gongan huiyi jueyi," p. 12.

[81] Shanxi sheng gonganting, "Guanyu jiehe zhenggai jinxing baomi jiancha de zongjie" (Summary of a Rectification and Reform Investigation into the Maintenance of Secrecy), *Gongan jianshe*, No. 252, June 25, 1958, p. 13.

[82] The simultaneous appearance of the *Agent Work Manual* and *Case Group Manual* in 1954 indirectly supports Michael Dutton's contention (in *Policing Chinese Politics*, p. 178) that "at this time, there occurred something of a move . . . toward a more formal professional justice system. Expertise, not mass involvement, now appeared as the order of the day."

[83] *Sufan yundong wenjian xuanbian*, p. 37.

[84] Wang Jinxiang, "Zai di yi ci quanguo caizheng maoyi baowei gongzuo huiyi shang de zongjie" (Summary at the End of 1st National Conference on Protection Work in Finance and Trade), *Gongan jianshe*, No. 166, July 6, 1956, p. 10. See also Dutton, *Policing Chinese Politics*, p. 187.

in force during the Elimination of Counterrevolutionaries. With Mao eagerly encouraging the widespread outsourcing of investigation, interrogation, and similar tasks to organizations of the revolutionary masses, disarray promptly ensued as far as Case Groups were concerned.[85]

Investigations involving case agents were most commonly launched in the political realm. For example, by extensively using a low-ranking policeman pretending to be "bent" as a penetration agent in a number of daring exploits, Case Groups under the Railroad Public Security Office in Hengyang had by 1952 succeeded – or so they claimed – in breaking up no less than six different Guomindang operations and arresting over fifty "important counterrevolutionaries." Most of the Guomindang operations (about which only scant details are known) had in one way or another been linked to the so-called Anti-Communist National Salvation Army, a paramilitary entity managed in close cooperation with the CIA.[86] But Case Group priority areas were never constant, as illustrated by the national CMPS plan for the third quarter of 1952, which spoke specifically of a need to put case agents to better use in the ongoing struggle against corruption, waste, and bureaucracy in government departments and state enterprises (the so-called Three-Anti Campaign), and against bribery and tax evasion, among others, in private industrial and commercial enterprises (the so-called Five-Anti Campaign).[87]

When created to target a particular organization, a Case Group would attempt whenever possible to employ two separate and entirely independent penetration case agents. The second agent was known as a "duplicate line" (*fuxian*), the word "line" here not to be confused with KGB usage as designating a specific sector of operations, such as scientific and technological intelligence ("Line X") or counterintelligence and security ("KR Line"). The Case Group might either attempt to infiltrate the organization from the outside or seek to recruit an agent from among its

[85] See Michael Schoenhals, "Outsourcing the Inquisition: 'Mass Dictatorship' in China's Cultural Revolution," *Totalitarian Movements and Political Religions*, Vol. 9, No. 1, March 2008, pp. 3–19. On case groups in the Cultural Revolution, see also (now somewhat dated) Michael Schoenhals, "The Central Case Examination Group, 1966–1979," *The China Quarterly*, No. 145, March 1996, pp. 89–111; Michael Schoenhals, ed., *Mao's Great Inquisition: The Central Case Examination Group, 1966–1979*, published as *Chinese Law and Government: A Journal of Translations*, Vol. 29, No. 3, May–June 1996.

[86] Tiedaobu gonganju, "Guanyu tielu zhencha gongzuo de jianyao zongjie" (Brief Summary of Operational Work on the Railroads), *Tielu gongan tongxun*, No. 13, December 8, 1952, p. 13.

[87] Zhongyang gonganbu, "Liuyue zhi jiuyuefen gongzuo buzhi baogao" (Work Deployment Report for the Months of June through September), *Tielu gongan tongxun*, No. 11, August 12, 1952, p. 3.

members. Both options were discussed in a primer distributed to regional railroad public security officers in Northern China in 1952:

Penetration operations: There are two kinds, one by inserting someone from the outside [*daru*], the other by turning someone already on the inside [*niyong*]. To find someone to put in from the outside is the most reliable option, but such qualified individuals are very hard to come by. To turn someone who is already on the inside is easier, but is rather more unreliable. Regardless of the option chosen, the selection of a suitable person for a penetration operation must only be carried out when an important prior lead of some reliability has already been obtained.[88]

Under all but the most extraordinary circumstances, a penetration agent was not meant to assume any kind of *leadership* position within a counterrevolutionary organization. According to the CMPS, this was because leadership inevitably entailed organizing and planning so-called counterrevolutionary activities. It furthermore called for a high degree of visible and substantial activism on the part of the agent if he or she was to avoid drawing the suspicion of his or her (enemy) superiors. The only circumstance under which a case agent on the inside would be permitted to assume a (by comparison minor) leadership role within a targeted organization was if the organization was exceptionally large and complex. Then a minor leadership position might permit the agent to acquire otherwise unobtainable and crucial intelligence on the organization as a whole. In its textbook cases, the CMPS saw the latter as a reason sufficiently compelling to permit exceptions to what was otherwise meant to be a firm rule.[89] The ideal positions that officers, where possible, sought for their penetration agents to occupy were those involving secretarial duties, any kind of mimeographing work, and/or other elements of communication. In their postmortems of actual cases, operational departments often highlighted the crucial contributions made by such agents.[90]

In analyzing the results of major Case Group operations, attempts were made to draw conclusions of general validity about where, for example, to penetrate an organization and what kind of individuals to recruit as

[88] *Gongan yewu xuexi cailiao* (*Public Security Vocational Study Material*) (Tianjin: Tianjin tielu guanliju gonganchu, 1952), pp. 18–19.
[89] "*Teqing gongzuo*," p. 12.
[90] "Chaling xian gonganju zhenpole yige ancang de fangeming jituan an" (The Chaling County Bureau of Public Security Has Broken Up a Hidden Counterrevolutionary Clique), *Jingji baowei gongzuo*, No. 9, April 1958, p. 5; Shenyang shi gonganju di er chu, "XXX jiuhe fangeming yinmou an shi zemyang pohuode" (How the Case of XXX's Counterrevolutionary Networking Plot Was Cracked), *Jingji baowei gongzuo*, No. 9, April 1958, p. 10.

agents. The following excerpt from a 1954 report from the CCP Center's East China Bureau in Shanghai describes how the city's public security organs had approached dealing with local Trotskyites after 1949:

Since the high-level organized core and activities of the Trotskyite bandits are extremely covert and cunning... it is only by opening up potent penetration agents that operational work can effectively be launched against them and a full picture of their organization may be gained. In our agent work, in view of the fact that the elements that make up the high-level core of the Trotskyite bandits are ideologically obstinate and very firm in their reactionary stand, and given that they will not in the near future give in, low-ranking elements turn out to be of little use to us. Hence we should normally target those mid-ranking Trotskyite bandit elements who are fairly weak yet able to get close to the leadership nucleus. We should subject them to crash recruitment in secret and open them up as agents. Prior to doing so, prospective agents should be investigated and studied in detail as far as their past crimes, degree of poisoning, ideological transformation, and personal characteristics are concerned – all part of a thorough preparation. In order not to alert the enemy, one may when necessary adopt the method of "luring the tiger out of the mountains" when attempting a secret and swift recruitment of agents.[91]

In one twenty-four-hour coordinated operation in December 1952, public security officers in cities all over Eastern China, aided by the work already performed by their case agents, broke up what was described as a regional Trotskyite network. The CMPS ordered the account of how this had been achieved to be disseminated "for reference" to operational departments in other parts of China engaged in the "struggle to wipe out the Trotskyites."[92]

A different report, which documented the breakup of the small, and by comparison politically insignificant, China Democratic Party (a network of mostly students between the ages of seventeen and twenty-eight in three counties on the Hunan-Hubei provincial border) in the winter of 1957, also conveys a sense of how to find and recruit penetration case agents. In this case, the members of the organization targeted with the use of such agents were clearly far less sophisticated than Shanghai's "covert and cunning" Trotskyites:

The decisive factor that made it possible to rapidly develop a clear picture of what transpired on the inside, obtain criminal evidence, and crack the case was the recruitment of a penetration agent capable of performing operational tasks

---

[91] Huadongju, "Su-Tuo gongzuo zongjie" (Trotskyite Elimination Work Summary) [June 1954], *Gongan jianshe hedingben*, p. 21.
[92] Ibid., p. 15.

on the inside. With respect to targets, profiling, and recruitment, one may either attempt to find and recruit someone already on the inside holding a fairly senior position (other than the central hard-core elements) and subject him to a crash recruitment, or one may look for someone on the outside able to get inside the enemy and close to the central individuals, and just let that agent move like a boat with the flow of the current. Of the two strategies, the first is the superior one, that is, to open up a fairly advanced agent. This is because in cases of this nature, unlike in cases of operatives sent in from overseas and networks of remnant historical counterrevolutionaries, the organization is typically not that strict. Even though its members may be very reactionary, they have numerous weak spots, and unlike *tewu* and historical counterrevolutionaries, they are not that ideologically obstinate. As long as the conditions are present and one is well prepared, it is neither very difficult to cultivate and educate someone nor very hard to execute a successful, swift recruitment. In cracking this case, we pulled out and recruited a target already on the inside, a target on the "ministerial" level, as well as put in a person from the outside to serve as the group's "secretary." As a result, it did not take us long to develop a clear picture of what went on inside the enemy [camp], acquire all of the necessary criminal evidence, and reach the goal of breaking up his organization in a timely fashion.[93]

"We consider it a success," the local Bureau of Public Security wrote of this case. The China Democratic Party, it should be pointed out, was in a sense typical of what local public security officers confronted in terms of organized political dissidence. A CMPS Party Group analysis of the nationwide total of 3,156 cases of "counterrevolutionary networking organizations" disrupted in 1960 found that a majority of those operating in urban areas, like the China Democratic Party, did not pose a violent threat but merely "spread reactionary ideas, rumors, and slogans."[94]

Critical Asset Guardians

The third and final distinct category of domestic agents recognized by the CMPS were those individuals covertly recruited as part of what in the Soviet Union was spoken of as the "counterintelligence servicing of installations" (*kontrrazvedyvatelnoye obsluzhivaniye obyektiv*), which PRC operational officers, in turn, simply called "guarding critical assets and production processes."[95] Agents tasked with guarding had a

---

93 Hunan sheng Xiangxi tujiazu miaozu zizhizhou gonganju, "Guanyu Yongshun," p. 20.
94 Gonganbu dangzu, "Muqian duidi douzheng qingkuang de huibao tigang" (Outline Report on the Current Situation in the Struggle Against the Enemy), *Gongan jianshe*, No. 420, April 1, 1961, p. 5.
95 "*Teqing gongzuo*," p. 11; *KGB Lexicon: The Soviet Intelligence Officer's Handbook*, edited and introduced by Vasili Mitrokhin with a foreword by Peter Hennessy (London: Frank Cass, 2002), pp. 238–39, 268.

narrower remit than secret investigation agents. As a rule, they were meant to be positioned in proximity to advanced scientific or industrial equipment (including infrastructure and highly classified information) in, for example, state institutions, government offices, factories, mines, corporations, enterprises, infrastructure, and so on.[96] Here their largely passive role was to help reduce the risk of enemy sabotage. A NEMPS document from 1950 defined sabotage very loosely to include arson, interrupting the electrical power supply, explosions, exploiting officials' technical ignorance by willfully allowing accidents to occur, and "diminishing productivity by fomenting discord, spreading rumors, and attacking activists."[97]

The cost of enemy sabotage in purely financial terms proved on the whole to be relatively insubstantial. Beijing Director of Public Security Feng Jiping, addressing the 1st Beijing municipal Conference on Economic Protection Work in 1950, estimated that losses caused by accidents and poor management were greater than those known to have been caused by sabotage.[98] A simple cost-benefit analysis may thus explain why the mission of critical asset guardians increasingly acquired more of a counterintelligence component. The reasons for this had also to do with changes in the corresponding priorities of the hostile intelligence services against which the CMPS was working. By 1961, priority targets of hostile intelligence services included individuals with access to highly classified information concerning the economy, the military, the defense industry, science and technology, and, last but not least, China's fledgling nuclear program.[99] In the case of the last, to complement the information obtained by U-2 spy planes, hostile services were actively engaged in trying to gather human intelligence on facilities and assets in some of the remotest corners of China. "It is reported," *Public Security Intelligence* revealed on March 18, 1960, "that Chiang Ching-kuo himself recently dispatched a number of Muslim *tewu* to China's Northwestern region" to collect information on the "most advanced defense-related branches of science."[100] In this context, this could only have been an oblique

---

96 "Teqing gongzuo," pp. 12–13.
97 Dongbei renmin zhengfu gonganbu, "Guanyu jingji baowei gongzuo de zhishi" (Instructions on Economic Protection Work), *Gongan baowei gongzuo*, No. 17, February 15, 1950, pp. 27–28.
98 Feng Jiping, "Zhi kaimuci," p. 10.
99 *Zhonghua renmin gongheguo falü guifanxing jieshi jicheng* (Collected Normative Interpretations of Laws and Regulations of the People's Republic of China) (Changchun: Jilin renmin chubanshe, 1994), p. 1557.
100 "Jiangbang tewu jiguan jiji souji wo guofang jianduan kexue qingbao" (Chiang Kaishek Gang *Tewu* Organs Actively Collecting Intelligence on Our Most Advanced National Defense Science), *Gongan qingbao*, No. 25, March 18, 1960, p. 3.

reference to China's attempt to develop its own nuclear bomb. Just how little human intelligence, however, the Guomindang and the United States were in the end able to collect may be judged from the Top Secret August 1964 CIA photographic interpretation report "Probable Atomic Energy Complex Under Construction Near Chih-Chin-Hsia," in which not a single shred of information collected on the ground is adduced in support of alternative interpretations of what imagery from satellite overflights of Yumen, Gansu province, depicted.[101]

Most of the critical assets that agents were meant to guard were part of China's economic infrastructure. At the end of the 9th NPSC, in August 1958, CMPS Vice-Minister Wang Jinxiang, responsible for overseeing the work of the 2nd Bureau, gave a long speech on "economic protection work under new circumstances." In his speech, he advocated that resources available for such work generally be concentrated in economic entities that were large, important, complex, handled rare products, and/or were highly secret. In a detailed breakdown by sector, he mentioned defense industry plants, scientific research institutes, geological surveys, large capital construction engineering projects, warehouses containing combustibles and explosives, economic planning departments, major infrastructure facilities, and harbors open to foreign vessels.[102] Albeit not specifically mentioned in his speech, an important sector where agents were to be deployed was post and telecommunications. In Guangdong province, the deployment of agents in major post offices and telephone exchanges had already been discussed in a work plan for 1955, drawn up specifically in response to demands from the CMPS. It specified the following:

Agent development must proceed in accordance with the principles of "necessity and capability." Post and telecommunications bureaus that already have protection units or officers should develop critical asset guardians in those critical sites where secrets are concentrated and where important equipment and lines that an enemy might easily use to transmit intelligence are located.... Ordinary county bureaus that lack protection units or officers, and that possess only simple equipment, need not develop any critical asset guardians.[103]

---

[101] National Photographic Interpretation Center, *Probable Atomic Energy Complex Under Construction Near Chih-Chin-Hsia, China*, The National Security Archive, George Washington University, http://www.gwu.edu/~nsarchiv/NSAEBB/NSAEBB186/index .htm (accessed October 19, 2011).

[102] Wang Jinxiang, "Xin xingshi xia," pp. 12–13.

[103] Guangdong sheng qingli youdian yaohai weiyuanhui, "Guanyu 1955 nian qingli you-dian yaohai renyuan fucha panding gongzuo de bushu" (On Deployment of Work to

Positioning agents in the radio and telecommunications sector was, interestingly enough, for many years not deemed a top priority. As a result, a survey conducted by the CMPS Party Group in 1961 found that "as a result of broadcasting stations for a long time not having been subject to the kind of [security] demands put on secret and critical infrastructure," their personnel were often "highly impure." Consequently, there had over the years been numerous and repeated "political accidents and mishaps" in which broadcasters had made politically significant gaffes on the air or otherwise manipulated broadcasting content so as to make a statement obviously critical of the regime. A broadcaster (a former Sanminzhuyi Youth Corps member) in Tianjin had referred to a certain "special grade labor hero" (*tedeng laodong mofan*) as a "*tewu* and labor hero" (*tewu laodong mofan*); one of his colleagues (a former member of the Guomindang) had spoken on the air of Chiang Kai-shek's armed forces as facing "certain victory" (*bisheng*) and not, as his script had it, "certain defeat" (*bibai*). A broadcaster in Sichuan (a "reactionary element") had, instead of referring to the CCP as "our helmsmen" (*duoshou*), described it as "our adversaries" (*duishou*). In replies to letters from readers, broadcasting stations had on numerous occasions (in Shanghai, thirty-one times in the first six months of 1960), either intentionally or inadvertently, leaked classified economic and defense-related information. The leaks were seen as particularly serious given that the CIA's Foreign Broadcast Monitoring Service on Okinawa was known to constantly monitor the airwaves in search of "intelligence on our nation's politics, economy, defense, diplomacy, and most advanced science and technology."[104] The event that in the end fundamentally changed the CCP leadership's view of the importance of maintaining strict control of broadcasting stations was the CIA-backed coup d'état in Iraq on February 8, 1963. The fact that, as Mao put it, "one tank regiment and the use of one broadcasting station managed to overthrow the regime of Qasim" showed the "need to stress the security and protection of broadcasting stations."[105]

In obviously critical sites like the large industrial plants built with Soviet and East European assistance as part of the 1st Five Year Plan, the

Reinvestigate and Assess Personnel in Critical Positions in the Posts and Telecommunications Sector in 1955), *Gongan jianshe*, No. 123, April 16, 1955, p. 4.
[104] Gonganbu dangzu, "Guanyu guangbo diantai baowei baomi gongzuo qingkuang de baogao" (Report on Situation with Respect to Protection and Secrecy Work in Broadcasting Stations), *Gongan jianshe*, No. 414, March 10, 1961, pp. 1–4.
[105] *Mao zhuxi Lin fuzhuxi guanyu baokan xuanchuan de zhishi* (*Chairman Mao's and Vice-Chairman Lin's Instructions on Press and Propaganda*) (Beijing, 1970), p. II/260.

CMPS had from the outset sought to copy what in the Soviet Union went by the name operational "agent cover."[106] What scant detail there is to document this suggests that it resulted in an overrecruitment of agents who proved to be of only limited use. This is illustrated by a report on the situation in the Baogang *kombinat* in Baotou, Inner Mongolia, a giant steel mill built with Soviet assistance. The plant in the spring of 1958 employed more than 26,000 persons, and according to a report circulated by the CMPS in June 1958:

> There were at one time 176 agents in the Baogang plants, but of these, some 26 have been weeded out, 29 are no longer of any use, and 8 were found to have leaked secrets. Only 113 agents remain, a very small number. More importantly, their quality is low. In Factory No. 447 [also located in Baotou and managed by the 2nd Ministry of Machine Building], there were originally 29 agents, of which now only 15 remain. In view of the complexity of the [security] situation ... it is obvious that our covert resources are weak.[107]

The asset to be guarded against sabotage in large industrial plants did not just include technical equipment, but also the technician or scientist operating the equipment. Guarding these critical human assets (often the PRC's elite scientists) was by no means a straightforward matter as far as the CMPS was concerned. Among the 357 university students who had returned from the United States between 1954 and 1958, 11 had by 1960 been conclusively identified by the CMPS as American *tewu*; an additional 17 were strongly suspected of being *tewu*.[108] But while resources had to be invested in guarding against spies or saboteurs among them, it was also necessary to control, but not excessively curtail access to, those *cleared* scientists against whom hostile intelligence services might seek to conduct operations inside China. Commenting on the medical profession, for example, one senior PLA officer emphasized in 1955 that while many senior physicians and professors kept in touch with relatives and former colleagues in the United States and the United Kingdom, in Hong Kong, and on Taiwan, this did not mean that they were themselves

---

[106] A term defined as "Operational protection, using KGB agents, for installations targeted by the enemy"; *KGB Lexicon*, p. 157.

[107] Biligbaatar, "Guanyu canjia Baotou shi zhencha gongzuo huiyi he dui jige zhongdian gongchang baowei gongzuo de kaocha baogao" (Report on Participation in Baotou Municipality's Operational Work Conference and Survey of Protection Work in Some Key Factories), *Gongan jianshe*, No. 244, June 12, 1958, p. 23.

[108] "Di-Jiang tewu jiguan jiji xiang woqu paiqian tewu" (The *Tewu* Organs of the Imperialists and Chiang Kai-shek Actively Dispatch *Tewu* to Our Region), *Gongan qingbao*, No. 8, February 3, 1960, p. 3.

necessarily counterrevolutionary, but it did pose a security risk in that "the enemy may exploit some of their complex circumstances to embark on counterrevolutionary activities."[109] It was in part in order to reduce the likelihood of this happening that the embassies and consulates of so-called imperialist and capitalist countries in the PRC were kept under constant surveillance, and the movements of diplomats and their staff systematically recorded. The CMPS calculated that in 1960 there were more than 2,000 different individuals with whom diplomats from imperialist and capitalist countries had been in touch during 1958 and 1959; of these, regular contact was maintained with 582. The British mission in Beijing, the CMPS noted, had by the end of the 1950s begun to cut down on the overall number of its ordinary contacts, and concentrated instead on maintaining links with a "small number of high-level intellectuals considered to be most reliable." The Swiss ambassador and the Pakistani attaché, meanwhile, had each "developed their own intelligence sources," and the Pakistani attaché was particularly eager to develop contacts inside China's Institute of Nuclear Physics.[110] To counter such efforts, the stated aim of the CMPS was to exercise total control over all known or suspected *tewu* elements among the foreign community in China.[111]

The operational protection of critical assets nationwide obviously involved a coordination of resources, of which the use of agents was only one dimension. To thus isolate the role of agents and assess their relative importance in this context is impossible: the only thing that can be said with certainty is that critical asset guardians did play a significant role during the early years of the PRC. As time progressed, however, some of the tasks they would have been called upon to perform in, for instance, a power plant only recently "liberated" from its original non-Communist owners no longer necessitated the use of agents. There was, it was presumed, little or no need for agents to monitor in secret the activities of CCP member managers of a recently nationalized plant.

The recruitment of agents to guard critical assets in industry was never higher on the agenda of the CMPS than during the Korean War. When the PRC entered the conflict in October 1950, the ministry issued instructions calling for emergency measures that stipulated an even more than usually rigorous control of engineers and technicians from a bourgeois

---

[109] *Sufan yundong wenjian xuanbian*, p. 142.
[110] "Dizi guojia zhu woguo shilingguan de jiandie huodong zai buduan jiaqiang" (Espionage by Imperialist and Capitalist Diplomatic Missions in China Steadily on the Rise), *Gongan qingbao*, No. 9, February 4, 1960, pp. 3–4.
[111] "1964 nian gongan," p. 3.

background and intensified covert monitoring of anything deemed critical.[112] After the signing of the 1953 armistice, the CMPS called for an overview of the use of agents in guarding critical assets, the outcome of which appears to have been a scaling down of activities. Indeed, local branches of the Beijing municipal Bureau of Public Security spoke in 1954 of henceforth only positioning agents "among technicians and staff in factories *that are fairly large.*"[113] In 1957, the Guangdong Bureau of Public Security announced in its work plan that, from now on,

in average units that are small and employ only a limited number of people who are politically pure, the use of agents to guard critical assets should as a rule be discontinued. Protection agents should only be developed in units where the circumstances are complex, that are large and employ many staff, and where the resources of the party and Youth League are weak. Leadership over those agents that already have been developed should be reinforced.[114]

Other provinces and entities voiced similar intentions in other plans from this period, including the CMPS 10th Bureau, responsible for operational work on China's national railroad grid.[115] In those *danwei* where staff and their families had been repeatedly screened and found to be "pure," and where the Communist Party and Youth League had a strong and visible presence, the CMPS's stated preference was by 1957 "to mainly rely on public work of a mass character for protection purposes, and not necessarily to develop agents."[116]

Restrictions on Where to Run Agents

The CMPS was duly empowered "according to operational needs and for clearly defined purposes" to recruit and deploy agents "in selected state

---

[112] Zhongyang gonganbu, "Guanyu jiaqiang yaohai bumen huwei de zhishi" (Instructions on Reinforcing the Safeguarding of Crucial Assets), *Tielu gongan tongxun*, No. 4, February 10, 1951, p. 6.

[113] Beijing shi gonganju Xisi fenju, "Guanyu guanche zhixing di liu ci quanguo gongan huiyi jueyi de shishi jihua" (Plan on How to Put into Effect the Implementation and Carrying Out of the Resolution of the 6th National Public Security Conference), *Shoudu gongan zengkan*, Vol. 6, No. 1, February 21, 1955, p. 54. Emphasis added.

[114] Guangdong sheng gonganting, "1957 nian gongan," pp. 19–20.

[115] Zhongyang gonganbu jiaotong baoweiju, "Guanyu hangyun gongan baowei gongzuo xiang Zhongyang gonganbu he Zhongyang jiaotongbu dangzu de baogao" (Report to the Central Ministry of Public Security and the Party Group of the Ministry of Communications Concerning Public Security and Protection Work in the Shipping Sector), *Gongan jianshe*, No. 202, October 17, 1957, p. 15.

[116] *"Teqing gongzuo,"* p. 13.

institutions, factories and mines, and enterprises."[117] Its provincial and lower-level equivalents enjoyed similar powers, albeit circumscribed in territorial terms: only in very exceptional circumstances was a Bureau of Public Security in one province permitted to run an agent in a different province.[118] Most importantly, public security organs across China were *expressly forbidden* from running agents and engaging in operational work inside the PRC diplomatic service, procuracy, courts, and "institutions of CCP committees" (*gongchandang dangwei jiguan*) – for example, a provincial CCP Propaganda Department or municipal CCP Organization Department. The use of agents for operational purposes *inside* the public security organs themselves was also strictly forbidden.[119]

Limits on where agents could be positioned were justified, first of all, with reference to the basic principle that all forms of operational work had to submit to CCP committee leadership and supervision. Limits of the same kind applied equally to all other forms of operational work inside the CCP.[120] Presumably this was well known to officers, but at the end of his discussion of operational and agent work at the 1st National Conference on Protection Work in Finance and Trade in April 1956, Wang Jinxiang saw fit to reiterate that "to engage in operational work inside the party is forbidden. In specific cases where it becomes necessary, a request for permission must be presented to the party committee in advance, and only when permission has been granted will the public security organs be tasked with carrying it out."[121] Later the same year, Luo Ruiqing touched on this same point at the 8th NPSC, reaffirming that "the public security organs are not empowered to conduct operational work inside the party – this rule was laid down way back, and it should still be observed at all times."[122] In its instructions to officers, the CMPS stressed that the operational work of public security organs had to be coordinated with the kind of supervision exercised by the procuracy and the courts. The claim was made that Communist *Party* institutions were in principle "internally pure and reliable." To secretly position agents run

---

[117] Ibid., p. 21.
[118] Chongqing shi gonganju, "Guanyu jinian lai teqing gongzuo jianshe de jiben qingkuang ji jinhou gongzuo de yijian de baogao" (Report on the Basic Situation in Recent Years with Respect to Agent Work Development and Views on Future Work), *Gongan jianshe*, No. 132, July 16, 1955, p. 14.
[119] "*Teqing gongzuo*," p. 21.
[120] Ibid.
[121] Wang Jinxiang, "Zai di yi ci quanguo caizheng," p. 10.
[122] Luo Ruiqing, "Zai di ba ci quanguo," p. 17.

by the operational departments of the public security organs among their staff – be they leading cadres or just ordinary staff – was, or so it was said, tantamount to committing "a mistake of principle."[123]

If the use of agents by operational departments inside public security organs was banned on grounds of principle, other no less powerful forms of surveillance and counterintelligence were present in their place to prevent "enemies" from infiltrating the security organs. The record shows that the CCP was indeed unwilling to put its trust entirely in the presumed "purity and reliability" of screened officers, and in 1953, what had started out in 1949 as the CMPS 6th (Personnel) Bureau was replaced by what has been called a "specialized ideological policing unit," the Political Department of the CMPS.[124] Tasked with internal security, it was replicated at lower levels in the system. A not insignificant number of officers who worked for it would, in 1967, be accused by their ordinary officer colleagues of being *tewu* who did nothing more constructive than build up "black dossiers" (*hei dang'an*) on the people around them.[125] While they obviously differed from operational agents in many crucial respects (not least in the fact that they were themselves officers, albeit with an unusual and no longer "public" security remit), one of the most fundamental differences was their background, which, unlike that of agents, was always impeccably "red" and politically beyond refute. In the case of agents, as the next chapter demonstrates, it was surprisingly often irredeemably backward.

---

[123] "*Teqing gongzuo,*" p. 21.
[124] Dutton, *Policing Chinese Politics*, pp. 146–49.
[125] *Liu Deng Peng Luo zai Shanghai shi gonganju de dailiren – Huang Chibo* (*Huang Chibo – Proxy of Liu Deng Peng and Luo in the Shanghai Bureau of Public Security*) (Shanghai: Shanghai shi yuan gongan renyuan doupigai xiaozu, 1967), pp. 9–20.

3

The Recruitment Base

Where Utility Trumps Class

"As you all know," officer cadets were told in the Central People's Public Security Academy in 1957, "agents are secretly recruited from all social strata, and include party and Youth League members, revolutionary masses, backward elements, as well as elements of the hostile classes and *tewu* elements. There are some of them who can be trusted politically, some who cannot altogether be trusted, and even some who are altogether untrustworthy and for whom special measures have to be devised for the sake of making controlled use of them."[1] As this observation suggests, the reality of the agent–officer relationship was some distance removed from the class struggle fare that the CCP was feeding China's population at large. It provided no easily actionable answer to the questions posed in the very first line of the first page of the *Selected Works of Mao Zedong*: "Who are our enemies? Who are our friends?"

The CCP would certainly have preferred under no set of circumstances to rely on hostile classes and *tewu* elements. But, as Mao had famously remarked in 1937, "practice is the criterion of truth," and practice proved that there were, and seemingly always would be, times when the services of a coerced "class enemy" or turned enemy operative had to be relied upon to attain an operational goal.[2] An agent recruited from within the ranks of the Communist Party's own membership or activist constituency was obviously preferable when a mission's goal entailed guarding critical assets and production processes. However, when a mission involved infiltrating a counterrevolutionary organization or "reactionary sects and

[1] "*Teqing gongzuo*," p. 8.
[2] *Selected Works of Mao Tsetung*, Vol. 1, p. 297.

societies," activists rarely got very far before their covers were blown, for to be credible (as studies of the use of informers by the FBI have also shown), the agent had to share at least some of the key attributes of the group he or she was expected to work against.[3] Stated with unusual forthrightness by a senior public security officer in the city of Zhengzhou, Henan province, the problem with activists was that, "needless to say, they are reliable and expedient, but not really suitable as penetration agents."[4]

Good agent material was often found among urban China's so-called backward masses. Characterized by public security officers involved in the formulation of doctrine at the highest ministerial level as important "societal assets" (*shehui liliang*), elements of the "backward masses" were seen as somewhat problematic by officers on the ground, since they could be expected to side with the enemy as easily as with the security organs. Long-term policy permitted operational officers to employ "a flexible strategy that increases the contradiction between [backward elements] and the enemy while reducing the distance that separates them from us," but the realization of such a strategy was subject to occasional failure.[5] Highly classified statistics from sixteen provinces and municipalities circulated by the CMPS in January 1960 showed that "bourgeois elements and their offspring," "backward masses," and "degenerate cadres and staff" had in the previous year generated 45 to 60 percent of the total number of "new counterrevolutionaries."[6]

Public security officers preferred to discuss the backgrounds of the agents they ran in terms of social strata and political "attitude" rather than in strict Marxist class terms. Although the CMPS was marginally involved in the grand ideological project launched by the CCP Center after 1957 to *theorize* about the continued existence of classes, class contradictions, and class struggle in socialist society, most of the time the ministry was simply interested in fine-tuning the best and most efficient ways of resolving practical problems – what Liu Shaoqi called maintaining "the public's tranquility." At the Central People's Public Security Academy in Beijing, lecturers explained that they applied quasi-sociological categories

---

[3] Marx, "Thoughts," pp. 409, 417.
[4] Li Ping, "Women de zhencha gongzuo kaishi youle zhuanbian" (We Have Seen the Beginning of a Turnaround in Our Operational Work), *Gongan shouce* (*Public Security Handbook*), No. 37, March 31, 1955, p. 29.
[5] "*Teqing gongzuo*," p. 11.
[6] "Xinde fangeming dou shi shenme ren?" (Who Are the New Counterrevolutionaries?), *Gongan gongzuo jianbao*, No. 93, January 27, 1960, pp. 7–10.

to agent backgrounds only for the sake of clarifying where to draw a line in terms of policy and, in so doing, facilitate agent direction, control, and management.[7] Immediately after the founding of the PRC, those categories had still been in flux, as it took time for senior officers to agree on what they ought to be and why.

Identifying the Recruitment Base

Senior party theorists at the CCP Central Party School in 1965 would claim that "One cannot possibly do a good job of socialism unless one stresses the primacy of thought and holds high the red banner of Mao Zedong Thought... and the factor that determines whether someone is a good guy or a bad guy is whether good thought or bad thought dominates [that] person's mind."[8] Certainly in the 1950s, and probably also in the first half of the 1960s, public security officers appear to have experienced problems with translating this particular notion into action. They preferred to allow a combination of rather more tangible factors than "thought" to help them determine who the "good guys" (*haoren*) and the "bad guys" (*huairen*) were, not to mention decide who should be placed in the fluid in-between category of those who belonged to neither group. Worth noting is that the CMPS and successful agent handlers were not – or, more accurately perhaps, could not afford to be – professionally prejudiced against agents simply because of their background. In the words of a section chief in the Beijing Bureau of Public Security, "the *dao* of utilization here is not to inquire about political stand, ideological consciousness, working style or morals. If the struggle against the adversary calls for it, *any* person capable of playing a role may be cultivated."[9]

For purposes of appraisal, the CMPS split the agent recruitment base as a whole into three parts. On the right were the so-called bad guys, a category presumed to be shrinking in size, if not in importance, over time and made up of individuals who came from what was – or had been until very recently – the enemy camp. On the left were the good guys, already a sizable – and presumed to be steadily growing – cohort made up of CCP and Youth League members and progressive members of China's

---

[7] "*Teqing gongzuo*," p. 8.

[8] *Xuexi Mao zhuxi zhexue zhuzuo de fudao baogao* (*Lectures to Guide the Study of Chairman Mao's Philosophical Works*) (Nanjing: Nanjing junqu zhengzhibu, 1965), p. 22, 70.

[9] Wang Lin, "Zai huiyi shang de zongjie baogao" (Summing Up Report at the Conference), *Renmin gongan zengkan*, No. 20, December 25, 1950, p. 29.

revolutionary masses. Occupying the middle ground were backward elements. Determining who belonged where was problematic at times, but not for the reasons debated at the CCP Central Party School or because of the insufficient grasp of Marxism that so many officers shared. In addition, there were, of course, criteria that were designed to completely disqualify some potential recruitment targets. Operational blueprints like the Shenyang Bureau of Public Security's Top Secret Agent Work Initiation Procedures from 1950 listed the kinds of people deemed to be unsuitable as agents:

- suspicious elements or people whose circumstances we have not fully grasped and about whom we have only scant information;
- those whose crimes are monstrous and who are truly hated by the broad masses;
- those who harbor a deep-seated hatred toward us, while we, at the same time, do not have sufficient incriminating evidence on them to be able to control them;
- the weak and incompetent who are incapable of playing a role.[10]

Just how strictly officers on the ground followed guidelines like these is not known. How "monstrous," for example, a crime had to be in the eyes of the CMPS in order to disqualify a potential agent is not known. That the meaning of "incapable of playing a role" depended entirely on the circumstances must be assumed. While nothing further was elucidated in the Agent Work Initiation Procedures, in a list of people not to be relied upon when mounting surveillance operations, a branch of the Beijing Bureau of Public Security mentioned, among others, "cripples and the sick."[11]

The Bad Guys

The *Lectures on the Subject of Agent Work* prioritized its discussion of the pros and cons of agents by firstly considering members of the revolutionary masses, then backward elements, and lastly elements from the hostile classes and *tewu* elements.[12] It was tacitly recognized by experienced

---

[10] Shenyang shi renmin zhengfu gonganju jingji baoweichu, "Guanyu jianli," p. 34.
[11] Haidian fenju, "Guanyu baowei gongzuo jige wenti de zongjie" (Summary of Some Matters Relating to Protection Work), *Shoudu gongan zengkan*, No. 35, September 15, 1952, p. 4.
[12] "Teqing gongzuo," pp. 8–11.

officers early on, however, that the coopted bad guys – hostile class and *tewu* elements – were often the most valuable agents. Wang Jinxiang was merely being forthright when he remarked in the summer of 1950 that "In our work of developing agents, we mainly utilize alien-class elements and hostile elements." After admitting that "these elements . . . cannot be trusted politically," he stressed that, in spite of this, "they have prerequisites that permit us to exploit them in attacks on the enemy."[13] Later the same year, the most senior operational officer in the Beijing Bureau of Public Security remarked that "as long as we manage to resist the advances of their women, aren't tempted by their money and wealth, don't let any of their filth rub off on us, and stay clean in spite of everything – then why should we be afraid of exploiting in a sharp-witted way those individuals [among them] whom we are able to exploit?"[14]

Who, then, were these so-called bad guys? In the autumn of 1950, the Economic Protection Office of the Shenyang Bureau of Public Security had forty-three "hostile elements" serving as secret investigation agents in the city's factories and enterprises. Fourteen were former "reactionary political party" (e.g., Guomindang) officeholders, including four who had once held county-level posts and seven who had held urban district-level political posts. A further five agents had been officeholders representing other "reactionary political organizations" (e.g., the Sanminzhuyi Youth Corps), including two former urban district-level officeholders. Another twelve had once served as *tewu*, six having been ex-military police officers, three former military officers, and three former police officers. One further agent was almost certainly about to lose his agent status, the Economic Protection Office reported to the NEMPS in October 1950, as he had been caught "spreading rumors." The final five – their backgrounds unclear – were cryptically referred to by the bureau as recently having suffered "accidents" (*chu shigu*).[15]

The information on the situation in Shenyang's economic protection sector was received by the NEMPS only days prior to the CCP Center's launch, in October 1950, of the Suppression of Counterrevolutionaries campaign, a nationwide drive motivated in part by what was seen as the excessive leniency on the part of public security organs and courts

[13] Wang Jinxiang, "Zai dongbei zhengzhi jingji," p. 21.
[14] Wang Lin, "Zai huiyi shang," p. 35.
[15] Shenyang shi renmin zhengfu gonganju jingji baoweichu, "Guanyu jianli," pp. 31–33, 36.

in dealing with enemies of the new order.[16] Just how many of the bad guys serving as agents in Shenyang's factories and enterprises survived the campaign unscathed is not known, nor is it known how the working conditions of those survivors may have changed by the time the campaign drew to a close. When it ended, detailed internal regulations, like the following from the Shanghai municipal Bureau of Public Security, explicitly sanctioned operational departments to continue to exploit some of them as agents:

Those whose histories are not tainted by serious crimes or the anger of the people [*minfen*], who are able to get close to and uncover the enemy – penetrate the enemy – or who have fairly good personal contacts inside the *tewu* organizations on enemy-held territory for us to exploit may, assuming the presence of conditions that definitely allow us to control them, be developed and utilized as agents subsequent to examination and approval by the municipal Bureau of Public Security of an application to do so, submitted in accordance with the routines governing the development of agents.[17]

To serve the public security organs as agents was one of the exit strategies that the CCP offered selected targets of campaigns like the Suppression of Counterrevolutionaries. In 1956, the Central Group of Ten, in a highly significant policy development, had decreed that even Guomindang and "imperialist stay-behind and dispatched *tewu* and spy elements" caught carrying out "counterrevolutionary destructive activities paid for and executed on behalf of the enemy" were not only eligible to escape punishment, but also were eligible for material rewards *as long as* they "not only make a sincere confession, but also are able to actively assist the government in its efforts to eliminate counterrevolution by identifying major counterrevolutionary elements and crack major cases of counterrevolution." The cost of the "material rewards" would be covered by the public security organs at the central or provincial (and corresponding) levels; lower levels, in other words, did not need to budget for them.[18]

Some hostile class and *tewu* elements enjoyed a different kind of immunity (in line with the practice of "using a long line to catch a big fish") from what might otherwise have befallen them in the course of

---

[16] Zhonggong zhongyang zuzhibu bangongting, ed., *Zuzhi gongzuo wenjian xuanbian 1949 nian 10 yue–1952 nian (Selected Organization Work Documents: October 1949– 1952)* (Beijing: Zhonggong zhongyang zuzhibu bangongting, 1980), pp. 44–47. See also Dutton, *Policing Chinese Politics*, pp. 141, 170–71.

[17] *Sifa zhengce xuanbian (Selected Judicial Policies)* (Shanghai: Shanghai shi gaoji renmin fayuan and Shanghai shi sifaju, 1982), p. 31.

[18] *Sufan yundong wenjian xuanbian*, pp. 48, 50.

political campaigns. A deputy director of the CMPS 2nd Bureau once decreed that some individuals, known with absolute certainty to have links to hostile intelligence services, were *not* to be touched in mass movements. Instead, attempts were to be made to position agents next to them and secretly keep them under surveillance.[19] While serving a clear operational aim, such a strategy could have paradoxical consequences, as Yang Qiqing learned on a visit to Anhui in February–March 1958. A number of known hostile intelligence assets in the province had de facto enjoyed protection in the course of every political campaign since 1949. "They themselves noticed already a long time ago," the vice-minister observed, and by now the "masses are unhappy and we find ourselves on the defensive in our work."[20]

One important segment of the agent recruitment base consisted of bad guys subject to so-called probationary control (*guanzhi*), a regimen described by political scientist Michael Dutton as "local community supervision through mass-line security organs" and meant to ease the burden on the PRC prison system.[21] After some initial grassroots-level confusion, it had been decided at the 4th NPSC that in urban China, the total number of persons subject to this regimen was not to exceed 0.2 percent of the entire local population (*dangdi renkou*) at any given time.[22] It was not uncommon for urban public security officers to tempt persons under control with various informal privileges and rewards, including the early suspension of control, if they showed signs of being willing to serve as agents. Little is known about how successful this was, but it is certain that the practice was poorly managed at times. For example, in its 1956 survey of the "overhaul and consolidation of agent work" in Jiexiu county, Shanxi, Li Guangxiang's CMPS Bureau for Operations Against Guomindang *Tewu* discovered that two "elements subject to control" who had been recruited as agents

had provided some important leads initially, but then became gradually quieter. Our study revealed that the reason was that although they had served their time in full, control had yet to be suspended and although their attitude was normally quite good – they had made achievements in their work – they had grown to

[19] Yan Dingchu, "Zai di yi ci quanguo," p. 19.
[20] Yang Qiqing, "Guanyu Anhui sheng dangqian gongan gongzuo de jige wenti xiang bu dangzu de baogao" (Report to the Ministry Party Group on Some Matters Concerning Public Security Work in Anhui Province at Present), *Gongan jianshe*, No. 259, July 1, 1958, p. 4.
[21] Dutton, *Policing Chinese Politics*, pp. 167–68, 188–89.
[22] Guofang daxue dangshi dangjianshi, *Zhonggong dangshi jiaoxue*, Vol. 19, p. 342.

resent this. Once control was suspended through administrative channels, they volunteered their services asking for assignments and moved even closer to us.[23]

The fact that such poor management was in evidence more than six years after the system had been put in place leads one to assume that management immediately after 1949 must have been even more chaotic. Indeed, in its progress report to the CMPS for September and October 1950, the NEMPS noted that, in places, local police stations had some individuals registered as requiring a regimen of control, when in actuality the individuals in question had already joined the CCP or the party's Youth League.[24]

The domestic operational utility of agents from hostile social backgrounds changed as Chinese society itself changed. Immediately after 1949, when the CCP's hold on power was still relatively weak, metropolitan Shanghai was, in the words of historian Frederic Wakeman, Jr., "indeed swarming with special service agents [*tewu*] left behind by the Bureau to Protect Secrets [*baomiju*] and other secret police units of Chiang [Kai-shek]'s regime."[25] In circumstances like these, significant operational resources were devoted to "attacking poison with poison" (*yidu gongdu*), as the recruitment of bad guys was called. Between 1949 and the spring of 1951, the public security organs in Shanghai, according to one account, "bought the services of more than 3,300 *tewu*, renegades, and counter-revolutionary elements to act as so-called 'antiespionage backbones' [*fante gugan*]."[26] By the second half of the 1950s, however, the CCP was firmly established in power, which prompted some questioning among public security officers of whether there still remained, inside the borders of the PRC, any circumstances that motivated the continued use of bad guys as agents. The cautious but authoritative answer provided by the CMPS was that "although our current threat assessment has changed and some of our agents who come from the hostile classes have already seen the disappearance of their sector of operations (and the conditions

[23] Gonganbu erju sichu, "Jiexiu xian," p. 21.
[24] Dongbei renmin zhengfu gonganbu, "Jiu shi yuefen gongzuo baogao" (Work Report for September and October), *Gongan baowei gongzuo*, No. 20, November 25, 1950, p. 13.
[25] Jeremy Brown and Paul G. Pickowicz, eds., *Dilemmas of Victory: The Early Years of the People's Republic of China* (Cambridge, MA: Harvard University Press, 2007), p. 52.
[26] *Chedi suqing Liu Deng Peng Luo zai Shanghai gongan bumen de liudu* (Thoroughly Eradicate the Poison That Liu Deng Peng and Luo Spread Throughout the Organs of Public Security in Shanghai) (Shanghai: Shanghai shi gonganju lianhe doupigai xiaozu, 1967), p. 1.

under which they were meant to serve us), we must not from this be led to believe that in the future we need no longer recruit hostile class elements as agents."[27] A drawing down – but no more – was, in other words, logical. A sense of just how big the *potential* recruitment base remained is provided by a set of aggregate figures compiled by the CMPS on the tenth anniversary of the founding of the PRC. The figures were intended to illustrate the size and composition overall, after a decade of revolution, of those categories of the population considered "counterrevolutionary elements and [other elements who make up the] social foundation of counterrevolution." Their total nationwide, the CMPS claimed, was a staggering (and ridiculously precise) 18,650,498 people and included hostile class as well as *tewu* elements.[28] In terms of sheer numbers alone, public security operational officers were clearly in no danger of running out of bad guys against whom to direct recruitment efforts.

The Backward Gray Masses

"It has to be pointed out," Luo Ruiqing remarked in May 1950, "that our so-called targets for recruitment as agents are by no means *only* to be sought inside the enemy camp. Among certain backward masses or even among the neutral gray masses, we should also look for agent resources, since the enemy invariably targets these people. They provide us with excellent opportunities to penetrate the enemy and carry out work on the inside."[29] The 1957 *Lectures* had surprisingly little to say about the agent recruitment base referred to by Luo, and one reason for this may have been confusion concerning how to circumscribe and define it. They did, however, provide an authoritative answer to a question linked to this confusion, asserting unequivocally that agents recruited from this base constituted "elements who come within the category of the people." Any contradictions arising between "them" and "us" were to be resolved by means fundamentally different from those used to resolve the antagonistic contradictions that supposedly defined "our" relationship with agents recruited "from within the enemy camp."[30] But how did one

---

[27] "*Teqing gongzuo*," p. 10.
[28] "Quanguo you duoshao fangeming he fangeming shehui jichu?" (How Many Counterrevolutionary Elements and Foundations of Counterrevolution Are There Altogether Nationwide?), *Gongan gongzuo jianbao*, No. 80, November 25, 1959, pp. 11–12.
[29] Luo Ruiqing, "Zai quanguo jingji baowei," p. 15.
[30] "*Teqing gongzuo*," p. 10.

define "backward"? How to operationalize a characterization like that of Luo Ruiqing's "neutral 'gray'"?

To develop a sense of how an erudite Marxist might define "backward," public security officers needed to look no further than their own in-house media. In June 1950, as a gap filler on what would otherwise have been a half-empty page, the Beijing Bureau of Public Security reproduced in *People's Public Security: Supplements* an entire paragraph lifted from Liu Shaoqi's 1945 "Report on the Revision of the Party Constitution." In it, the CCP vice-chairman noted, among other things, that "among the masses everywhere there is always a relatively active part, a part that's in an intermediary state, and a backward part, and the activist elements are always in a relative minority, while it's those who are in an intermediate and backward state that end up making up the broad masses."[31] The category comprising those deemed backward was sizable and amorphous, but – and this was crucially important – not to be conflated with the irredeemably reactionary. Assuming correct "methods of leadership," the hearts and minds of the backward were there for the Communist Party to win.[32]

Liu Shaoqi did not have the everyday concerns of public security officers in mind when he elaborated on backwardness. The CMPS authors of the *Lectures* did, on the other hand, when they stressed that the term backward should be interpreted broadly, rather than narrowly, as standing for "politically neutral elements."[33] An extended discussion of the utility of backward elements as agents in Northeast China had already been attempted by Wang Jinxiang in the summer of 1950. Fully endorsed by the CMPS, Wang made the following points:

These people are able to perform tasks for us because of their gray appearance and the breadth of their substantive personal relationships [*shehui guanxi*], and because some of them are in a position to close in on the enemy and discover hidden enemies. Their professions, class status, and attitudes all differ, and while some of them may be progressive or middle of the road, there are also those who are backward or reactionary even. Hence, when utilizing them, one should neither deal with them as one might when dealing with a member of the enemy camp, nor should one dispense with making a distinction between insiders and outsiders and treat them all [identically]. Our attitude toward utilizing them should be that, with the exception of the occasional political hooligan or ideological reactionary, they should in principle serve us of their own free will, and we should mainly seek

[31] *Renmin gongan zengkan*, No. 9, June 25, 1950, p. 82.
[32] *Selected Works of Mao Tsetung*, Vol. 3, pp. 117–22.
[33] "*Teqing gongzuo*," pp. 9–10.

to convince them or educate them to do just that, rather than force or order them [to do so]. How to proceed should depend on the concrete circumstances in each instance.[34]

Wang went on to describe four such concrete circumstances with suggestions on how to proceed when encountering them. One involved targets presumed to have a sense of justice and patriotism to which appeals could profitably be made. A second involved targets with whom, presumably over some period of time, an amicable personal relationship had been established by the officer. A third involved making tactical use of the target's weaknesses, whether economic or physical, and by helping to overcome them create a sense of indebtedness on the part of the target. The fourth and last circumstance involved what Wang called "exploiting the contradictions" present in the community to which the target belonged and exploiting the target with this in mind:

For example, one can exploit Protestant elements to mount surveillance of enemy operatives [*dite fenzi*] inside the Catholic Church; have the enlightened elements keep the reactionary ones under surveillance; or use Chinese priests to keep the foreign spies in the churches of the capitalist countries under surveillance. One can exploit people at lower levels in industry and commerce to keep counter-revolutionary elements at higher levels under surveillance, etc.[35]

Wang ended his list of examples with a routine reminder, emphasizing that the aim was always and only to recruit and use members of the backward masses to "work for us" with a clear purpose in mind.

The audience addressed by Wang consisted of senior Northeast China operational officers, some of whom in the second half of 1950 would embark on pilot programs to recruit agents among backward elements. The progress report on one such program, in the port city of Yingkou, submitted to the Liaodong provincial Bureau of Public Security in September 1950, described how local officers had gone about their recruitment task and managed to recruit two backward elements, both of whom were technicians:

The technician (from Southern China) in the Paper Mill enjoys having a good time (dancing, making music, singing, playing ball, etc.), so we joined him in this and began building up a relationship (proceeding from being mere acquaintances to becoming friends). In due course, the relationship went from being exclusively private to involving politics as well, deepening gradually. Once we had achieved our breakthrough, we managed to realize our goal of having him work voluntarily

---

[34] Wang Jinxiang, "Zai dongbei zhengzhi jingji," pp. 18, 23.
[35] Ibid., p. 24.

for us. The technician XXX in the Textile Plant is someone who is loyal and honest, hesitates to seek the limelight, rarely has the eyes of the masses on him, has been around, and has an active social life. By studying technical matters and investigating glitches together with him, paying him due respect and treating him as our teacher, we managed to make friends with him, and in the end succeeded in having him volunteer to work for us. So, for example, when we told him, "We were hoping you might be able to help us in our work," he responded without hesitation, saying, "How could I not? Of course I will help you."[36]

This report drew a positive comment from the provincial Bureau of Public Security, which awarded the Yingkou officers good marks for the way in which they had gone about recruiting the technicians as agents.[37]

But while pilot programs like the one just cited did yield positive results, problems still persisted in how to apply any lessons learned. The CMPS favored highly personalized training activities matching the needs of the individual agent, as well as monitoring more generally tailored to the traits or qualities associated with his or her social background. With respect to agents who came from the "backward masses," for example, it argued:

Backward agents should be given political and ideological training regularly, their awareness should be raised, and they should be given a sense of being masters of their own affairs. Their particular weaknesses should be pointed out to them (those weaknesses are always likely to be exploited by the enemy) and they should be given help to overcome them, thus making it possible for them to operate more effectively. There was, for example, one ideologically backward agent who, after we had begun utilizing him, insisted he had nothing to report, and who only after a period of fostering and training began to provide us with information. In the continuing process of utilizing and training him, as his degree of awareness gradually increased, and by way of concrete assistance extended to him, not only did he provide us with a wealth of important information, but he even picked up an important lead on a case with links to Hong Kong.[38]

Once the difficult years of initial regime consolidation had passed and the danger that the CCP might, in Mao's words, "make a mess of everything" diminished, the CMPS started to feel increasingly confident about the recruitment of backward elements, which was now said to have become

---

[36] Quoted in Schoenhals, "Recruiting Agents in Industry and Trade," p. 20.

[37] Yingkou shi gonganju, "Yingkou shi qi ba yue kaizhan gongchang qiye teqing gong-zuo zongjie" (Summary of Work at Developing Agents in Factories and Enterprises in Yingkou Municipality during July and August), *Gongan baowei gongzuo*, No. 20, November 25, 1950, p. 47.

[38] Gonganbu erju sichu, "Jiexiu xian," p. 22.

easier.[39] The total number of backward elements among some critically important categories of potential agents was shrinking – if the official statistics could be trusted. No cumulative figures like those for the nationwide total of allegedly counterrevolutionary and similarly hostile elements were ever made public, but according to a survey of universities in Beijing, Tianjin, and Qingdao, those deemed to belong to the backward intelligentsia comprised a substantial 28 percent of the intelligentsia as a whole in 1956, a figure that had declined to 15 percent by 1962.[40] At the same time, the overall number of good guys was said to be growing.

The CCP's Activist Constituency

The preferences of public security officers with respect to the background of agents did not remain static. Immediately after the founding of the PRC, as has already been noted, there was concern about how to square the operational employment of bad guys with the new revolutionary order. At the time, Luo Ruiqing had to tell officers pointedly that "you can't beat about the bush and limit yourself to dealing only with Party and Youth League members."[41] However, after a few years, this clearly was no longer an issue. In fact, at the 6th NPSC, Luo instead had to caution officers against recruiting only hostile elements as agents. Things could get dangerously out of hand, he said, if agent work were to become "entirely or for the most part" dependent upon more or less unsavory and ultimately unreliable elements – and added that it would make effective monitoring of agent work "very difficult." It was imperative, he concluded, that operational departments also set out to "recruit a batch of politically trustworthy and professionally suitable elements as agents."[42] After all, as the authors of the *Lectures* felt compelled to stress, it was "not the case that the basic masses possess *none* of the prerequisites needed to get close to the enemy."[43]

From a purely administrative point of view, recruiting a greater number of agents from social groups and communities deemed by the CCP to be politically trustworthy made sense and made agent supervision easier. But from an operational point of view, discrimination in favor of agents from the revolutionary masses actually created a number of problems,

---

[39] *Selected Works of Mao Tsetung*, Vol. 5, p. 145; "*Teqing gongzuo*," p. 10.
[40] *Renmin ribao*, January 30, 1956.
[41] Luo Ruiqing, "Zai quanguo jingji baowei," p. 15.
[42] Luo Ruiqing, "Zai di liu ci quanguo gongan huiyi shang de baogao," p. 41.
[43] "*Teqing gongzuo*," p. 9.

proving that there was often a gap between the reality on the ground and the party's revolutionary rhetoric. The *Lectures* spelled out some of the pros and cons of using members of the revolutionary masses as agents. In favor of their recruitment was the fact that such agents could normally be trusted politically. Whereas an agent whose background was that of a backward element, it was said, needed to have his or her performance "*strictly* observed and monitored" (*yange kaocha*), the performance of an agent who happened to be a progressive element or a CCP or Youth League member merely needed to be "observed and monitored" (*kaocha*).[44] Hence, in recruiting agents for the purpose of guarding critical assets (rather than penetrating the enemy), officers were advised to choose, when possible, members of the revolutionary masses. On the flip side of the coin, the operational utility of the latter as agents was limited by what amounted to an open secret – that they stood out in the hostile environments where the public security organs needed agents to blend in:

However, progressive elements will on the whole be unfamiliar with . . . the enemy. A contradiction exists between, on the one hand, the energy with which they devote themselves to their work and the progressive way in which they think, and, on the other hand, the gray image that they need to project if they are to be able to close in on the enemy in the covert struggle.[45]

The conclusion drawn from this in the *Lectures* was that, much as they might have wanted to, "operational departments cannot rely primarily on progressive elements to get close to and penetrate the enemy."[46]

   This begs the question of where suitable members of the revolutionary masses were to operate as agents. The Christian Church, described in one aggressively worded *People's Daily* editorial as home to no small number of "imperialist spies," was one of the communities that operational departments were encouraged to target early on.[47] In a NEMPS political protection directive from February 1950, it was stated that

[t]he political protection offices and sections of urban bureaus of public security everywhere should avail themselves of the opportunity represented by the preaching and proselytizing activities of Protestant, Catholic, and other religious organizations to identify adherents and believers whose thinking is by comparison progressive or who also happen to be members of our Party or Youth League and

---

[44] Ibid., pp. 45–46.
[45] Ibid., p. 9.
[46] Ibid., p. 8.
[47] *Renmin ribao*, July 16, 1953.

to recruit such insiders, train them, and task them with operating on the inside of the organizations in question. This initial operational work should be completed during the three spring months and should have as its aim to gradually establish control over the activities of the churches and thus lay a foundation for our work in the future.[48]

In the same directive, the NEMPS also asked political protection officers to profile for agents among labor union activists in various sectors of industry. Here, it was said, as in the churches, men and women deemed "politically reliable and in a position to do work" were very much sought after. Even though the NEMPS confidently spoke of the labor unions as organizations that "we" – here obviously meaning the CCP – already "control and lead," the potential threat that organized labor might under certain circumstances pose to the new authorities was evidently not taken lightly. Trustworthy secret investigation agents would be in a position to gain advance knowledge of any wildcat strikes in the offing or receive a steady stream of up-to-date information about the mood among organized labor. Upon recruitment, the NEMPS explained, the new agents were to be "individually educated, trained, tested, and put to work reporting on the situation."[49]

A different NEMPS directive from 1950 touched upon the delicate tactical matter of just how agents recruited from among the revolutionary masses were to handle themselves in public. Apparently, some public security officers had suggested that, in order to become effective as sources of information, subsequent to recruitment agents should consciously tone down their "progressive" side somewhat and pretend to be less activist and less committed to the new order than they actually were. The idea that this tactic would yield positive results in, for example, the company of one's colleagues at work (in this particular case, state-owned enterprises), however, was refuted in the directive: the rookie agent should continue to behave exactly as he or she had in the past. Behavior in general was to continue to be "commensurate with the individual's status and position. He should not stand out *too* much, as this is likely to compromise him and render him useless [as an agent]. But to be avoided even more is to feign passivity and backwardness, break away from the masses, and isolate oneself [from them]."[50] Just how controversial this issue may have been, and for how long, is not known, but it was still mentioned in

[48] Dongbei renmin zhengfu ganbanbu, "Guanyu jiaqiang zhencha," p. 20.
[49] Ibid.
[50] Dongbei renmin zhengfu ganbanbu, "Guanyu jingji baowei," p. 31.

public security training manuals and textbooks some seven years later. The *Lectures* described it in no uncertain terms as a tactic that had been tried but abandoned as counterproductive. It had, it was alleged, "seriously confused the thinking of the masses and put the activists in an isolated position vis-à-vis the masses." Not only that, it had reinforced the "arrogance of counterrevolutionary elements" and damaged the CCP politically. It was "erroneous and must be rectified and forbidden."[51]

One particular context in which agents from a "good" class background were valuable, possibly even uniquely so, was in sting operations against hostile intelligence services. In the words of a CMPS task force surveying operational work in Tianjin in late 1954, this entailed "proceeding to recruit as agents the targets that the enemy might seek to rope in, and then spread our net and wait, alternatively watching for an opportunity to embark on an overseas mission."[52] It was well understood that hostile intelligence services sought to exploit the weaknesses that even a person from what the CCP saw as a good class background might have. On August 5, 1960, *Public Security Intelligence* informed senior public security officers that the Guomindang Intelligence Bureau (*Qingbaoju*) had recently promulgated a set of Mainland Work Development and Infiltration Implementation Measures that called for assets to be recruited in the CCP, Communist Youth League, and PLA, in public security organs, industry, and overseas diplomatic and trade missions, as well as among members of the PRC's so-called democratic political parties. One of the Guomindang's primary measures consisted of securing the defections of those strategically placed, such as confidential secretaries, archivists, design and statistics staff, managers of military storehouses, and cadres posted overseas.[53] The CMPS clearly realized that such a tactic could also be turned to the advantage of operational departments. By allowing "trustworthy agents" to be dangled in front of, or even recruited by, the enemy, they might ultimately succeed in "penetrate[ing] his innermost [core]."[54]

Ambitious sting operations targeting hostile intelligence services placed extremely high demands on the agent. Operational officers mounting such operations were instructed to keep in mind that

[51] "*Teqing gongzuo*," p. 9.
[52] Gonganbu Tianjin shichazu, "Guanyu Tianjin shi," p. 4.
[53] "Jiangbang tewu jiguan zuijin shiqi dui woqu de zhuyao yinmou huodong" (The Major Plots Targeting Our Region Presently Plotted by Chiang Kai-shek Gang *Tewu* Organs), *Gongan qingbao*, No. 75, August 5, 1960, p. 3.
[54] "*Teqing gongzuo*," p. 9.

when engaging overseas enemies in struggle, the agent has to convince the enemy that here is a reliable person whose commitment [to the enemy] is firm, but who is wanting when it comes to operational capacity and the means of gathering intelligence. On the one hand, the enemy must not be made to begin to doubt the agent's bona fides if he carries out his assignments with apparent ease; on the other hand, he must also not be allowed to arrive at the conclusion that the agent has no future and therefore suddenly sever all relations with him [when he fails to carry out an assignment]. On the one hand, the agent must not provide the enemy with genuine intelligence; on the other hand, he must through contacts and communication with enemy operatives develop an understanding of their activities and movements. In the process, he must convince the enemy overseas that unless he himself sends someone to the Chinese mainland, he will not see his plans unfold as hoped for. Ultimately, the agent is to attain the goal of having lured the enemy across the border.[55]

As was also the case with bad guys and backward elements, the results of aggressive operations involving good guys as agents were regularly presented to the CMPS by regional, provincial, and lower public security organs. One retrospective on two years of operational work in the railroad sector, presented to the CMPS in August 1952, illustrated how the Northeast China Railroad Bureau of Public Security had apparently "employed two of our young Youth League members, grasping opportunities that presented themselves, to penetrate the enemy, win his confidence, and ultimately break up his 'Sanminzhuyi Young People's National Salvation Society.'"[56] On a different occasion, a Youth League member with a cousin who worked for a hostile intelligence service in Hong Kong was used in a classic sting operation (described as "a major success") to gain detailed information on "how the enemy dispatches *tewu*, what they're up to, and more."[57]

Gender Matters: No Sex Please, We're Chinese!

German historians have concluded that the *inoffizielle Mitarbeiter* serving the Stasi were predominantly male.[58] It appears certain that in Mao's China, the agents recruited by the public security organs were also predominantly men: in all PRC sources, the default gender of the agent as well as the public security officer is, not surprisingly, male. There is no

---

[55] Wang Dongning, "Zai Hebei quansheng," p. 11.
[56] Tiedaobu gonganju, "Guanyu tielu," p. 13.
[57] "Teqing gongzuo," p. 9.
[58] Jens Gieseke, *Die hauptamtlichen Mitarbeiter der Staatssicherheit: Personalstruktur und Lebenswelt 1950–1989/90* (Berlin: Christoph Links Verlag, 2000), p. 268.

explicit weighing of the relative merits of gender and little discussion of the possible advantages that men might have over women (or vice versa) in certain operational situations or on certain types of missions. The only thing that sources do confirm is that women, albeit to a limited extent, were also used as agents.[59]

Prior to 1949, women had served with distinction in all of the various native and foreign intelligence and security services then active in China. Chiang Kai-shek's personal stenographer for more than a decade, Anna Shen, had been an undercover CCP operative, and in the words of one historian, many of "the most flagrant security blunders, made both by the Americans and Chinese, were direct results of intelligence officers' susceptibility to sexual attraction to female agents of hostile forces."[60] How many of the latter may have sought or managed to engage CCP members of the opposite sex (and what, if anything, they achieved) will probably never be known; but, after the founding of the PRC, older party members clearly enjoyed telling young public security officers stories of "incidents" as edifying or cautionary tales. At the 1st municipal Conference on Economic Protection Work, one of Beijing's vice-mayors revealed how, years earlier, the "bodyguard of a responsible comrade was seduced by a female *tewu* who paid him off to assassinate his boss. But in the end his conscience would not let him do it, so instead he committed suicide, leaving behind a note explaining what had happened."[61] In Shanghai, the public security director bragged in front of his officers of how "when we were pursuing cases back in Yan'an, we could spend a whole night in bed in the company of a woman without being moved and without taking our trousers off. Let me see you dare to attempt something like that!"[62]

In the PRC, public security operational departments continued to employ female agents when it was deemed that circumstances warranted

[59] An attempt to break down some widely held Chinese stereotypes concerning women in intelligence is made in Yi Bei, *Keyi baolie keyi wenrou: sifang yuedu nü jiandie* (*Fierce and Gentle: A Confidential Reading of the Female Spy*) (Guilin: Guangxi shifan daxue chubanshe, 2011).

[60] "Shen Anna: Jiang Jieshi shenbian de hongse nüdie" (Anna Shen: The Red Female Spy by Chiang Kai-shek's Side), Xinhua News Agency, news.xinhuanet.com/theory/2008-12/19/content_10526532.htm (accessed February 2, 2012); Yu Maochun, *OSS in China: Prelude to Cold War* (New Haven, CT: Yale University Press, 1996), p. 290.

[61] Zhang Youyu, "Zai huiyi shang," p. 14.

[62] *Gaoju geming de pipan daqi chedi dadao Shanghai shi gongan xitong de fangeming xiuzhengzhuyi fenzi Huang Chibo* (*Hold High the Big Banner of Revolutionary Criticism and Thoroughly Topple the Counterrevolutionary Revisionist Element in the Shanghai Public Security Sector Huang Chibo*) (Shanghai: Shanghai shi gonganju geming zaofan weiyuanhui, 1967), p. 10.

their use; and their use by no means went unacknowledged in reports to the CMPS. Here is the first paragraph of such a report, drafted in October 1963 by the national interagency task force running Class A Case No. 12, an operation against a network of saboteurs controlled by the Guomindang out of Hong Kong:

> The enemy specializes in various forms of sabotage to our railroad network and had already on our territory established a "Beiping–Tianjin Operations Station" and a "Communications Station." In order to target these activities by the enemy, we put in place two principal agents: one is S, mistress of the [central operational target] bandit G (S is thirty-nine years old, of *hui* nationality, and has a junior middle school education. During the Japanese occupation, she served as G's underground messenger and became his mistress. She currently works for a Tianjin Trade Corporation). She was to seek to become head of the enemy's operations station. The other is L, an old acquaintance and friend of the bandit G.[63]

This particular operation, in which the mistress of the "bandit G" played a central role, was spectacularly successful. Two CMPS officers, with personal knowledge of the case, claimed four decades later that "over a period of more than ten years, we were able to catch 110 *tewu* elements connected to this case, who either had been sent in from abroad or remained underground [after 1949]."[64]

The use of female agents notwithstanding, after 1949 a ban was imposed on what could be called certain "instrumental" uses of promiscuity as a tactic or technique to attain operational goals. The so-called honey trap (known in China since remote antiquity as the "stratagem of the beautiful woman") was said to have no place in New China.[65] "All other means are permissible, except that of the honey trap," an older officer who for many years had worked in the CSAD's 1st Office explained in a lecture on tradecraft to junior officers from the Beijing municipal Bureau of Public Security in 1949. The older officer was apparently well qualified to speak on the subject, having had direct personal experience with setting such traps (this according to someone who was on intimate enough terms with him to know that he had at one time contracted syphilis).[66]

---

[63] "Shier hao zhuan'an huibao tigang," p. 1.

[64] Yan Youmin, *Gongan zhanxian*, p. 178.

[65] *Chedi qingsuan Luo Ruiqing*, p. 7.

[66] Guojia kewei jiguan dalianwei zhenggongzu dazibaozu, ed., *Wuchanjieji wenhua dageming dazibao xuanbian* (Selected Big Character Posters from the Great Proletarian Cultural Revolution), 14 vols. (Beijing, 1968, 1969), Vol. 9, 1968, pp. 7, 10.

Sexual entrapment was terrifyingly effective. Some indication of just how potentially susceptible Chinese men were to such entrapment can be gleaned from occasional reports on gender-related problems in the public security sector. Particularly easy prey to honey traps set by the enemy were New China's young and upwardly mobile crop of urban police officers, including as it did many politically reliable but simple-minded villagers (who had joined the CCP when it was still primarily a rural-based force for change) now interacting for the first time in their lives on a daily basis with the urban bourgeoisie. Knowing the temptations to which these officers were exposed in the course of their daily work, the CMPS tried to provide, if not counseling, at least the occasional "agony aunt" type of replies to readers' letters in *Public Security Handbook*, a short-lived periodical for police officers edited by Shi Luoming, the wife of Luo Ruiqing's political secretary.[67] One such piece of advice, dated March 31, 1955, was given in response to a young, unmarried Beijing police officer's letter, extracts of which were published in the periodical:

I haven't committed any kind of error, but the nature of my work puts me in daily contact with the darker side. I keep having to deal with *tewu*, traitors, capitalists, hooligans, and dancing hostesses constantly making advances. Take Nie XX, the wife of a former Japanese puppet regime Kempetai [military police] and *tewu*; she keeps saying things to me like: "Old Yin, please feel at home in our house, come and have a bite or a drink any time you like."; "What do you think of young Miss Bai, who lives in our courtyard?"; "Your button's coming off, let me sew it on for you!"... I can cite any number of examples of this sort. Each time, I always sternly tell these people off and subject them to some criticism, but I am unable to keep an entirely cool head and I often fail to appreciate that this is the bourgeoisie on the offensive.[68]

The obvious danger here was, of course, that someone like "young Miss Bai" might be able to tease all kinds of classified information out of the officer. Sometimes officers needed no persuasion whatsoever, and simply volunteered the information up front as a means of impressing a member of the opposite sex. In 1953, a young operational officer and CCP member employed in the Nanjing Bureau of Public Security's 1st Section had dated the daughter of one of the city's industrialists. At the time of the May 1 celebrations, when she asked him twice why he did not take part in the parades, the young officer had promptly blown his own cover

---

[67] Sun Mingshan, *Lishi shunjian III*, pp. 27–33.
[68] "Tigao jingti yanfang zichanjieji sixiang de qinshi" (Be More Vigilant and Firmly Guard against the Corrosive Power of Bourgeois Ideology), *Gongan shouce*, No. 37, March 31, 1955, p. 39.

by responding, "You all just go ahead and demonstrate. We've got our assignment to take care of." According to a circular on serious leaks of party and state secrets issued by the municipal CCP Secrecy Committee, the officer in question had sometimes been in uniform and sometimes in plainclothes when telling his girlfriend that he was on duty, an obvious indicator of the clandestine work his profession occasionally entailed. In the same circular that exposed his fellow officer's transgressions, it was revealed that a Communist Youth League member, also employed in the Nanjing Bureau of Public Security's 1st Section, had been pursuing a girl "lacking in moral integrity" and that, in order to impress her, he had told the girl that he did "secret work and specialize[d] in fighting the hidden enemy"; moreover, he said that "[o]ur work involves secrets that some of the section chiefs don't even know about." He had even shown her a group photograph of his colleagues, pointing out to her who the section head and deputy heads were.[69] This, needless to say, was a major security breach that, once uncovered, did not go unpunished.

Such were the temptations faced by young male officers who, if they did well, might one day be recruiting and running their own agents of the opposite sex.[70] Senior officers who already did just that were reported as grappling with delicate sexual relationships already well past the stage of mere temptation.[71] The CMPS 2nd Bureau serial *Economic Protection Work* mentioned in 1953 an incident involving an officer in the city of Qingdao who "in January [of] this year developed a female agent, failed to utilize her as intended and sought instead to have an affair with her... whereafter she came in person to the municipal Bureau of Public Security, looking for a certain Comrade, insisting he be held to account."[72] The CMPS Top Secret serial *Public Security Construction*

---

[69] Zhonggong Nanjing shiwei baomi weiyuanhui, "Guanyu XXX XXX yanzhong xielu dang he guojia jimi shoudao kaichu dangji tuanji chufen bing song fayuan yifa chengchu de tongbao" (General Circular on XXX and XXX Being Expelled from the Party and League and Sent to the Court for Punishment According to the Law for Having Seriously Leaked Party and State Secrets) [December 6, 1954].

[70] In the 1970s, an operational rule came into effect that banned men from running women as agents and vice versa. No such rule existed in the 1950s and 1960s.

[71] Two-thirds of reported violations of law and discipline in the Chongqing Bureau of Public Security in the first eight months of 1957 involved illicit sexual relations. See Zhongyang gonganbu zhengzhibu, "Guanyu gongan bumen mouxie reyuan zhong weifa luanji he wu zuzhi wu jilü qingkuang de tongbao" (General Circular on the Situation in Public Security Departments with Respect to Certain People Violating the Law and Discipline and Flouting Organization and Discipline), *Gongan jianshe*, No. 214, January 31, 1958, p. 17.

[72] Shandong sheng gonganting erchu, "Xiang Zhongyang," pp. 9–10.

reported in 1954 the case of an officer in Fuan county, Fujian, who was
having an extramarital affair with a female agent described by one of
his superiors as a woman who is "very reactionary, curses our leader,
has tried to start a fire in a hospital, and steals things."[73] Further, a
1957 *General Circular* from the CMPS Political Department mentioned
"operational officers committing adultery with female agents, or bringing
women of dubious political background to clandestine premises to commit adultery with them there."[74] Another case, which was mentioned
in the CMPS Top Secret serial *Public Security Work Bulletin* in 1959,
was that of a deputy head of political security in a county on the border
between China and Burma, who disappeared without a trace on December 1, 1959. In reporting the matter to the CMPS, the provincial Bureau of
Public Security described how he had recently "committed adultery with a
female agent and therefore been ordered to engage in self-examination."[75]

None of these reported cases were extensively documented. One that
was – the CMPS Political Department devoted an entire separate *General
Circular* to it – concerned a twenty-eight-year-old operational officer in
the Inner Mongolia Autonomous Region. In his case, the problem was
more than just having sex with an agent: it ended in his divorcing his wife
as well as almost ruining her health; she had been six months pregnant
at the time. The following excerpt from the extended report on his case
also throws interesting light on an international dimension of what the
CMPS called the officer's "degeneracy":

In 1955, for professional reasons, D set about developing an agent (female) of
mixed blood whose [Chinese] name was E. On numerous occasions, D used their
[handler–agent] meetings as a pretext for good food and drink, chitchat, and
gossip. They then began an illicit sexual relationship. . . . In February 1957, when
Director Zhao of the Bureau of Public Security was to meet with a delegation from
one of the Soviet security services and exchange with them intelligence to come out
of the investigations of certain individuals, including someone called "Masha,"
D worried initially that "Masha" might be E, since her Soviet name happened
to be "Masha." Later D revealed the identity of the target under investigation to
her and asked: "Is there really a shop assistant by the name of Masha who works
for that firm?" to which E responded, saying: "The short form of that woman's
Soviet name is Masha." Later, on a number of occasions, D asked E about certain
people who were being investigated and told her: "Don't have anything to do

[73] "Jianxun" (News in Brief), *Gongan jianshe*, No. 107, November 23, 1954, p. 30.
[74] Zhongyang gonganbu zhengzhibu, "Guanyu gongan bumen," p. 18.
[75] "Lingxun" (Miscellaneous News), *Gongan gongzuo jianbao*, No. 83, December 14,
1959, p. 12.

with these people, since they may have problems and we're right in the middle of an investigation of them!"[76]

The report also mentions D's squandering of operational resources intended for travel to Hebei and Shandong "to conduct an investigation." Instead, he had spent nine days and nine nights with his agent E in a hotel (where D later claimed he had been bedridden due to ill health) in Harbin, some 1,000 kilometers by train away from Hebei and even farther away from Shandong. The report ends by revealing that D had since been expelled from the CCP and handed over to the court to be punished "in accordance with the law."[77]

Little is known about where operational departments under normal circumstances might have recruited female agents from and with what specific aims in mind. In September 1964 – when, for reasons unknown, the question of just how strongly the honey trap ban was to be enforced was on the political agenda – Mu Fengyun insisted that his 1st Bureau "had not been employing female agents to work on male operational targets, and needless to say had never employed female agents to trick anyone into committing a crime."[78] The CMPS knew full well that its enemies sought to recruit widely and for a wide range of purposes. *Public Security Intelligence* reported in November 1960 that the National Security Bureau (*Guojia anquanju*) on Taiwan had recently called for more resources to be devoted to identifying potential "female *tewu* among overseas Chinese, skilled workers, and maids, in cultural and film circles."[79] Chiang Kai-shek's armed forces, *Public Security Intelligence* reported three months later, sought specifically to recruit *tewu* among young female (rather than male) ethnic Chinese going to the PRC from Indonesia to attend university. While such students – male and female – were judged to have great potential as long-term assets if they could be recruited, it was believed that this was the case with "female students in particular."[80] If the PRC's own operational officers had sought to set a honey trap of the cruder kind,

---

[76] Zhongyang gonganbu zhengzhibu, "Guanyu tuihua bianzhi fenzi XXX suo fan cuowu de tongbao" (General Circular on the Errors Committed by the Degenerate Element XXX), *Gongan jianshe*, No. 216, February 21, 1958, p. 14.

[77] Ibid., pp. 14–15.

[78] Sun Mingshan, *Lishi shunjian II*, p. 544.

[79] "Jiangbang 'guojia anquanju' zuijin tichu dui woqu paiqian huodong de jixiang cuoshi" (Some Recent Measures by the "National Security Bureau" of the Chiang Kai-shek Gang Involving Dispatch to Regions We Control), *Gongan qingbao*, No. 108, November 9, 1960, p. 5.

[80] "Mei-Jiang tewu jiguan gaibian zai huaqiao zhong wuse paiqian duixiang de zuofa" (American and Chiang Kai-shek *Tewu* Organs Are Changing Their Profiling for Targets

they would probably not have found a shortage of women prepared to act as bait. Brothels may have been closed down shortly after 1949, but in urban China in the 1950s there were still significant numbers of what today might be called active "independent sex workers" available. A survey conducted by the Heping city district branch of the Tianjin Bureau of Public Security in 1954 found that there were some 137 active prostitutes in that central part of the city: of these, only 3 had been forced into prostitution because they were genuinely destitute; a full 75 had no economic obligations whatsoever and simply enjoyed the better material quality of life that sex work provided them.[81]

The official CMPS view of the relative merits of the honey trap, as distinct from the use of female agents per se (as in operations targeting other women), differed markedly from that of the KGB. According to the husband of the officer responsible for the agony aunt column cited earlier, the topic had been broached in conversation during a 1957 visit to Moscow to celebrate the fortieth anniversary of the founding of the Cheka. On that occasion, Luo Ruiqing had been told by the KGB that it "regarded it as an important instrument, and [revealed that] some of the [Soviet] experts in China had in the past personally employed the 'honey trap.'" To his own colleagues, Luo then sought to explain why he disagreed with the Soviet view and was not prepared to condone it:

[Luo Ruiqing] told the comrades [that] they must not advocate this. He maintained that the right road to take for our public security work was that of the mass line. In the course of dealing with crafty enemies, he said, we must in our struggle of course make use of every kind of effective instrument. But the use of an instrument like the "honey trap" is inappropriate, since even though it may allow us to strike at our enemies, we will also find that we ourselves become corroded [by employing it]. On occasion, it may even see us squander the wife and suffer the loss of our soldiers all the same – the losses simply outweigh the gains![82]

It is possible that Luo chose to frame his opposition to the setting of honey traps in terms of Maoist politics (the so-called mass line) for personal reasons: he may have genuinely believed that they had no place in New China. The fact that male handler–female agent relationships were generally poorly managed no doubt made him additionally reluctant to permit their use. Similar reluctance was echoed at the highest political

to Dispatch among Overseas Chinese), *Gongan qingbao*, No. 16, February 27, 1961, p. 4.

[81] "Jianxun" (News in Brief), *Gongan jianshe*, No. 120, March 21, 1955, p. 26.

[82] Sun Mingshan, *Lishi shunjian III*, p. 326.

levels: during a 1964 briefing by Xie Fuzhi, Zhou Enlai himself argued in favor of strong enforcement of a ban on honey traps.[83]

By the time Sino–Soviet relations had fundamentally changed "from 'eternal friendship' to 'eternal enmity,'" as one British intelligence historian put it, public security officers in China were told that the KGB had raised the widespread use of sexual entrapment as an operative instrument to hitherto unheard-of levels of professionalization.[84] In a set of lectures on counterintelligence, a PLA officer explained that the Soviet Union, "for the sake of [turning] simple and good-hearted young men and women into sex spies," was operating a "special 'sex-spy' training school." The school's graduates, he said, were called "crows" if they were male and "swallows" if they were female. One of the swallows, he said, had once managed to seduce the head of a Chinese train crew serving on the Trans-Siberian Beijing to Moscow route, forcing him to "provide the KGB with much secret intelligence."[85] In their discussions of the CMPS's own training programs, Chinese sources failed to hint at whether the establishment of similar training schemes had been attempted in Mao's China. Even in the context of the intricate process of identifying the ideal agent – the person to recruit for a given mission – where one might have expected the issue of sex to have been touched upon, there was no discussion of it. On paper, operational profiling, to be discussed in Chapter 4, had no gendered dimension.

[83] Zhonggong zhongyang wenxian yanjiushi, ed., *Zhou Enlai nianpu 1949–1976 (Chronicle of the Life of Zhou Enlai 1949–1976)*, 3 vols. (Beijing: Zhongyang wenxian chubanshe, 1997), p. 666.

[84] Andrew and Mitrokhin, *The KGB and the World*, p. 271; Ye Jianying, "Zai di shiliu ci quanguo," p. 3.

[85] Xue Guozheng and Jing Yongsheng, *Fangjian baomi gongzuo jianghua (Lectures on Antiespionage and Secrecy Work)* (Beijing: Guofang daxue chubanshe, 1987), p. 86.

4

Finding the Right Person for the Job

Operational Profiling

Operational profiling can be described as a process of selecting a suitable person to make a good agent. One popular introduction to the subject, a book accompanying the BBC television series *Spy*, highlights the role of the specialized "profiling team" that "most intelligence services will have . . . devoted to this hunt."[1] For its part, the CMPS in the 1950s focused much of its attention on the role of the individual field officer in identifying persons of operational interest. It was the officer's active involvement in the profiling process, the ministry argued, that more than any other factor determined whether or not the outcome would be successful – finding an ideally positioned individual who, in due course, would be recruited.[2]

CSAD veterans had learned from personal experience in hostile pre-1949 environments just how crucial a task operational profiling was. Biographical sketches of the men and women who served the party on the covert front in the 1930s and 1940s record their efforts – some spectacularly successful, some disastrously misconceived – at identifying targets for recruitment who possessed in sufficient measure such key agent qualities as discretion, nerve, and self-motivation.[3] The esoteric behavior observation skills and ability to "read" personality traits and types called for on the part of the profiler had been employed – and in a sense been turned on their head – in the Yan'an Rectification Campaign of 1942–44,

---

[1] Harry Ferguson, *Spy: A Handbook* (London: Bloomsbury, 2004), pp. 94–101.

[2] "*Teqing gongzuo*," pp. 1, 20–21.

[3] See Mu Xin, *Yinbi zhanxian tongshuai Zhou Enlai* (*Supreme Commander on the Covert Front, Zhou Enlai*) (Beijing: Zhongguo qingnian chubanshe, 2002), passim.

in the phase known as the Rescue Campaign. Led by the then CSAD director, Kang Sheng, the Rescue Campaign had as its goal the identification of enemy agents and assets that had already penetrated or otherwise posed a potential threat to the Communist Party. Perfected and refined, the profiling skills of CSAD officers were subsequently put to good use in the Chinese Civil War (1945–49), years that Chinese intelligence historians today, quoting Mao Zedong, claim were when the party's "intelligence work was the most successful."[4]

Immediately after the founding of the PRC, a new generation of operational officers received systematic training in the ins and outs of profiling. The crucial importance of possessing as much reliable information as possible about a target was repeatedly driven home to officers. "First of all ... if you do not possess knowledge," they were bluntly reminded, echoing Mao Zedong's rural surveys some two decades earlier, "you have no right to speak. This is even more so [than elsewhere] the case in agent work."[5] In due course, general principles were established concerning how to go about profiling and what exactly to focus on: "Your emphasis should be on clarifying the recruitment target's history, political thinking, moral character, personality traits, living situation, relatives and substantive personal relationships, as well as any and all positive and negative factors relating directly to the recruitment target as an individual."[6] It was further required that any findings always be checked and double-checked. As readers of the CMPS *Public Security Handbook* were reminded in 1954, major damage or worse was likely if and when "we utilize elements from the hostile classes as agents ... without having put them through an in-depth [background] check."[7]

There were inevitable discrepancies between how profiling work functioned in reality and in textbook cases. But in the main, according to the *Lectures on the Subject of Agent Work*, three key considerations (in addition to gauging the overall likelihood of success) were meant to inform it. They were, firstly, to always have a *clear purpose* for which a target, if ultimately recruited as an agent, was to be used; secondly, to determine how *suitable* the individual in question was for the agent task(s) to be

[4] Hao Zaijin, *Zhongguo mimi zhan* (China's Secret Wars) (Beijing: Zuojia chubanshe, 2007), pp. 366–90.

[5] Shenyang shi renmin zhengfu gonganju jingji baoweichu, "Guanyu jianli," p. 38.

[6] "*Teqing gongzuo*," p. 28.

[7] Zhao Derun, "Jianli shiyong teqing yao shenzhong kaocha" (Careful Observation and Study Should Precede the Recruitment and Utilization of Agents), *Gongan shouce*, No. 21, May 10, 1954, p. 28.

performed; and thirdly, to have – or develop in the course of profiling – a sense of his or her likely *dependability* as an agent.[8] Just how officers went about the task of profiling was not always recorded, but retrospective analyses of actual cases and other sources provide a fairly good picture of the operational uses made of archives, information obtained from a target's employer or friends and neighbors, physical surveillance, and interrogation of persons in custody – to mention but a few optional elements in the process as a whole.

Rationale and Purposeful Engagement

In line with their ability to profile potential agents, field officers were expected to have a ready answer to the question *why* the prospective agent was needed in the first place. In the *Lectures*, this was referred to as profiling "purposefulness." It was stipulated that officers should always be on the lookout for suitable agent material, but that any further action on their part was only to be attempted for a concrete reason. Only when a specific mission called for it was so-called purposive profiling of a *new* agent to be embarked upon. Otherwise, if the services of an already existing agent could be enlisted, this was the preferred option.[9]

That the CMPS felt a need to stress something as seemingly commonsense as the principle of purposefulness has to be understood in the political context of the 1950s, when many officers shared an understanding of the quantifiable as for all purposes equal to the scientific and a large quantity as by default superior to a medium or smaller one. In November 1952, the regional Railroad Public Security Bureau of Northeast China described a situation where "potential agents are being blindly developed, without considering whether or not they will be able to be of any use or not. Mere numbers are enough: quality is not asked for."[10] Critical of this trend, the Beijing Bureau of Public Security had already in 1951, in its Plan for Implementing the Resolution of the 4th NPSC, stressed that profiling officers were under an obligation to ensure that "the agents developed are all able to serve [the resolution of] cases and aren't cultivated just for the sake of it."[11] But despite the recognition

---

[8] "*Teqing gongzuo*," p. 21.

[9] Ibid.

[10] Dongbei tielu gonganju, "Guanyu liangnian lai zhencha gongzuo de jiantao" (Self-Criticism for the Past Two Years of Operational Work), *Tielu gongan tongxun*, No. 13, December 8, 1952, p. 16.

[11] Beijing shi gonganju, "Zhixing di si ci quanguo," p. 45.

early on of the shortcomings of existing profiling practices, the problem of purposefulness was one that was never fully resolved.

In order to improve the *quality* of profiling work, it became more or less obligatory early on to conduct formal appraisals (postmortems) of concluded missions. To overcome "deviations and defects," the NEMPS had noted in the summer of 1950, "in the wake of every relatively large case, immediate and close attention has to be paid to summing up how it was cracked and analyzing enemy activity characteristics."[12] Appraisals were, among other things, meant to elaborate on the considerations that had prompted the initial need to profile for, and in the end recruit, one or more agents. In the following account – excerpted from an appraisal submitted to the CMPS 2nd Bureau by the Hunan provincial Bureau of Public Security in 1958 – profiling officers explain how they had reasoned when recruiting a case agent to penetrate a network of political dissidents led by a cadre ("L") who worked in the personnel section of the Chaling county Pharmaceuticals Corporation. It explained how, early on, Case Group officers had sought to identify an individual able to serve as an agent positioned as close as possible to him:

Crucial to speeding up the unfolding of the case was the development of an agent who would be in a position to serve as an operational penetration asset. With this aim in mind and in the hope of finding someone whom we could recruit, we launched an in-depth investigation of the key targets P, O, N, and M. As it turned out, M was the one whose qualifications seemed to match our needs the best. He was a Youth League member and had been acquainted with L for quite a long time. After being turned down for Party membership, he had become disgruntled, at which point L had sought to rope him in. In everything he did, great or small, L consulted with M, and the two became intimate friends. When the [first] Socialist Education Movement got underway, M gradually "made a left turn" and took the initiative to contact his superiors and unburden himself of some problems. The county Bureau [of Public Security] grasped this opportunity to educate, inspire, and develop him as a penetration agent.[13]

After four months of systematically collecting evidence and information through its agent, the county Bureau of Public Security on October 17, 1957, broke up the dissident network and arrested its senior members. In analyzing the entire operation from start to finish, the utility of the agent M was duly highlighted. It was also noted that in order to reduce the

---

[12] Dongbei renmin zhengfu gonganbu, "Wu liu liangge yue de gongzuo zonghe baogao" (Comprehensive Summary of Work in the Months of May and June), *Gongan baowei gongzuo*, No. 19, September 15, 1950, p. 39.
[13] "Chaling xian gonganju zhenpole," p. 4.

likelihood of his feeding the authorities false or exaggerated information, a second individual had been sought and found by the Case Group to serve as a "duplicate line." In this way, the Case Group explained, "full confirmation of the truthfulness of the information supplied by the earlier agent was obtained."[14]

When an officer determined, in the course of his or her work, that rather than profile for a new agent, an already deactivated agent could again perform a purposeful role, it was the responsibility of the officer to assess, on the basis of a careful reading of the former agent's closed file, the precise reasons for the original deactivation of the agent. If those reasons proved to be unproblematic, an investigation into the former agent's current circumstances was launched in preparation for his or her reactivation; particular attention was paid to how the agent had behaved since deactivation, when he or she may not have been subject to close scrutiny by the authorities. The final decision as to whether contact with the former agent was to be reestablished was made (as when recruiting a new agent) by the leadership of the given public security organ. Even when permission had been granted to contact him or her, officers were expressly cautioned against reactivating the agent until they had managed to establish satisfactorily that it was safe to do so.[15]

Nerves and Discretion: Qualities of a Good Agent

In 2004, the BBC in the TV series *Spy* asked a panel of intelligence professionals what qualities they looked for in a good agent. The experts came up with a list of five key qualities: resourcefulness, observation skills, nerve, empathy, and discretion.[16] Half a century earlier, it was also these very qualities that Chinese "agent spotters" were on the lookout for. Textbooks instructed officer cadets learning the basics of profiling to pay particular attention to determining, for example, "whether or not the potential agent is in a position and able to get the operational target to develop a positive opinion of him, establish an 'amicable' relationship with the operational target, and control the operational target."[17] Additional personal qualities to look out for – and any remedial action to be undertaken in this context – might depend on the ultimate operational

[14] Ibid., p. 5.
[15] "*Teqing gongzuo*," p. 68.
[16] Ferguson, *Spy*, pp. 1–2.
[17] "*Teqing gongzuo*," pp. 25–26.

purpose for which someone was to be recruited. A timid, faint-hearted individual would be unsuited to a Case Group mission where there was considerable personal risk. A wavering, indecisive agent might well compromise an operation altogether. Meanwhile, a person with little or no self-confidence could perhaps be worked on to develop greater confidence, while an overconfident person who might underestimate the difficulty of an assignment could be lectured concerning the seriousness of the mission.[18] If the problem with a target appeared to involve the absence of particular abilities or skills, the officer was to devise a plan for how the agent, once successfully recruited, could be trained to acquire those abilities or skills as quickly and effectively as possible. "A new agent," the *Lectures* stressed, "cannot possibly from the very start possess every one of the qualities he needs."[19]

Highest on the list of the work-related qualities that profiling operational officers sought in their targets was undoubtedly discretion. Obviously, those who could not be trusted to keep their agent identities secret would be useless as agents. While the value of discretion was in a sense absolute, that of other – often more specific – qualities depended largely on the nature of the mission. In the case of guardians of critical infrastructure, they were described in a CMPS task force survey of the situation in the Anshan Steel Works as needing to be "firstly, technically quite proficient, able to perform [operational tasks], and having a professional position that permits discovery of problems; secondly, willing and interested in executing protective tasks; and thirdly, not already totally overburdened with multiple professional obligations."[20]

Operational officers often inclined toward targets who drew little or no attention to themselves. In Yingkou, officers profiling targets whose backgrounds were those of backward elements at one point disqualified a potential agent because he was too visible. "In the Paper Mill," they concluded, a certain technician "stands out among the masses and they always have their eyes on him, hence he is likely to be of little use [as an agent] and would [at best] be able to serve as a common informant [*ermu*]."[21] Admittedly, the priorities of one profiler might obviously be at variance with those of another, depending again not least on the nature

[18] Ibid., p. 46.
[19] Ibid., pp. 8, 27.
[20] Gonganbu Liaoning shicha xiaozu, "Guanyu Anshan shi gonganju zhencha gongzuo de kaocha baogao" (Investigation Report Concerning Operational Work by the Anshan Municipal Bureau of Public Security), *Gongan jianshe*, No. 113, January 10, 1955, p. 3.
[21] Quoted in Schoenhals, "Recruiting Agents in Industry and Trade," p. 15.

of the mission. For instance, in Chongqing in 1955, the qualities sought in a particular secret investigation agent were the near opposite of those just described: someone who "meets a wide range of people, is on top of things, maintains complex substantial personal relationships, is an extrovert and has accumulated a wealth of social experience."[22]

Irrespective of exactly what task the profiler had in mind for the prospective agent, he or she would be looking for someone able to establish a relationship with the operational target(s), hence the emphasis in the *Lectures* on officers considering such qualities as the agent's profession, educational level, and hobbies. Of particular importance was anything that could trigger the interest of a particular operational target and therefore serve as a basis on which to establish a relationship. If, for example, the agent was to operate among and report on members of the expatriate community in Beijing, then an informed, extroverted, and articulate member of the capital's opera scene might be just the kind of target that profilers were looking for. The *Lectures* further explained that if no prior basis for a relationship existed or was hard to find, a resourceful agent, with the assistance of his handler and the public security apparatus, would have to create the necessary preconditions.[23]

The discussion in the *Lectures* may be assumed to have been based on actual cases, albeit reduced to the bare essentials in order to better serve a didactic purpose. More substantial and informative accounts of what profiling really entailed on the ground are to be found in operational postmortems such as the one excerpted here, submitted to the CMPS 2nd Bureau by the Anshan municipal Bureau of Public Security in October 1957. It throws some interesting light on the profiling concerns of officers working in the economic protection sector:

When the Anshan Steel Corporation employee Q went to visit the home of his mother-in-law at the time of the 1956 Spring Festival, he bumped into R (Q and R were past acquaintances, R being the neighbor of Q's mother-in-law). In the course of their conversation, Q sensed that R was spreading reactionary remarks, for example when he told him: "Your father-in-law sits at home unemployed and is having a hard time economically. Surely in the old days it would never have come to this, would it?" "I hear you were once arrested and then released. I bet during the Campaign to Eliminate Counterrevolutionaries you were struggled against (*douzheng*) because of this!" "How come you tell your brother-in-law just about everything? That you were a military policeman in Yingkou and a member of the Nationalist Party, that you had a gun and killed a guy, why . . . these are

22 Chongqing shi gonganju, "Guanyu jinian lai teqing," p. 13.
23 Ibid., p. 26.

really serious things!" Q felt that R was spreading reactionary remarks and so went to inform on him.[24]

In this particular case, operational officers might have wanted to enlist the services of an agent to determine what, if anything, R was up to. But to do so simply on the basis of the information that Q had volunteered would have been to overreact. In the end, R *and* Q (who had informed on him) were both subjected to what could be described as internal security checks; what is important to note is that, at this early stage, the checkup on Q was indistinguishable from the profiling exercise that would have sought to determine his suitability as an agent *if* mounting an operation against R had been called for. Upon receiving the information, the operational department proceeded to conduct a tentative investigation:

> It discovered that the informant Q had been a member of the Sanminzhuyi Youth Corps, and that at one point prior to Liberation, he had gone to Yingkou, to the home of one of his in-laws (a military police squad leader), in search of a job, but had been unsuccessful. It also found that there was no truth to the matter of his having had a gun and having killed someone. Q is presently a member of our [Communist] Youth League and has a good attitude.... A tentative analysis of the information obtained in the course of our investigation indicates [that] Q does not hold a grudge against R, and the claims he makes in the information he provided on him appear, against the background of R's actual behavior since Liberation, entirely possible. That R could be plotting to engage in counterrevolutionary activities is also entirely possible. To thoroughly clarify the true state of affairs would necessitate in-depth operational work.[25]

Once the decision to organize a Case Group and mount an operation involving an agent had been taken, the utility of the information tentatively gathered on Q – to clarify his precise relationship with the man on whom he had informed – now changed. It was now seen as the first positive indication of his potential recruitability as an agent. With this aim in mind, and augmented with other relevant information gathered by operational officers, a successful attempt was made to recruit Q as an agent:

> The conclusion drawn, after some research, was that to use the informant Q as an agent in the course of the operational work to be conducted would be the best course of action. Firstly, given his past and because R is actively trying to rope

---

[24] Anshan shi gonganju, "Zhenpo 'Zhongguo guomindang fangong jiuguotuan' an jingyan jieshao" (Presenting Experiences from Cracking the Case of the "China Guomindang Anti-Communist Nationalist Salvation Regiment"), *Jingji baowei gongzuo*, No. 9, April 1958, p. 11.

[25] Ibid., p. 12.

him in, which means he is in a position to get close to R. Secondly, Q informed on R to the organization on his own initiative, which meant that it was entirely possible that he would agree to work for us. Forthwith, the outcome of in-depth checking and training resulted in Q being developed as an agent.[26]

The analysis of the case went on at length, detailing the entire operation from start to finish. Q's contribution was critical, but in order to reduce their dependence on him, operational officers also, in the absence of a duplicate line agent, made use of recording equipment and the perlustration of mail to verify the information he provided. R and four other persons were in the end arrested and charged with attempting to organize a "China Guomindang Anti-Communist National Salvation Regiment." No firm link of any kind between them and their "regiment" and the Guomindang on Taiwan was ever uncovered.[27] They are likely to have been given prison sentences of varying lengths, but no information about this (or about the ultimate fate of the case agent Q) has come to light.

A Question of Trust

Once it had been decided that a clear purpose existed for an agent to be recruited and, furthermore, a prospective individual was available, profilers were expected to assess how trustworthy the target was likely to be as an agent. This was *not* tantamount to assessing the target's politics but amounted to something different. It was, in short, simply to determine whether the agent could be made to serve his handler loyally. This element of the profiling process was crucial: if it was mismanaged, there could be no talk of guaranteeing what the CMPS called the "purity, consolidation, and fighting power" of the agent contingent. Officers were warned that if what was known about the target was insufficient to prove that he or she could be trusted, then the target was "not to be rashly recruited."[28]

That external developments could also influence an agent's trustworthiness became apparent in the autumn of 1950. After the UN forces in Korea had crossed the 38th parallel, as part of their preparation for a possible expansion of the war on the Peninsula to Chinese territory, officers from the NEMPS Political Protection Office surveyed the current state of mind of those agents who had been previously recruited from among bad guys and backward masses in urban centers. In effect, what the survey sought to gauge was how the war was affecting the overall reliability of

[26] Ibid.
[27] Ibid., pp. 14–15.
[28] *"Teqing gongzuo,"* p. 23.

agents. Were they wavering or did they appear to remain loyal to New China? The findings, circulated in a Top Secret report on October 29, 1950, found significant changes in agents' state of mind and behavior. Indirectly, the survey also provides a window – not just in times of war – on the degree of trustworthiness that operational officers could expect to encounter in the targets they profiled.

The first kind of agent described in the survey was, to put it simply, one considered to be trustworthy. It included individuals who "proved they had a good attitude" – like that of a husband-and-wife team of agents in Anshan, who were quoted as saying, "If we don't put in a good performance at this time, then when?" Most of the agents who belonged in this category had already served the public security organs for quite some time, had been tried and tested in the past, and had supposedly concluded, in the words of the survey, that a time of war was "the [right] moment to render meritorious service to make up for past misdeeds."[29]

The second kind of agent was deemed unreliable and more or less blatantly opportunistic, including agents suspected of secretly attempting to elicit information from their handlers to feed to hostile intelligence services. The NEMPS report described about half a dozen such cases. Most involved former Guomindang *tewu*, but one intriguing case also involved an agent in Shenyang – a fortune-teller whose nickname was "Pacific Ocean" and who, anticipating regime change, had recently told an old lady her fortune, saying, "My dear lady, you are about to enjoy a happy life! Within another three months or less, there will be a change in the weather. At the very least, the 'Pacific Ocean' you see before you will become a county magistrate or better!" The author of the report commented on opportunistic agents by saying that a majority of them were behaving the way they did because they were deeply afflicted by reactionary ideology, had been counterrevolutionary for a long time, and in any case had decided to throw in their lot with the CCP "for impure reasons." Their opportunism and fickleness of commitment was clear: "In the present situation they show their true colors and dream of restoring the old order."[30]

One particular type of individual – a subgroup of the one just described – against whom profilers were expected to be on guard was

---

[29] Dongbei renmin zhengfu gonganbu zhengzhi baoweichu, "Guanyu muqian teqing renyuan de dongtai yu women shiyong duice" (On Current Trends among Agents and Our Utilization Responses), *Gongan baowei gongzuo*, Vol. 20, p. 25.

[30] Ibid., pp. 25–26.

the bogus activist. Senior public security officers repeatedly expressed reservations about persons whom (in a worst-case scenario on behalf of hostile intelligence services) they said merely "pretend to be progressive and exploit every kind of substantive personal relationship to penetrate our inside."[31] In Tianjin in 1950, the municipal Bureau of Public Security was particularly attuned to this type. In a report describing two former *tewu* working for the Investigation Bureau of the Guomindang Interior Ministry (*Neidiaoju*) in two of the city's state-owned textile plants, it was found that the said *tewu*, in the eyes of the factory managers, were both behaving in an exemplary fashion and hence had recently been taken off their watch list, but that this had very much irked operational department managers, who suspected that their "progressive attitude" was little more than a charade.[32] In Beijing, senior operational officers proposed that by comparison relatively harmless bogus activists were to be shunned or, when it proved to be a better option, be tactically exploited in some very limited capacity.[33]

The third category described in the NEMPS survey included those agents who, for whatever reason, were seen to be retreating from an initially proactive stance and exhibiting a waning enthusiasm for agent work. The survey stated that, in private, such wavering agents were pessimistic about the future and were alleged to be making statements such as "The situation has deteriorated too far and we can no longer continue the way we used to!" or "If we go on working for the Communist Party now, once there is a change in the weather, how do we know who'll end up running things?" Their handlers noted that, when debriefed, these agents were becoming increasingly inclined to "speak only of distant matters, and not about present circumstances," to "talk only in general terms, and not about concrete things," and to "only report about things rumored to have happened, and not about what's actually going on."[34] Those who

---

[31] Feng Jiping, "Zhi kaimuci," p. 11.

[32] "1949 nian xiabannian tehu guanli gongzuo zongjie" (Summary of Special Household Management Work in the Second Half of 1949), *Tianjin gongan*, Vol. 1, No. 4, September 30, 1950, p. 14; "Yinian lai tehu guanli gongzuo de shouhuo ji jingyan jiaoxun" (Gains, Experiences, and Lessons Learned from a Year of Special Household Management), *Tianjin gongan*, Vol. 1, No. 4, September 30, 1950, p. 16; "Guanyu fandong dangtuan tewu renyuan dengji chuli zongjie baogao" (Summing Up Report on the Registration and Disposal of Reactionary Party and Organization *Tewu* Personnel), *Tianjin gongan*, Vol. 2, No. 1, January 31, 1951, p. 26.

[33] Guo Yumin, "Zai huiyi shang guanyu Shijingshan," p. 20.

[34] Dongbei renmin zhengfu gonganbu zhengzhi baoweichu, "Guanyu muqian teqing," pp. 26–27.

had been recruited from society's backward elements wavered, it was reasoned, because they

do not see the present situation for what it is, do not see the powerful force of the people, but believe that the Chiang Kai-shek bandits are going to come back again. As a result, in their minds, this gives rise to much apprehension and they think they ought to ... act early [rather] than late, have something to fall back upon, or wait and see what color the sky will turn.[35]

The fourth and final category consisted of agents who were fundamentally uncomfortable in their role, uncertain of how they were performing, and terrified of what the future might hold. They included an agent in Shenyang, who insisted he be told by his handlers what they had in store for him if and when "the situation becomes critical." Some agents could not bring themselves to believe that the PRC stood any chance of emerging victorious from a military confrontation with the United States. In conversation with their handlers they raised questions such as "How many aircraft do you have?" "Do you have any B-29 bombers?" "When the situation turns really tense, will I be able to go with you?" In an assessment of the reliability of the agents in this category, the authors of the survey wrote as follows: "The reason a majority of these elements are terrified and keep sounding us out is mainly because ... they have committed crimes and are afraid we will suppress them, a feeling reinforced by reactionary rumors and agitation."[36]

The NEMPS Political Protection Office concluded its assessment (of how a major external event like the war on the Korean Peninsula had affected the trustworthiness of agents) with a few points of general advice to officers. The most important point was not to underestimate the degree to which agent work constituted a "complex struggle" that called for adaptability and flexibility.[37] And the key to success in finding a trustworthy agent whose services could be relied upon even under adverse conditions was thorough research, utilizing every avenue available.

Exploiting Archives

In order to decide whether or not to attempt a recruitment, the public security profiler was to conduct a thorough background investigation of the target in absolute secrecy. Typically, this involved a number of steps.

[35] Ibid., p. 27.
[36] Ibid.
[37] Ibid., pp. 27–28.

The first, in order of relative importance, was to use the preexisting in-house resources of public security organs to build up a picture of the person identified as a potential agent. Especially if the target was a hostile class or *tewu* element, it was likely that public security archives already contained information about him or her.

The founding of the PRC saw the concentration of numerous archival resources in the hands of public security organs. One had already been developed prior to 1949 by the CCP's central, regional, and local social affairs departments; another comprised what came to be called the "enemy and puppet archives" of the ancien regime. On November 20, 1948, in preparation for the impending takeover of Tianjin and Beijing, the CSAD had issued a directive dealing inter alia with Nationalist as well as former Japanese security service and police archives. It stated that "all documents and archives etc. relating to enemy *tewu* are to be trans-ferred in their entirety to the public security departments for safekeeping and management. The public security departments are furthermore to actively collect them, and no person may tear up, throw away, or des-troy them."[38] After the founding of the PRC, the cumbersome process of combining various disparate records into a truly useful operational resource slowly got underway. At the end of 1951, in the context of talking to public security officers in Beijing about decisions taken at the recently concluded 4th NPSC, Luo Ruiqing called on "all branches of public security bureaus as well as bureau vocational departments to weed out old leads and then proceed to set up a system of archives and card files."[39]

The *scope* of the new combined archives may have been impressive, but retrieving information from them for operational purposes posed many challenges. On the practical level, one problem was the often entirely dif-ferent and incompatible indexing systems of inherited and new archives. Initially, the most common organizing principle whereby files on spe-cific individuals could be retrieved was the so-called Four Corner system (which assigned a unique four-digit number to each Chinese character), but in 1953 this system was abandoned in parts of China in favor of the *bopomofo* system (a Republican-era phonetic, albeit not alphabetic,

---

[38] Zhonggong zhongyang zhengce yanjiushi, ed., *Zhengce huibian (Collected Policies)* (N.p.: Zhonggong zhongyang Huabeiju, 1949), p. 126.

[39] Luo Ruiqing, "Zai Beijing shiju xuexi di si ci quanguo gongan huiyi jueyi zongjie dahui shang de baogao" (Report to the Concluding Meeting of the Beijing Bureau of Public Security to Study the Resolution of the 4th National Public Security Conference), *Renmin gongan zengkan*, No. 30, November 20, 1951, p. 37.

system that used non-Roman "letters"). The superiority of the latter system (superseded by the *pinyin* system at a later date) was that it was unaffected by the reform and simplification of the Chinese writing system begun at this time. In the "struggle against the enemy," registration of names according to phonetic criteria was proving superior to a character-based system, readers of the CMPS magazine *People's Public Security* (classified "for official use only") were told.[40] In spite of this, some public security archivists at the grassroots level favored yet another ordering and retrieval system, the so-called stroke order arrangement, involving the number of strokes in a character. Differences in the systems being used did not necessarily impact on the ease with which information could be retrieved in each separate instance, but it made any merger or combination of archives difficult.

Public security archives were used extensively; of this there is little doubt. In 1956, the Harbin municipal Bureau asserted that six years of work on building up a new and detailed population database had provided operational departments with "powerful support in the struggle against enemies." In 1955 alone, operational departments in the city had consulted the files of more than 22,190 individuals. In the following case, reported by the Harbin bureau, the specific use of archives may well in the end have involved spotting and assessing a target capable of serving a Case Group as an agent:

For example, in the course of mounting an operation against the *tewu* F [who is known to be] set to enter the PRC on a mission, a timely examination of census records revealed that there were cards on some ten individuals called F. After examining and eliminating some, it was possible to locate F's paternal cousins and fellow natives. Prior to F's arrival, we were already in control of the premises where he was likely to attempt to take up residence, and had managed to grasp the initiative.[41]

A problem with the archives and the information they contained was that profilers had no way of knowing whether anything in a file might in fact be grossly inaccurate.[42] Careless recording of data was commonplace: senior officers, who often had to shoulder the blame for serious mistakes or instances of negligence, admitted as much in their speeches. In December

---

[40] Hao Dianwen, "Renkou kapian guanli de fangfa haochu duo" (Numerous Things Good about Census Card File Management), *Renmin gongan*, No. 12, October 31, 1956, p. 18.

[41] Ibid., p. 19.

[42] Shaw, *Social Control in China*, p. 77.

1952, Feng Jiping criticized the inclination of "some comrades" involved in recording information to just "invent things, out of the blue, and make things up." He cited the example of a police officer who had previously worked in the old Nationalist police force and who had been retained in the Dongsi branch of the Beijing Bureau of Public Security: "[Having] at one time had his picture taken in the company of some Americans in front of the gates of the old [Republican] Bureau of Police, [one] of our cadres made a note of this, writing down that the 'said police officer is a *tewu* with the Sino-American Cooperative Organization.'" "Fairly common" was how Feng further described the sloppy recording of particulars, such as writing "member of Guomindang Military Statistics Bureau (*Juntong*)" instead of "Central Statistics Bureau (*Zhongtong*)" and writing "*tewu*" instead of "Guomindang party member." In a few instances, participation in revolutionary work even came to be recorded as engagement in "counterrevolutionary activities." One man who had arrived in Beijing from Nanyang, in the province of Henan, was registered by the police as having arrived from Southeast Asia (also pronounced *nanyang*); this was reported to the 1st Office of the municipal Bureau of Public Security, which, as a result, kept the man under surveillance for almost two years.[43]

The cards (*kapian*) mentioned by the Harbin Bureau of Public Security were convenient shortcuts to essential information on individuals. In theory, they were meant to be compact, easily accessible "miniatures" (*suoying*) of the fuller archival file holdings on a person. However, they admittedly sometimes failed in this respect and simply recorded a mass of contradictory information. Indeed, careless corroboration meant that the content of a file might very well be at odds with what the card claimed. In late 1950, an examination of cards documenting fifty-three PLA officers and personnel in the Logistics Department of the 68th Corps uncovered numerous anomalies. The *nature* of their alleged problem (whether or not, for example, it amounted to an unalterable "antagonistic contradiction") was often assessed in an obtuse and seemingly haphazard fashion, and it would have been difficult to actually use only the cards as a shortcut toward an assessment of agent potential.[44]

---

43 Feng Jiping, "Zai ganbu huiyi shang chuanda di wu ci quanguo gongan huiyi jueyi ji jiancha zhenya fangeming gongzuo de baogao" (Report to a Meeting of Cadres Transmitting the Resolution of the 5th National Public Security Conference and Investigating the Work of Suppressing Counterrevolutionaries), *Shoudu gongan zengkan*, No. 38, December 2, 1952, pp. 14, 18.

44 68 jun zhengzhibu baoweibu, "Dui 53 fen kapian yanjiu de zongjie" (Summary of Research into 53 Card Files), *Baowei gongzuo jianshe*, No. 7, January 15, 1951, pp. 15–19.

Eventually, public security organs began disseminating to those with a need to know even more comprehensive information resources – printed lists with basic information copied from the cards just mentioned. A typical entry on one such list of no less than 17,000 names from the city of Jinzhou reads as follows:

#2614. Name: [. . .]. Alias: n/a. Native place: n/a. Originally one of our scouts. In the thirty-sixth year of the Republic, when dispatched by us from Shashi to a certain locality in He [*sic*] [Hebei?], availed himself of the opportunity to abscond, only to be arrested. Turned traitor and went over to the enemy on June 19 in the thirty-seventh year of the Republic.[45]

Again, the *quality* of the listed information left a lot to be desired. Also to be found on the Jinzhou list, the following entry contained information pointing to a file (record group 3, catalogue #8, file 277) in the archive of the municipal Bureau of Public Security:

#2353. Name: [. . .]. Alias: n/a. Native place: n/a. Jin county, fifty-six years of age, Soviet spy. Having been developed by Soviet intelligence officer Zhang Jitong since the thirty-fifth year of the Republic, he was in April the following year inducted by Zhang into the Soviet Communist Party and recruited as a spy. Provided information about Harbin's Majiagou airport. Arrested by the Japanese Kempetai in Harbin in May in the thirty-sixth year of the Republic.[46]

Here the date of the subject's arrest by the Japanese two years *after* the end of World War II is almost certainly incorrect. In view of such inaccuracies, senior officers are known to have impressed upon their subordinates not to take information for granted and not to conduct an "investigation without analysis, or superficial analysis without detailed analysis."[47]

Information, again, appears to have been added in a somewhat haphazard fashion, but often included (when known) an update on the individual's whereabouts. "Prior to the Liberation of Beijing he fled to Taiwan, where he is a teacher in Taizhong municipality," is how one person's entry in a list of around 20,000 former Central Statistics Bureau *tewu* active in Beijing (compiled on the basis of the archive of the Beijing municipal Bureau of Public Security) ends; the information about another person on the same list ends with "After Liberation fled to Hong Kong,

---

45 *Diwei renyuan chazhao xiansuo huibian* (*Collected Leads in Search for Enemy and Puppet Personnel*) (Jinzhou: Liaoning sheng Jinzhou shi geweihui qingcha diwei dang'an bangongshi, 1970), Vol. 6, p. 34.
46 *Diwei renyuan chazhao*, Vol. 6, p. 16.
47 Wang Dongning, "Zai Hebei quansheng," p. 10.

where he lives at No. 2 Liren Street."[48] When nothing more precise was known about the *tewu*'s current whereabouts, information about relatives or friends was added, for example: "Fled to Nanjing prior to Liberation. His parents reside here in Beijing, outside the Anding Gate, where they sell firewood" or "His friend Z lives at No. 22 Sibaoli, Xi'an Road, District No. 10, Tianjin municipality."[49]

The cards – and, obviously, the archives – maintained by public security organs duly recorded if and when the status of a hostile class or *tewu* element underwent any fundamental change after the founding of the PRC (including if he or she had been executed). In the following case, a former captain in the Guomindang Military Statistics Bureau (some 717 *tewu* belonging to the bureau had registered with the new authorities in Beijing within one year of "Liberation"[50]) would clearly no longer have been of value as a potential agent, since he had gone on to become a bona fide officer with the Beijing Bureau of Public Security. Had he possibly been an agent for the CCP Social Affairs Department prior to 1949? Deemed sensitive, such information was not included in the entry on him in a massive list (referring to files held in the archive of the Beijing Bureau of Public Security) of *tewu* of the former Military Statistics Bureau active in Beijing. His entry read as follows:

Name: [. . .]. Captain and member of the 3rd Intelligence Group [of the Guomindang Military Statistics Bureau Beiping Garrison Command 2nd Section] in 1948. Male. Originally resident of 1 Pailou 10th Alley, Dongsi, Beijing municipality. Had previously served as intelligence staff officer in the bandit Beijing Garrison Command 2nd Section and as member of Group 284 under the bandit Ministry of National Defense 2nd Office. In 1951, worked in the 2nd Office of the Beijing Bureau of Public Security.[51]

The card summaries thus only provided the minimum information that would allow someone to identify a person with some accuracy. They were, in the words of those who compiled lists on the basis of them, meant only to serve as "leads" and little else.

---

[48] Zhongguo renmin jiefangjun Beijing weishuqu qingcha diwei dang'an xiaozu, ed., *Fei Beiping zhongtong tewu ziliao (Material on Bandit Central Statistics Bureau Tewu in Beiping)* (Beijing, 1969), pp. 26, 87.

[49] Ibid., pp. 38–39.

[50] "Yinian lai fandong dangtuante dengji gongzuo zongjie" (Summary of a Year's Registration of Reactionary Party and Organization Members and *Tewu*), *Renmin gongan zengkan*, No. 7, May 25, 1950, p. 26.

[51] Zhongguo renmin jiefangjun Beijing weishuqu qingcha diwei dang'an xiaozu, ed., *Fei Beiping juntong tewu ziliao (Material on Bandit Military Statistics Bureau Tewu in Beiping)* (Beijing, 1969), p. 548.

The actual public security files on individuals on the lists held more substantial information. Take, for example the man U, who from 1949 to 1951 had worked on the island of Okinawa as a senior monitor with the CIA's Foreign Broadcast Monitoring Service and who returned to Beijing in 1952 to work as a translator, first for the Peace Conference of the Asian and Pacific Regions, later for the North China regional and Beijing municipal government. In a list of former Military Statistics Bureau *tewu* on which the Beijing Bureau of Public Security had information in its archive, the entry on him was a mere four lines long, ending with "arrested in March 1958, sentenced to ten years."[52] The full file (#7133) on U, however, was a massive repository of information. Maintained, while still active, by the 5th Office of the municipal Bureau, it not only documented U's years in the Qinghe Labor Reform Camp, but also his activities prior to being arrested. Like so many files of its kind, it contains much contradictory information. In a résumé prepared by U in 1953, he wrote:

When I arrived back in Hong Kong [from Okinawa] in September 1951, I made contact with the local [CCP] organization, but was found not to qualify for membership of the community.... The local [CCP] organization in Hong Kong may have investigated me [at the time], and it is possible that the Central Personnel Department passed an official verdict on me. Comrade Yang Banliu (contact telephone number: Beijing 4 2083) should be able to provide a reference.[53]

In a different résumé, written three years later and attached to an employment registration form, he describes the same period in his life as follows: "Engaged in underground revolutionary work in Hong Kong (1951–1952) (Introduced by and worked under the leadership of W)."[54] In a list of fifty-two of his substantive personal relationships, written in February 1964, he sticks to the "underground work" story, stating about an old contact that "he participated in underground work with me in Hong Kong. Current address unknown. Have not been in touch for eight years."[55] What this illustrates was just how difficult the public security files would have been to use. They were in effect repositories of contradictory information far removed from an accurate summary of straightforward facts about a particular individual.

[52] Ibid., pp. 1172–73.
[53] "Ganbu jianlibiao" (Cadre CV Form) [January 30, 1953].
[54] "Gongzuo renyuan dengjibiao" (Staff Registration Form) [1956].
[55] "Baogao" (Report) [February 7, 1964].

A Visit to the Grass Roots

Further stages in the profiling process often involved gathering information about the target from the place where he or she lived or had lived.[56] The assumption, obviously, was that here the local CCP organization, neighborhood and village committees maintaining household registration records, as well as ordinary people, might have knowledge of the target's past and present work as well as private life. If and when profilers in this context proceeded in person to access written records or interview people, secrecy was paramount. In order not to expose the real purpose of an investigation, officer cadets in the Central People's Public Security Academy were told as part of their training to "conduct this kind of reading of records and interview of people under a suitable cover or excuse."[57] A 1952 document drawing lessons from a prolonged investigation conducted out of Tianshui municipality, Gansu province, proposed that when covert investigations of employee records and files needed to be carried out, the investigators should adopt designations like the "Task Force for Temporary Workers' Promotion to Regular Workers" or claim to be members of a "Salary Reform Group."[58]

If and when the information was collected by way of written inquiries, equally strict security had to be maintained: it was *not*, the CMPS found itself compelled to point out in 1954, permissible, as some economic protection units had gotten into the habit of doing, to use ordinary mail for this purpose and to address a request for information directly to the grass roots. The correct way of going about it was to send a letter by registered mail to the local public security unit and ask it to act as an intermediary.[59] Findings were, whenever feasible, to be returned not by ordinary mail, but with the help of the confidential courier service operated by the CCP and PLA, a process referred to in a set of regulations from 1951 as "forwarding through the military mail (intraparty communications)."[60] This nationwide internal courier service system was highly secure; however,

---

[56] "*Teqing gongzuo*," pp. 28–29.

[57] Ibid., p. 29.

[58] Xibei ganxian gongchengju gonganchu, "Guanyu modi gongzuo qingkuang de baogao" (Situation Assessment Work Report), *Tielu gongan tongxun*, No. 13, December 8, 1952, p. 18.

[59] "Piping yu jianyi" (Criticism and Suggestions), *Gongan shouce*, No. 31, December 10, 1954, p. 43.

[60] Zhonggong zhongyang zuzhibu bangongting, *Zuzhi gongzuo wenjian xuanbian 1949 nian 10 yue–1952 nian*, p. 316.

it did not always operate as intended. In Nanjing, for example, it was meant to be used exclusively (or so the regulations stipulated) to forward *official* "Top Secret, Secret, Important (*yaojian*), urgent, or ordinary mail (the latter will not be registered, nor will inquiries about lost items be conducted) ... between party, government, and mass organizations." But a meeting of officials responsible for the operation of the system reported to the municipal party authorities in December 1954 that it was in fact abused to pass on everything from personal mail and photographs in the category of Top Secret mail to envelopes containing private movie and theater tickets in the category of urgent mail.[61] A lack of resources meant that the system was under constant strain. Secure it may have been, but the estimated delivery time for documents sent long distance by courier and routed via provincial bureaus of public security was often far longer than that of mail sent via the ordinary postal system.[62]

As one might expect, the management of census and other relevant records in rural China by townships (or, after 1958, by People's Communes) was poor by comparison with the qualified professionalism that characterized the CMPS or major urban bureaus of public security.[63] In remote and impoverished parts of the countryside in particular, it took years before the real-world value of archives was appreciated and began to have an impact. In 1958, *People's Public Security* published an article specifically aimed at convincing skeptical rural police officers of the good uses to which an archive could be put. The article, describing and commenting on the situation in a county in Fujian province, asserted that the "creation of a vocational archive is not only a matter of planning for the long haul but also has very great significance in the actual, current struggle."[64] It went on to quote a township party secretary as repeatedly telling a visiting county public security officer that "a public security archive is a substantial resource in the struggle against the adversary and should be valued accordingly."[65]

[61] Zhonggong Nanjing shiwei bangongting mishushi, "Guanyu jiaotong, shoufa gongzuo zhong liangge juti wenti de tongzhi" (Notification Concerning Two Concrete Problems in Communication and Dispatch Work) [December 22, 1954], p. 2.

[62] "Renmin gongan weishenme you youju faxing?" (Why Is *People's Public Security* Distributed by the Post Office?), *Renmin gongan*, No. 19, April 10, 1957, p. 5.

[63] On the PRC household registration system, see the chapter "The Emergence of the *Hukou*" in Michael Dutton, *Policing and Punishment in China: From Patriarchy to "the People"* (Cambridge: Cambridge University Press, 1992), pp. 189–245.

[64] "Xiangxiang shixian dang'anhua" (Each and Every Township Its Own Archive), *Renmin gongan*, No. 50, October 5, 1958, p. 16.

[65] Ibid., p. 17.

People's Public Security published in the same year a detailed retrospective on the development of a township archive in Xiangxiang county,
Hunan province, as told by the archive's creator and curator to a visiting
cadre from the provincial Bureau of Public Security. Flicking through his
filing cabinet, the township archivist was in April 1958 able to boast to
his visitor that it contained

> individual files on every landlord element, rich-peasant element, counterrevolu-
> tionary element, and bad element; ideology and attitude registration forms of
> party and Youth League members from different periods; forms recording the
> findings of examinations of coop and team cadres and members; and every mili-
> tia member's personal vitae as well as forms and material documenting their
> ideological stance and performance at work. We are in control here of the cir-
> cumstances of altogether 8,496 people, or 85 percent of the adult population in
> the entire township. The files of individuals are sorted by the coops (villages) and
> production teams to which they belong, and arranged according to the number
> of strokes in the surname, which makes retrieval very convenient.[66]

Historians would hence be mistaken if they assumed that these grassroots
files contained little more than census records.[67] They also provided crucial community of interest data by throwing light on substantive personal
relationships. Exactly how aggressively managers of archives pursued
additional information to incorporate varied from place to place. For
some of those who raised the matter in the public security sector, nothing
was too insignificant to be recorded. Accordingly, in the words of one
1951 year-end work report on "social intelligence" emanating from the
Public Security Office of the Tianjin Railroad Management Bureau, "a
few words or snippets of information picked up here or there may not
be sufficient to prove anything, but once accumulated they may turn into
something very useful."[68] In the PLA, with respect to the files of vaguely
"backward" persons, this philosophy was applied with impunity: "The
remarks, behavior, and attitude of suspect elements (*xianyi fenzi*) and all
corroborating information are to be recorded regularly and registered in
a timely fashion, as well as analyzed and studied at regular intervals and
arranged in a comprehensive fashion," the security section of the North
China Military Region Political Department demanded in the winter of

---

[66] Zhang Yulin, "Yige xiang de gongan dang'an gongzuo" (A Township's Public Security
Archive Work), *Renmin gongan*, No. 45, July 1, 1958, p. 16.

[67] A comprehensive official list of what files were to contain can be found in Shaw, *Social
Control in China*, p. 75.

[68] Quoted in Michael Schoenhals, *Public Security in the People's Republic of China*, p. 52.

1950–51.[69] In the civilian sector, on the other hand, in society at large, senior officers would eventually begin to ask just how much information on people it was necessary to collect. "What's the point of recording all this information?" a deputy director of public security in Shanghai said to local police officers in 1965. "There are ten million people in Shanghai: if you keep records like this from when a person is sixteen, by the time he's in his grave, his stack of records will be a meter high. With six million adults in this city, even two Park Hotels will not be sufficient to store it all."[70]

The township archivist in Xiangxiang county was in 1958 able to provide his visitor with some recent examples of the political uses to which his files (and the "control of the circumstances of people" that they permitted) had been put:

This time around, in the rural rectification movement, we were able to extract information, from the files of party and Youth League members and coop and team cadres alone, on a variety of errors committed by altogether 122 people. We submitted timely reports on all of these to the [coop] party committee and furthermore dealt with [the individuals affected] accordingly, one by one. In this way, not only did we cleanse the grassroots level organization, but also gave added impetus to rural rectification and the Great Leap Forward in [agricultural] production. As part of the documentary preparatory groundwork that preceded the launch of our all-out attack on the enemy, in less than ten days we managed to complete both the compilation and the verification of documentation, and of the 103 items submitted to higher levels for ratification, some 61 resulted in arrests, detentions or [the imposition of probationary] control. The people affected included some who had never caught anybody's attention because they "never committed any major mistakes, while constantly committing minor ones." Because we, under normal circumstances, made a point of noticing and accumulating information on these so-called "minor errors," it finally became possible to spot the big problems. The archive has also played many roles over the years in the context of assisting in the external investigation of cadres and in the verification and provision of information.[71]

Because the information they contained was deemed to be of such enduring intelligence value, the archives of public security organs across China were in 1960 exempted from the rule that the contents of closed files – like

[69] Huabei junqu zhengzhibu baoweibu, "Guanyu xianyi cailiao zhuanyi deng wenti de jidian yidian" (Some Views on the Transmission of Suspects' Documentation and Other Matters), *Baowei gongzuo jianshe*, No. 7, January 15, 1951, p. 14.

[70] *Lu Zheng zuixinglu* (*Record of Lu Zheng's Crimes*) (Shanghai: Shanghai shi ganganju zhengzhibu bangongshi nongbaochu geming zaofandui, 1967), pp. 11–12. Shanghai's twenty-two-story Park Hotel was the tallest building in China at the time.

[71] Zhang Yulin, "Yige xiang de gongan dang'an gongzuo," pp. 16–17.

those of other state institutional archives – be automatically transferred to the corresponding state district, municipal, or provincial archive after a fixed period of time.[72]

Tapping Additional Sources

Just how often agent profiling work went much further than what has been described so far is not known. A truly in-depth background check of a prospective agent may have involved the use of other agents.[73] However, since the CMPS decreed that it was only permissible to employ agents when deemed absolutely necessary and with the approval of a superior officer, how often or how easily approval was granted for conducting background checks as a means of profiling cannot be determined. A trusted and proficient agent who had been used before might be relied upon to conduct a one-on-one investigation of the target to obtain information that could not be gained by other means. The CMPS stressed, however, that the actual motive behind such an investigation was not to be divulged to the agent tasked with carrying it out.[74]

Another way of collecting further information on the prospective agent was by reading his or her mail.[75] When interception and perlustration of an individual's correspondence functioned as it was meant to, and records were properly kept, it was possibly more accurate (because it amounted to surreptitiously accessing firsthand information) than any intelligence based on rumors about the target known to local police officers. An intimate – but not always very smooth – working relationship existed between the public security organs and China's postal services insofar as the interception of mail was concerned. Some six months before the founding of the PRC, the Tianjin municipal Bureau of Public Security had ordered its operational offices to have their staff contact local post offices to work out a system whereby mail to and from addressees in the city could be examined.[76] In Northeast China, the NEMPS in February 1950 spoke of "building further on the foundations already established" in this way and of calling a regional meeting specifically on the topic, to push

---

[72] Guojia dang'anju bangongshi, ed., *Dang'an gongzuo wenjian huiji* (*Collected Documents on Archive Work*) (Beijing: Dang'an chubanshe, 1986), Vol. 1, pp. 124–25.

[73] Compare Schoenhals, "Recruiting Agents in Industry and Trade," pp. 13–14.

[74] "*Teqing gongzuo*," p. 29.

[75] Ibid.

[76] Tianjin shi renmin zhengfu gonganju, "Zhishi" (Directive), *Tianjin gongan*, Vol. 2, No. 1, January 31, 1951, p. 24.

for greater professionalization and regularizing a system of recording, developing leads, cross-checking, and exchange of information between post offices and the public security organs.[77]

Local post offices were expected to monitor the contents of certain categories of mail, including letters to and from individuals on watch lists compiled by the public security organs.[78] These watch lists were not limited to "suspect elements"; for security reasons, the international correspondence of senior scientists and employees in government ministry research institutes was also scrutinized as a matter of routine. Of the 26,000 employees in the Baotou Steel Works in 1958, 190 were known by the Bureau of Public Security in Inner Mongolia to have links of one kind or another to persons abroad, and of these individuals, 9 had links to what were said to be *tewu* working for Japan or the United States.[79] A survey conducted by the CMPS discovered in 1960 that between September 1959 and March 1960, employees in the PRC Ministry of Metallurgy, Ministry of Construction Engineering, Ministry of Geology, Ministry of Agricultural Machinery, and Ministry of Hydropower, among others, had, on no less than twenty-eight separate occasions, revealed state secrets in correspondence with individuals in the Soviet Union, Mongolia, Romania, East Germany, Thailand, Malaya, and Hong Kong.[80]

That the mail was being read was an open secret in much of urban China, and this fact frustrated security-conscious public security officers. A letter to *People's Public Security* in the spring of 1957 expressed outrage at the fact that an ordinary urbanite had recently suggested in an informal chat to a public security officer that "there is something very suspicious about so-and-so. Are you reading his mail or are you not?"[81] The letter writer – possibly encouraged by Mao Zedong's recent call for a "gentle breeze and mild rain" type of identification and settlement of "contradictions among the people" – identified the root of the "open secret" problem as one of officers disclosing confidential information to members of the public without authorization. Whereas ordinary correspondence with a relative in Hong Kong or on Taiwan was of limited

[77] Dongbei renmin zhengfu gonganbu, "Guanyu jiaqiang zhencha," p. 24.
[78] Dongbei renmin zhengfu gonganbu, "Dui youdian jiancha de jige wenti" (Some Problems in Postal Examination), *Gongan baowei gongzuo*, Vol. 17, pp. 40–42.
[79] Biligbaatar, "Guanyu canjia Baotou," p. 21.
[80] "Xiemi shimi shijian buduan fasheng" (Constant Leaks and Loss of Secrets), *Gongan gongzuo jianbao*, No. 18, March 1, 1960, p. 12.
[81] "Jianjue xiang shimi xingwei zuo douzheng!" (Resolutely Fight Behavior Compromising Secrecy!), *Renmin gongan*, No. 19, April 10, 1957, p. 13.

interest most of the time, it could also – when officers were profiling for agents – prove to be useful to operational departments, in particular if a relative was suspected or known by the authorities to be a *tewu*. Indeed, there were times when a target was recruited as an agent for a single purpose – to help convince his or her *tewu* relative that it was safe to return to the Chinese mainland.

Further feeding into the profiling process might be information obtained through physical surveillance of the target. The authors of the *Lectures* stressed that covert tracking and trailing was "of very great help" when the immediate aim of a Case Group was to gain a fuller picture of how a target interacted with the larger organization or network, the penetration of which was the ultimate purpose of his or her planned recruitment.[82] Unfortunately, the literature on the subject is limited, and recollections of the work of plainclothes officers in tracking the movements of targets in urban China in the 1950s and 1960s are scant and not very informative. However, an anecdote hinting at the hardships and problems such work involved can be found in Feng Jiping's official biography:

> In 1960, because of the crop failure caused by natural and manmade calamities, people all went around hungry. At one time, the legs of our undernourished officers tasked with conducting nighttime physical surveillance were so badly affected by edema that pursuing the enemy on foot proved impossible. Deng Kai, the beleaguered head of the [Beijing Bureau of Public Security] Physical Surveillance Office at the time, told Director Feng of this when the two men happened to meet. A distressed Feng commented, "This won't do! They are vanguards fighting on the front lines. How can we let them go hungry?!" and immediately wrote a special report to Comrade Liu Ren [on the municipal Party Committee] asking the Municipal Committee to provide each officer on the surveillance front with an extra daily ration of half a *jin* of grain.[83]

Just how many surveillance officers Beijing's Bureau of Public Security had in 1960 is not known, but the number of those proficient at their job may have been fairly limited – it took years of training combined with natural talent to become a good surveillance officer – which might explain why the bureau had to push those at its disposal beyond the reasonable call of duty.[84] In many parts of China, operational departments had to contend with untrained officers who performed rather less than satisfactorily. A

---

[82] *"Teqing gongzuo,"* p. 29.
[83] Liu Guangren, Zhao Yimin, and Yu Xingqian, *Feng Jiping zhuan* (*Biography of Feng Jiping*) (Beijing: Qunzhong chubanshe, 1997), p. 137.
[84] Ferguson, *Spy*, p. 186.

CMPS task force visiting Shanxi province in the winter of 1954–55 found that in the provincial capital, residents never had a problem spotting a plainclothes officer in a crowd: "Their caps, shoes, and mode of transport give them away in an instant! They're worse than useless," the CMPS complained.[85]

The interrogation of persons in custody was also viewed by the CMPS as capable of yielding useful profiling information, but the authors of the *Lectures* emphasized that any information obtained in this way "is not to be given easy credence."[86] On the basis of past experience in such matters, senior officers were well aware of how certain dubious interrogation techniques were prone to providing information that could not be trusted. This may well have been why Yang Qiqing, in a major lecture on operational case work on November 26, 1955, stressed that "we admit that confessions obtained through *correct interrogation procedures* are on the whole quite reliable, but no matter what, they must all be corroborated by investigation."[87] The same problem with confessions had been raised three months earlier at a high-level conference on the progress of the Elimination of Counterrevolutionaries campaign in China's armed forces, where it was noted that "merely having a confession, and no investigation, does not count as having clarified a matter."[88] In its discussion of the ins and outs of the profiling process, it is worth noting that the *Lectures* mentioned but did not elaborate on the interrogation of persons in custody. By comparison, it was not given the same priority as other forms of investigation and research.[89]

A final stage in the profiling process might involve giving a senior operational officer with extensive agent-handling experience an opportunity to personally observe the target up close. In textbook cases, the officer would use this opportunity to assess whether or not the information already accumulated on the target appeared to confirm what he or she was able to observe firsthand. The senior officer's assessment of the target would be carried out under some suitable cover: the authors of the *Lectures* suggested that "whenever possible, some public function should be used as a pretext, allowing for a direct encounter with the target and

---

[85] Gonganbu Shanxi shichazu, "Guanyu Shanxi sheng zhencha gongzuo 'guoguan' wenti de kaocha baogao" (Investigation Report into Whether Operational Work in Shanxi is "Up to Scratch"), *Gongan jianshe*, No. 118, March 7, 1955, p. 9.

[86] *"Teqing gongzuo,"* p. 29.

[87] Yang Qiqing, "Zhuan'an xiaozu," p. 73. Emphasis added.

[88] *Sufan yundong wenjian xuanbian*, p. 151.

[89] *"Teqing gongzuo,"* p. 29.

personal scrutiny, the purpose of which need not be revealed." What this
meant was that it was permissible for the encounter to be arranged by the
public security organs in a variety of ways, depending on the "nature of
the target's work, his lifestyle, etc." In some cases, the name of the public
security organs might not be mentioned at all, while in others it might.
Under certain circumstances, it was admitted in the *Lectures*, the officer
might find his or her ability to probe the target limited, which meant
that one or more additional meetings would be called for. If this was so,
a reason for a second meeting had to be arranged at the first meeting.
CMPS experience showed that these assessment meetings "must not be
too numerous, since if they are, the pretext under which they are conducted may no longer work." And if the officer meeting with the target
was at this point adopting a cover, then it was important that his or her
true persona – and, therefore, the real nature of the meeting(s) – never be
revealed to the target after his or her recruitment as an agent. This was
necessary in order to avoid awkward questions arising later or provoking
"displeasure" on the part of the target.[90]

The ultimate purpose of the involvement of the senior officer was to
assess the likelihood of deception and to make a judgment, based on
whatever criteria the officer might use given past experience and profes-
sional/functional responsibilities. A careful reading of the available record
suggests that the skills called for to recognize possible deception would
at the very least have included a consideration of motive, anomalies, and
inconsistencies. On rare occasions when senior figures went on record
with their views on deception, however, they rarely spoke of how they
had reasoned in such measured terms, but simply referred to gut feelings.
The following is an excerpt from an address by Kang Sheng (with a brief
significant interjection by Zhou Enlai) to a delegation from Inner Mongolia in the spring of 1967, in which the one-time head of the CSAD explains
why he had become convinced that a long-standing leading member of
the CCP leadership in Inner Mongolia was not what he claimed to be:

I didn't know Wang Yilun before, and had only seen him once at a reception
for the Party Committee of the [Inner Mongolia] Autonomous Region. Now, as
soon as I look at him, I'd say he's not a Communist Party member at all, nor is
he an ordinary person. *There's something about his appearance, the way he does
things, his manner, his speech and movements, which keep suggesting to me that
he is a tewu.* I asked him: are you really a Communist, or are you Guomindang?
He kept hesitating and couldn't give a clear answer. People like me, we've met a

[90] Ibid., pp. 29–30.

lot of Communists and quite a few Guomindang as well (Premier [Zhou Enlai]: *We can smell when something is wrong!*), so I asked him: Where did you join the party? He kept on hesitating.[91]

The heuristic appraisals of specific targets by people like Kang and Zhou may appear to have been far from careful and responsible, but the substantive base of their knowledge of agent and intelligence work in general can hardly be said to have been fragmented or skewed. Their curious references to gut feelings (e.g., "something about... suggesting to me") and olfactory sensibilities ("We can smell when ... ") are not cited here to suggest that the painstaking profiling work that used archives, confidential interviews, perlustration of the mail, surveillance, and other means described in this chapter was ultimately of no importance and that leaders' subjective views determined everything, but merely as a reminder of its *relative* real-world value. Ambitious and motivated PRC profilers undoubtedly strove to become something akin to Marxist applied social scientists, and at times their procedure *did* by itself produce approximately correct answers to the all-important operational question "Is this person likely to become a good agent?" Later, if an analysis of a mission gone wrong suggested that the responsibility for its failure was really theirs, the profilers were always able to seek consolation in the *Selected Works of Mao Zedong*, in which the CCP Chairman asserted that "failure is the mother of success... [and] the lessons learned from failures are the basis for future triumphs."[92]

---

[91] *Zhongyang guanyu chuli Neimeng wenti de youguan wenjian he zhongyang fuze tongzhi jianghua huibian* (*Center's Decision on Resolving Matters in Inner Mongolia and Collected Central Leaders' Speeches*), 2 vols. (Huhehot: Huhehaote geming zaofan lianluo zongbu, 1967), Vol. 1, p. 101. Emphasis added.

[92] *Selected Works of Mao Tsetung*, Vol. 2, p. 56.

5

Recruitment

There were no uniquely "socialist" ways of recruiting an agent: there were only those ways that worked and those that did not. Experienced operational officers had learned the hard way the importance of tailoring their approach to the target and understood only too well the meaning of the following injunction by Mao Zedong, included in a reader compiled under the aegis of the CMPS in the winter of 1959–60: "The most fundamental method of work that all Communists must firmly bear in mind is to determine our working policies according to actual conditions."[1]

Notwithstanding the pragmatism of Mao's statement, officers had to identify the most suitable recruitment strategies under the conditions prevailing in urban China after 1949. While, for example, the Shenyang Public Security Bureau Agent Work Initiation Procedures stressed the "absolute impermissibility of employing a fixed formula or attempting to follow the same rigid procedure every time," it nevertheless described a finite number of strategies open to modification.[2] Later textbooks attempted to strike a similar balance: the *Lectures on the Subject of Agent Work* devoted a full three chapters to the subject of recruitment, to be studied by officer cadets attending the Central People's Public Security Academy; at the same time, cadets were reminded that "there is no fixed rule that says where or in what capacity one should personally observe and study – or under what kind of cover one should meet and get to know – the target. Everything is determined by hard facts such as what the nature of the target's job is, what kind of life it leads, etc." While stressing that, as a rule,

---

[1] *Mao Zedong tongzhi lun*, p. 209.
[2] Shenyang shi renmin zhengfu gonganju jingji baoweichu, "Guanyu jianli," pp. 34–35.

the actual recruitment of the target was to be made "in the name of" the public security organs, the *Lectures* explained that the initial approach might also, under some circumstances, be attempted "under some other flag."[3]

Ultimately, the CMPS emphasized, successful agent recruitment was a matter of the operational officer bringing into play his or her full range of "political skills, tradecraft, and professionalism." It was for didactic purposes *only* that blueprints and textbooks often limited their discussions of recruitment strategies "based on our current experience" to a mere three prototypes. The first of these was the "patriotic pitch," the successful execution of which assumed that the target was a Chinese citizen who could be made to work for the public security organs by appealing to a preexisting "patriotic political self-awareness." The second was the lengthy and often highly delicate procedure of operational cultivation, known in house as "gradually engaging, educating, and influencing" a potential agent. The third was a coercive routine that involved blackmail or threat of exposure, which basically entailed the target agreeing to collaboration under duress and the pressure of circumstances. This strategy, however, often tended to produce agents whose cooperation was minimal and, thus, was officially seen as limited in its applicability to hostile class and *tewu* elements.[4]

As much as it emphasized the need for flexibility as far as recruitment strategies were concerned, the CMPS also stressed the need for the regularization of bureaucratic and other routines that had to be completed prior to and after the agent recruitment interview. Exactly how officers were meant to manage such routines was outlined in the *Lectures*. Accordingly, officer cadets were told at the Central People's Public Security Academy that the mere recruitment of the agent did not mean the job was finished: it should be immediately followed by the compulsory completion of paperwork – even where the recruitment of an agent had failed – including the opening of a personal file on the agent.[5]

Preparation Is Key

Once profiling work was complete, operational departments would begin preparing for the recruitment of the prospective agent. In practical terms,

---

[3] "*Teqing gongzuo*," p. 29.
[4] Ibid., pp. 33–36.
[5] Ibid., pp. 38–40.

this involved – but was not limited to – deciding upon a time and a place to attempt recruitment and determining which strategy would likely yield the greatest chance for success. Setting the stage involved advance preparation of a cover or pretext under which recruitment could be safely conducted in absolute secrecy. In the words of one Shanghai Bureau of Public Security document, the fact that "a person, with due permission, is to be developed and utilized as an agent is on no account to be made public."[6] Preparations were expected to pay due attention to even the most minute details. Operational officers were supposed to have committed to memory Mao Zedong's ten so-called principles of operation, the fifth of which stated: "Fight no battle unprepared, fight no battle you are not sure of winning."[7]

The *Lectures* instructed future agent handlers to empathize with the target and bear in mind that he or she would soon be confronting an altogether novel, highly stressful, and potentially dangerous set of circumstances:

His recruitment as an agent will be a major event in a person's private life. Having been recruited, he is faced with having an entirely new set of duties and obligations to the state and to the public security organs. These duties and obligations may well be ones to which he has never previously given any thought. In today's political situation, an absolute majority of people will be happy to shoulder this task [of being an agent], but this still does not mean that everyone will be willing to do so. Some people whose thinking and understanding is flawed, and who hold certain erroneous opinions about our public security work, may also come up with pretexts for rejecting the operational officer's request. Therefore, prior to making the decision to attempt the recruitment of an agent, one must first of all investigate and clarify the situation of the agent in its entirety, and make an assessment of how likely he will be to allow himself to be recruited and of the difficulties one is likely to encounter in this respect.[8]

Retrospective analyses of successful agent recruitments often illustrated just how much applied psychology had gone into preparing for a successful recruitment.

Timing was an important factor governing recruitment attempts and was by no means simply a tactical matter of picking the right day of the week. There were other, longer-term factors to be taken into consideration as well. Experience showed, for example, that the positioning – including the recruitment – of a penetration agent inside an organization

---

[6] *Sifa zhengce xuanbian*, p. 32.
[7] Zhonggong zhongyang zhengce yanjiushi, *Zhengce huibian*, p. 7.
[8] "*Teqing gongzuo*," p. 27.

deemed hostile or potentially hostile to the CCP was preferably to be done strategically, within a particular window of opportunity in the evolution of that organization. Perhaps the most important lesson learned in the course of the breakup of a trans-provincial Guomindang network of railroad saboteurs in 1950, according to the public security organs in Zhengzhou, was that the "opportune moment for us to put a penetration agent in place is when the enemy is in the very process of building up and expanding his organization."⁹ Obviously, there were times when such considerations did not apply, but even in the recruitment of an essentially passive critical asset guardian, for example, some thought might need to be given to whether threat levels were seen as rising or falling and how this might influence recruitment timing.

A different kind of time frame related to the psychological state of mind or physical movements of the recruitment target. Here timing was obviously a matter of mounting an attempt when the target was most amenable to persuasion and likely to consent to serving as an agent. The following description by two officers from the Changsha municipal Bureau of Public Security illustrates the significance of seizing the ripe moment. The account describes how an operation run out of Hong Kong by the Guomindang Central Committee Group Two was broken up by recruiting a penetration agent, a woman already "on the inside," who had begun to have second thoughts about what she had gotten herself into:

In order to achieve greater clarity about the concrete tasks that C had been sent back [to Changsha] to execute, we needed to penetrate deep into the tiger's lair and mount a surveillance operation. Initially, due to limitations posed by various circumstances, this had not been possible and hence little progress had been made. We then investigated the circumstances of H and arrived at the conclusion that she was just a run-of-the-mill exploitation asset [*yiban liyong fenzi*] under C's leadership. If only we did our job well, she might well quickly wake up to her error and agree to work for us. At around this same time, C reported in secret to the enemy as follows: "Not long after I had returned, I discovered H and gave her the secret writing chemicals. . . . " He also told H to assume responsibility for his communication with Hong Kong. *H, however, remained in a state of indecision, neither daring to refuse C nor daring to turn him in to the authorities: she was planning to leave for Lanzhou in order to get away from C. This meant, from the looks of it, that the conditions under which we might be able to win her over*

⁹ "Zhengzhou gonganchu pohuo wei 'Yu-E suijingqu dihou gongzuo weiyuanhui zanbian di yi lu di yi zongdui' an" (Zhengzhou Public Security Office Cracks Case of Puppet "Henan-Hubei Regional Pacification and Enemy Rear Work Committee Temporary 1st Route 1st Column"), *Tielu gongan tongxun*, No. 4, February 10, 1951, p. 8.

and make use of her had ripened. After having subjected her to persuasion and education, and after making our policy clear to her, she basically confessed to all of the activities that C and she had been engaged in, [and] furthermore handed over the secret writing chemicals, writing brush, and letters written to her in secret writing by her husband in Hong Kong, and expressed a readiness to work for us and offer meritorious service to atone for crimes committed.[10]

In their discussion of timing an agent recruitment attempt, the authors of *Lectures* highlighted tactical matters and spoke mainly of the need to take into account the nature of the target's profession as well as his or her personal habits. It was paramount, for instance, not to arouse the suspicions of family or colleagues by allowing the recruitment to take an excessively long time (during which the target's absence might be hard to explain). If the target was a "person of habit who always leaves and returns home at very regular hours," officer cadets were reminded, then suspicions might easily be aroused if the recruitment were ill-timed and he or she failed to "return home or arrive at a particular place at the normal time." If asked under these circumstances by family members or colleagues about the reason for the late arrival, the *Lectures* warned, "the target may well reveal what had actually happened."[11]

In addition to timing, the actual place where the recruitment interview was to take place had to be selected bearing a number of crucial factors in mind, including location, accessibility, and surroundings, as well as the social status, professional position, and gender of the target in question. Operational departments obviously wanted to ensure that any recruitment proceeded in absolute secrecy. Any location that satisfied this requirement was, in theory, a suitable one. Under normal circumstances, the official premises of the public security organs themselves were viewed as unsuited to the task of recruitment, since the fact that the target had visited them might be difficult to keep secret. But in those cases where the target was an "antagonistic class element" whose "crimes are well documented and substantial," and his or her recruitment basically amounted to one optional culmination of an extended interrogation, his or her recruitment there was deemed permissible.[12]

Prior to the actual recruitment interview, the recruiting officer had to consult his or her superior officer as to whether or not the target should,

---

[10] Huang Yingke and Xie Yinhui, "Zhenpo 'Zhongweihui erzu' tewu XXX an" (Cracking the Case of the "Central Committee Group Two" *Tewu* XXX), *Renmin gongan*, No. 18, March 25, 1957, p. 17.

[11] "*Teqing gongzuo*," pp. 30–31.

[12] Ibid., p. 30.

immediately upon recruitment, be required to provide certain basic personal information in writing. The information (e.g., a brief résumé and a written pledge pertaining to his or her new role) was slated to eventually end up in the agent's personal file. In some cases, depending on the circumstances, an oral commitment would suffice: the CMPS, for example, granted operational departments the right to waive or make some recruitment formalities optional in the case of agents who were Communist Party (or Youth League) members.[13] Presumably, the reason for such a full or partial waiver was the simple fact that agents from such backgrounds would have already provided the CCP with the relevant biographical information more than once in the past.

The rationale behind the need to complete a number of formalities at the same time as recruitment was to ensure that the target would mentally commit him- or herself to the role of agent. If the agent was deemed to be a hostile class or *tewu* element, such formalities also served as an additional means of control – similar to those that the KGB included under the rubric of "consolidation of agent recruitment."[14] The latter were euphemistically described as measures that "give the agent additional incentives to fulfill conscientiously the commitments he has made."[15]

Worth noting is that the CMPS, possibly more so than the KGB, was prepared to recognize the subtle dialectic involved in asking agents to commit themselves in writing: it was well understood that doing so might provoke very different responses in targets from different backgrounds. At the Central People's Public Security Academy in Beijing, it was impressed upon officer cadets that individuals who had agreed to serve as agents and who were "ordinary members of the masses or backward elements, and elements of the [old] elite in particular," often looked positively on such formalization. It was, in their eyes, proof of trust and legitimization of their new agent role as being a very honorable one. On the other hand, cadets were told, they should expect to occasionally come across individuals who reacted differently. These included those who were genuinely prepared to work as agents but were – or had reason to be – afraid to formally commit themselves in writing. They also included persons who saw the very fact that they were being asked to go through formalities as proof of a *lack* of trust. In such cases, it was up to the recruitment officer to decide how best to proceed and choose the most appropriate course of action.[16]

[13] Ibid., pp. 38–39.
[14] Ibid., p. 39.
[15] *KGB Lexicon*, p. 210.
[16] "*Teqing gongzuo*," p. 39.

In the final preparatory phase, operational officers had to obtain permission from the relevant authority to recruit the agent in question. To this end, they were required to submit a request to their own CCP Committee and to the higher-level administrative (immediate supradepartmental) leadership. The CMPS *Agent Work Manual* described what the special form to be used for this purpose was meant to look like. Known as the Agent Opening Authorization Form, it was similar to the Agent Registration Form described in greater detail later in this chapter.[17] It was the responsibility of the officer managing the planned recruitment to complete the form. Higher-level authority to recruit had to be given by all of the parties involved and had to be explicit: for a superior officer to merely circle his or her name on a preprinted list of recipients was not enough. CMPS regulations stipulated that "each one of the organs to which a request is presented should append to it explicit opinions of examination and verification, and the organ providing authority to recruit should do this formally in writing."[18] The involvement of the superior officer (and what he or she was expected to keep in mind when giving the go-ahead) appears to have been one of many issues debated at the 2nd National Conference on Operational Work and the 3rd National Conference on Economic Protection Work held in the summer of 1952. Debate at both conferences centered on the role of the head of the public security organ involved, and concluded that it was to be the most senior officer who had "the power to decide whether to open up an agent or not.... He should have a clear and concrete idea of the problem that is to be resolved [with the help of the agent]."[19]

Normally, the request for permission to recruit did not have to elaborate on the precise and practical details of the planned recruitment: it was only on those occasions when the target was especially important, or the recruitment was complicated, that a detailed plan of execution had to be attached to the Agent Opening Authorization Form. If an unforeseen event impacted on recruitment before the plan was executed, it was to be revised accordingly and an updated version presented to the relevant organ.[20] The following is the text of an original 1956 request (without the attached biographical data on the prospective agent) for permission to recruit an agent, as preserved in a file of the Taiyuan municipal Bureau

---

[17] "Chengqing jianli teqing pishi biao" (Agent Opening Authorization Form) [n.d.].

[18] *"Teqing gongzuo,"* p. 32.

[19] Li Woru, "Zai di wu ci quanguo tielu gongan huiyi shang de zongjie" (Summary at the 5th National Railroad Public Security Conference), *Tielu gongan tongxun*, No. 12, September 17, 1952, p. 13.

[20] *"Teqing gongzuo,"* p. 32.

of Public Security. It begins with the following brief explanation of the matter that was to be tackled by way of an agent's recruitment: "The stay-behind *tewu*-suspect element T is employed as a worker in a retail department belonging to one of our vehicle agencies. The department in question constitutes a 'blank space' as far as we are concerned, where we have no resources capable of exercising control over him."[21] The Taiyuan request went on to propose a solution, explaining why a particular profiled individual should be recruited to fill this "blank space" as an agent:

Consequently, we must first of all open up a monitoring agent in the agency, in order to facilitate a gradually more in-depth operation. We have profiled X, a member of the CCP, who is a backbone force in the retail department in question and in a position to keep tabs on its staff. If we subject him to additional training, he may be able to serve us in a capacity that monitors and controls the *tewu*-suspect element T – his thinking, his actions, and active substantive personal relationships. For this reason, we intend to open up X as an agent and herewith seek authorization to proceed.[22]

At the top of the sheet of paper on which the request was written, a senior officer evidently authorized to do so had simply written "Agree to open up as agent. Zhao, June 15."[23]

In recruitment preparations, as everywhere else, there were discrepancies between praxis on the ground and the routines described in textbooks and regulated by directives from the CMPS. Some were minor and of little or no consequence: the above request for authorization had, for example, not been made on the proper Agent Opening Authorization Form, but rather on common office stationery; it nonetheless contained all of the information needed by the authorizing body. Suggesting that more serious irregularities were by no means uncommon is the fact that CMPS regulations explicitly forbade operational departments from letting the recruitment target complete the Agent Opening Authorization Form him- or herself![24]

The Recruitment Interview

The most critical part of the recruitment process as a whole was undoubtedly the recruitment interview, described in one Shanghai

---

[21] Taiyuan shi gonganju di yi chu, "Wei jiang XXX jian wei teqing you" (Motivating the Opening Up of XXX as Agent) [June 6, 1956].
[22] Ibid.
[23] Ibid.
[24] *"Teqing gongzuo,"* p. 32.

operational directive as a "secret, one-on-one conversation."[25] (Recruitment of agents in groups or batches was forbidden.[26]) While the KGB in this context explicitly stated that the "recruitment interview is based on the recruiter using words to influence directly the mind of the person being recruited," the CMPS seems to have taken this more or less for granted, stressing instead that the recruiter in each instance had to "decide the substance and form of the conversation based on the agent target's concrete circumstances."[27]

The *Lectures* contained a simple step-by-step description of how a model recruitment interview was to be conducted. It began by noting that the recruiter should begin simply by engaging the target in a very ordinary conversation concerning his or her current circumstances, work, family and friends, or whatever topic came up naturally. The purpose of this approach was threefold. It was designed, firstly, to put the target at ease and reduce the chances of him or her feeling nervous, uncomfortable, or simply fearful. Secondly, it allowed the recruiter to indirectly check the accuracy or completeness of the information already in his or her possession concerning the target. And thirdly, it enabled the recruiter to make one final assessment regarding the suitability of the target as an agent. The *Lectures* noted that, at this critical juncture, the interviewer could still decide, for whatever reason, that the target would prove unsuitable as an agent and that the recruitment should be aborted. Should this occur, the topic of conversation was not to deviate from the original excuse for the meeting and the meeting was to end on some inconsequential topic. That the meeting had originally been planned as a recruitment operation was not to be divulged.[28]

If, in the course of their conversation, the would-be agent happened to mention the particular individual a mission (of which he or she would become part) was to target, the recruiter was to avoid saying anything substantive about the person in question. The *Lectures* explained the operational logic behind this:

[The recruiter] should instead seek to lead the [prospective agent] on, by way of letting him broadly discuss the circumstances of his friends, and in this way mention himself the operational target as well as volunteer his private views of him and suggest that he might be someone the public security organs ought to

---

[25] *Sifa zhengce xuanbian*, p. 32.
[26] "*Teqing gongzuo*," pp. 21, 32.
[27] *KGB Lexicon*, p. 174; "*Teqing gongzuo*," p. 37.
[28] "*Teqing gongzuo*," p. 37.

keep an eye on and why. In this way, the target will believe that the reason we are interested in that person is because of information the target himself provided. In this way, we can keep our intentions secret. We can also, by listening to what the target says about the operational target, further determine the likelihood of the impending recruitment of the agent proving a success.[29]

Even during the interview, therefore, the CMPS was adamant that the option be left open of aborting the recruitment process as if nothing had happened.

Only once the recruiter had become firmly convinced that the target was suitable, and that he or she would agree to work for the public security organs as an agent, would the subject of recruitment be broached in the course of their conversation. The *Lectures* stressed that this should be done in as natural a way as possible so as not to appear to come out of the blue. The following model scenario illustrates how this was to be done in the case of a target presumed to be amenable to the patriotic pitch:

For example, in the course of their conversation, the operational officer might have broached the subject of acts of sabotage being attempted by the imperialists and the Chiang Kai-shek gang, which might in turn have prompted the target to reveal his suspicions about certain people being possibly engaged in hostile activities. This would in itself already to some extent have created the preconditions under which the operational officer could raise the matter with the target and invite him to help the public security organs expose hidden imperialist *tewu* elements and other counterrevolutionary elements. Under normal circumstances, when broached in this way, the patriotic sentiment of the target is easily brought into play, making him willing to serve the public security organs.[30]

In the rare event of the target expressing strong reservations and hesitating – to the point of resisting – to be recruited as an agent, the officer was to inquire into the reasons for this unwillingness and "find a way of clearing up the target's incorrect ideas."[31] In the case of those who were Communist Party or Youth League members and political activists, a final recourse would presumably have involved invoking Leninist principles of revolutionary discipline. How the CMPS interpreted those principles may be deduced from its selection of quotes from the *Diary of Lei Feng*, reproduced in *People's Public Security* in 1963, which gave due prominence to Lei's words: "I think the greatest happiness lies in

[29] Ibid., p. 37.
[30] Ibid., pp. 37–38.
[31] Ibid., p. 38.

giving one's everything to the party's undertaking."[32] The *Lectures* did not discuss this further; its authors simply asserted that "As soon as the principle has been explained to them, they will agree."[33]

With respect to the reluctance of some hostile class and *tewu* elements to be recruited as agents by the public security organs, the CMPS seems to have been mildly optimistic, believing in 1957 that it would lessen with the passage of time. The assumption on which this optimism rested was that the stronger and more powerful the PRC became, the more "divided and demoralized" its enemies and the enemies of socialism would in turn become. Under these conditions, the likelihood that some hostile class and *tewu* elements could be recruited would increase, it was said, and the instances when "under our control, they can be made to serve us of their own will rather than because they are compelled to do so, will also grow in number."[34] It is hard to say whether actual developments on the ground after 1957 validated these assumptions.

Wang Jinxiang once explained how, at the end of the recruitment interview, if the agents were "alien-class elements," then "we give them neither titles nor identity papers or arms, in order to make it impossible for them to abuse the opportunity of working for us to carry out illegal acts." If the agents belonged to the gray middle stratum of backward elements, he went on to say, "again, we give them neither titles nor identity papers, so as to prevent the impure elements among them from abusing the situation to swindle and bluff, practice fraud and irregularities, and adversely influence our political standing." If, finally, Wang noted, the agents were members of the "basic masses," it was important to continue to deal with them in a comradely spirit.[35]

The Power Ladder

An important aspect of the agent recruitment process discussed in studies based entirely (or almost entirely) on European or Western data is that of the power ladder. This essentially postulates that, firstly, targets are unlikely to allow themselves to be recruited by someone they regard as inferior to themselves, and that, secondly, "there is unlikely to be trust between an agent and an officer if the agent feels the officer is *too far*

---

[32] *Renmin gongan*, No. 150, April 20, 1963, p. 12.
[33] "*Teqing gongzuo*," p. 38.
[34] Ibid., p. 11.
[35] Wang Jinxiang, "Zai dongbei zhengzhi jingji," pp. 21–25.

above him on the power ladder."[36] In the first of these two respects, Mao's China was no different from any other milieu in which the recruitment and running of human agents might be attempted. The Chinese power ladder, however, differed slightly from the European one in the second respect, in that Chinese agents appear, in many cases, to have been quite ready to put their trust in an officer significantly above them on the power ladder.[37]

The CMPS authors of the *Lectures* touched upon the power ladder mainly in the context of postrecruitment matters. Here, in their discussion of the factors affecting agent training, they attached critical importance not only to the "party spirit" of the handler, but also – and in equal measure – to his political, cultural, and professional sophistication. "Only when," they stressed, "the operational officer is superior to the agent in these respects will he enjoy the kind of prestige with the agent that is a precondition for exercising influence over him. In the absence of this kind of prestige, it will become impossible to properly educate the agent."[38]

That this kind of prestige was not always present in handler–agent relations was something the CMPS was acutely aware of. A ministry task force that visited factories and mines in Jilin in 1955 commented on how the power ladder impacted on recruitment and urged senior officers not to delegate the recruitment of highly educated, proud, and refined scientists and technicians as agents to simple, unsophisticated junior officers:

When developing and controlling high-level agents, senior officers have to involve themselves in person. This is because, at present, quite a few technicians do not yet have the kind of understanding that they ought to have of public security and protection work, while at the same time our officers are not sufficiently familiar with the characteristics and circumstances of technicians and have little experience in how to deal with them.... [Under these circumstances] deviations easily occur that in turn have a negative impact.[39]

In this case, it was implied that, in time, the problem might diminish as the target category for recruitment – (bourgeois) technicians – and the public security officers got to know each other better. No such optimism,

---

[36] Fergusson, *Spy*, pp. 122–24.

[37] Needless to say, much more research would have to be done to assert this confidently; for now, this claim is more of a speculation than an empirically grounded finding.

[38] "*Teqing gongzuo*," pp. 58–59.

[39] Gonganbu Jilin shichazu, "Guanyu changkuang zhineng keshi baowei gongzuo qingkuang de kaocha baogao" (Investigation Report Concerning Protection Work in Functional Offices of Factories and Mines), *Gongan jianshe*, No. 123, April 16, 1955, pp. 11–12.

however, was reflected in a report from Chongqing, also from 1955. Here what was conceived of as not so much a matter of social distance but very much one of "face" was treated as a more enduring problem. The solution proposed using a suitably highly placed intermediary as a kind of go-between:

> In the case of persons holding senior technical positions, high-level intellectuals, and elite personages, it is even more necessary to pay attention to their ideological and personality traits and to be particular about the tactic – and the form or method – of their recruitment. Normally, it should be the responsible comrade on the CCP Committee who makes the introduction or the administrative head who entrusts them with working for us.[40]

This particular solution, to what was clearly a common real-world problem, was not discussed in the *Lectures*. It fudged the issue of who actually carried out the recruitment – the officer or the "responsible comrade" making the introduction.

An example of a very senior CCP official recruiting an agent on behalf of the operational organs (as suggested in the Chongqing document) concerned the actor Ying Ruocheng. The account warrants retelling in the context of the power ladder because at the time, as individuals, the actor Ying and his recruiter, the Beijing mayor and CCP Politburo member Peng Zhen, could hardly have been further apart in terms of social distance. However, as is evident from the way Peng conducted the recruitment interview, since Ying came from a *family* that was both highly intellectual and a member of the old elite, his recruitment as a secret investigation agent by a member of the new postrevolutionary elite was entirely appropriate and would make operational sense in the years to come.

In his memoirs, Ying writes of how one evening in 1952 he was asked to stay on after a curtain call because someone important wished to see him. He suspected that it was a high-ranking CCP official when he was taken by car to a huge courtyard not far from the Beijing People's Art Theater, where he worked. In the end, his well-wisher turned out to be none other than Peng Zhen, the mayor of Beijing himself. After greeting Ying and engaging in some small talk about the theater, Peng got around to what Ying describes as the "real purpose" of the visit:

> "We have seen the list you handed in about your foreign acquaintances and classmates," he began. "It could be very useful to the country, to the party, and

---

[40] Chongqing shi gonganju, "Guanyu jinian lai teqing," p. 13.

to the army if we could enlist your help – especially now when Japan is beginning to have ambitions again."

I was overwhelmed by his proposal, and I responded, "But I'm a totally nonpolitical person. I don't see how I can be of any help."

"Oh yes, you can be," was his reply. "We don't want you to do anything mysterious. Just go on associating with these people, and whatever their reactions are – especially when it's about some big event – give us a nod so that we'll know and be prepared. We don't want to be taken by surprise." He continued in this vein, and talked quite a bit about Japan. "I've read your résumé. Your father [on Taiwan] is someone we respect. He is a good scholar – a famous scholar – and was imprisoned by the Japanese for quite a few years." Nobody had ever acknowledged that to me before. The Nationalists never said it, even though it was them my father was supposedly working for both times the Japanese arrested him. . . .

I agreed to Peng Zhen's request. But actually they made very little use of my services. I suppose they didn't need me. . . . They continued to call on me from time to time, though they didn't ask me to do anything out of the ordinary.[41]

The meeting between Peng and Ying can only be described as a text-book "introduction" of the kind proposed in the Chongqing report – which stressed the need to "respect the status, position, and dignity of the agent" – followed by the subsequent "entrustment" of the agent to the operational organs (the latter, of course, being the anonymous "they" mentioned by Ying in the last paragraph).[42]

The cluster of issues involving power, prestige, and face that agent recruiters were forced to deal with was a bafflingly complex one, and their attempts to reduce it to a few simple rules met with little apparent success. As a loose statement of principles, the following advice from the conveners of a meeting on protection work in the cultural sphere in Jiangsu province began well, but then it quickly turned into something reminiscent of (and as inflexible as) a *nomenklatura* list of cadre by rank:

Some secret investigation agents should be developed among high- and mid-level intellectuals. This should be done according to the principle of "common soldiers approaching other common soldiers" and "generals approaching other generals." Agents who are university professors, researchers in scientific research institutes, hospital chief surgeons, or holders of positions equivalent to these should be led personally by the municipal director [of public security] himself or by section chiefs whose abilities correspond to those of a [bureau] director. Agents who are university lecturers, surgeons, assistant researchers in scientific research institutes,

[41] Ying and Conceison, *Voices Carry*, pp. 51–52.
[42] Chongqing shi gonganju, "Guanyu jinian lai teqing," p. 14.

or holders of positions equivalent to these, should be led by the relevant section chiefs or by suitably able section staff.[43]

Sometimes problems emerging in the power ladder context were not due to an insufficient appreciation of the issue as such, but simply to a lack of suitably qualified high-level recruiters. A CMPS task force visiting Shanxi found – using the same metaphor used in the preceding quote – that the employment of "common soldiers" to approach "generals" was causing no end of problems "with respect to profiling, recruitment, fostering, training, control, and utilization of agents."[44] But, having no "generals" at their disposal, there was little Shanxi operational departments could do to solve the problems.

The Patriotic Pitch: Your Country Needs You!

In the words of the CMPS, it was imperative to have developed *in advance* "a clear conception of the ideological foundation on which the agent's work for the public security organs could be made to rest."[45] No doubt significant is the fact that in this context, the 1957 *Lectures* made no use of the word "revolution." After the founding of the PRC, the first scenario and concomitant recruitment strategy to be considered was the one that appealed to patriotism.

The aim of the patriotic pitch was to arouse the target's sense of responsibility for what the CMPS called "national construction and the collective enterprise."[46] It assumed that the target could be made to accept the mission because he or she shared with the CCP, and its public security organs, an understanding of patriotism defined as an allegiance to "People's China" (and not Chiang Kai-shek's Republic of China on Taiwan). It assumed that the mission, regardless of what it entailed, would be looked upon as an honorable assignment. In the words of the *Lectures*:

Because their work in its entirety has as its lofty goal the protection of the mother-land, the people, and the interests of the working class, the public security organs are able in that work to count on the aid and support of the broad masses and all progressive public figures. It is for this reason that it is possible for the public security organs to first and foremost employ this method to recruit agents.[47]

---

[43] "Jiangsu sheng wenhua baowei gongzuo qingkuang he 1955 nian gongzuo jihua" (The Situation in Cultural Protection Work in Jiangsu Province and Work Plan for 1955), *Gongan jianshe*, No. 131, June 25, 1955, pp. 7–8.
[44] Gonganbu Shanxi shichazu, "Guanyu Shanxi sheng," p. 10.
[45] "*Teqing gongzuo*," pp. 32–33.
[46] Ibid., p. 34.
[47] Ibid., p. 33.

Appeals to patriotism worked most effectively when the adversary against whom operational departments sought to recruit Chinese citizens was a foreign state actor. A former KGB officer, Konstantin Preobrazhensky, indirectly concluded as much from his own largely unsuccessful recruitment activities: "The Chinese have extremely strong feelings of ethnocentrism and patriotism. I understood this from the very beginning of my own recruitment activities [among them]."[48] An example of a successful recruitment by the PRC's public security organs based on an appeal to patriotism was described in a Yingkou program progress report from 1950. It noted that the target (a technician) had previously worked for the British and believed he had been treated very unfairly by them. He was, it was said, now quite happy to serve under Chinese management and tried his best to make a positive impression on "us." His recruitment, therefore, proved remarkably easy.[49]

The CMPS by no means believed that appealing to patriotism alone was an easy recruitment strategy, however. The recruiter, it stressed, had to keep in mind that every target had a different attitude toward politics in general, and that his or her views of what the work of the public security organs entailed could never be assumed to be the same. Moreover, because the patriotic pitch assumed and sought to reinforce a target's hatred (presumed to be present a priori) of *tewu* and foreign spies, and in this way make him or her sympathize with the work of the public security organs, it was recognized that it was of limited use among members of the sociopolitical categories of the hostile classes and *tewu* elements. Yet, while officers might have sought to recruit an agent from these categories by appeals to material or personal self-interest, they were still expected to make an appeal to patriotism, if only as a matter of routine.[50] It was further understood that love of one's country alone might not be sufficient to commit even the most reverently patriotic citizen to becoming an agent; hence, the *Lectures* reminded operational officers to "care for and attend to" the target both in terms of politics and in terms of the target's material circumstances.[51] On this point, the PRC and Soviet experiences seem to have been similar. The KGB claimed that the "political-ideological grounds for recruiting secret collaborators among Soviet citizens are, as a rule, their patriotism." But, it went on to add, different "grounds for recruitment are generally used in combination,"

---

[48] Konstantin Preobrazhensky, "Russian Espionage on China," International Analyst Network, http://www.analyst-network.com/about.php (accessed March 10, 2010).
[49] Schoenhals, "Recruiting Agents in Industry and Trade," pp. 18–19.
[50] "*Teqing gongzuo*," p. 33.
[51] Ibid., p. 34.

the second most important grounds on the KGB list being "material gain or other personal interest."[52]

The Gradual Pitch: I Thought You'd Never Ask

The second recruitment method described by the CMPS involved the gradual cultivation of a target over a fairly extended period of time. In the *Lectures*, such targets were described in the following way:

They may, for example, not yet have managed ideologically to draw a clear line of demarcation between themselves and *tewu* and counterrevolutionary elements; or they may have misapprehensions about the work of the public security organs; or they may entertain certain old moral viewpoints, etc. For reasons like these, if an operational officer were to propose to them right away that they work for the public security organs, they would be altogether unprepared and might even reject the proposal.[53]

Addressing specifically the situation that public security officers should expect to encounter in cultural circles, PRC Vice-Premier Chen Yi in November 1954, at a CMPS conference on the subject, cautioned against "forcing oneself upon" scientists, educators, members of the medical profession, and so on. "As soon as you show up," he pointed out, "they will know that you've come to do protection work, that yours is a different profession altogether." What needed to be done first of all was to overcome resistance, develop a "common language" (the difficulties involved in doing so were not to be underestimated, Chen explained), and build up trust over a fairly extended period of time.[54] In the end, while the procedure as such may have differed, the narrow grounds for recruitment nonetheless often involved some variant of those used in the patriotic pitch.

In the textbook case, the gradual approach was broken down into discrete stages. It might begin by arranging a first contact in the workplace under the pretext of a chance encounter over some professional matter. It might also be set up with the assistance of a suitably positioned third party to take place during off hours or at a party. The possibilities were endless – on the whole, limited only by the imagination and judgment of the

[52] *KGB Lexicon*, pp. 288–89.
[53] "*Teqing gongzuo*," pp. 35–36.
[54] Chen Yi, "Zai ganbu di yi ci quanguo wenhua baowei gongzuo huiyi shang de baogao" (Report to the Ministry of Public Security's 1st National Conference on Cultural Protection Work) [November 29, 1954], pp. 2–3; *Jianguo yilai gongan*, p. 75.

recruiter. During their initial meeting(s), the operational officer's purpose was merely to build up trust – that is, to "cultivate" the target.[55] As the authors of the Shenyang Agent Work Initiation Procedures put it, "there are those targets who agree to get on the agent track [*zoushang teqing renyuan de guidao*] only after having been worked on repeatedly."[56]

During stage two of the gradual approach, the recruiter would ask the target to perform some very simple task – essentially a favor that was in itself innocuous and unlikely to be refused by the target. If things proceeded smoothly according to the intentions of the recruiter, the first request might be followed by a second, a third, and so on. As part of their training, it was impressed upon officer cadets that one crucial factor that could make or break the successful recruitment of the agent was whether or not they were able to provide a task that the agent could successfully execute – and one that the agent was genuinely interested in carrying out. Once the task was completed, it should ideally make the agent feel that he or she had "been of service to his country, himself, and his friends." The point of this exercise was, as explained in the *Lectures*, "to lead the target into performing agent work without really being aware of it [*buzhibujuede bei yin xiang teqing de gongzuo*]." This would in effect prepare the way for the third and final stage: the recruiter asking the target whether or not he or she would be willing to assist the public security organs on a regular basis. Since the groundwork had been laid over a period of time, it was surmised that this request would not come as a surprise. It was the experience of the CMPS that, if everything had been handled properly up to this point, the target would "normally agree" to become an agent.[57]

In an ideal scenario the entire process of cultivation and recruitment was, from start to finish, handled by an operational officer working under-cover. In reality, however, this norm was not always adhered to at the local level. In February 1954, the Jiangsu provincial Bureau of Public Security admitted in a report to the CMPS that in some universities in Nanjing, agent cultivation as well as recruitment among senior intellectu-als was to some extent being carried out by nonprofessionals who, only after the targets had been recruited, would hand over control of them to the public security organs. The Jiangsu bureau defended this practice with arguments similar to those found in the Chongqing Bureau of Public

---

[55] "*Teqing gongzuo*," p. 35.
[56] Shenyang shi renmin zhengfu gonganju jingji baoweichu, "Guanyu jianli," p. 36.
[57] "*Teqing gongzuo*," pp. 35, 36.

Security discussion of the power ladder. It was, in short, a recognition of (and an ad hoc solution to) the problem that the Jiangsu bureau simply did not have any officers who might successfully cultivate senior professors or nationally prominent academics. Hence, in its report to the CMPS, it explained how, "during the early stage of the opening up process, it is best to have a senior party member with high prestige in their university engage them in conversation and education, and provide them with a specific investigative task as a means of testing them. Then, once the conditions are ripe, they may be handed over to the public security organs for control."[58] The targets, so the bureau implied, simply would not have allowed themselves to be recruited by a lowly public security officer many rungs below them on the power ladder.

The Hard Pitch: An Offer You Can't Refuse

In a purely domestic context, the CMPS did not speak of the third recruitment method as blackmail, but admitted that it involved getting a "handle" (*babing*) on a target and ensuring "coercively," with the help of the handle, that the agent was recruited and performed his or her assigned tasks. If they were considering using as agents "persons who have not committed any crimes that give us a handle on them," the *Lectures* emphasized that officers must *not* "fabricate and coercively employ handles."[59] Whereas the KGB, for its part, claimed (in what may have illustrated the CMPS's claim that Soviet officers "did not understand the Chinese situation"[60]) that because of an apparent obsession with loss of face, "the use of compromising material is a strong lever to make a Chinese collaborate," the CMPS made a particular point of downplaying the operational value of the handle that consisted entirely of no more than a "stain" on a target's morals or private life.[61]

Early on, regional and local public security organs like the NEMPS ensured that tactical advice in matters of coercive recruitment was disseminated to those with a need to know. In its blueprint Agent Work Initiation Procedures, the Shenyang Bureau of Public Security affirmed the value of the coercive approach and confidently reminded officers of the fact that the CCP was now in power:

One has to be good at making positive use of our political superiority and the excellent circumstances in which we find ourselves. Vis-à-vis these people [our

[58] Jiangsu sheng gonganting di si chu, "Guanyu Nanjing shi," p. 14.
[59] "*Teqing gongzuo*," p. 35.
[60] See Chapter 1.
[61] Andrew and Mitrokhin, *The KGB and the World*, p. 286; "*Teqing gongzuo*," p. 35.

former enemies], one must give expression to our boldness of vision: we are the public security organs of the state, as well as the state's punitive organs. We represent the state and the people when presenting them with agent tasks, and we have the right to ask of them to execute such tasks conscientiously and responsibly. At the same time, we shouldn't lower our guard or hesitate to subject [our former enemies] to education. The [policy of combining] leniency and suppression is to be put into play with imagination and substance.[62]

The blueprint suggested to officers that the coercive approach be considered when dealing with hostile classes and *tewu* elements as follows:

With respect to those that have not yet registered with the authorities or whose registration is perfunctory, the moment when they get off work or are about to return home for the holiday, they are to be secretly arrested and subjected to crash [*tuji*] recruitment. Then, once the matter has been settled, they are to be secretly released again. If the recruitment cannot be taken care of swiftly, they are to be ordered to make a phone call or write a note asking for leave [from work].[63]

As used here, the expression "crash" recruitment referred to a swiftly executed opportunistic recruitment – as opposed to prior cultivation of the agent – invariably involving an element of coercion and the use of compromising material.

The Shenyang blueprint outlined a coercive recruitment scenario, using as an example the detention of a senior former Chiang Kai-shek "bandit." It suggested that the recruiter begin by engaging the target in a general conversation gradually leading to a more specific discussion of how the target had come to join a "reactionary organization." In thus doing, the target would be encouraged to describe his or her work for the organization, the people with whom he or she was in contact, and what he or she thought of them. The rationale for this second step, the authors of the blueprint pointed out, was a desire to optimize the way in which the agent could eventually be exploited. In the third and final stage of the interview, the nature of the target's errors or crimes would be raised, and it would be pointed out in no uncertain terms that they were tantamount to "opposing the people and endangering the motherland." The target would be encouraged to "make up for past crimes by rendering meritorious service" and agree to "work for us." If the target refused, the recruiter was to announce that he or she would be severely punished in accordance with the law.[64] If the coercive recruitment attempt was a success, the *Lectures* later noted, it was important that the newly recruited

---

[62] Shenyang shi renmin zhengfu gonganju jingji baoweichu, "Guanyu jianli," p. 39.
[63] Ibid., p. 34.
[64] Ibid., p. 35.

agent be released from custody within the twenty-four-hour time frame stipulated in the 1954 Arrest and Preliminary Hearing Work Temporary Statutes.[65]

A Chiang Kai-shek bandit or *tewu* like the individual mentioned in the Shenyang blueprint would have been only too familiar with the coercive approach to recruiting agents outlined here. In 1940, Chen Yun had described it in some detail in the intraparty journal *The Communist*, albeit as employed prior to the founding of the PRC by the security services of the Guomindang in their attempts to penetrate the CCP. "The entire process," he stressed, was completed "within a very brief time span." It typically started with the target being detained in secret – "not in the home by armed uniformed officers," but perhaps "in the street, by plainclothes *tewu*." In this way, the assumption was that news of the detention "will not spread and it will become possible later to release the target and have him serve [the Guomindang] as an agent in place [*dang neijian*]." While in custody, the target would be made to sign a statement (Chen Yun outlined some of the good cop/bad cop routines and other techniques of coercion used to achieve this aim) expressing support for the Guomindang cause, as well as accept a sum of money for which a receipt had to be signed. Chen Yun stressed that this statement and the receipt would not be made public by the *tewu* organ, but would be retained by it (and added to the recruited individual's file) as a means of exerting pressure on the agent, should it become necessary. Upon having "surrendered to the enemy," the "element" would then be "released in secret, without bail." His release would occur "in the dark of night or before dawn, so as to avoid anyone noticing. Everything beginning with the secret detention and ending with the secret release was very swift and would normally not have taken more than a few hours or half a day." Commenting on the technique, Chen admitted that it could be dangerously effective and allowed for "easy penetration" of the CCP by its enemies in those cases where a "leading party organ [was] not vigilant" or failed to follow up on the reasons for "a certain person [briefly] having gone missing."[66]

By the time of the 2nd National Conference on Operational Work in the summer of 1952, the coercive approach to agent recruitment was said

---

[65] "*Teqing gongzuo*," p. 31; Zhongyang gonganbu, "Guanyu daibu ji yushen gongzuo de zanxing tiaoli" (Arrest and Preliminary Hearing Work Temporary Statutes) [August 14, 1954], p. 5.

[66] *Chen Yun wenji 1935.10–1949.09* (*Chen Yun's Collected Writings, October 1935– September 1949*), 3 vols. (Beijing: Zhongyang wenxian chubanshe, 2005), Vol. 1, pp. 252–53.

to have been instrumental in the successful breakup of a number of hostile intelligence operations on PRC soil. In Tianjin, for example, a concerted Guomindang effort to collect railroad traffic intelligence was thwarted thanks to the "swift recruitment of a wavering element on the enemy's inside who agreed to serve as our penetration agent."[67] In Xi'an, public security officers managed to secretly assume control of a Guomindang network, the so-called New Society Revolutionary Party, which had over 100 members, "by targeting the enemy's weak link and swiftly executing a crash recruitment of a member who had submitted voluntarily to the authorities [*mimi zishou*]." In a textbook case of "using a long line to catch a big fish," the officers had allowed the network to operate under their control for over a year before breaking it up and arresting all of its leading members.[68]

In its discussion of the conditions under which an officer might attempt to recruit a target using compromising material, the *Lectures* distinguished between – but did not elaborate at length on – two distinct sets of circumstances. One was essentially the one hinted at in the Shenyang blueprint, consisting of compromising "material exposing activities while a participant in a *tewu* organ of the imperialists or the Chiang Kai-shek clique, or a certain other counterrevolutionary organization, sufficient to ensure a criminal prosecution in court if exposed." In the other set of circumstances, the public security organs would be able to threaten the target with "facts that he would not dare have the enemy or his own contacts know about." To recruit an agent in this way was essentially one of "cutting off his escape route" and making it impossible for the agent to turn on the handler. This strategy was primarily applicable to the recruitment of members of hostile intelligence services.[69]

The Agent's Personal File

Once the recruitment of the target had been successfully carried out, the officer involved was expected to inform his or her superiors of this in a written report that summed up the recruitment interview and the forms

---

[67] Tiedaobu gonganju, "Guanyu tielu," p. 13. It had been a steep learning curve for operational officers in Tianjin: in the spring of 1949, they had admitted, in a review of how the takeover of the city had been conducted, to *not* being good at "swiftly grabbing the opportunity to build up covert operational assets in the course of carrying out arrests"; "Rucheng soubu gongzuo zongjie baogao" (Summary of Location and Detention Work since Entering the City), *Tianjin gongan*, Vol. 2, No. 1, January 31, 1951, p. 18.

[68] Tiedaobu gonganju, "Guanyu tielu," p. 13.

[69] "*Teqing gongzuo*," p. 34.

of contact and communication agreed upon between recruiter and agent. The recruiting officer's report was also to indicate what initial task(s) had been or would be assigned to the agent. It was at this point that the operational departments would open a file on the agent. Known as the Agent Personal File, it would be maintained by the specific public security unit to which the officer running the agent belonged. This meant, for example, that while active, the file of an agent being run by an officer in the *n*th Office of the Bureau of Public Security in municipality X would be kept, physically, in the *n*th Office. Once closed, however, the file would be transferred laterally to the archive of the bureau, accompanied by a completed so-called Agent Personal File Handover Form. These latter forms were generic and could also be used in those cases when control of an agent was to be shifted from one unit or locality to another – that is, involving the transfer of a still active file.[70]

The personal file brought together operational documents with personal data on the agent as well as various other relevant papers. Such papers might include the original authorization to attempt the target's recruitment, specifying for what operational purpose and on what grounds. This authorization was, as explained earlier, to be made on a uniform Agent Opening Authorization Form designed specifically for this purpose. If a Bureau of Public Security did not recruit or run large numbers of agents, or was otherwise strapped for resources, the authorization might also appear on ordinary office stationery. An agent's performance would be evaluated and documented in his or her file, again either on plain paper or – as in the case, for example, of agents being run out of the Beijing municipal Bureau of Public Security in 1956 – on a different, custom-made so-called Agent Work Accumulated Achievements Form.[71]

If the agent was someone who had been recruited from within the enemy camp, possible operational records of incriminating evidence were also meant to be deposited in the personal file. The *Lectures* stressed in this context that "crimes as admitted by the target are to be mentioned in the written interrogation record, which is to be deposited and preserved in the agent's personal file. The written interrogation record may be relied upon to investigate and affix criminal responsibility, should this become necessary."[72] The power to assess "necessity" in this last

---

[70] Ibid., pp. 40–41. Cf. *KGB Lexicon*, p. 246.
[71] "Teqing gongzuo chengji jileibiao" (Agent Work Accumulated Achievments Form) [1956].
[72] "*Teqing gongzuo*," p. 38.

respect was vested in the public security organs, *not* the PRC courts or the procuracy. It found expression in the CMPS Arrest and Preliminary Hearing Work Temporary Statutes, which stipulated that if and when the public security organs "deem it necessary to exploit the accused for intelligence [collection] or surveillance purposes," the interrogation of a suspect "whose unlawful acts have been exposed in full and who has confessed his crimes . . . should be suspended [*dei tingzhi*]."[73]

The Shenyang Agent Work Initiation Procedures stated that the new agent was "to be told to produce a written pledge," the wording of which was to "conform to procedural regulations."[74] In line with efforts to standardize agent recruitment formalities as much as possible, operational departments maintained mimeographed copies of more or less uniformly worded "offer of service" statements, which new agents were to sign at the time of recruitment. Following is the full text of one such prepared statement; its wording indicates that it was meant to be given to agents recruited from the ranks of hostile class and *tewu* elements. Having been duly signed by the agent and stamped with his or her personal chop, this statement was placed, together with an Agent Opening Authorization Form, in an Agent Personal File maintained in a state-run enterprise in Southwest China in May 1952:

Voluntary Offer of Meritorious Service to Atone for Crimes Committed

I volunteer to faithfully safeguard the long-term interests of the people's motherland and voluntarily accept a work assignment to resolutely fight all destructive elements who sabotage national economic construction. I shall strive to perform meritorious service to atone for crimes committed and resolve to transform myself into a genuine servant of the people. In my work I will categorically obey the leadership of the organization, scrupulously honor the laws of the people's government, and abide by work discipline. Should I fail to exert myself or violate discipline etc., I am prepared to submit to the severest punishment meted out by the people's government.[75]

Accompanying the statement, on the same mimeographed single sheet of paper, were four points spelling out the rules of conduct by which the agent had just promised to abide. The wording, mentioning among other things the need to maintain secrecy and not fabricate information, was almost identical to the points of agent discipline discussed (in the context

73 Zhongyang gonganbu, "Guanyu daibu ji yushen," p. 13.
74 Shenyang shi renmin zhengfu gonganju jingji baoweichu, "Guanyu jianli," p. 35.
75 "Ligong shuzui ziyuanshu" (Voluntary Offer of Meritorious Service to Atone for Crimes Committed) [May 8, 1952].

of formalities to be observed at the time of recruitment) at a 1950 meeting of operational officers in Northeast China, which would suggest a fair degree of nationwide standardization.[76] Worth noting is the fact that the word "agent" is used in neither text. This was by no means coincidental: in fact, CMPS regulations stated explicitly, for the sake of secrecy, that recruited individuals were *not* to be told that this was how they were referred to "in-house."

Arguably one of the most important documents in an agent's personal file was his or her completed Agent Registration Form. Such forms were meant to be more or less uniform across China (with the usual degree of extra flexibility permitted in ethnic minority regions), and the CMPS provided lower-level bureaus of public security with templates spelling out what they were meant to contain. The forms were then designed and produced locally, being either printed, typed, or mimeographed. While the ministry's *Agent Work Manual* listed the compulsory identifying particulars and essential data concerning the agent that were to appear on all forms, a local Bureau of Public Security might add to its own forms extra space for data not explicitly demanded by the central authorities.[77] The following description of an Agent Registration Form is based on the *Agent Work Manual* instructions to operational officers and on a form preserved in the file of the Taiyuan agent X, whose Agent Opening Authorization Form was excerpted earlier in this chapter.

At first glance, X's Agent Registration Form looks very much like most PRC personnel registration forms from the 1950s: the overall design doesn't differ from that of contemporary government cadre or factory worker registration forms.[78] But there are significant differences with respect to content. Preprinted in the upper-left-hand corner are the words "Agent No.," and here the number 404 has been stamped by the authority opening the file on X. The number suggests that he was the *n*th agent in a sequence of registered ones: he could, for example, have been the 404th agent opened by the Taiyuan municipal Bureau of Public Security since an unknown date. More likely, however, is that the first of the three digits making up the number represented the particular section of the Taiyuan bureau that had opened the agent. The contents of the file reveal that he had been opened by the bureau's 4th Section, 1st Office, and in this case

[76] Wang Jinxiang, "Zai dongbei zhengzhi jingji," p. 22.
[77] Cf. *KGB Lexicon*, p. 398.
[78] "Teqing renyuan dengjibiao" (Agent Registration Form) [June 15, 1956]. For a description of ordinary enterprise personnel files in the PRC, see Dutton, *Policing and Punishment in China*, pp. 222–26.

Agent 404 is thus more likely to have been the fourth agent opened by the section since some unknown date.

CMPS regulations specified that each agent was to choose a code name immediately upon recruitment. This code name was then recorded in the agent's personal file "so as to henceforth facilitate contact."[79] There is no designated space for a code name on the Taiyuan Agent Registration Form, but on one of the other documents in the file on X he is referred to as "Agent 404, controlled by Comrade Wang Jinrong in the 4th Section."[80] This may suggest that, at the time, an agent's internal registration number may have been used among public security officers in Taiyuan as a substitute for a code name. CMPS regulations, in fact, stated that an agent's number was to be used in-house as a way of referring to the agent; furthermore, the number was not to be divulged to the agent. In case studies detailing operations involving agents presented in the *Lectures*, "real" code names in the form of aliases rather than numerical designations are used and clearly identified as such. If this proved necessary, the recruiter was meant to explain to the new agent why there was a need for a code name. If the agent at first hesitated or even refused to use one, the *Lectures* noted, its use should not be forced upon the agent. The matter was, however, to be raised again at some later point. One important purpose for which the agent was meant to employ a code name was to sign any future intelligence reports to be handed over to the handler.[81] In his memoirs, Ying Ruocheng reveals that the code name he and his wife (with whom he cooperated) used to sign their reports was the semitransparent Wu Ying, meaning "martial hero" and homophonous with their respective last names.[82]

Cases of a less than stringent implementation of the rule that agents' true identities were to be protected at all cost were occasionally mentioned in *People's Public Security*. "In February this year," a junior public security officer in the communications sector wrote in the "Letters from Readers" column in 1956,

I went to the Ocean Shipping Bureau in Guangzhou to investigate and verify material on the historical crimes of a target in the campaign to eliminate counter-revolutionaries in our office. In the files that the Counterrevolutionaries Elimination Office in the bureau allowed me to consult I found to my surprise material that

---

[79] "*Teqing gongzuo*," p. 40.
[80] "Teqing anjuan yijiaoshu" (Agent File Transfer Form) [n.d.].
[81] "*Teqing gongzuo*," pp. 39–40, 55.
[82] Ying and Conceison, *Voices Carry*, p. 201.

compromised institutional secrets involving operational work and agents, material that said "so-and-so is an agent, recruited by so-and-so, he's been approached on so-and-so many occasions, and in the course of his recruitment he has..." etc.[83]

Ordinary files on counterrevolutionaries such as those referred to here, regulations stipulated, were not to contain any information indicating that so-and-so had at some point agreed to serve as an agent.[84] Evidently, in this case, the Ocean Shipping Bureau in Guangzhou had failed to keep operational records separate from ordinary files, and the junior officer writing to *People's Public Security* was very much concerned about this and other examples of what he called "serious leaks." By publishing his letter, the journal's editors in effect concurred, but it is worth noting that they did *not* feel it was necessary to add any additional or extended comment of their own other than a headline that read: "In the course of investigations carried out as part of the internal elimination of counter-revolutionaries, one must take strict precautions against leaking secrets concerning operational work and agents."[85]

The CMPS *Agent Work Manual* asked for the following identifying particulars to be recorded on the Agent Registration Form: name, sex, age, ancestral home, residential address, status (*shenfen*), educational level, and present occupation. On the Taiyuan form, the space for "name" is followed by one for "aliases" (predating the agent recruitment) and, as one would expect, the manual's abbreviated reference to "status" information is divided into two parts: one space to record the agent's class background (*chushen*), the other for his or her own personal circumstances (*chengfen*). Other data asked for on the Taiyuan form concern the agent's ethnicity and religion.[86] A known Agent Registration Form from Beijing, also from the mid-1950s, specifically included a space in the upper-right-hand corner for a standard 3.4 × 2.4 cm size photograph of the agent.[87] On the Taiyuan form, there is no such space on the form.

On the generic form described in the *Agent Work Manual*, the political stance of the agent was meant to be recorded under the heading "political

---

[83] "Duzhe laixin" (Readers' Letters), *Renmin gongan*, No. 11, September 30, 1956, p. 24.
[84] On the compartmentalization (in legal and quasi-legal records) of information mentioning operational work, see Zhongyang gonganbu, "Guanyu daibu ji yushen," pp. 2, 11.
[85] "Duzhe laixin."
[86] "Teqing renyuan dengjibiao."
[87] "Teqing renyuan dengjibiao" (Agent Registration Form) [1956].

and/or organizational affiliation(s)" and "political attitude." On the Taiyuan form, information concerning the agent's "political affiliations" was to be recorded in a space set aside for this purpose in the basic identifying particulars section. A note at the bottom of the form explained that affiliation here referred exclusively to *progressive* political affiliations such as "membership of the Communist Party, Youth League, Democratic Youth League, etc." Past membership, the same note went on to explain, in political organizations like the Guomindang or the Shanxi Fellowship of Self-Strengthening and National Salvation was to be recorded on the form in a different space set aside for information on affiliations with "reactionary organizations." The precise data requested concerned "Previous membership in what reactionary political organizations and which position held."[88] The request for information on "position held" was routine: as part of its so-called policy of distinguishing between antagonistic and nonantagonistic contradictions, the CCP made a point of distinguishing between the officers and the rank and file of "reactionary political organizations" prior to 1949. Additional biographical data asked for on the generic form described in the *Agent Work Manual*, but not explicitly mentioned on the Taiyuan form, concerned special skills and hobbies. The Taiyuan form left some, albeit not much, space for a brief chronological résumé, followed by rather more space where information on the following subject was meant to be recorded: "Behavior since opened (including recorded successes and failures, or behavior since surrendering)." The space is blank in the file kept on Agent 404.[89]

Information to be included on the registration form pertaining directly to the agent's actual execution of the tasks for which he or she had been recruited was, according to the *Agent Work Manual*, meant to comprise the following: "grounds for utilization," "terms of utilization," and "aims and methods of utilization."[90] On the Taiyuan form, this and related information was recorded under slightly different headings. Firstly, space was set aside on the form for information on when and where the agent had been recruited; space was also set aside to record specifically the "method and process" whereby the agent had been recruited (Agent 404 had been "opened in a positive conversation by way of education," his handler had written on the Taiyuan form.) Instead of a heading called "grounds for utilization," the heading on the Taiyuan form was

[88] "Teqing renyuan dengjibiao."
[89] Ibid.
[90] "*Teqing gongzuo*," p. 32.

titled "agent's present tasks": here it was entered that he was engaged in surveillance of T. Instead of "terms of utilization," the Taiyuan form next had the heading "terms of operation," and here the information about Agent 404 was that he was engaged in "secret investigation." Presumably, in the case of other agents, the terms might have included guarding critical assets or serving an operational Case Group. The third heading requested information on "area and site where agent is active": here it said that Agent 404 was active in the small factory that employed both him and his investigation target.[91]

The penultimate space on the Taiyuan form was set aside for information on the agent's substantive personal relationships. On this point, the form followed the template described in the *Agent Work Manual*. On employers' registration forms for ordinary Chinese citizens, information on substantive personal relationships meant the names of "relatives and friends who have exercised an ideological influence, *good or bad*, on the individual."[92] On the agent registration forms, it meant something slightly different. Here, it was a far more narrowly defined selection of individuals, as a note at the bottom of the Taiyuan form explained: "Major social connections here refers to those located within the social foundation likely to be exploited by the enemy."[93] That the concept of substantive personal relationships was to be interpreted in this narrow fashion on agent registration forms is likely to have been specified by the CMPS.

Finally, the *Agent Work Manual* called for space to be reserved on the registration form for "other." On the Taiyuan form, the space is labeled simply "notes," and in the file kept on Agent 404 nothing was recorded here.[94] That this space was normally left blank on similar forms is evidenced by the author's cursory examination of some fifty different worker, cadre, and PLA officer registration forms from the 1950s and 1960s: only one in the end turned out to have anything at all written in this space.

When Recruitment Fails

A former employee of Britain's Secret Intelligence Service once claimed that "it is estimated that fewer than one in five [recruitment] operations

[91] "Teqing renyuan dengjibiao."

[92] Explanation quoted here from *Zhongguo renmin jiefangjun ganbu lülishu* (*Chinese People's Liberation Army Officer Curriculum Vitae Form*) ([Beijing]: Zhongyang renmin zhengfu renmin geming junshi weiyuanhui zongganbubu, 1953), p. 2. Emphasis added.

[93] "Teqing renyuan dengjibiao."

[94] Ibid.

is a success."⁹⁵ Although it is not known whether the CMPS managed to achieve a higher success rate, it is arguable that in what the *Lectures* described as "our current *domestic* working conditions" it managed to do so. The question of who was to take responsibility if and when a recruitment attempt *did* go wrong was a delicate one, as was the issue of responsibility for any other operational failures. In 1951, Feng Jiping described a widespread and systematic dodging of responsibilities:

The section chiefs in some Public Security Bureau branches say that "above me, there's the head of the Public Security Bureau branch, and below me there's the deputy section chief and the desk officers, so I'm in the clear, should there be a problem." And some of the heads of Public Security Bureau branches maintain that "problems may be raised later: first one just passes them on to the superior level, where they will be examined by the municipal Bureau." Because certain cadres have this idea of layer-by-layer dependency, it has resulted in each level reporting up the chain of command, but with no level of command actually assuming responsibility.⁹⁶

Although Feng here spoke of the paperwork/routines preceding the arrest of a suspected counterrevolutionary, there is little reason to believe that responsibilities for the recruitment of an agent were managed in a drastically different fashion.

A recruitment attempt could fail for any number of reasons, and operational departments, as a matter of course, collected information on just what those reasons were and what could be done to eliminate at least some of them. At the Central People's Public Security Academy, officer cadets in 1957 were asked to remember that the "circumstances surrounding a failed agent recruitment are to be reported in writing by the operational officer to the superior leadership that approved the recruitment attempt, and the report should contain a detailed explanation of the reasons for the failure."⁹⁷ Presumably drawing on their personal experiences as well as on any number of such reports, the CMPS authors of the *Lectures* mentioned a couple of the more common reasons for failure. First of all, they noted, the target might cite a compelling reason for not wanting to work for the public security organs. In the following case, a busy factory technician in Shenyang, who initially, albeit reluctantly, had agreed to

---

⁹⁵ Ferguson, *Spy*, p. 91.
⁹⁶ Feng Jiping, "Zai quanju ganbu huiyi shang guanyu Beijing zhenya fangeming gongzuo de zongjie baogao" (Summing Up Report at a Meeting of All Cadres in the Bureau on the Work of Suppressing Counterrevolutionaries in Beijing), *Renmin gongan zengkan*, No. 30, November 20, 1951, p. 27.
⁹⁷ "*Teqing gongzuo*," p. 41.

serve as an agent, sought to explain at the first postrecruitment meeting with his handler why he was changing his mind:

Each and every day, I devote myself flat out to my administration duties: will I still be able to do this in the future? I carry out my administration duties conscientiously: assuming I *don't* do this kind of work for you, will I still be able to wash away the stains of the past on my politics? These duties I am meant to perform for you: do I report on them to my administrative superiors as well? If I don't report them, does that not amount to flouting organization and discipline? And if I don't do this kind of work, and encounter problems [as a result], am I still not meant to report this to my administrative superiors?[98]

The local Bureau of Public Security commented, saying it was obvious that the man was really not prepared to serve as an agent, but the reasons were unclear and needed to be determined and then addressed.[99] In cases like this one – where the agent or potential agent was quite confident in his or her professional position and not worried about losing his or her job – operational officers were encouraged to negotiate a compromise solution, as in the following reminder to officers in Southwest China:

Some agents, because they are quite busy in their [normal] professional activities, do not have ample time to work for us. In addition to educating them to "squeeze" out more time at their own initiative, the main solution should be to task them in a way that permits them to combine it with their regular professional activities, since otherwise the agent may become worried and lose confidence in his work [for us].[100]

Ultimately, the authors of the *Lectures* realized, no amount of advance preparation could eliminate completely the prospect of failure. Something could always go wrong, officer cadets were reminded; hence, it was important to be prepared for what needed to be done in the eventuality of failure. Most important, in the case of an unsuccessful recruitment attempt, the target was to be prevented "from revealing secrets."[101] What this entailed was to ensure that a failed recruitment attempt remained forever a secret.

The *Lectures* noted that, in some cases, sheer incompetence could explain a failed recruitment attempt, but they did not elaborate further on this or cite actual examples. A rare example of incompetence and criminal misconduct (on the part of the officer responsible) was how the Liaoning

[98] Shenyang shi renmin zhengfu gonganju jingji baoweichu, "Guanyu jianli," p. 37.
[99] Ibid., p. 38.
[100] Chongqing shi gonganju, "Guanyu jinian lai teqing," p. 14.
[101] "Teqing gongzuo," p. 41.

provincial People's Procuratorate described a 1954 case of a recruitment gone badly wrong and resulting, ultimately, in the suicide of the agent, a forty-two-year-old illiterate peasant from suburban Shenyang. J was described as an extroverted and industrious man with a checkered past who found it hard to control his temper after a few drinks. After arguing with a local police officer and being caught complaining about the state's grain- purchasing policy, rumors were circulated that he had been an ex-con man, a former Guomindang spy, and an informer for the Republican police. Soon afterward, when two public security officers arrived, on orders from above, to find and recruit a suitable local informer (on the local criminal underworld), they decided to mount a coercive recruitment targeting J and to use embellished versions of the unsubstantiated rumors about him to force him to agree to serve as an agent "to atone for crimes committed." Terrified by what might happen to him should he refuse to cooperate, J agreed to serve, but quickly discovering that he had absolutely nothing of substance to report to his handler and feeling increasingly troubled by this, he asked to have his recruitment ended and to be relieved of his duties. When his handler refused to do so, J turned to two local CCP cadres for advice, but this only got him into deeper trouble. Arrested for having revealed "state secrets" (his recruitment) but at the same time accused in public of having fabricated the story (in front of the local cadres, the public security officers denounced J's claim to having served as a source of theirs as pure fantasy), J broke down completely and took his own life during his first night in police custody.[102] The CMPS disseminated a highly critical detailed account of the entire affair to public security officers nationwide and in a follow-up report (devoted to the punishments of varying severity meted out to the officers involved), called it a "human rights violation" of the most serious kind.[103]

---

[102] Liaoning sheng renmin jianchayuan, "Guanyu Shenyang shi gonganju Jiaodong fenju weifa luanji bisi 'teqing' XXX shijian de baogao" (Report on the Incident of the Eastern Suburb Branch of the Shenyang Bureau of Public Security in Violation of Law and Discipline Hounding the "Agent" XXX to Death), *Gongan jianshe*, No. 122, April 12, 1955, pp. 23–26.

[103] "Shenyang shi gonganju yansu chuli bisi 'teqing' XXX shijian" (Shenyang Municipal Bureau of Public Security Deals Seriously with Incident of "Agent" XXX Being Hounded to Death), *Gongan jianshe*, No. 128, June 5, 1955, pp. 16–17.

6

Training and Tradecraft

Behind the Covert Front

In its editorials, the *People's Daily* in the 1950s came down hard on those unnamed "members of our revolutionary ranks" who failed to appreciate the supreme importance of having the correct political stance.[1] More or less by default, PRC news media attributed the operational successes of public security organs to the superior *political* qualities of the men and women involved. Behind closed doors, however, senior public security officers assessed somewhat differently the relative importance of politics and professionalism – or the qualities of "redness" and "expertise," as they were also known. "Talking about politics day in and day out is not going to put food on your table!" Shanghai's director of public security impressed upon his subordinates in 1959. Operational officers, he emphasized, also had to develop the requisite professional skills and *tradecraft*: in the words of a British writer on the ethics of the subject, the "arts of deception."[2]

Nobody was more fully aware than the CMPS leadership of the fact that, in reality, the victories that officers and their agents scored on the covert front had everything to do with first-rate tradecraft. During his tenure as minister, Luo Ruiqing made the development and improvement of professional skills among his officers a priority: "We not only need to master primitive forms of struggle," he noted specifically in his 1953 New Year's address, "but in particular need to master sophisticated

---

[1] *Renmin ribao*, July 12, 1955.
[2] *Huang Chibo zuixing lu* (*Huang Chibo's Criminal Record*) (Shanghai: Shanghai shi gonganju lianhe doupigai xiaozu, 1967), p. 6; Andrew, Aldrich, and Wark, *Secret Intelligence*, p. 401.

forms of struggle."[3] Three years earlier, in 1950, Wang Jinxiang had told operational officers:

You need to conduct research into the techniques of where, when, and how you meet with your agent and how to ensure you will not be spotted by the enemy. Otherwise, the result of just a moment's carelessness, a breach of security, may well be that all your running and cultivation of the agent will have been wasted and your work will have been compromised.[4]

For public security officers, the norm after 1949 became to develop proficiency and expertise through systematic training as well as learning on the job. In the 1960s, Xie Fuzhi promoted the slogan "to train hard to perfect one's skills."[5] Although he remained personally ambivalent about the appropriateness of some of his officers' techniques and at one point sharply criticized what he called putting "little" – presumably dirty – "tricks in command," Xie after 1959 nonetheless oversaw the public security sector's growing operational use of a range of increasingly sophisticated technical gadgetry.[6]

The initiation of the agents themselves in the ins and outs of tradecraft invariably took place under suboptimal conditions. There were, after all, no specialized schools, as handlers were reminded during their own basic training, "where one can foster politically reliable backbone agents (*gugan teqing*) and allow them to become tradecraft proficient."[7] For the individual agent, acquiring the necessary skills thus often became a matter of what Mao Zedong in 1936 had called "learning warfare through warfare."[8] The CMPS stressed that, as a matter of policy, the training of the agent in elements of tradecraft "must be intimately integrated with the actual work performed by the agent."[9]

Many of the dimensions of tradecraft deemed to be crucial to agent work essentially amounted to human ones (such as living undercover, elicitation skills, and nerve), while others contained what might be called "infrastructural elements." Focusing more on the technical aspects of

---

[3] *Luo Ruiqing lun renmin gongan gongzuo* (*Luo Ruiqing on People's Public Security Work*) (Beijing: Qunzhong chubanshe, 1994), pp. 165–67.
[4] Wang Jinxiang, "Zai dongbei zhengzhi jingji," p. 26.
[5] Xie Fuzhi, "Xuexi jiefangjun dalian guoying benling" (Learn from the Liberation Army and Train Hard to Perfect Your Skills), *Renmin gongan*, No. 184, October 15, 1964, p. 2.
[6] Liu Xingyi, *Yang Qiqing zhuan*, p. 403.
[7] "*Teqing gongzuo*," p. 45.
[8] *Selected Works of Mao Tsetung*, Vol. 1, p. 190.
[9] "*Teqing gongzuo*," p. 60.

operational work, this chapter looks at how these ranged – from officers following developments in intelligence both in China and abroad, to acquiring knowledge in the art of setting up and managing safe houses, handling impersonal agent–officer contact routines, and making operational use of "material technical resources."[10]

Training in the Academy

In the words of Frederic Wakeman, Jr., the pre-1949 security operations of the CCP were "based upon a combination of Moscow tradecraft and [the CCP's] own inventiveness" and as such were "extremely effective."[11] Moscow tradecraft was something the nascent CCP had first become acquainted with in 1926, when three young party members – men in their early twenties – were sent to the Soviet Union for training in intelligence and security work. Chen Geng, Xie Fuzhi's erstwhile colleague, was one of those sent. Gu Shunzhang was another; he would later help set up the party's first security service, the Central Special Services Section, only to turn traitor after being arrested by the Guomindang in 1931. Young party members selected as showing promise continued in the 1930s, under the auspices of the Comintern, to be dispatched to the Soviet Union for training, among them Chen Long, future director of the CMPS 1st Bureau. By the end of the decade, a select but impressive list of Soviet-trained men and women held key positions in the CSAD in Yan'an.[12] Here they helped run what has been described by one historian as "Moscow's effort to train intelligence officers for Communist revolutions in Asian countries." To all intents and purposes an intelligence school, it offered one-year courses in operational tradecraft to students "carefully selected by both the CCP and the Comintern headquarters in Moscow from [among] Communists in China and many other Asian countries."[13] One of the teachers was the resident Comintern translator Boris Aleyev, who shared with the young students his knowledge of intelligence work, technical aspects of wireless communication, drawing, and photography. His students would in due course form the backbone of the PRC public security apparatus.[14]

After the end of the War of Resistance against Japan, the CSAD continued in the second half of the 1940s, under what were logistically difficult circumstances, to organize crash courses, rarely lasting longer than six

[10] *KGB Lexicon*, p. 383.
[11] Wakeman, *Spymaster*, p. 147.
[12] Mu Xin, *Yinbi zhanxian tongshuai*, p. 35.
[13] Yu Maochun, *OSS in China*, p. 41.
[14] Zhu Chunlin, *Lishi shunjian I*, p. 356.

months, in tradecraft for new recruits to its ranks. The officers who entered Beijing in January 1949 to establish a CCP security presence in the city – set to become the future capital of the PRC – included more than 100 graduates of a recent CSAD Intelligence, Protection, and Public Security Training Course, organized in Yellow Mud Village, in eastern Hebei province.[15]

In Beijing, courses like those given in Yellow Mud Village were regularized and became a permanent institution – the North China Public Security Cadre School.[16] At the 1st NPSC, Luo Ruiqing stated that the mission of the school was to "train high-level backbones."[17] The school was the flagship institution of its kind, and by the end of 1952 it had trained more than 2,500 officers and, according to a former staff member, "to a certain degree resolved the need for officers in the initial phase of creating the Ministry of Public Security and [establishing control over] cities like Beijing and Tianjin."[18] In January 1953, the CMPS received the go-ahead from Zhou Enlai's cabinet to transform the Public Security Cadre School into a full-fledged university. Luo Ruiqing gave a speech four months later in which he impressed upon officer cadets studying at what would henceforth be called the Central People's Public Security Academy the importance of becoming "tradecraft proficient, being in possession of all the knowledge and technical skills needed, and learning how to be resourceful and capable in fighting counterrevolutionaries."[19] Knowing full well that active senior public security officers were often too busy to find the time to formally teach and lecture to their "revolutionary successors," the CMPS leadership sought to elevate the standing of the public security educator, even if this meant making intentionally provocative comparisons, like this one by one of Luo's deputies in 1954:

Some officers working in schools maintain that school work is not important. There's no future in it, and it commands no respect, they say. This is clearly wrong, and on this point, these comrades of ours are not as clever as our enemies. Both the first United States president Washington and the current president Eisenhower were once university presidents. Chiang Kai-shek began his career as president of the Huangpu Military Academy.[20]

[15] Mu Yumin, *Beijing jingcha*, p. 360.
[16] Zhu Chunlin, *Lishi shunjian I*, p. 609.
[17] Ibid., p. 609.
[18] Ibid., p. 82.
[19] *Luo Ruiqing lun*, p. 192.
[20] Wang Zhao, "Zai di yi ci gongan xuexiao jiaoyu gongzuo huiyi shang de zongjie" (Concluding Summary at the 1st National Conference on Educational Work in Public Security Schools), *Gongan jianshe*, No. 194, July 15, 1957, p. 12.

By 1958, the Central People's Public Security Academy had trained a total of 6,400 officers.[21] Not all of them became specialists in operational work, however: the academy also trained officers who would move on to very different public security sectors, such as prison management and homicide investigation. In 1959, the academy was reorganized and merged with the Central Political and Legal Cadres' School, set up shortly after the founding of the PRC, to also train officers of the courts and procuracy.

Partially replicating what was being done in Beijing under the aegis of the CMPS were the regional ministries of public security and their corresponding schools in Shanghai, Xi'an, Chongqing, Shenyang, and Wuhan. These regional public security schools were, in the words of Luo Ruiqing, tasked with "training intermediate level backbones."[22] In terms of future agent handlers, the kind of young men and women the schools were looking to recruit and train was described in an internal document drawn up by the NEMPS in the autumn of 1950. It stressed first and foremost that the key to successful operational work was the "fostering of large numbers of 'agent controller backbones.'" With this aim in mind, it announced the launch of a special program of classes in how to run agents, perform operational work, and conduct interrogations. The program targeted officers who satisfied the following criteria:

(1) firm political stance and three years of work experience; (2) sharp-witted and alert, experienced and able to cope in a wide range of social settings; (3) minimum higher elementary school educational background and physically fit; (4) correct ideology and development potential.[23]

The NEMPS expected to be able to find individuals who satisfied these criteria in Northeast China's provincial and municipal public security organs, but it also asked the regional CCP Organization Department to assist it in locating additional recruits among students in the region's ordinary schools.[24]

That public security academies would favor students with a "firm political stance" is hardly surprising. But that they also selectively favored students from certain ethnic backgrounds is less well known. As noted in

---

[21] Zhu Chunlin, *Lishi shunjian I*, pp. 81–89.
[22] Tao Siju, *Xin Zhongguo di yi ren*, p. 203.
[23] Dongbei renmin zhengfu gonganbu, "Guanyu gaijin zhencha gongzuo wenti" (On the Problem of Improving Operational Work), *Gongan baowei gongzuo*, No. 20, November 25, 1950, p. 23.
[24] Ibid.

Chapter 2, the CMPS 1st Bureau from the outset prioritized operational work, including the use of agents, in China's ethnic minority and frontier regions. A severe shortage of officers from other than Han Chinese background, however, often hampered work on the ground in these regions, and as a result, the CMPS ordered public security schools and academies to launch special courses to remedy the situation.[25]

A senior delegate from Inner Mongolia at the 6th NSPC highlighted the political logic of the intensified training and promotion of ethnic minority public security officers as one of reducing interethnic tension: "Even though some Mongolian masses are discontented with our policies," he said, when they see them being implemented and defended by officers of Mongolian descent, their discontent "does not provoke ethnic conflict."[26] Beginning in 1954, the Central People's Public Security Academy organized special classes for officers from some of China's larger ethnic minority groups. Some sixty junior public security officers from Xinjiang – members of thirteen different nationalities including Uighurs and Kazakhs – made up the special Nationalities Class I, members of which attended the academy for twelve months in 1954–55.[27] Altogether 207 Tibetans (mostly youths with no public security background) made up the special Nationalities Class II, founded in Tibet as the Tibetan Public Security Training Class in September 1956, and transferred to Beijing in July 1957. The Tibetan contingent was initially supposed to receive an elementary education, become acquainted with Marxism-Leninism, and beginning in late 1957, develop basic operational skills over a period of five years. When the revolt in Tibet broke out in 1959, however, their studies were interrupted, and they were sent back to help with damage limitation and the reassertion of CCP control.[28] Prior to leaving Beijing, in conversation with a reporter from *People's Public Security*, they had pledged to "thoroughly smash the sinister plot of the rebels and work hard to build our new Tibet in accordance with the instructions of the Central People's Government."[29] Assuming they remained true to this pledge, they would

[25] Zhongyang gonganbu, "Guanyu zai shaoshu minzu," p. 7.
[26] Wu Tong, "Zai di liu ci quanguo," p. 15.
[27] *Jianguo yilai gongan*, pp. 74–75.
[28] Ibid., p. 135; "Xizang jingguan gaodeng zhuanke xuexiao jiben qingkuang" (Basic Introduction to the Tibet Police College), Tibet Police College, http://www.tpa.net.cn/show_gk.asp?id=5 (accessed February 2, 2012).
[29] "Fensui panluan fenzi de yinmou, nuli jianshe xin Xizang" (Smash the Plot of the Insurrectionist Elements and Strive to Build a New Tibet), *Renmin gongan*, No. 68, May 28, 1959, p. 19.

have played a crucial role in executing the shift away from the openly confrontational policies of the late 1950s in Tibet toward the long-term stance welcomed by the CMPS in 1961 of "strengthening operational work and build[ing] up capacity in the form of agents."[30]

Textbooks and Extracurricular Reading Matter

The lack of good up-to-date textbooks for training purposes initially represented a problem, with the CMPS having to fall back on texts written or compiled prior to 1949. While it is impossible to say with certainty what kind of balance they may have struck between advocating "Moscow tradecraft" and the specific experiences of the CCP, the following Cultural Revolutionary denunciation of an officer who had held a leading position in the CMPS 1st Bureau after 1954, and who had originally been involved in the production of operational work textbooks in Northeast China, indicates the preferences of the CMPS at the time:

During his time in the Northeast, he used every ounce of his energy to tout the mysticism and isolationist model of the Soviet revisionist OGPU [*Gebowu*]. He personally wrote and compiled so-called "operational work primers" on the basis of texts emanating from the departments of the Soviet revisionist OGPU and invited their staff to "train [our] operational officers."[31]

Translated into more neutral language, this criticism suggests that Moscow tradecraft was initially held in high regard and that much was done to impart it to Chinese officers. The unnamed so-called primers probably included books like *What You Need to Know about Urban Protection Work* (four volumes), *Traitor Elimination Primer*, and *Mandatory Readings for Intelligence and Protection Officers*, all known to have been sponsored and distributed by the Harbin Bureau of Public Security in 1948–49.[32] In principle, learning from the Soviet elder brother was emphasized in the early years of the PRC, with a particular focus on scientific and technological aspects of operational (and forensic) work, including the use of sophisticated equipment.[33] It is likely to have influenced the content of classes at the Central People's Public Security Academy (in 1953 and 1954) on how to "respond to the threat

[30] Gonganbu xibei gongzuozu, "Dui jiaqiang shaoshu minzu," p. 5.
[31] *Dadao litong waiguode*, p. 11.
[32] Dai Wendian, *Zhongguo gongan tushu*, pp. 902–5.
[33] Sun Mingshan, *Lishi shunjian IV*, pp. 91–92.

posed by foreign spies" and how to "guard capital construction against sabotage."[34]

It was not until May 1956 that an ad hoc committee chaired by Yang Qiqing was set up by the CMPS to organize and oversee the production of a new set of textbooks on vocational subjects to be taught in the Central People's Public Security Academy and regional/provincial schools.[35] It may have been a coincidence, but this was less than a month after Mao Zedong at an expanded session of the CCP Politburo had called for lessons to be drawn from the Soviet Union while exploring new ways of building socialism in China suited to the country's specific conditions. The relatively relaxed political atmosphere of 1956 probably proved conducive to the production of new vocational textbooks "with Chinese characteristics." Yang Qiqing had already accumulated some experience with developing such texts before 1949 while serving as director of the Social Affairs Department of the Shanxi-Hebei-Shandong-Henan Base Area. At the time, he had been personally in charge of editing and overseeing the production of primers and textbooks with titles like *What You Need to Know about Operational Work, Teaching Notes on Physical Surveillance and Intelligence Work*, and *Teaching Notes on Interrogation Work*.[36]

After some initial disagreements over the quality and scope of the new textbooks (the first drafts were regarded by those who received them as "excessive in content, and their chapters too long"), they were officially approved for classroom use in 1957.[37] In the present context of the use of agents, the most interesting one is textbook No. 4, entitled *Lectures on the Subject of Agent Work*. Written by an elite group of experienced operational officers brought together specifically for the task from different parts of China, it was ratified by Yang Qiqing's committee and printed in a first edition classified as Top Secret by the Central People's Public Security Academy in April 1957. Divided into three sections and containing more than a dozen chapters, it covered in a very hands-on fashion the following subjects: the tasks and categories of agents; management, leadership, and oversight of their work; the identification of potential agents and the proper recruitment strategy; caring for and training/educating agents; and elementary tradecraft, including the dos and don'ts of communication, safe houses, and so on. Just how it was used in class is

---

[34] Dai Wendian, *Zhongguo gongan tushu*, pp. 254, 610.
[35] Tao Siju, *Xin Zhongguo di yi ren*, p. 209.
[36] Liu Xingyi, *Yang Qiqing zhuan*, pp. 166, 254; *Zhongguo renmin gongan shigao*, p. 233.
[37] Tao Siju, *Xin Zhongguo di yi ren*, p. 209.

difficult to say, but presumably it served as a point of departure for a more extended discussion of each subject, with the teacher adding supplementary material and commentary based on his or her own individual operational experience. Copies are unlikely to have been printed and distributed in quantity to students, and security concerns mandated that if and when officer cadets were permitted to take notes during lectures, they could only do this in special "confidential notebooks" (*baomi bijiben*), the safekeeping of which was stringently regulated.

The *Lectures* did not cover the use of agents in the fight against ordinary crime, nor did it deal with physical surveillance (mobile, static, etc.) or countersurveillance. These were among the subjects covered in other textbooks used in other, separate classes.[38] Whether the Central Academy textbooks were also used in regional and provincial schools of public security is uncertain, but the fact that a copy of the *Lectures* dated 1958 survives in the library of the Shaanxi provincial People's Police School suggests that this may well have been the case.[39] If so, one would have to assume that they complemented other, intermediate-level textbooks produced locally. One 1955 primer from Nanjing – geared to the needs of officers serving in political protection departments – on the examination and interpretation of crime scenes can only be described as quite elementary: its most detailed section dealt with the forensic examination of handwriting and was, one presumes, meant to teach officers how to identify the writer of "counterrevolutionary slogans" or "reactionary handbills" they might come across in their work.[40]

The kind of extracurricular reading matter that officers were encouraged to read was as a rule produced by the commercial publisher The Masses Publishing House, founded in 1956 and attached to the CMPS. Having started out as The Masses Bookshop in April 1949, it had originally operated as an ordinary commercial establishment as well as an operational safe house.[41] The books published for official use only by The Masses Publishing House included translations of foreign books meant to illustrate how "the enemy" operated, as well as, occasionally, works that gave the reader a better understanding of the world beyond China's borders. Titles appearing in the first half of the 1960s included

[38] "*Teqing gongzuo*," p. 14.
[39] Dai Wendian, *Zhongguo gongan tushu*, p. 250.
[40] Nanjing junqu zhengzhibu baoweibu, ed., *Xianchang kancha yewu cankao ziliao* (*On-the-Scene Investigation Vocational Reference Materials*) (Nanjing, 1955), pp. 20–34.
[41] 1956–2006 *Qunzhong chubanshe chengli 50 zhounian* (*1956–2006: Fifty Years of the Masses Publishing House*) (Beijing: Qunzhong chubanshe, 2006), p. 14.

Ellis M. Zacharias's *Secret Missions: The Story of an Intelligence Officer*, advertised in the PRC as the memoirs of someone with twenty-five years of experience in "intelligence activities"; the April 1963 *Harper's Magazine* article "The Craft of Intelligence" by the U.S. director of the Central Intelligence Agency, Allen W. Dulles; veteran journalist Andrew Tully's 1962 bestseller *CIA: The Inside Story*, the first work of its kind to expose in some detail a succession of failed and successful CIA operations; and an abridged translation of David Wise and Thomas B. Ross's 1964 exposé *The Invisible Government*, described by the CIA's legal counsel at the time as "uncannily accurate."[42]

On a lighter note, cadets and officers seeking to improve their tradecraft were also told to read and enjoy the translated exploits of Arthur Conan Doyle's fictional hero Sherlock Holmes. In 1961, at a conference on surveillance work in Shanghai, the municipal director of public security was heard observing that "whereas we cannot put our faith in Holmes's repertoire of feudal, bourgeois, and fascist tricks – but must come up with our own proletarian and revolutionary Holmes – some of that old stuff may still prove to be useful here and there." Finally, if learning from fictional foreigners was not to everyone's taste, it was possible instead to take some cues and tips from the heroes and villains of Chinese history and classical opera. Indeed, Shanghai's director of public security once asked his officers to learn how to "adopt clever disguises and move about observing things incognito" by emulating Kuang Zhong, the upstanding Suzhou governor of the Ming dynasty in the Kunqu opera *Fifteen Strings of Cash*. The director himself boasted in private that he had been able to visit Shanghai's Big World entertainment complex incognito and easily, he claimed, distinguished the "ladyboys" (*yaoguai*) from the common prostitutes plying their trade there.[43]

Learning on the Job

British intelligence historians have estimated that "it takes perhaps ten years for an agent-runner to achieve their full potential."[44] In view of this, it is hardly surprising that public security organs in Mao's China after 1949 desperately strove to speed up the training and learning process of its operational officers. In addition to the formal courses in

[42] Dai Wendian, *Zhongguo gongan tushu*, p. 283.
[43] *Huang Chibo zuixing lu*, p. 27.
[44] Andrew, Aldrich, and Wark, *Secret Intelligence*, p. 160.

tradecraft-related subjects on offer at the Central People's Public Security Academy and its lesser comparable institutions elsewhere in China, some public security bureaus also used more praxis-oriented schemes that essentially amounted to training on the job. Such schemes complemented the text-centered training typical of the academies.

After having established their presence as the "People's Police" in China's cities in 1949–50, many new recruits to the force confronted a plethora of practical problems, not least in terms of acquiring simple vocational skills. Older and experienced officers who had been retained from the Republican police, according to a survey conducted in Tianjin, often "regard the young newcomers on the job as little more than inexperienced children who don't know the ways of the world. They look down on them and don't want to help them acquire any vocational skills. They worry that once the [newcomers] have learned the ropes, they themselves will be given the boot."[45] Tasked with the difficult job of improving the situation, and quickly, were intermediate-level municipal public security leaderships. A self-critical NEMPS document from the autumn of 1950 specifically claimed with respect to agent work that "leaderships have not done their part. They have not been setting examples, taking on apprentices, coming up with practical ideas, or otherwise setting things in motion. And officers at lower levels not only lack ways and means, but also find the whole idea [of recruiting agents] awkward and cannot bring themselves to overcome their inhibition."[46]

Striking a similarly critical albeit slightly more upbeat note only a few months earlier, a deputy public security director in Beijing, Zhang Minghe, had proposed the following solution: "There are many young intellectuals in our Bureau of Public Security at present: if each and every one of us responsible cadres takes one of them on as an apprentice, and helps them develop their vocational skills, then within a few years, they would surely manage to grow into formidable public security sector cadres."[47] What, if anything, came of this idea during Zhang's own tenure in Beijing is not known. However, after his transfer to neighboring Hebei province in 1953, and his colleague Feng Jiping's (the two men, it

---

[45] "Pingji dingxin gongzuo zongjie" (Summary of Rank and Salary Setting Work), *Tianjin gongan*, Vol. 1, No. 2, August 15, 1950, p. 15.

[46] Dongbei renmin zhengfu gonganbu, "Guanyu gaijin zhencha," p. 21.

[47] Zhang Minghe, "Zai kuoda juwu huiyi de baogao" (Report to an Enlarged Bureau Affairs Meeting), *Renmin gongan zengkan*, No. 9, June 25, 1950, p. 5.

appears, did not get along[48]) promotion to the post of director of public security in the capital, apprenticeship schemes were to become a reality. The first scheme was set up and run on a trial basis by the Beijing Bureau between February and October 1955. The apprentices, in this case, were inexperienced officers from the operational sections of the local branches of the municipal bureau: deputy section chiefs, ordinary field officers, and desk officers. They were each assigned to a section chief or senior officer in the corresponding offices of the municipal bureau. The latter serving as their tutors, apprentices would follow and learn from them in the course of normal duties, such as officer–agent meetings. According to the CMPS, apprentices were at the beginning so inexperienced (and therefore obviously uncomfortable) in operational matters that "they blushed when encountering an agent face-to-face, and would not know what to say." While they studied relevant literature like the *Agent Work Manual* during their eight-month apprenticeships, it was, most importantly, by watching and learning from their tutors that they "developed their vocational skills."[49]

Feng Jiping advertised the apprenticeship scheme at a mass meeting of CCP-member public security officers serving in Beijing in October 1955, telling his colleagues why "at the same time as we strengthen our schools and vocational training classes, each sector needs to pay full attention to make use of, in their actual work, the 'taking on of an apprentice' as a method of fostering and improving officers."[50] Before the end of the year, the scheme would receive a very positive review by the CMPS in the form of a write-up in the ministerial serial *Public Security Construction* under the headline "A Good Way of Fostering Operational Officers."[51] The CMPS claimed that the inexperienced Beijing officers had very quickly managed to improve various aspects of their tradecraft: they had acquired a command of elementary "methods of investigation and research" and learned how to open up and control agents. The deputy section chief and some of the field officers, under the direction of their tutors, had even learned how to handle independently the operational aspects of dealing with simpler cases and leads. The CMPS insisted that

[48] "Yike yongyuan buhui yunluo de jiangxing – Zhang Minghe" (Zhang Minghe – A Never-Setting Star of a General), Xy-yanxin's blog, March 24, 2010, http://blog.sina.com.cn/s/blog_606dd3950100hsjb.html (accessed January 18, 2011).
[49] "Jianxun" (News in Brief), *Gongan jianshe*, No. 148, December 29, 1955, p. 27.
[50] Feng Jiping, "Jianjue guanche di liu ci," pp. 45–46.
[51] "Jianxun," *Gongan jianshe*, No. 148, December 29, 1955, p. 27.

if experienced officers, not just in Beijing but also elsewhere, could each take on one apprentice for six months or a year, such a scheme would quickly provide a major boost to the quality of operational work across China.[52]

Although in time the skill and competence of operational officers undoubtedly improved due to formal training and apprenticeship schemes like those detailed here, it was also clear that there remained significant room for improvement. This is evident from the results of a test that some 175 protection officers had to take in 1963 in the Central Political and Legal Cadres' School (as the People's Public Security Academy was by then called). The test comprised sixteen questions on vocational matters as well as general policy (for example, "What is our basic long-term policy for the elimination of counterrevolutionaries?"). Forty-six – more than a quarter of the officers – either got all of the answers wrong or simply handed in a blank questionnaire, ninety-five got a majority of the answers wrong, and only thirty-four managed to get nearly all of the answers right. In commenting on the very disappointing results, the editors of *People's Public Security* said that they should serve as a lesson to everybody and that further "vocational tests" should be encouraged.[53]

Keeping Clandestine Premises

One of perhaps the most important subjects on which officer cadets received training in the academy and on the job, in apprentice schemes like the Beijing one, was that of safe houses. The English-language term "safe house" conventionally refers to an innocuous-looking premise established by an intelligence or security service for the purpose of conducting clandestine or covert activity in relative security. In the PRC, a single term with the same broad meaning never gained currency, at least not within the public security sector. Instead, terminology similar to that used in the Soviet Union was adopted early on, one that firmly distinguished between "clandestine premises" (*Kvartira konspirativnaya* in Russian, *mimi judian* in Chinese), on the one hand, and "secret rendezvous premises" (*Kvartira yavochnaya* in Russian, *jietou judian* in Chinese) on the other.

---

[52] Ibid.
[53] "Pingshi bu xuexi kaoshi chu xiaohua" (Those Who Do Not Study Regularly Make Fools of Themselves When Taking Exams), *Renmin gongan*, No. 147, February 20, 1963, p. 12.

The KGB defined clandestine premises as an official building covertly at the disposal of public security officers for operational purposes.[54] In the context of agent work, the CMPS used the term to refer to premises (a building or suite of rooms in a building) belonging to the public security organs, where operational officers were able to meet undercover with the agents they ran or conduct other business.[55] An early NEMPS directive explained that the creation of such premises was to be prioritized "in those regions where seaports and communication checkpoints are located, in order to erect clandestine lines of defense against traitors and spies."[56] More than half a century later, a retired public security officer from the port city of Yingkou recalled what this entailed in practical terms:

After the Spring Festival in [February] 1950...Zhou Yutang, the head of surveillance, called me in one day for a talk, to inform me that the organization had decided to use the Liao River Bookshop as operational premises for clandestine meetings with agents. My cover was to be that of "shopkeeper" and Comrade Wang Chunxiang was to work together with me as my "shop assistant." [In those days] the Liao River Bookshop was located in a small two-story building just east of the old post office on central Liao River Street. It served as our front. We ran a small everyday business, selling writing materials, stationery, paper, etc. The shop had a front entrance and a back entrance, which made it easy to come and go in secret.[57]

Agents would, in this particular case, meet with their handlers in an apartment above the bookshop. The officer tasked with managing the premises remembered how, on occasion, he would go out to buy dumplings for the agents to eat. He also remembered the agents leaving by the back entrance.[58]

In reading between the lines of contemporary records, it is apparent that novice operational officers had only the faintest of ideas about the what and wherefore of clandestine premises. When an internal investigation and rectification campaign conducted by the NEMPS in the summer of 1950 laid bare the extent of the problem (particularly in the economic

---

[54] *KGB Lexicon*, p. 223.
[55] "*Teqing gongzuo,*" pp. 68–69.
[56] Dongbei renmin zhengfu ganganbu, "Guanyu jiaqiang zhencha," p. 21.
[57] Wei Dianjiu, "Huimou mimi judian" (A Safe House Remembered), Zhonggong Liaoning sheng lao ganbu ju, http://www.lnlgb.gov.cn/lgb/website/informationShow.jsp?id=402880e425667d7001256d454be600b4&type=8a8080e911585fa80111159354f940007 (accessed February 2, 2012).
[58] Ibid.

protection sector), the ministry responded by putting some general principles on paper to "resolve matters in the future."[59] Very much part of
the package of policies and routines aggressively promoted by Chen Long
at the 1st National Conference on Operational Work, the principles dealt
with selected organizational aspects of agent running and were mentioned
in a Top Secret NEMPS review circulated after the conference. The review
explained how

> in those places – factories and mines – where there are protection sections [*baowei
> kegu*] but as yet no backbone officers running agents, the sections need to carry out
> agent work in parallel with their other work, but should do so outside the factory
> or mine premises. Here they need to establish rendezvous and liaison premises
> and pay attention to clandestine work. In the case of smaller factories and mines
> lacking protection sections or agent-running backbone officers, the economic
> protection organs may set up external agent direction premises from where agent
> work inside a number of smaller factories and mines may be developed and
> controlled. Premises from where agent work may be directed should [also] be set
> up in complex urban areas. Where the resources needed are not yet available,
> the local branches [of municipal bureaus of public security] may designate and
> appoint specific individuals to carry out the task [of setting up such premises].
> Where municipal bureaus of public security do not have local branches, they may
> themselves directly dispatch individuals to set up and control such premises.[60]

This particular review did not have anything more specific to say about
the day-to-day management of clandestine premises. Presumably while
there were other NEMPS documents that did, officers on the ground
were likely given room for maneuver to resolve any issues as they saw fit.

The ideal location for clandestine operational premises in an urban
environment was wherever large numbers of people came and went. It
was not in a quiet side street where a stranger was likely to arouse the suspicion – or at the very least draw the attention – of the vigilant "masses."
According to the *Lectures*, however, the entrances to clandestine premises
were to be located where they could *not* be readily observed by neighbors
or ordinary passersby. The actual room or suite of rooms on the premises
where an agent might meet with his or her handler, or where operational
officers might confer with each other, was to be sealed off from all other
rooms and not otherwise accessible from adjacent apartments or visible
from the outside. To the outside world, the clandestine premises were
to have the appearance of an ordinary residence, office, or shop. ("Some

---

[59] Dongbei renmin zhengfu gonganbu, "Guanyu gaijin zhencha," p. 21.
[60] Ibid., p. 24.

small shops located in critical places are operated directly by the public security apparatus," sociologist Ezra F. Vogel concluded in 1969 on the basis of interviews with refugees, including public security officers, arriving in Hong Kong.[61]) Officer cadets were reminded in the *Lectures* that even items of furniture, among other decor, had to correspond to what one would expect to find in a real apartment, shop, or office. Public utilities such as water, gas, electricity, sanitation, and garbage collection were furthermore to be used in ways and to an extent that in no way differed from what might to an outsider appear normal.[62]

The establishment of clandestine premises was meant to follow stringent management routines laid down by the CMPS. While it is not possible to reliably ascertain to what extent these routines were actually followed, praxis is likely to have differed depending on the time and place. Nevertheless, the most important routine was the written request for permission to open a safe house in the first place, which had to be submitted in advance to the head of the public security organ concerned. CMPS rules stipulated that a request for permission had to spell out and list inter alia the following:

- the rationale behind the setting up of the clandestine premises: why were they needed?
- the exact location of the clandestine premises (city district, name of street, exact address, etc.);
- the cover under which the clandestine premises were to be kept/used;
- technical operations equipment, if any, that needed to be installed;
- the need, if any, for furnishings.[63]

Only once permission had been obtained was establishment of the premises allowed. At this point, they would be registered as an entity on which a running file was to be kept, containing (a) all of the records and documentation relating to the creation, inspection, upkeep, and maintenance of the premises and (b) a supposedly up-to-date list of all agents who had met there, or were meeting there, with their handler(s). It would appear to be the case, judging from the description in the *Lectures* of the routines involved, that political protection and economic protection operational departments each managed their own clandestine premises

---

[61] Ezra F. Vogel, "Preserving Order in the Cities," in John W. Lewis, ed., *The City in Communist China* (Stanford, CA: Stanford University Press, 1971), p. 88.

[62] *"Teqing gongzuo,"* p. 69.

[63] Ibid.

separately. As a rule, for the sake of minimizing the risk of their being compromised, clandestine premises were only to be used to meet with a relatively limited number of agents who had passed a stringent background check as to their trustworthiness. Registration and safekeeping of the file on particular clandestine premises was the direct responsibility of the operational department using them.[64]

The keeper of the clandestine premises was likely to be (as in the case of the Liao River Bookshop) a public security officer working undercover; this was not a firm rule, however. In any case, he or she, the CMPS insisted, had to be a very trustworthy individual who had passed a stringent background check. Since the cover under which the premises were used had to withstand outside scrutiny, this meant that the person in charge of the premises had to sever all *public* links with the public security organs. The Yingkou "shopkeeper" recalled how "discipline was very strict and we were not allowed to have any [overt] contact with people from the Bureau [of Public Security]." Deemed of paramount importance, secrecy was also strictly enforced when using public telephone lines in and out of the premises. When an agent arrived at the premises for a meeting, "I would phone and, using a code name, notify Director of Public Security Wang Lie, his deputy Ma Hongquan, or the head of the Political Protection Section to come in secret to the bookshop to meet up with the agent."[65]

The covers under which clandestine premises were kept ranged from the simple and straightforward to the complex and elaborate. The daughter of a member of the CCP underground prior to 1949 – a man whose public persona in the 1950s was that of a registered and ostensibly reformed Guomindang counterrevolutionary *tewu*, but who was actually an undeclared member of the CCP – recalled decades later the clandestine premises managed by her father in which she herself spent her childhood:

In accordance with the needs of the class struggle at the time, the party organization decided – and the public security organs put up the money – to build a large shop on Xinhua Street, right in the busiest section of downtown Xinxiang [in Henan]. They named it the Progress Sports Equipment Emporium and put my father in charge: he became known as the "shopkeeper." That shop became one of our party's clandestine operational premises. Later the public security organs built our family a tile-roofed house with five rooms and a big courtyard on Xinle Street, on the very site where [my parents] had once managed an underground intelligence forwarding station. Facing the street, under a huge archway, were a pair of large black doors, with identical large copper rings on them. The house stood in striking contrast to the other houses on the street, all of which at the time were low, dark, and dilapidated. From the looks of it, ours was the home of quite a wealthy family. Those who asked were told that a capitalist had built the house with money he had himself earned. In actuality, it was from here that our public security organs conducted their covert work. Our whole family lived in this big courtyard, and we served as crucial cover for my father and mother and their comrades-in-arms who, in this way, were able to continue to lay low and operate clandestinely. After having served as an underground intelligence forwarding station for the party prior to the founding of the PRC, our family home continued after the founding of the PRC to serve the party as clandestine operational premises.[66]

Not all ex-*tewu* who had been undeclared members of the CCP continued to serve under such relatively comfortable cover as this girl's father after 1949. In Zhengzhou, some 80 kilometers to the south of Xinxiang, it is recorded how a former CCP penetration agent in the Guomindang Central Statistics Bureau had wanted to "come out" when the PLA assumed control of Henan, but that he was ordered to continue serving undercover. With a deputy director of the provincial Bureau of Public Security's 1st Office serving as his handler, he was first given the rather humble cover of an itinerant peddler in very modest circumstances, then in 1954 had his cover (and position) changed to that of a clerk in a downtown hotel. Whether that hotel was itself a clandestine premise is not known, but it appears likely.[67]

One important region of China where clandestine premises were set up as part of a broader strategy immediately after the establishment of the PRC was the uniquely difficult terrain (in every respect, physical as well as political) of western Sichuan and (prior to 1955) Xikang province. On the strategically important road from Chengdu via Ya'an and Kangding to Chamdo and, ultimately, Tibet, the priority location for such premises was in the vicinity of major bridges (likely targets of sabotage by enemies of the new regime). In late 1954, the provincial Bureau of Public Security reported to the CMPS that it was looking toward "further consolidating" such already existing "protection premises" in Ya'an and Feixianguan, as well as establishing an additional four in the counties traversed by the road. In the by comparison large municipality of Kangding,

[66] Qi Baozhu, "Fuqin de 'qianfu' shengya" (My Father's Career "Under Deep Cover"), Zhongguo jingcha wang, http://www.cpd.com.cn/gb/newspaper/2010-01/19/content_1274057.htm (accessed January 18, 2011).
[67] *Zuojia wenzhai* (*Writer's Digest*), No. 1413, March 1, 2011.

additional clandestine premises were to be set up specifically for purposes of liaison between operational officers and special case agents engaged in neutralizing "enemy operatives."[68]

One set of clandestine premises on the border with Tibet came to be widely known to the public when a fictionalized drama of an operation led by a young public security officer and a contingent of "turned" former Guomindang *tewu* was broadcast on national television in 2008. A brief history of the real – as opposed to fictional – Station 208 located in the Ngawa region, on the northern route west out of Chengdu, also appeared in Chinese newspapers at the time of the broadcast:

When New China had only just been established, the total number of people living in Zagunao was less than a thousand. They included Tibetans, Qiang, Hui, and Han Chinese. In the interior, with a population of that size, it would have amounted to no more than a small village, but in the sparsely populated Ngawa region, Zagunao counted as a bustling town. In late July 1951, an itinerant Han peddler purchased a three-room Qiang-style stone house here, located on a hillside east of town, and hired some Qiang carpenters to spruce it up like new. The peddler was really acting on behalf of someone else, a business proprietor preparing to set up shop in Zagunao. In mid-August that year, a young Han business proprietor arrived in Zagunao, leading a trade caravan of more than a dozen people. The many bundles of merchandise that they and their Yaks had been carrying were offloaded and stored in the stone house. Salt, tea bricks, odds and ends needed for sowing, and all kinds of merchandise that would sell really well in the Tibetan community were stored in two rooms set aside to become a shop, while the third room was to serve as a doctor's consultancy and lodgings. From the eaves of the house, a white cotton banner with the words "Liyuan Traders" in Chinese and Tibetan was suspended. The proprietor of Liyuan Traders was the Head of Station of "Intelligence Station 208" Li Shoufu, and the people in the caravan were his station staff. Liyuan Traders became the very first intelligence station that Li Shoufu and his reconnaissance squad established upon entering the Ngawa region. It also became the hub of a "208" intelligence network, the collection points of which could be found all across the snow-covered mountains and grasslands.[69]

Although Liyuan Traders was designed simply to serve as a front, it sold much sought-after merchandise at a good price and did brisk business among the Tibetan community. Within months of opening, Station 208 had more or less managed to recover the money spent on purchasing the

---

[68] Xikang sheng gonganting, "Guanyu guanche di liu ci quanguo gongan huiyi jueyi jia-qiang jingji baowei gongzuo de jihua" (Plan for the Implementation of the Resolution of the 6th National Public Security Conference and Strengthening Economic Protection Work), *Gongan jianshe*, No. 111, December 20, 1954, pp. 6–7.

[69] "Jiemi mimi qingbaozhan '208'."

premises. Furthermore, Liyuan Traders not only provided the intelligence operatives with means to live, but the profit alone sustained the entire operation of the station.[70]

Undoubtedly one of the bolder stratagems involving the use of clandestine premises for operational needs was that of actually running them for an unsuspecting hostile intelligence service. In order to exercise "tight control of the rendezvous between our agent and the enemy's couriers," the national task force that ran the Class A Case No. 12, the massive CMPS operation against Guomindang railroad saboteurs fielded from Hong Kong, in early 1954 – after having, in a spectacular example of the "arts of deception," sought and received the go-ahead as well as funding from an unsuspecting enemy – established clandestine commercial premises in downtown Tianjin specifically for use by the Guomindang Central Committee Group Two Mainland Railroad Work Group! The liaison premises, which to the unsuspecting eye looked like an ordinary private nickel and dime store, were managed for three years by one of the task force's principal agents (the mistress of the "bandit G" mentioned in Chapter 3) and an undercover operational officer before being shut down. Here they regularly intercepted Guomindang intelligence requirements and other communications by mail or courier (coopted sailors on shore leave) as well as operational funds in the form of bank transfers from the Guomindang in Hong Kong.[71] In the late 1960s, after Xie Fuzhi's order in 1967 to suspend the use of agents and safe houses nationwide, it was denied that these particular premises had ever deceived the Guomindang. It was alleged, to the contrary, that they had been part of an attempt by high-level CCP "traitors, *tewu,* counterrevolutionary revisionist and alien-class elements" to "aid and abet the enemy, look after the enemy, and let the enemy get away."[72]

Using Secret Rendezvous Premises

The CMPS had by the mid-1950s already begun to caution lower-level public security organs against allowing operational departments to proceed with the unchecked establishment of large numbers of clandestine premises. The CMPS did not, however, have the same reservations about

---

[70] Ibid.

[71] "Shier hao zhuan'an huibao tigang," pp. 9, 21–22.

[72] Yi chu junguan xiaozu 12 hao an zhuan'anzu, "Guanyu chongxin shencha di 12 hao an gongzuo baogao" (Report on the Reexamination of Case No. 12), [November 30, 1968], pp. 3, 10.

secret rendezvous premises. These could by comparison be opened and
shut down with relative ease, and at the Central People's Public Security
Academy in 1957, officer cadets were specifically encouraged to make
more use of them.[73]

Similar to the KGB, the CMPS defined secret rendezvous premises
as private residential (occasionally official) premises that did not actually belong to the public security organs, but were used through special
arrangement with the proprietor for clandestine meetings between operational officers and agents.[74] When the rendezvous premises were a private
residence, the proprietor would normally be a Communist Party or Youth
League member or a "trustworthy member of the masses or agent" who –
like a manager of clandestine premises actually belonging to the public
security organs – had passed a stringent background check. In the winter
of 1954, the most senior public security officer overseeing operations in
county seats and harbors along the South China coast favored using the
residential premises of "basic masses," descendants of martyrs, or "reliable relatives or friends of agents."[75] One 1955 operational document
from Chongqing on how to direct and exploit agents referred specifically
to deactivated former agents (assuming they could be trusted politically)
as suitable proprietors for premises where "liaising undercover" was to
take place.[76] According to the *Lectures*, furthermore, the ideal proprietor
was also someone "who has few family members and who can keep a
secret."[77] For classificatory purposes, neither the KGB nor the CMPS considered "keeper of rendezvous premises" (*Soderzhatel yavochnoy kvartiry*
in Russian, *jietou judian de fangzhu* in Chinese) to constitute an agent
category in itself. Whereas in English one might have expected to come
across a term such as "facilities agent," the reference in the *Lectures* was
simply to that of "proprietor" (*fangzhu*).[78]

The boldness and ingenuity with which CCP operatives serving on the
covert front had set up and maintained secret rendezvous premises in
hostile territory prior to 1949 was the stuff of lore in intelligence circles.
Yang Zhihuai – one-time member of the CCP underground in Northeast
China and, by the time he retired in 1982, chief editor of *People's Public
Security* – wrote decades later of how in "Manchukuo" close to the end of
World War II, a network of agents and officers ultimately reporting to the

[73] "*Teqing gongzuo*," p. 70.
[74] *KGB Lexicon*, p. 224; "*Teqing gongzuo*," p. 69.
[75] Wen Minsheng, "Dali jiaqiang yinbi douzheng," p. 6.
[76] Chongqing shi gonganju, "Guanyu jinian lai teqing," p. 14.
[77] "*Teqing gongzuo*," p. 69.
[78] Ibid.; *KGB Lexicon*, pp. 224, 378.

CCP Jin-Cha-Ji Social Affairs Department had set up one of their safest and best meeting points in the official residence of the prime minister of the Japanese puppet government, Zhang Jinghui. Zhang's son had been induced by a relative to join and support the Communist cause and "quickly grew to be an ideal underground operative." In his home, officers and agents "met and exchanged intelligence in the safest of all possible surroundings. It served us excellently in our work."[79]

In what would have been a setting significantly less hostile than that of "Manchukuo," public security operational officers were after 1949 expected to negotiate with the proprietor (who would have been sworn to secrecy, including on behalf of all adult members of his or her household) a contract of sorts that guaranteed unobstructed and exclusive public security access "for work purposes" to one or a couple of rooms on certain dates for a certain duration. As part of the contract, the proprietor would be provided with an appropriate cover story to use if and when other persons (including, presumably, any children that the proprietor might have) asked questions.[80] If commercial (rather than private residential) premises were to serve the needs of operational officers for a certain duration, the practical arrangement between the public security organs and the proprietor may well have resembled the contract between the CCP Center and the Beijing municipal government drawn up in 1955 to regulate the operation of the Beijing Hotel. At the time, the hotel (and its car pool, predecessor of one of the capital's two big state-run taxi firms, the Shou Qi Group) already employed on a permanent basis many ex-members of the ad hoc contingent of plainclothes officers established to provide security during the celebrations in Tiananmen Square on October 1, 1949.[81] Although it was supposed to operate primarily as a competitive business enterprise, it was also tasked with arranging banquets, accommodation, and other services for the State Council and CCP Center. On this last point, the contract stated explicitly that "when a contradiction arises between the operation [of the hotel] as a business, and the fulfillment of a political task, [the hotel management] is to prioritize the political task."[82]

---

[79] Zhu Chunlin, *Lishi shunjian I*, p. 211.

[80] "*Teqing gongzuo*," pp. 69–70.

[81] Wang Fan and Dong Ping, *Lingxiu shenbian teshu weidui* (*The Leadership's Special Bodyguard*) (Beijing: Zhongguo wenshi chubanshe, 2009), p. 281.

[82] *Guowuyuan jiguan shiwu guanliju dashiji 1950–1995* (*Record of Major Events in the State Council Department of Administraive Affairs 1950–1995*) (Beijing: Guowuyuan bangongting mishuju, 1995), p. 97.

Like clandestine premises, secret rendezvous premises could only be established and operated with the express permission of the head of the public security organ involved. A written report from the operational department requesting permission to go ahead had inter alia to spell out the following points:

- the rationale for utilization of the secret rendezvous premises: why were they needed?;
- their exact physical location;
- the background and circumstances of the proprietor (and family members) to whom the premises to be utilized belonged.[83]

Additionally, the CMPS called for the inclusion, with the report, of an appendix that documented the background check made on the proprietor and his family members. Once new secret rendezvous premises had been registered, they would become the subject of a running file in which all relevant information pertaining to them and their utilization would be recorded and preserved.[84] The CMPS on the whole favored changing premises at regular intervals, since prolonged use was seen as increasing the risk of their being compromised.

Coded Conversations

Public security officers and their agents were expected by the CMPS to manage their contacts in Tianjin or Guangzhou with the same attention to secrecy as in a foreign hostile setting such as Tokyo or Geneva. For obvious reasons, the ministry viewed the direct face-to-face meeting between handler and agent as the ideal form of contact. Only when such a meeting proved impossible were other agent communications channels to be employed. Alternative "ordinary and commonly used means of contact" approved by the CMPS included coded telephone conversations and the use of clandestine postal addresses.[85]

In the early 1950s, China's telephone network was still deemed to be highly insecure. To err on the side of caution, senior operational officers stressed, telephones were only to be used as a last resort and always under the assumption that an unauthorized party might be listening in.[86]

---

[83] Cf. "*Teqing gongzuo*," p. 70.
[84] Ibid.
[85] Ibid., pp. 65, 67–68.
[86] Wang Lin, "Zai huiyi shang," p. 36.

A survey conducted in late 1954 in Jiangsu province by the provincial Bureau of Public Security found that the situation was "extremely serious" and that curious telephone operators often eavesdropped on confidential conversations between public security officers. In one prefecture, the survey found operators specifically and systematically listening in on officers talking about military operations conducted by the Guomindang and the defensive measures taken by the PLA in response.[87] The security of the public telephone network began to improve in 1954 when, having been ordered to do so by the CCP Center the year before, the CMPS and the Ministry of Posts and Telecommunications took a joint decision to invest more funds and personnel in its protection.[88] This would have been of particular concern in the critically important provinces and large cities on the Eastern China seaboard, where between 70 and 90 percent of the staff in the post and telecommunications sector were at the time still holdovers from the "old society" and, thus, susceptible to Guomindang penetration.[89] An investigation conducted by the CMPS found that in those parts of China where CCP control had been established fairly early, 7.5 percent of the staff still posed a likely security risk and needed to be reassigned to jobs elsewhere. The corresponding figure for staff in those parts of China that had been "liberated" later on was 11.3 percent.[90]

Little substantial information is available on the operational aspects of officer–agent communication using telephones. Almost nothing is known about the actual telephone numbers that agents were given to call from which it would be possible to trace the receivers. If operational departments copied the practice of the KGB, they are likely to have belonged to so-called keepers of clandestine telephones. These were "persons who have personal access to a telephone, and who spend a large part of their time at home, because of the state of their health, age or other reasons." Basically, the person answering the clandestine telephone would serve as an intermediary, helping to establish urgent contact or pass on a message in case of an emergency. Agents were not to disclose their identity to him or her but only give their aliases.[91]

---

[87] Jiangsu sheng gonganting, "Guanyu gongkuang qiye neibu diqing zonghe baogao" (Comprehensive Report on the Threat Level in Factories, Mines, and Corporations), *Gongan jianshe*, No. 111, December 20, 1954, p. 14.

[88] *Deng Xiaoping nianpu 1904–1974*, Vol. 2, pp. 1114–15; *Jianguo yilai gongan*, p. 67.

[89] Huadong ganganju. "Guanyu zai Huadong qu qingli youdian xitong yaohai renyuan de qingkuang baogao" (Situation Report on the Weeding Out of Critically Positioned Persons in the Post and Telecommunications Sector in East China) [June 1954], *Gongan jianshe hedingben*, p. 31.

[90] Zhongyang ganganbu, "Guanyu quanguo youdian xitong," p. 26.

[91] *KGB Lexicon*, p. 393.

Telephone directories in Mao's China were regarded as for official use only. When a copy was found to have fallen into the wrong hands, the matter was serious enough to be noted in the public security sector's internal communications. In April 1960, the CMPS revealed in *Public Security Intelligence* that an American news agency in Hong Kong had managed to obtain a Guangzhou telephone directory.[92] In November 1960, it reported that "American and Chiang Kai-shek spies" had recently "once more" been able to get hold of an unspecified PRC telephone directory.[93] What the system of telephone numbers in a large city looked like at the time may be gleaned in part from the last edition of the directory for Beijing to appear prior to the Cultural Revolution. At the time, telephone numbers in the capital consisted of six (occasionally five) digits, of which the first two identified the exchange and the probable part of the city in which a subscriber was located. For example, numbers beginning with 66 indicated a subscriber in the western part of central Beijing, numbers beginning with 75 one in the Chongwen district, and so on. (The two numbers to the switchboard of the municipal Bureau of Public Security, located in central Beijing, were 55 41 20 and 55 28 40.) The telephone directory revealed that the city had thirteen automatic urban telephone exchanges and an additional seven semiautomatic rural ones.[94] There was also, in addition to these, one exchange the existence of which was not revealed in the telephone directory, but which all resident foreigners knew, because it was the one that handled all calls to and from foreign embassies and residences (the numbers of which all began with 52). Finally, there was the secret Exchange No. 39, which handled calls going into and out of Zhongnanhai and to and from members of the senior leadership. By 1967, a handful of telephone numbers in the 39 00 00 series had been revealed to Red Guard and "rebel" leaders on a need-to-know basis, among them the ones manned by Premier Zhou Enlai's personal liaison officers. And so it is that historians now know that one way of reporting something of political import directly to the staff of the nation's most senior leaders was by dialing 39 61 94, or 39 67 38, or 39 66 10, or 39 26 00.[95]

---

[92] "Lingxun" (Miscellaneous News), *Gongan qingbao*, No. 46, April 29, 1960, p. 4.

[93] "Mei-Jiang tewu zai Gang you neng shougou dao wo difang baokan" (American and Chiang Kai-shek *Tewu* Are Again Able to Obtain Our Local Newspapers in Hong Kong), *Gongan qingbao*, No. 108, November 9, 1960, p. 5.

[94] Beijing shi shinei dianhuaju, ed., *Bufen dianhua haoma 1967* (*Beijing Telephone Directory 1967*) (Beijing, 1967).

[95] Xiang Yang, work diary [June 25, 1967–August 29, 1968], last page.

The prearranged codes employed by agents and handlers when speaking over the phone may, depending on the circumstances, have ranged in complexity from the relatively transparent to the highly sophisticated and innovative – again, close to nothing of substance is known about the subject. When ordinary Chinese were discovered to be communicating in code over the telephone, it was viewed with great suspicion by the authorities.[96] Prior to 1949, CCP members operating underground are known to have told each other "brother deceased" or "father's funeral" to signal that a meeting was off or had to be aborted. Conversely, "is well again and has checked out of the hospital" or "injury now healed" meant that somebody's release from prison had been secured.[97] Whether or not the users of code after 1949 drew inspiration from CCP history and communicated in a similar manner is not known.

Secret Writing

Clandestine postal addresses were used for communication far more frequently than the telephone. The KGB defined such an address as a "clandestine handover point to which an intelligence or counterintelligence agent sends information by post...using ciphers, prearranged signals, secret writing or microphotography." The CMPS *Lectures*, using similar language, described it as an "address to which one or more agents send letters or reports in which they, using agreed-upon codes, report on the progress of their assignments to operational officers." Whereas the KGB noted that an "operational officer may also use a clandestine address to pass his instructions and operational material to the agent," the *Lectures* stated in nearly identical terms that an "operational officer may also in the name of the keeper of the clandestine address use it to send his instructions to the agent, using a code or secret writing."[98]

The first set of what were quite simple procedures for managing secret writing, at a time when the CCP's "domestic working conditions" had

---

[96] Compare Zhou Enlai's and Kang Sheng's warnings to Red Guards in Jiangsu sheng shengji jiguan geming zaofanpai dalianhe zongbu, ed., *Mao zhuxi dang zhongyang ji zhongyang shouzhang guanyu Jiangsu wuchanjieji wenhua dageming de zhongyao zhishi huibian* (*Collected Instructions from Chairman Mao, the Party Center, and Central Leaders Concerning the Great Proletarian Cultural Revolution in Jiangsu*) (Nanjing, 1968), p. 119.

[97] Fei Yundong, *Zhonggong dang'an wenxian zhengji* (*Collecting CCP Historical Archive Material*) (Beijing: Zhongguo dang'an chubanshe, 2004), pp. 96–97, 130.

[98] *KGB Lexicon*, p. 164; "*Teqing gongzuo*," p. 67.

been radically different, were spelled out as far back as December 1928 in a special notification from the Party Center to provincial-level leaders. Entitled "On Technical Aspects of Document Work," it spoke of secret writing as a "means of struggle" and favored strict regulation of the use of secret inks.[99] A one-time member of the Central Special Services Section recalled well over half a century later how "at the time, we all wrote between the lines of an [ordinary] letter using either chemical ink or rice gruel, and the recipient would then heat it up which made the secret writing visible."[100] The notification ruled that communications in secret writing had to be preceded, accompanied, or followed by a so-called bill (*fapiao*) on which the person issuing the communication indicated to the recipient which specific procedure, out of a number of different alternatives, was to be employed to make it legible. When a separate bill could not be issued, the same indication could assume the form of a coded signal on the document itself, for example three dots (...) or three zeros (000), which indicated to the recipient by which means the writing would be rendered visible. The notification also explained that sometimes "ordinary family letters" might be the safest means of sending a message, and that in such cases certain coded words had to be used to let the recipient know that what seemed an ordinary letter was in fact something more significant. *A Brief History of CCP Confidential Work* explains how an extra graphic element like *shi*, *mu*, or *shan* – "stone," "wood," or "mountain" – might be added to a character on the envelope. This signaled to the recipient that secret writing was present and which chemical could be used to make it legible.[101] The *Lectures* reminded officer cadets to devise *in advance* a suitable cover under which the agent would be sending and receiving letters from the clandestine address. On the off chance that he or she was asked, the agent had to give convincing answers concerning whom he or she was communicating with and why.[102]

Many of the simple but effective techniques used by the CCP in the early days probably remained in use after 1949. The Guomindang, for its part, certainly continued to use such techniques well into the 1960s. In 1963, for example, the CMPS knew the code contained in letters between the Guomindang Central Committee Group Two Mainland

---

[99] Fei Yundong, *Zhonggong dang'an*, pp. 92–93.
[100] Mu Xin, *Yinbi zhanxian tongshuai*, p. 135.
[101] Fei Yundong, *Zhonggong dang'an*, p. 93.
[102] "*Teqing gongzuo*," p. 67.

Railroad Work Group in Hong Kong and the group's assets in the PRC: the words "commerce" or "business" meant intelligence work; "brother" or "sister" was used to indicate the gender of a contact; age was used to refer to something in percentage terms; reference to a person being "in the hospital" meant that he or she had been arrested; and "cousin" meant a superior intelligence officer. Ways of concealing secret messages in a letter included reading only the fourth character on the third line, the fifth character on the fourth line, and so on. The various chemical or other secret inks in use were well known to the CMPS, as were the specific techniques used to make text written with them legible. Also known was how to decipher the Guomindang's transposition ciphers, created by offsetting the numbers in the ordinary Chinese numeric telegraph code by a number (between 1 and 9) indicated by the date of the month in which a message was sent.[103]

Gadgets and Gizmos: Covert Technologies

Operational work in Mao's China remained for many years decidedly low-tech, and tradecraft was almost entirely a matter of perfecting the same human skills that an officer or agent might have had to rely on in a premodern context. Especially outside of Beijing, the use of technology could be particularly haphazard. In its report to the CMPS 2nd Bureau on experiences gained in the course of cracking a case of suspected counterrevolutionary activity in the Anshan Steel Corporation, the Anshan municipal Bureau of Public Security wrote of how "in November 1956, we thought of a way of installing (without his knowledge) recording equipment in the agent's home." At the critical moment when the equipment was to be used to record the agent's conversation with an operational target, "because of a technical malfunction, it proved almost entirely impossible to hear what [the agent and the operational target] were saying to each other." It was only when, in January 1957, the location at which the agent was to meet with the target changed to Beijing that the Anshan officers were able to call on their better-equipped colleagues in the capital to come to their assistance. "We first dispatched people to Beijing to liaise," the bureau report explained, "and then were able under the direction of the 2nd Bureau of the Ministry of Public Security and in close cooperation with the protection section of the Beijing [Ferrous Metallurgy] General Design Institute to install recording equipment in the

[103] "Shier hao zhuan'an huibao tigang," pp. 10–12.

XX Hotel." This time the apparatus worked as intended, and "there was a perfect match between what the agent reported and what our recording showed."[104]

In the winter of 1953–54, a number of experts on technical operations from the Soviet Union arrived in China. Hosted by the CMPS, over the next couple of years they shared with their Chinese counterparts the "basics of modern operational science and technology."[105] The first significant attempts to improve technical operational capabilities prioritized selected key cities rather than represented a nationwide effort.[106] The resources of the Beijing municipal Bureau of Public Security were bolstered in December 1954, giving a significant boost to technical operations in the national capital.[107] In November 1955, the CMPS set up a Technical Operations Bureau to manage and oversee the same kind of work nationally. The bureau was for many years headed by Di Fei, who, prior to joining the ministry, had been in charge of operational work (including technical operations) within the Beijing Bureau of Public Security. The CMPS prioritized the training of officers in all aspects of the new technical equipment as it became available in cities across the country. In Liaoning province, home to numerous key defense industry research institutes and plants built with Soviet assistance, the provincial public security work plan for 1957 listed Shenyang, Lüshun (Dalian), Anshan, and Fushun as cities where "there will be a gradual further buildup of technical surveillance in order to raise combat ability to fight hidden enemies."[108]

Planning documents indicate that the fields of science and technology were always high on the CMPS agenda. The ministry plan for 1958 called specifically for more resources to be channeled into the development of instruments used in technical operations and projected how, by the end of the year,

in seven large key municipalities, the full range of technical surveillance instruments should be in place and up and running. In other municipalities, in accordance with the principles of necessity and capability, there is to be a step-by-step buildup of one or more new technical surveillance instruments. There is to be a

---

[104] Anshan shi gonganju, "Zhenpo 'Zhongguo guomindang,'" pp. 13–14. The CMPS 2nd Bureau here refers to the Bureau for Operations Against Guomindang *Tewu*. See Chapter 1.
[105] Sun Mingshan, *Lishi shunjian IV*, pp. 91–92.
[106] "Di ba ci quanguo gongan huiyi guanyu 1956 nian," p. 9.
[107] Zhu Zhencai, *Jianguo chuqi Beijing*, p. 350.
[108] Liaoning sheng gonganting dangzu, "Guanyu 1956 nian quansheng," p. 10.

focused improvement of the technical equipment employed in physical surveillance and a correct implementation of the principle of key-point examination of postal communications. Research into technical aspects of postal examination is to be strengthened and technical surveillance is to be aggressively utilized in the struggle against the enemy.[109]

The 1st National Conference on Technical Operations, convened in the final week of March 1958, drew up a five-year plan for long-term capacity building to cope with the "situation on the covert front."[110] In 1962, Di Fei's Technical Operations Bureau was able to report to the CMPS that a new electronics factory (No. 811, built on the basis of a KGB blueprint) operating on a trial basis since 1958 was finally able to produce "an already basically complete line of products."[111] How to deploy such products on the covert front is likely to have been debated at a later National Conference on Technical Operations that met in 1963.[112]

In the Soviet Union, the KGB's use of "technical operations measures" meant in essence the covert installation and use of audio or optical facilities, for example listening devices or cameras.[113] The CMPS, for its part, was in the 1950s particularly worried by its own lack of – and clearly wanted to be able to acquire for operational purposes – what the KGB called "operational sound recording" equipment such as miniaturized bugging equipment.[114] Half a century later, a former CMPS confidential secretary recalled how

[i]n the cold war decade of the 1950s, the media reported that the two superpowers were both accusing each other of bugging each other's embassies. In order to make sure that our own embassies abroad were not being bugged, the Ministry of Foreign Affairs asked the Ministry of Public Security to send specialists to some of our embassies in the West to carry out a security examination. As expected, they found bugging devices that had been planted there. When the specialists returned and in the course of reporting back to Vice-Minister [of Public Security] Xu [Zirong] displayed the bugs, it was the first time that I myself saw these "little gadgets." We were told they had been placed in ceilings, desks, legs of chairs, in

---

[109] Zhongyang gonganbu, "1958 nian quanguo gongan," p. 4.

[110] *Jianguo yilai gongan*, p. 148.

[111] Zhang Zhaojin and Ding Zhaojia, "Guanyu yuan 811 chang jianchang chuqi bufen qingkuang de huiyi" (Recalling the Early Years of Factory 811), Feiyang junshi blog, August 8, 2007, http://www.fyjs.cn/ bbs/read.php?tid=1050200 (accessed January 18, 2011).

[112] Yu Jianping et al., eds., *Jianguo yilai fazhi jianshe jishi* (*Record of Events in Legal System Building since the Founding of the Nation*) (Shijiazhuang: Hebei renmin chubanshe, 1986), p. 169.

[113] *KGB Lexicon*, pp. 250–51, 278–79.

[114] Ibid., p. 274.

concrete beams and pillars, even, and that they included wire- as well as wireless-controlled ones. Even so, no matter how much effort had gone into concealing them, we had all the same been able to find and remove them.[115]

Despite this discovery, a PLA source from the end of the cold war notes that "between 1960 and 1978, in our embassies abroad, significant numbers of surreptitious listening and optical recording equipment were uncovered."[116] This indicates that concealed listening devices often went undetected despite the best efforts of "bug-sweeping" officers to find them.

While the CMPS, due to financial constraints, may have been unable to provide its own operatives on the covert front with much sophisticated gadgetry or equipment to enhance offensive capabilities, the ministry from the outset made sure, at the very least, to keep a careful eye on the kind of sophisticated equipment deployed by its enemies. It regularly collected and disseminated to those officers with a need to know information from open sources about the latest gadgets and gizmos being developed and used by enemies. A case in point was an article in the CMPS journal *People's Public Security* on June 12, 1957, which briefed Chinese public security officers nationwide on the range of electronic eavesdropping devices currently being used by so-called American *tewu* organs:

The American weekly *Time* recently reported as follows: today, in many large companies and plants, American *tewu* organs already employ a variety of electronic eavesdropping devices to listen in on what employees and workers are saying in rest rooms, dining rooms, and elsewhere.

It is said that if you have a conversation in an ordinary room, there are small microphones that will pick up what you say and carry it – either through hairlike wires or radio transmitters – to a person listening in the next room or two blocks away. A tiny and effective pocket microphone and recorder unit can be operated undetected in any ordinary briefcase planted in a conference room, and is able to record what is said for five hours without interruption.

If you want to listen in on people's muted conversations, then you can employ a so-called wireless microphone packed into a transmitter smaller than a pack of cigarettes and so sensitive [that] it can pick up whispers in an average room and transmit them by radio to a receiver hundreds of yards [*jibai ma*] away. The equipment works continuously for up to four days.

Perhaps you think that if a conversation takes place in a car then everything will be fine. Not so: a wireless unit can be hidden in the car to pick up passenger

[115] Sun Mingshan, *Lishi shunjian III*, p. 407.
[116] Xue Guozheng and Jing Yongsheng, *Fangjian baomi*, p. 87.

conversation as well as record and transmit signals reporting the starts, stops, and changes of direction to another car following behind.

Then there is the microphone that resembles a "shotgun." From several hundred yards away, carefully aimed at the target, it is able to pick up even a whispered conversation. This kind of a microphone is very effective when it comes to eavesdropping on conversations in a nearby house, a skyscraper across the street, or a boat on a lake.[117]

The *People's Public Security* piece was an almost word-for-word translation of a brief report entitled "Manners & Morals: Who's Listening?" that had appeared in *Time* magazine three weeks previously.[118] Nothing is known about whether the CMPS managed to actually obtain any of the more sophisticated commercially available American gadgetry specifically mentioned in the article, only that similar items were indeed successfully acquired from some foreign manufacturers. Illustrating this is an incident in 1967, when a group of Red Guards from Beijing's most prestigious science and technology university discovered that a competing Red Guard group had planted a surreptitious listening device on their campus. Showing the device to Kang Sheng, saying, "We're not sure, but we think it could be U.S.-made," they received the following response by the one-time head of the CSAD: "No. It might be Japanese though."[119]

Corruption and Complaints

In the early 1960s, the balance in domestic operational work between "Moscow tradecraft and [the CCP's] own inventiveness" gradually shifted from learning from the Soviet Union to a greater emphasis on developing China's own experiences (including insights and modes of operation that predated the modern era) as well as learning from foreign (nonsocialist) countries more broadly – the latter an implicit admission of the limitations inherent in looking only to Moscow. The shift generated mixed results: any *negative* impact it may have had was insignificant compared to the suspension of all forms of regular tradecraft vocational

---

[117] "Meiguo tewu jiguan yong dianzi toutingqi lai kongzhi renmin" (American *Tewu* Organs Employ Electronic Eavesdropping Devices to Control the People), *Renmin gongan*, No. 22, June 12, 1957, p. 17.

[118] *Time* magazine, May 20, 1957. The only important parts of the report not translated in *People's Public Security* were contextualizing paragraphs in which the readers of *Time* had been given the source of the information, a U.S. Senate Judiciary Committee report based largely on testimony from private investigators and equipment manufacturers.

[119] *Jinggangshan bao* (*Jinggangshan Report*), No. 25, April 5, 1968.

training after 1966. Where serious problems in applied tradecraft emerged, but on a timetable that had nothing to do with the deterioration of Sino–Soviet relations or the onslaught of the Cultural Revolution, was in the twin sectors of running clandestine premises and utilizing the latest material technical resources.

Irregularities plagued the way clandestine premises were used from the outset, and the Three-Anti and Five-Anti campaigns saw the CMPS order a compulsory overhaul of them nationwide during the third quarter of 1952.[120] By the early 1960s, they had long since been identified as a major problem by the CMPS leadership, and the extent to which their management and utilization had become riddled with corruption was exposed in the course of the Socialist Education Movement and debated at a six-week-long National Conference on Political Protection Work in late 1964. The draft minutes of the conference circulated by the CMPS on January 28, 1965, noted the need to "separate the management from the utilization of clandestine premises" and affirmed a ban on the operation of such premises for profit and economic gain in the trade or services sector. They were *not* to be used as "guest houses or rest homes," the minutes stressed, or indeed as a cozy retreat for a young officer and his bride on their honeymoon, as the minutes could have added by citing a Guangzhou Bureau of Public Security report.[121] A CMPS *Notification* revealed that

[q]uite a few [clandestine premises] are *not* being run for work purposes, but for the sake of profiting and making money. They're "accessible through the back door" and [those who run them] maintain all kinds of privileges, take more than their fair share, feather their nests at the public's expense, even running illegal money-making operations, evading taxes, practicing graft and embezzlement, speculating, and profiteering. They're being operated by some to employ friends, or even make indiscriminate use of bad people, or to shield or connive with counterrevolutionary and bad elements. In this way, not only are our secrets compromised and our cadres corrupted, but we become divorced from the masses, which has a negative impact.[122]

It was imperative, the CMPS pointed out, that a thorough review and rectification of the use of clandestine premises nationwide be carried

---

[120] Zhongyang gonganbu, "Liuyue zhi jiuyuefen gongzuo buzhi baogao," p. 3.
[121] Jianguo yilai gongan, p. 280; Guangzhou shi gonganju, "Guanyu XXX panbian toudi qingkuang baogao" (Situation Report on the Defection of XXX), *Gongan jianshe*, No. 236, May 8, 1958, p. 4.
[122] *Jianguo yilai gongan*, p. 278.

out. In particular, the practice of utilizing them for all kinds of money-generating extrabudgetary schemes rather than as intended for operational purposes was to be clamped down with impunity.[123] There is little reason to doubt that Xie Fuzhi's 1967 order to simply decommission all safe houses was a reaction to problems that had been simmering for some time.

Secondly, the domestic use of the technical equipment that the CMPS desperately craved, most notably surveillance equipment including cameras and surreptitious listening devices, also caused a multitude of problems. Showing themselves to be (unknowingly, no doubt) adherents of what a junior British diplomat in Beijing at the time dubbed the First Law of Diplomacy (which states that "It is not the other side you need to worry about, but your own"[124]), senior officers increasingly employed such equipment in security operations targeting their own subordinates rather than in operations against Guomindang, "imperialist," or Soviet "revisionist" *tewu*. Because these operations, carried out by internal Political Departments, involved intrusive surveillance of "our own people," they generated intense resentment among officers and others who insisted that they were being unfairly targeted – being listened to or spied upon in secret. "When one man is out there executing a task," they complained, "a second man with a camera will be trailing him, taking pictures of every move he makes in order to 'see what he is up to.'"[125] In Shanghai, officers unprepared to accept this new modus operandi complained about the elevation of surveillance technology use to a level higher than that of politics and traditional Maoist means of dealing with possible "internal contradictions."[126] In Beijing, the CCP Chairman himself would have probably lent a sympathetic ear to the complaints of officers: in 1967, the leadership of the CMPS Technical Operations Bureau was accused by Cultural Revolutionary rivals of having used "investigating technical surveillance matters" and a test of listening devices in the Beijing Hotel in 1961 as a cover for surreptitiously positioning bugs in proximity to

[123] Ibid.
[124] Sir Percy Craddock, quoted in J. E. Hoare, *Embassies in the East: The Story of the British and Their Embassies in China, Japan and Korea from 1859 to the Present* (Richmond, VA: Curzon Press, 1999), p. 85.
[125] *Liu Deng Peng Luo zai Shanghai shi gonganju de dailiren*, pp. 14, 26.
[126] *Lin Deming de zuixing* (*Lin Deming's Crimes*) (Shanghai: Shanghai shi gonganju zhian huzheng chu dou-Lin xiaozu, 1967), p. 9.

Mao.[127] When Mao discovered that his flirtations with a young female member of staff had been recorded on tape, he is rumored to have become livid.[128] Like the mismanagement of safe houses, the abuse of sophisticated technical equipment was by the mid-1960s used by critics to paint the darkest picture possible of domestic operational work.

[127] *Gaoju geming de pipan daqi*, p. 15.
[128] MacFarquhar and Schoenhals, *Mao's Last Revolution*, pp. 36–37.

7

Agent Running

Beijing Rules

The CMPS inclined toward a holistic view of agent running. While for didactic purposes it may have been prepared to separate the process into its constituent parts, including direction and control, briefing and debriefing, agent welfare, and so on, in the operational real world these parts were so closely intertwined that it was impractical to isolate them. How well or how badly *any* one part was managed inevitably impacted on the quality of the whole. In this respect, problems on the ground were plentiful. "In some public security sectors," one 1952 report from the Northeast Railroad Public Security Bureau lamented, "not only does the officer in charge of the sector not personally exercise control [of the recruited agents], even his section chiefs show no concern and delegate [the running of] agents to the rank and file, in this way preventing efficient control, utilization, and hence use of agents in the struggle against the enemy."[1] The CMPS leadership expressed its disquiet on innumerable occasions after 1949 concerning how agent running was being managed, pointing out that agents without direction and control were agents in name only.

The situation was undoubtedly better in some sectors than in others, and better in some parts of China than in others. Where it was mismanaged, it may have resembled the state of economic protection in Jiangsu province, where, according to the provincial Bureau of Public Security's self-critical assessment of October 1954, "there are serious deficiencies with respect to the direction of agents and a state of chaos prevails wherein things are just left to drift: in the provincial-level organs in the trade

[1] Dongbei tielu gonganju, "Guanyu liangnian lai," p. 16.

and finance sector, contact has been altogether lost with approximately 60 percent of agents."[2] In one of the province's factories, some twenty agents had been recruited, but more than a year after having agreed to serve and having had their Agent Registration Forms opened, not a single one of them had actually been contacted again, much less been given or executed an actual operational task.[3]

A damning critique of the domestic use of agents in the first seventeen years of the PRC circulating in Shanghai in 1967 showed that officers were under intense pressure to each run a specific quota of agents. In what the critique described as the uncritical adoption lock, stock, and barrel of Soviet practices, the CMPS had – in its 1956 Operational Work Plan to Counter *Tewu* and Spies of the Imperialists and Chiang Kai-shek Bandit Gang – stipulated that operational officers were to each run "at least fifteen agents," and more senior officers were each to run "between three and five high-level agents."[4] Ultimately, fulfilling quotas like these proved impossible if the quality of agent running was to attain and remain at an acceptable level. In the end, some operational officers got around such directives by simply inventing the agents they supposedly ran and notching up their fictional successes. In the winter of 1953–54, the newspaper *Railroad Public Security*, published for official use only by the Bureau of Public Security under the PRC Ministry of Railroads, exposed instances of railroad protection staff claiming credit for having prevented what were entirely fictitious acts of enemy sabotage. Officers scathingly characterized by the paper as unprincipled and individualist employed this particular ruse in their attempts to secure promotions, job transfers, CCP membership, and bonuses.[5]

The reality of agent running in Mao's China does not lend itself to easy analysis and assessment. Just how effective, for example, *were* the 10,000 agents deployed on and along the national railroad grid in the mid-1950s?[6] There is no clear-cut answer: the historical record of everyday life on the covert front in the PRC is opaque, fragmented, and open

---

[2] Jiangsu sheng gonganting, "Guanyu jingji baowei," p. 10.

[3] Ibid.

[4] *Dadao litong waiguode*, p. 12. Compare the following claim by a Soviet intelligence officer who defected to the United States in 1954: "In the Soviet Union today there are thousands of case officers.... Each case officer has between five and ten agents working for him." Peter Deriabin and Frank Gibney, *The Secret World* (Garden City, NY: Doubleday, 1959), p. 75.

[5] *Tiedao gongan (Railroad Public Security)*, January 21 and April 23, 1954.

[6] Wang Jinxiang, "Zai di qi ci quanguo tielu," p. 25.

to alternative interpretations. The paper trail that officers and agents generated is particularly challenging to historians, not least for the reason given by Peter Jackson in his introduction to the seminal study *Exploring Intelligence Archives: Enquiries into the Secret State*: "Deception, deceit and manipulation are central elements in many of the day-to-day practices of many intelligence agencies."[7] Attempted in this final chapter is merely a tentative bare-bones reconstruction – to the extent that this is possible – of how agent running was conducted inside the borders of the PRC. The points covered include direction, briefing and debriefing, operational control, agent welfare, and last but not least, how operational relationships between officers and agents were terminated.

Direction

Direction (*lingdao*) was seen as the many ways of ensuring that the agent executed a mission successfully and also, in the long term, as perhaps the most effective form of agent training. "It is only possible to gradually raise an agent's political awareness and improve his tradecraft in the course of actual work and with the help of the concrete direction and assistance provided by the operational officer," it was emphasized in the *Lectures*.[8] For the public security organs to reach this goal, it was imperative that the officer's direction was personalized and adapted to the individual target. One of the essential purposes for which operational departments collected data about the social background of agents was to improve and tailor direction, control, and training to the unique needs and circumstances of the individual agent. At the Central People's Public Security Academy, officer cadets were told the following:

That each agent will need to be handled differently simply means that each agent has to be directed, controlled, and trained differently depending on ability and working conditions. It is not permissible to manage all agents in an identical fashion. The reason why it is necessary to deal with each agent on his own unique terms is because all agents come from different social and family circumstances and differ with respect to their political background, educational level, working ability, social standing, profession, standard of living, personality traits, habits and hobbies, attitude toward serving the public security organs, etc. If one fails to consider the unique circumstances that characterize each agent as such, then

---

[7] R. Gerald Hughes, Peter Jackson, and Len Scott, *Exploring Intelligence Archives: Enquiries into the Secret State* (London: Routledge, 2008), p. 3.

[8] "*Teqing gongzuo*," p. 45.

one will not be capable of correctly directing and controlling agents or effectively training them.[9]

Regardless of the unique circumstances of the agent in question, there were routines to be followed. The first preliminary act upon successful recruitment was for the officer and agent to determine the date and location for their next meeting. Drawing from experience, the *Lectures* asserted that, if possible, not too much time was to elapse between recruitment and the second meeting:

> It very often happens in the case of agents recruited from hostile strata that once back home again, after recruitment, they start having second thoughts and waver. At this point, there is a particularly grave danger of the operational target noticing and the agent being compromised. Hence, if the conditions permit it, the operational officer is to initially meet quite frequently with this kind of agent in order to be in a position to train and observe him.[10]

As part of their training, handlers were encouraged to establish as soon as possible some form of agreed-upon timetable according to which they could regularly meet with their agents. This also included the details of where and when to meet – including, in an emergency, how to alter plans at the very last moment. In the *Lectures*, it was explained that "when, at the first meeting, it is decided when the next meeting is to take place, the best thing to do is to establish two alternative times, so that if for some unforeseen reason the agent is unable to make contact at the first time agreed upon, he has the second time to fall back upon."[11]

Operational officers were required to inform their superiors of the timetable for meetings with their agents. The reason given by the CMPS was that it allowed officers at superior levels to examine how work was proceeding and/or personally exercise some supervision over the contact between handler and agent. Ever mindful of the need not to cause an embarrassing loss of face to lower-level officers, textbooks stressed – reflecting the euphemistic language favored by the CCP – that this "oversight" was necessary and was merely designed to "help" them.[12] Handlers were meant to impress upon their agents the importance of arriving at meetings on time, and furthermore to emphasize that they were *never* to seek out the meeting place without prior agreement and authorization.

---

[9] Ibid.
[10] Ibid., p. 40.
[11] Ibid., p. 66.
[12] Ibid.

Handlers were themselves to ensure – when approaching secret rendez-vous premises to meet with an agent – that they were not being followed and that the premises were not under observation. So as not to draw the attention of neighbors, the handler was to arrive *before* the agent and not at the same time. Arriving ahead of time also allowed officers to make whatever advance preparations might be necessary.[13]

Whether the agent was immediately upon recruitment to carry out a specific task depended on the circumstances, including the purpose for which the agent had been recruited and the qualities he or she might have. In principle, the agent's first task was not to go beyond what had already been discussed during recruitment. Above all, the execution of a set task was meant to give the handler a first real indication of the agent's ability and reliability. The *Lectures* spoke in terms of "gradually guiding" the agent toward focusing on the operational target and the task to be executed.[14] A 1955 Chongqing text on the direction of agents spoke of a "trial process" during which the agent's political and operational dependability could be tested, followed by a first assignment of a "substantial task" at the appropriate time.[15] A postrecruitment trial period was, for security reasons, viewed as compulsory under two particular circumstances, the first being when an agent came from the "hostile camp." The period during which such an agent would be carefully monitored in secret while executing relatively less important tasks could be an extended one. The *Lectures* urged officers that, if they absolutely had to assign a "substantial task" right away to a newly recruited agent from within the enemy camp, they should use all means at their disposal to "keep him under powerful control, utilize physical surveillance or duplicate line agents to monitor his behavior, examine his correspondence, all in order to make sure he does not collude with the enemy to sabotage us."[16]

The second, presumably rare, circumstance in which a trial period of monitoring was seen as appropriate was if and when a newly recruited agent was to perform a long-term task deemed to be extremely sensitive, such as the penetration of a hostile intelligence service. Here the time frame, following recruitment, for "long-term cultivation" (*changqi pei-yang*), as it was called, could be a matter of years. A 1963 report to the

[13] Ibid., p. 70.
[14] Ibid., p. 40.
[15] Chongqing shi gonganju, "Guanyu jinian lai teqing," p. 13.
[16] "*Teqing gongzuo*," p. 40.

CMPS from the task force running the Class A Case No. 12 documents just such a case:

> After L had returned from Hong Kong in 1956, subsequent to a detailed investigation that confirmed that he was not politically problematic, he was recruited and singled out for long-term cultivation. He is someone with a very rich social experience, and having been subjected to education he has acquired a fairly clear understanding of our government. He has no profession in the PRC and has no knowledge of any internal secrets of ours; at the same time, he has Hong Kong identification papers and can enter Hong Kong at will. His brother is a respected capitalist in Hong Kong. . . . In Hong Kong, L's cover and the conditions under which he could establish himself are excellent, and many of the friends he has made in Hong Kong happen also to be on intimate terms with [the operational target] K. Furthermore, L is in no way involved with our agents S and V. Hence the terms on which we should consider dispatching L to attempt to incite the defection of the bandit K are very good. Even if such an attempt were to fail, K would not dare to subject L to persecution. And, at the same time, it would not impact on the ability of S and V to keep the enemy under continued surveillance. Right now the cultivation of L is still ongoing. In 1962 he was sent to Hong Kong once, without being given tasks but as a way of testing him further. From the looks of it, we shall be able to exploit him in the future.[17]

In the end, L's potential as an agent was never exploited and he fared badly in the general inquiry ordered by Xie Fuzhi on December 1, 1967. Indeed, a 1968 investigation looking into this particular case, with a view toward determining, among other things, if the agents involved had "done any bad stuff," characterized L's role as entirely negative. Ever since the founding of the PRC, it was found that he had "consistently maintained a reactionary stance, looked upon our party with hatred, spread rumors wantonly, slandered and attacked the policies of our party, [and had] regularly been in contact with politically problematic persons. Suspicions persist that he was dispatched [to the PRC in 1956] by the bandit G."[18] The particulars of this case notwithstanding, L's fate demonstrates that postrecruitment monitoring could be lengthy and that agents, in the end, were not always fully developed.

Secrecy and the compartmentalization of information meant that, as a rule, operational officers as part of their direction efforts were *not* meant to inform agents of "what ultimately warranted the use of the agent in a specific operation."[19] The need-to-know principle was meant to be applied very strictly when it came to the sharing of information, not

---

[17] "Shier hao zhuan'an huibao tigang," pp. 29–30.
[18] Yi chu junguan xiaozu 12 hao an zhuan'anzu, "Guanyu chongxin shencha," p. 4.
[19] *"Teqing gongzuo,"* p. 43.

only in the handler–agent relationship but more generally as well. "Every party member," the general rules by which all CCP members had to abide stipulated, "should make a point of not inquiring about secret matters that are unrelated to one's own work. One is not to ask about secrets one's not meant to know, nor tell other people secret things they're not meant to know."[20] The CMPS augmented these rules with even stricter ones, spelled out in documents like the draft General Rules for Counterespionage and Confidentiality Work in State Organs, drawn up by the 2nd Bureau, and On Some Regulations Governing Counterespionage and Confidentiality Routines in State Organs, drawn up by the 1st Bureau.[21] But there were inevitably circumstances under which careless officers or agents nevertheless broke these rules.

Agent Briefing

The CMPS looked upon agent briefing as involving two distinct interrelated elements. The first was to outline to the agent, in clear and concrete terms, his or her operational task. The second was to explain to the agent the means and method(s) whereby the task was to be carried out. The CMPS also emphasized that the operational officer in charge was under an obligation to ascertain that the agent had fully and accurately understood everything he or she had been told during the briefing.[22]

Scattered evidence in the literature from the first half of the 1950s suggests that the agent briefing process was often poorly managed, especially by inexperienced lower-level officers. When ad hoc CMPS task forces in the winter of 1954–55 surveyed a number of provinces and municipalities to determine whether operational work was up to par, many of their findings failed to meet expectations. Sometimes the problems on the ground were quite elementary; one task force explained this by noting that "most of the staff waging the actual battles are still rookies [*xinbing*] with no experience." Their tradecraft was substandard, the

---

[20] Zhonggong zhongyang zuzhibu bangongting, *Zuzhi gongzuo wenjian xuanbian 1949 nian 10 yue–1952 nian*, p. 180.

[21] Zhongyang gonganbu erju, "Jiguan fangdie baomi gongzuo tongze (caoan)" (General Rules for Counterespionage and Confidentiality Work in State Organs [Draft]), *Tielu gongan tongxun*, No. 3, December 15, 1950, pp. 6–8; Zhongyang gonganbu yiju, "Guanyu jixiang jiguan fangdie baomi zhidu de guiding" (On Some Regulations Governing Counterespionage and Confidentiality Routines in State Organs), *Tielu gongan tongxun*, No. 3, December 15, 1950, pp. 8–10.

[22] "Teqing gongzuo," p. 55.

group's survey of Shanxi province noted, their analytical capacity inadequate, and their "political intuition" poor.[23] In an effort to try to rectify the situation, the CMPS in the summer of 1955, at the request of numerous lower-level bureaus of public security, disseminated descriptions of what it deemed to be successful and reasonably well-functioning operational routines. One of the descriptions (by the Chongqing Bureau of Public Security) raised the following basic points about what was to be kept in mind when tasking agents: if the overall mission was simply one of "keeping a suspicious element under observation," the operational officer had to make sure that the briefed agent knew precisely what *kind* of "suspicious" behavior to look out for. If the agent's mission involved the protection of a critical asset, the officer was to ensure that the agent knew just what (and what not) that "protection" was meant to entail in practical terms. And if the agent's task was investigative, it was the officer's responsibility to ensure that the agent knew precisely what his or her mission parameters were – what to focus the investigation on and what to leave aside.[24] Points like these, elementary as they were, touched on many of the key problems identified by the CMPS.

In an October 1950 Case Group retrospective of an operation targeting a network of Guomindang *tewu* in Henan province, the initial tasking of a penetration agent (here called a "contact") was described as follows:

After numerous conversations with the contact ([original] *Note*: the contact is the son of workers and was [before 1949] for a time a member of the Communist Party, before turning traitor and joining a *tewu* organization), through persuasion and education, by explaining to him what the future held in store and dispelling his misgivings, he came to express a willingness to work for us. Hereupon he was promptly tasked with: (1) finding out what the enemy was up to and reporting it to us in time; (2) allowing us as much as possible to review the enemy's correspondence and papers prior to their dissemination; (3) and reporting to us as the occasion demands the shifting internal makeup and personnel changes in the [enemy's] organization.[25]

Findings gathered from the first years of the PRC prompted a number of recommendations concerning agent tasking, touching, among other things, on how to make the best possible use of agents in a large operation. Though worded differently, the recommendations were in essence the same as those that in 1957 would find their way into the CMPS *Lectures*.

[23] Gonganbu Shanxi shichazu, "Guanyu Shanxi sheng," p. 10.
[24] Chongqing shi gonganju, "Guanyu jinian lai teqing," p. 13.
[25] "Zhengzhou gonganchu pohuo wei 'Yu-E,'" p. 7.

In the field, the instructions each agent received from his or her handler would have been one of many variations on the textbook theme. Highly specific requests might, for example, have been augmented by more general briefs that placed greater emphasis on the agent's own initiative and creativity. Illustrating this are the following notes found in the work diary of a Beijing schoolteacher who, for a brief period in the mid-1960s, served as an informer keeping an eye on the intercampus networking of radical student dissidents. Here are the operational demands that he himself felt compelled to satisfy:

1. Report immediately, at once; 2. Accuracy, exact; 3. No summing up. Time, place, persons, surrounding circumstances, causes of struggle, slogans, problems; 3 [*sic*]. Scope to be broad: urban to rural, schools to government offices ...; 4. Quality: besides the above, brief reports should contain analysis; 5. Highlight politics, grasp two-line struggle ...; 6. Grasp symptoms, trends; 7. Rapid reports and brief reports – keep it simple and to the point; 8. Major issues to be reported quickly. If no reports, investigate responsibility; 9. Some typical things... should also be reported; 10. Different *danwei* to cooperate, keep each other posted; 11. Maintain an intelligence network: telephone numbers, addresses, telephone numbers of key individuals.[26]

Meant to be understood only by the agent him- or herself, scribbled points like these are on the surface ambiguous: what did, for example, the claimed need for different *danwei* or work units to "cooperate" and "keep each other posted" refer to? Quite unlike the carefully written and logically structured postoperational accounts of agent briefings that Case Groups (like the one from Henan cited earlier) produced for the record, raw notes like these jotted down by agents at a briefing were not necessarily coherent or accurate, but they often constitute the sole surviving record of what agents actually took with them from briefings.

In the course of briefing an agent, a good handler was not only to listen to any ideas the agent might have as to how a task was to be best carried out, but also to consider any requests for assistance the agent might have that might improve the odds of success. Under normal circumstances, the *Lectures* declared without explaining why, it could be assumed that the agent's ideas were good and requests reasonable, and hence should be given consideration. The *Lectures* stressed, however, that it was important for operational officers not to leave the initiative entirely in the hands of the agent – tantamount to a loss of control – but

[26] "Extracts from work diary."

to basically proceed in accordance with the instructions they themselves would have been given by their own superiors.[27]

The *Lectures* called on the handler to thoroughly familiarize him- or herself with the agent's new mission beforehand, as well as read any and all documentation pertaining to previous meetings with the agent and earlier missions the agent might have previously carried out. In the course of tasking a case agent, a Case Group handler might initially have brought up matters that included, but were not limited to, the following:

- How to make use of matters of common interest or concern to establish contact with the operational target.
- At what point and under what circumstances the agent should possibly indicate a willingness to be of service to the target.
- At what moment and under what conditions the agent was to speak to the target of his or her own (false or real) background and hint at what he or she might be qualified to do for the target.
- If the agent and the target had previously known each other, explain to the agent under what cover he or she was to reestablish contact.
- How the agent was expected to meet again with the target (after initial contact had been [re]established).
- On what subjects the agent was to engage the target in conversation.
- What particular leading questions the agent was to raise with the target.[28]

These points were particularly important when dealing with a new and inexperienced agent on his or her first mission. It was further emphasized in the *Lectures*, in the context of what made a good agent, that he or she was not to pose any direct questions to the target that, instead of eliciting an answer, would trigger suspicion. Too many questions, even from friends, would put the target on guard: "When the operational target determines that his friend as such does not need this particular information and that his asking for it is not simply prompted by curiosity, he will at this point begin to suspect that there might be an agent of the public security organs among his friends."[29]

While the kind of briefing an agent would ultimately receive depended on any number of circumstances, including those about which no records were kept, a "model" briefing of agents employed to serve the operational

[27] "*Teqing gongzuo*," p. 56.
[28] Cf. Ibid.
[29] Ibid., p. 58.

need of countering the activities of hostile intelligence services on Chinese soil was described briefly in the *Lectures*. Where the aim of a mission was to prevent sensitive intelligence from falling into hostile hands (an alternative and slightly more sophisticated aim might also have been to seek to feed false information to the enemy), the first task given to an agent would often simply be to verify and confirm beyond a reasonable doubt (or reject, depending on the situation) the suspicions that had prompted the launch of the mission in the first place: that is, the belief that the operational target was indeed a spy. The *Lectures* could in this context have mentioned the kinds of operations that the Tianjin municipal Bureau of Public Security had been running against, among others, selected former employees of foreign hongs like Jardine Matheson & Co. Ltd. and Butterfield & Swire after 1949. In late 1954, a CMPS task force visiting Tianjin found that the operations had generated disappointing results since no more than a handful of actual cases of possible British and Japanese espionage had been uncovered.[30]

The next task that the same agent would be called upon to do was to ascertain exactly for which country or organization the operational target – assuming he or she had indeed turned out to be a spy – was working. Here the answer was of great strategic concern to the CMPS, whose 1st Bureau devoted considerable resources to the upkeep of wide-ranging threat inventories.[31] In public, CCP propaganda often opted when necessary for vague generic labels like "American and Chiang Kai-shek (*Mei-Jiang*) *tewu*," even in cases where a connection to *both* the Guomindang regime on Taiwan and the United States might in fact be tenuous and not fully established. For example, an official four-page flyer, publicly distributed in Beijing in 1966 documenting the crimes and sentences of seventeen named individuals, referred to some of them as "American and Chiang Kai-shek *tewu*" in its title, but in the actual text they were called "American operatives . . . recruited by the CIA"; no link to the Guomindang was even hinted at, much less explained.[32] While the PRC media rarely

---

[30] Gonganbu Tianjin shichazu, "Guanyu Tianjin shi," p. 2.

[31] The resolution of initial (1950) confusion over how to refer to Guomindang *tewu* in the employ of the "U.S. imperialists" is noted in Schoenhals, "Recruiting Agents in Industry and Trade," pp. 14–15.

[32] The other thirteen individuals were charged with murder, rape, and other violent crimes. "Guanyu jixu zhenya yi pi Mei-Jiang tewu, xianxing fangeming fenzi he xingshi fanzui fenzi de cailiao" (Documentation on the Continued Need to Suppress a Batch of American and Chiang Kai-shek *Tewu*, Active Counterrevolutionary Elements, and Criminal Elements) (Beijing, 1966), p. 1.

bothered to distinguish in public between organized opposition to the Communist Party that merely *claimed* links to Chiang Kai-shek's regime (like the homegrown Guomindang Anti-Communist National Salvation Regiment in the Anshan Steel Corporation mentioned in Chapter 4) and *tewu* that actually had such links, operational officers, in an effort to conserve resources, made determining whether such links existed one of the priority tasks of their agents. In publications designated for official use only, the distinction was made explicit. For instance, the Bureau of Public Security in Pingyue prefecture in Guangxi was reported at the 6th NPSC to have cracked "two homegrown counterrevolutionary organizations created by residual counterrevolutionary elements who had either sought to make contact with *tewu* organizations based in Hong Kong and Taiwan or claim for themselves to be operating in the name of one of the *tewu* organs of the Chiang Kai-shek bandit gang."[33] Further, the Bureau of Public Security in Shijiazhuang was at one point said to have thwarted an attempted riot by an organization calling itself the "Guomindang Hebei provincial government," whose leading members had sought *in vain* to "contact the Americans and Chiang Kai-shek and explore every means of obtaining explosives in their attempt to fabricate weapons."[34] In both cases, the reports made it clear that there was in fact no concrete link to the Guomindang.

The third step in the model briefing process saw the Case Group operational officer task the agent with identifying and exploring the channels of communication that the suspected *tewu* was using: specifically, how did he or she receive direction and instructions and pass on any intelligence collected? Following is a description by the Shenyang Bureau of Public Security's 2nd Office that illustrates the lengths to which a Case Group might go to allow penetration agents to pursue such answers:

The agent had already managed to penetrate the enemy without any problems, thus allowing us to be more aggressive. Given [that] the main culprit Y was lying

---

[33] "Xiang qu tepaiyuan, xiang zhian baowei weiyuanhui zhuren ji cheng, zhen paichusuo ganbu chuanda di liu ci quanguo gongan huiyi jueyi de baogao tigang" (Outline of Report Transmitting the Resolution of the 6th National Public Security Conference to Specially Appointed District Officers, Heads of Township Public Order Committees, and Officers in Urban and Market Town Police Stations), *Gongan shouce*, No. 26, September 3, 1954, p. 14.

[34] Shijiazhuang shi gonganju dangzu, "Guanyu pohuo 'Huadi zongbu,' 'Guomindang Hebei sheng zhengfu,' 'Zhonghua chixindang' san qi fangeming baoluan anjian de baogao" (Report on Cracking Three Cases of Attempted Counterrevolutionary Riots by the "China Region General HQ," "Guomindang Hebei Provincial Government," and "China Scarlet Hearts Party"), *Hebei gongan tongbao*, No. 19, April 1961, p. 2.

low in Beijing and that the suspected *tewu* A very much wanted to travel there to
see him but was unable to leave his job [in Shenyang], we reasoned as follows:
if we were... able to create the conditions under which the agent would end up
having to journey to Beijing, it might be possible for him to secure a position
for himself as a "liaison man" [between Y and A] and as such be able to obtain
evidence of crimes. Consequently, we arranged for the agent to be transferred
to a position as a component acquisitions officer that would involve a lot of
travel. At the same time, in order to maintain control over the enemy and avoid
arousing his suspicions (and in order to see if he would indeed attempt to exploit
the agent), we arranged for the agent to turn to A and – suggesting that he was
really unwilling to accept his new job and all that it entailed – ask for his advice
as follows: "The leadership is considering moving me to acquisitions, a job that
will force me to travel a lot. The paltry bonus I will get won't be enough to make
up for it: money-wise it's a losing proposition, and I really don't want to do it."
When A heard this he promptly criticized the agent: "How come all you can think
about is money? This is a great job. When you go to Beijing, you'll have a chance
to call on Y." He strongly encouraged the agent to take the job.[35]

In this case, the agent successfully managed to control communication
between the two "enemies" in Shenyang and Beijing, respectively, as well
as discover that – as in the previously cited cases – neither of them in fact
was in contact with foreign or Guomindang intelligence.

Agent Debriefing

The *Lectures* described the debriefing process in terms of the handler
receiving and assessing a report from the agent on a given mission. The
CMPS in this context impressed upon officers the importance of paying
attention to even the minutest details of the report, its content, and its
delivery. If at all possible, officers were to debrief agents in person. Having
listened to the agent delivering the report orally, the officer was to use the
face-to-face meeting to ask the agent to clarify any unclear points and to
elicit, when called for, any additional information of value not already
provided.[36]

If the case officer had reason to believe – either from experience or on
the basis of specific alternative sources of information to which the agent
was not privy – that the agent needed to alter the way(s) in which he or
she was carrying out the mission, the officer was to inform the agent of
this during the debriefing session. Often, sources reveal, this amounted to
a lot of harsh criticism, not always constructive. For this reason, as the

[35] Shenyang shi gonganju di er chu, "XXX jiuhe fangeming," p. 10.
[36] "*Teqing gongzuo*," p. 54.

CMPS felt compelled to point out, it was every frustrated case officer's duty to also spell out just *how* an underperforming agent should go about improving his or her work.[37]

The CMPS had no problem admitting that it was sometimes the agent who had developed a better idea (than the case officer) of how a mission should proceed, and that the agent therefore might be justified in expressing reservations regarding the officer's assessment and advice. The *Lectures* explained how officers were meant to proceed in such a scenario: "If the agent disagrees with the opinion put forward by the operational officer, then the officer is to give due consideration to the agent's reasons for disagreeing. If those reasons appear correct, the officer should accept them." Conversely, without elaborating on how this could be determined other than very subjectively, the *Lectures* added that "if they are incorrect, the officer should patiently explain this to the agent and convince him of this."[38] This attitude on the part of the CMPS reflected the same kind of pragmatism that Mao had discussed not long after the outbreak of the War of Resistance against Japan. Mao had acknowledged that behind enemy lines there was no alternative to acting independently and keeping the initiative in one's own hands. When the circumstances warranted – when securing prior consent was impossible – the agent might have to "act first and report afterwards" (*xianzhan houzou*), anticipating what might be agreed to or approved after the event. In Mao's words, this merely represented a proven effective policy that combined both independence and initiative.[39] Accordingly, the CMPS empowered case officers to accept the agent's assessment of a situation and make whatever adjustments might be needed to his or her own prior assessment. On this point, the *Lectures* made no mention of any need for officers to first elicit the opinion of their superiors.

In conjunction with each oral debriefing, the agent (assuming he or she was literate) was also expected to submit a written report. The information contained in this report was to be as objective, clear, precise, and concrete as possible. In the words of the *Lectures*, the agent was meant to put on paper only things "remembered accurately and known for certain."[40] The following sample illustrates what this raw information, as received by operational departments at the time of debriefing (and

[37] Ibid.
[38] Ibid.
[39] *Selected Works of Mao Tsetung*, Vol. 2, p. 213.
[40] "*Teqing gongzuo*," pp. 54–55.

destined, in this form, after analysis, to end up in the agent's file), may have looked like. Lifted from the file containing reports that Agent 404 in Taiyuan submitted to his case officer every Friday for six weeks in February and March 1957, it details the activities of the "stay-behind *tewu*-suspect element" T:

Recently, the Vehicles Agency announced that everyone should have their picture taken, by March 10 at the latest. The past few days, everyone has been to the studio, except for T and so-and-so, who claim they already have pictures of themselves. But when they were asked to produce them, so-and-so said something like anytime you want one is fine with me, while T didn't actually say when he would hand one in. When he had his picture taken, so-and-so asked "What's the point of having one's picture taken?"

So-and-so works in one of the agency's municipal departments. He was at one point given a two-year sentence for graft, but was released on health grounds after serving just over two months. When government bonds were being sold, he said: "Everyone is entitled to his own opinion, and given the circumstances of my family, [buying] bonds for a few yuan is about all I will agree to. Even if I don't buy a single bond, they're hardly going to brand me a counterrevolutionary."

On Thursday, everybody was still working full of energy when so-and-so said to T: "Did you serve in the past as the commander of a company or battalion?" T replied laughing, saying, "Fuck you!"

One day that same week, T said to X: "To whom did you pass on the [written] request I gave you, to quit the Agency? It's not with secretary Su." X replied, saying: "I gave it to the director. Go ask the director."[41]

The relevant CMPS regulations stipulated that a brief report like this one was to be signed by the agent using, for security reasons, his alias. None of Agent 404's six reports are, as it turns out, signed. The *Lectures* hints at what may have been the possible reasons for this, noting that "if given the constraints of education, timing, or circumstances, [the agent] is himself unable to submit a report in writing, the operational officer should summarize in written form the contents of what the agent has reported."[42] They may, in other words, be contents of reports that Agent 404's case officer had written down in his stead on the basis of an oral debriefing.

The seemingly insubstantial quality of his report doesn't necessarily mean that Agent 404 was unskilled as an informer: the problem, if there was one, may also have had to do with his case officer's debriefing skills.

---

[41] "Fanying qingkuang" (Report on Circumstances) [March 15, 1957].
[42] "*Teqing gongzuo*," p. 55.

A Changchun public security officer who was particularly interested in discovering and exploiting activists had mocked those of his colleagues who looked on debriefing an agent in simplistic terms. Blunt and "point-blank questioning" was to be "avoided at all cost," he stressed, and proceeded to explain why:

> For example, if you just ask "So what's the situation?" [the agent] may well, without giving it any further thought, respond by saying "There's nothing happening!" But if you proceed slowly, just by engaging him in a simple chat, he will in the end provide you with a lot of information. Take for example Mrs. B – when debriefed by Group No. 32 about a certain Central Statistics Bureau *tewu* – who at first was very hazy [on any details], but later after we just talked slowly for a while provided a lot of valuable information.[43]

In the context of agent debriefing, the CMPS put particular stress on the psychological element – on the officer always giving the agent praise where praise was due and on pointing out errors and flaws in such a way as to make criticism constructive and positive. This strategy echoed similar advice given by Mao Zedong on numerous occasions.[44] As the CCP Chairman put it in an informal conversation with colleagues, Kang Sheng among them, during the 1964 Spring Festival: "Praise should be the main thing, and criticism should be supplementary. Among those working for our cause, there are many good people."[45] There was a subtle instrumental psychological logic behind this, of which Mao (and Kang surely no less) was no doubt well aware.

Covert Information and the Courts

When debriefing the agent, the officer was expected to determine exactly *how* the agent had gone about executing his or her mission. Without a clear understanding of this, it was pointed out in the *Lectures*, it would be difficult to confidently and accurately assess the quality of the agent's work and/or, by extension, the quality of his or her reporting. If the agent's original task had involved direct contact with an operational target, the case officer would be particularly keen to build up a picture

---

[43] Lu Qian, "Zemyang faxian," p. 95.
[44] Cf. Michael Schoenhals, *Doing Things with Words in Chinese Politics: Five Studies.* (Berkeley: University of California Institute of East Asian Studies, Center for Chinese Studies, 1992), pp. 24–25.
[45] Stuart Schram, ed., *Mao Tse-tung Unrehearsed: Talks and Letters 1956–71* (Harmondsworth: Penguin Books, 1974), p. 201.

of how the agent had acted in the target's presence and anything else pertaining to the presence of other persons at the time.[46]

Motivating interest in this kind of contextual information was an important caveat that applied to covertly obtained information. Rarely if ever spelled out but known to all of those who handled it "in the raw," such information was inadmissible in Chinese courts and could not be invoked for any legal or judicial purposes. The CMPS Arrest and Preliminary Hearing Work Temporary Statutes of 1954 expressly stipulated that in the course of preliminary hearings there was to be *no* inclusion in the documentation used by the courts of information obtained by covert means.[47] In spite of this, such information did find its way into court proceedings. This was not an infrequent occurrence, moreover; it warranted a critical CMPS comment in *People's Public Security*, which specifically touched upon the problem with such (unattributable) information:

Some turn the information provided by agents into public evidence by having the operational officer process it and put his personal chop to it, but to proceed in this way is inappropriate. It not only fails to make legally admissible evidence out of secret operational information, but on the contrary compromises the secrecy of our operational work. . . . The same applies to information obtained through physical surveillance, which neither in processed form nor in the form of extracts [copied from the unprocessed record] may be entered into the preliminary hearing files.[48]

The rationale behind the interest in contextual information expressed in the *Lectures* had to do with resolving this problem. Perhaps because it was not strictly an operational matter, the authors of the *Lectures* did not dwell on it at length. They simply noted that *if* other persons had been present at a crucial juncture (e.g., at the moment when an operational target had revealed to the agent his or her intent to engage in destructive acts), circumstantial information would facilitate the invitation of one of those persons to come forward, thereby making the information (which then could be sourced to that person) utilizable in court. Elaborating on this in greater detail, the authors of a report from the CMPS 19th (Preliminary Hearing) Bureau in 1958 argued as follows:

The utilization of secret documentation as evidence has to be managed with great care. Henceforth, any evidence touching upon secrets such as agents, postal examination, technical operations, aerial (*tiankong*) [camera?] surveillance, etc.

---

[46] "*Teqing gongzuo*," p. 54.

[47] Zhongyang gonganbu, "Guanyu daibu ji yushen," p. 2.

[48] "Da duzhe wen" (Replies to Readers' Questions), *Renmin gongan*, No. 10, 1956, p. 17.

may not be utilized in public, and leaking it is strictly forbidden. One should to the maximum extent collect public evidence, such as documentation consisting of denunciations by the masses and oral admissions by coperpetrators, and substitute it for such evidence instead. However, there are cases where the secret evidence touches upon the main crimes of the perpetrator and it proves truly impossible to collect alternative public evidence. [When this is the case] one may first – through internal channels – manage the matter in the appropriate way by discussing it with the [CCP] leaderships of the courts and procuracy. When documentation (the content of which may be made public) provided by agents is to be turned into denunciations by the masses, witness statements, or admissions by coperpetrators, or when certain operational data are to be turned into reports by operational officers or operational departments, etc. the relevant procedures may be embarked upon only after careful research and checking and approval by the leaderships.[49]

This reasoning was applied to information from agents and its possible use in court proceedings. Important to note is that a very different set of considerations applied to "finished intelligence" serving a political rather than a legal need. Here the overriding concern was instead with anonymity and source protection. On this point, public security concerns differed little, if at all, from the concerns of the PLA General Staff managing defense-related intelligence. Spelled out in a set of regulations from the General Staff Headquarters was the firm rule that those responsible for dissemination had to "pay conscientious attention to concealing the source of the intelligence. When information that is to be shared with lower levels derives from technical operations or secret sources, it first of all has to be analyzed and arranged comprehensively. Parts of it that are of limited immediate concern ... are to be redacted."[50]

Control

In 1962, an experienced CIA operations officer defined control as "the capacity of a case officer (and his service) to generate, alter, or halt agent behavior by using or indicating his capacity to use physical or psychological means of leverage."[51] The CIA officer's counterparts in China

---

[49] Zhongyang gonganbu shijiuju, "Dangqian yushen gongzuo de qingkuang he jinhou renwu" (On Present Preliminary Hearing Work and Future Tasks), *Gongan jianshe*, No. 227, April 1, 1958, p. 9.

[50] Zhongguo renmin jiefangjun baomi weiyuanhui bangongshi, ed., *Baomi gongzuo wenjian huibian* (*Collected Documents on Secrecy Work*) (Beijing, 1987), p. 376.

[51] John P. Dimmer, Jr., "Observations on the Double Agent," in *Inside CIA's Private World: Declassified Articles from the Agency's Internal Journal, 1955–1992*, selected and edited by H. Bradford Westerfield (New Haven, CT: Yale University Press, 1995), p. 443.

would have had little difficulty understanding what he meant by this. In the words of the CMPS, control (*kongzhi*) was first and foremost about "purposefully and systematically influencing the agent's state of mind."[52] A 1950 retrospective of an operation that involved the coordinated use of agents – the target was a Guomindang stay-behind network of saboteurs in and around the east China railroad hub of Shangqiu – discussed it at some length, highlighting specifically the critical contribution that effective control of the state of mind and behavior of agents had made toward neutralizing the network.[53] Three general findings were, according to the authors of the analysis, particularly worth sharing with other public security operational officers.

The first general finding concerned the initial stages of operations involving inexperienced agents. Here it tended to be the agent's commitment and – above all – self-confidence that needed to be controlled. For what could be perfectly legitimate reasons, the agent might initially fail to obtain significant quantities of intelligence of the kind desired by the public security organs – and whatever information he or she *was* able to provide could turn out to be unspecific or not concrete. This was often the point at which the agent, mainly in order to prove his or her worth to the handler, would become overeager to acquire more and better intelligence too quickly. Paying insufficient attention to security and the means of collection would, as a result, significantly increase the agent's risk of exposure. The authors of the Shangqiu retrospective suggested that the agent would become anxious and worry about "not being able to gain the trust" of the handler because of problems with the quality of the intelligence he or she was able to provide. In this context and at this stage of an operation, therefore, they stressed, it was imperative that "we express our trust and concern." The agent had to be comforted by the handler, given a renewed sense of self-confidence, and encouraged to confidently proceed with the operational task while paying due attention to safety. To illustrate this, they referred to one agent who, after having penetrated the enemy, found himself working under unexpectedly harsh conditions, with the result that he was unable to execute his tasks with the success initially hoped for. "When our side on a number of occasions," they pointed out, "sent people to criticize him, he became despondent and nervous. But once we had realized this, we consoled him, and as a result his self-confidence rose again."[54]

[52] "*Teqing gongzuo*," p. 47.
[53] Shangqiu xingzhengqu gonganchu, "Guanyu pohuo fei 'Dixiajun,'" p. 14.
[54] Ibid.

The second general finding had to do with how a new or inexperienced agent reacted upon scoring his or her first major operational victory. Here it was concluded that the agents tended to believe that their contribution to a particular operation was bigger than it really was. (Left unstated was that this inflation of self-worth was an inevitable by-product of the compartmentalization of information that prevented officers from sharing the bigger picture with their agents, including details pertaining to the possible involvement and roles of additional, duplicate-line agents.) Frequently, an excited agent would argue passionately in favor of using the intelligence he or she had provided to crack the case immediately and, in thus doing, declare the operation a success. This had happened in the case of one agent based at a railroad stop 10 kilometers west of Shangqiu, on the strategically critical Lianyungang to Zhengzhou trunk line, whose surveillance had yielded information that would have made it technically possible to round up one particular cell of saboteurs. In actuality, what the public security organs in Shangqiu were interested in was not merely putting one cell out of action, but an entire network. Hence in this case, and in other similar situations, a handler's immediate priority, so the authors of the report emphasized, had to do with convincing the agent "to behave normally and not stand out too much." It was not up to the agent to decide how his or her contribution to the operation was to be exploited. It was believed that if calmly and carefully explaining this was not enough, then a thinly veiled threat just might make the agent see reason. In the case of the previously mentioned agent, "In order to educate [him]...we told him that if your cover were to be blown, it would be bad for both of us: for our operation, as well as for you personally."[55]

The third and final finding had to do with control of an experienced agent at the obviously decisive juncture when he or she could legitimately claim the right to be rewarded for services rendered, or even to retire, in a situation where the handler, on the other hand, might want to keep the agent in place to carry on working as before. In this context, it was noted that some agents might demand greater material rewards than was their due. Should this be the case, handlers were to encourage the agent to adopt a long-term perspective. If the agent's social background was one that was stigmatized in any way, the handler could hint vaguely at the possibility of a (much coveted?) reward in the form of what might be called "upward social mobility."

---

[55] Ibid.

Agent Rewards and Welfare

Agents, it was appreciated, could not be expected in the long run to perform their delicate, sensitive, and sometimes dangerous tasks without any kind of material rewards. In the early years of the PRC, the reward element of operational work went largely unregulated: in February 1950, talk was of senior officers still gaining experience in such matters, while the laying down of common ground rules would come later.[56] In a speech apparently inspired by deliberations at the 1st National Conference on Economic Protection Work later the same year, Wang Jinxiang spoke positively of so-called substantive rewards that could amount to anything from money and gifts to various kinds of preferential treatment.[57] In the end, official policy stipulated that officers should themselves "find a proper way of helping agents (in particular those who are backward elements) overcome any economic problems they may encounter, either in life or at work, and when necessary also provide them with suitable material assistance."[58] Ying Ruocheng claimed that prior to 1966, when officers from the Beijing Bureau of Public Security called on him in his capacity as an agent, he was usually "treated to a good meal." Still living at home at the time, Ying's son remembered decades later how "we could always get food that regular citizens could not get in their weekly and monthly rations in order to entertain the foreigners who would always come to our home – at a time when it was outrageous to have foreigners come to your home."[59]

But to develop and sustain just the right kind of balanced, mutually beneficial relationship between handler and agent was a challenge, and one that not all operational officers on the ground managed well. Originally published in *People's Public Security: Supplements*, the following is an excerpt from what an officer in Dalian had told his counterparts in Beijing on the subject of how *not* to go about "fostering vocational contacts":

Some [officers] are of the mistaken opinion [that] "there's nothing money can't buy" and believe that as long as one is prepared to provide one's contacts with financial assistance, they will in the end always oblige. As a result, [these] officers don't look carefully at – don't analyze or give much thought to – what kind of

---

[56] Dongbei renmin zhengfu gonganbu, "Guanyu jiaqiang zhencha," p. 22.
[57] Wang Jinxiang, "Zai Dongbei zhengzhi jingji," p. 24.
[58] Chongqing shi gonganju, "Guanyu jinian lai teqing," p. 14.
[59] Ying and Conceison, *Voices Carry*, pp. 53, xxii.

people they're fostering as their contacts. They don't plan for the long term: all they are is eager to achieve quick results here and now. They cannot be bothered with attentively and patiently training their contacts to a point where they become genuinely politically aware and cooperate with us as such when we strike back at renegades and eliminate adversary assets.... In some cases, every time the contacts have done a little something for them, [these officers] promptly invite them to a movie or a meal in a restaurant. As a result, their contacts get into the habit of expecting just that, and when it fails to happen they complain, moan and groan, insist times are hard, say they haven't eaten yet, and demand means with which to conduct business. They may even start to make up stories and say that if we want to see achievements, we need to provide them with funds for social intercourse, disguises, and any number of things. Everything then revolves around money.[60]

The "mistaken opinions" identified here may well have been indicative of how quite a few officers reasoned in the early 1950s. They were also among the problems targeted in the courses on offer in provincial and central public security academies. By 1957, however, the discussion of agent rewards and welfare at the Central People's Public Security Academy was conducted on a different level of sophistication altogether.

Affirmed in the *Lectures* was the policy of helping agents "when necessary and possible" to obtain employment or transfer from one job to another, to arrange for them or their family members to get medical treatment when called for, and to simply help them overcome any economic hardship. In this context, the *Lectures* stressed, it was important only to give rewards in recognition of actual achievements, since too much generosity for no apparent reason was "counterproductive." It was incumbent upon the handler to identify the right occasion to reward the agent and also the kind of reward. Obviously with security concerns in mind, the *Lectures* emphasized further that if and when agents were to be given "substantial rewards," it had to be done in such a way as not to arouse suspicion. The handler and agent needed to agree in advance on a cover story that the latter could use, if needed, to explain why and how the agent had come into the possession of a substantial sum of money, for example, or some expensive item such as a wristwatch.[61]

Not in the context of rewards, but in that of how the individual agent and his or her circumstances might change over time, the *Lectures* raised an issue that – it was widely recognized – had important long-term implications for agent welfare. Immediately after 1949, there had been a

---

[60] Quoted in Schoenhals, "Recruiting Agents in Industry and Trade," p. 16.
[61] "*Teqing gongzuo*," pp. 61–62.

window of opportunity for agents performing meritorious service to improve their public social status (*chengfen*), which – it is important to remember – in time would become the class background (*jiating chushen*) of any future and/or at this point still under-age children. The process was analogous to that by which it was possible for retained members of the Guomindang government administration, after a probationary period of no less than one year in the service of the PRC, to see their formal status changed from old-style mandarin (*guanli*) to "functionary" (*zhiyuan*).[62] Nothing is known about the details of the process involved, but serving as an agent had the potential of expediting the replacement of a stigmatizing or otherwise undesirable social status with a better one. In the words of the *Lectures*, "agents who have been recruited from among the typical backward elements may, by way of training and fostering, and passing the test of actual work, turn into politically aware revolutionary masses."[63] And for those agents who had been members of the CCP's activist constituency all along, the long-term incentive of becoming a bona fide public security officer (with all the perks that this potentially entailed) was a very real one.[64] Wu Shiliang, the wife of the actor Ying Ruocheng, had started out as an agent in 1951 while an actress in the Beijing People's Art Theater, and in 1958 became a formal employee of one of the operational departments of the Beijing Bureau of Public Security; the eulogy read at her funeral three decades later credited her with being an "outstanding soldier" on the covert front.[65]

Orderly Termination

Operational departments were meant to have routines worked out in advance for how to handle problems arising from a move or permanent relocation on the part of the agent. When an agent had to relocate permanently – whether because of his or her cover, his or her so-called social profession, or because it was mandated by the "needs of the struggle" – the handler was expected to follow a routine protocol, drawn up by the CMPS, to ensure the safe transfer of the agent's file and the responsibility for running him or her to the public security organ in the new location.

---

[62] Lanzhou junqu zhengzhibu zuzhibu, ed., *Zuzhi gongzuo wenjian huibian* (*Collected Organization Work Documents*), 3 vols. (Lanzhou, 1980), Vol. 1, pp. 477–78, 522–23, 535.

[63] "*Teqing gongzuo*," p. 14.

[64] Yan Dingchu, "Zai di yi ci quanguo caizheng," p. 19.

[65] Ying and Conceison, *Voices Carry*, p. 201.

In taking over the running of an agent, the officers concerned (not merely the new case officer, it seems, but others with a "need to know" as well) would study the agent's existing file and seek to become acquainted with his or her individual circumstances. A time and a place for a first meeting would then be arranged. If the agent's move was only temporary, a different routine protocol allowed the handler's superiors to decide, depending on the circumstances, between simply informing their counterparts in the new location of the presence of the agent and themselves, one assumes, briefly putting routine contacts with the agent on hold. Alternatively, and without necessarily informing their local counterparts of this, the agent's case officer might follow the agent to the new location and maintain regular contacts there for the duration.[66]

Relationships between agents and operational departments rarely lasted a lifetime. Writing about East Germany's *inoffizielle Mitarbeiter* in *Anatomy of a Dictatorship*, historian Mary Fulbrook observed that "informers were often only active for a few years, [and] turnover was relatively high."[67] In Mao's China, the average "life span," as it were, of an agent may have been roughly the same. Inevitably, at some point, the circumstances that had prompted the agent's recruitment in the first place would change: his or her services might simply no longer be called for, or the agent's utility might have been exhausted. Unless a different, alternative arrangement was deemed preferable, this called for an orderly termination of the operational relationship. The routines to be followed were not elaborated upon in the *Lectures*, but given that agents during their tenure invariably would have – in one form or another – come to acquire operational activity-related information, they are certain to have involved some form of protection against unauthorized disclosure by the (ex-)agent of what he or she had been doing.

Three documents related to the circumstances of his termination preserved in the Personal File of Agent 404 in Taiyuan give some idea of what the orderly termination of a low-level agent entailed. The first two are the draft and final texts, respectively, of a 1957 memo from the Taiyuan municipal Bureau of Public Security's 1st Section, which spelled out the reasons for the termination and asked for it to be approved. The memo began with a brief description of X's recruitment a year earlier, in the summer of 1956, copied almost verbatim from the original

---

[66] "*Teqing gongzuo*," p. 68.
[67] Fulbrook, *Anatomy of a Dictatorship*, p. 50.

request for authority to recruit him. It then proceeded to describe how the circumstances of X's utilization had changed so that the 1st Section of the municipal Bureau of Public Security no longer had any real need for his services:

In January 1957, the *tewu* T changed his workplace. As of then, because the two men had ceased to work and live close to each other, the circumstances that had permitted monitoring him were no longer present. Then, on May 29, [1957], he voluntarily surrendered to the Beicheng branch of the municipal Bureau of Public Security and basically admitted his criminal activities as a historical [pre-Liberation] *tewu*. As a result, there is no further need to exercise control over him (and in actuality X is no longer in a position to exercise such control), and T should be dealt with in accordance with the law as an element who has voluntarily given himself up.[68]

These contents were identical in the draft (dated June 28) and final text (dated July 9) of the memo. The final paragraph, which explained the rationale behind the proposed termination of X, was significantly longer in the draft, where it read as follows:

Comrade X constituted a penetration struggle asset employed for a particular period for a particular concrete reason. Due to changing circumstances, not only has he lost his usefulness, but the case in question has already proceeded to the resolution phase. Having analyzed the matter, we find that Comrade X does not have the qualifications that, from any particular angle, would warrant making [further] use of him. Given all of the above, we propose to terminate him. Furthermore, the leaders of his unit who have been aware of it should be informed of Comrade X's operational achievements and under these circumstances, the operation is to be suspended. At the same time, Comrade X should be told that the *tewu* T has already surrendered and the nature of his problem is already clear. Aside from telling him he need no longer specifically concern himself with the circumstances of this matter, he should be given personal encouragement and told to heighten his vigilance and take note of enemy *tewu* activities, report developments in time, and be prepared to serve on the covert front as one of our informers and eyes and ears.[69]

The final sentence, with its reference to serving as "eyes and ears," indicated that X may have been terminated as an agent, but could expect in the future to occasionally be approached by ordinary police officers

[68] Taiyuan shi gonganju di yi chu, "Wei tingzhi teqing XXX de cailiao" (On Terminating Agent XXX) [July 9, 1957].
[69] Taiyuan shi gonganju di yi chu, "Wei tingzhi teqing XXX de cailiao" (On Terminating Agent XXX) [June 28, 1957].

conducting assessments of popular sentiment or wanting to be updated on the situation in his *danwei*.

While the recommendations in the preceding memo were most likely acted upon, by itself the memo did not, strictly speaking, amount to the termination of X and the closing of the file on Agent 404. For the agent's termination to become effective, the memo also had to include a formal comment from a duly empowered senior officer. On July 8, 1957, the draft termination memo, it appears, was read by a senior public security officer by the name of Shi Wenhe – the same officer who almost exactly a year earlier had approved the original recruitment. It was his handwritten and duly signed comment on it that described what the future relations between the operational department and the (soon to be former) agent were to be:

> Matters involving T: some [suspicions] were confirmed through investigation, and as for the target himself, he has now given himself up to the police, so we should prepare to come to a conclusion. For this purpose, use of the agent in proximity of T should cease. But, given that the agent is a CCP member, contact with him may when called for be made in the future.[70]

Shi's comment on the draft was not reproduced on the final text of the termination memo, which was carefully written out by a clerk. At the bottom of it, someone had in different handwriting added in brackets at the very end that Shi had "issued spoken instructions," presumably to his officer colleagues, "explaining achievements and outcomes."[71] The third text documenting the termination was an otherwise empty generic preprinted intradepartmental cover letter form dated August 7, 1957, on which Shi, with his signature, formally put the proposal to "terminate the use of the agent X" into effect.[72]

Other instances of termination involved retaining suitably positioned former "agents with practical experience gained in the course of the struggle on the covert front" in alternative capacities. The municipal Bureau of Public Security in Chongqing, for instance, cautioned against terminating an agent relationship altogether without a very good reason: "When, temporarily, there are no tasks for an agent to execute, one should continue to foster the agent and stay on the lookout for opportunities when he can be utilized. He should not be summarily cast aside." The

---

[70] Ibid.
[71] Ibid.
[72] Taiyuan shi gonganju di yi chu, "Untitled document" [August 7, 1957].

option of keeping an agent "on the books" as the keeper of secret rendezvous premises has already been mentioned, and only what the Chongqing
Bureau referred to as a "very small number of agents who neither now
nor in the future will ever have any utility value" should be altogether cut
loose "in a way befitting the circumstances."[73] An example of the latter
kind of agent was one whose ad hoc recruitment from *within* a suspected
counterrevolutionary organization had occurred solely for the purpose
of cracking down on that same organization. With few exceptions, such
agents – like the informers whom the CMPS 2nd Bureau in 1958 claimed
had helped wipe out the People's Party and similar networks in the provincial finance and trade sector – would, in the end, receive very little in
return for the service they had rendered. In its 1957 report on the small
student-led China Democratic Party, the Xiangxi prefectural Bureau of
Public Security explained that "on the whole," the members who assisted
the authorities had pitifully few qualifications that justified keeping them
on the books. In the words of the report, just about the only thing they
could be used to do was take part in a post-crackdown propaganda
blitz, when officers could order them to "make public confessions and
denounce [other members of the China Democratic Party], and in this
way help educate the masses." Once their utility in this respect had been
exhausted, it was time to simply let them go.[74]

The harshest form of termination was meted out to those agents whom
the public security organs knew, or had strong reason to believe, had
attempted to intentionally deceive the public security organs in some way.
Luo Ruiqing described them early on as "bad elements" who exploited
their agent status "to engage in nefarious activities, in the sense that
they make up bogus intelligence and fabricate bogus cases to deceive
us, even going so far as to pursue a policy of the 'red skin, white core'
variety whereby they superficially back us while actually backing the
enemy."[75] In the most serious cases, such agents were likely to have been
"terminated" in the full sense of the word, not just metaphorically. In
less severe cases, meanwhile, Wang Jinxiang hinted during the Campaign
to Eliminate Counterrevolutionaries at the fate that would befall them.
"Agents," he said, "who have counterrevolutionary problems but refuse
to come clean, who swindle and bluff, merely feigning compliance, and

---

[73] Chongqing shi gonganju, "Guanyu jinian lai teqing," p. 14.
[74] Hunan sheng Xiangxi tujiazu miaozu zizhizhou gonganju, "Guanyu Yongshun," p. 20.
[75] Guofang daxue dangshi dangjianshi, *Zhonggong dangshi jiaoxue*, Vol. 19, p. 256.

engage in double dealing, should be exposed to the denunciation of the masses and then dismissed."[76] Grand Cultural Revolutionary designs aside, operational considerations like these also very much need to be taken into account when assessing and making sense of the demise of Mao's secret agents after 1967.

[76] Wang Jinxiang, "Zai di yi ci quanguo," p. 7.

Postscript

As I was finishing this book, I emailed a friend – a perspicacious social historian in Florence who for many years has written on both the Soviet Union and Mao's China – and admitted that I was still uncertain about what, if any, firm conclusions could be drawn about "the meaning of it all." He wrote back suggesting that I console myself with the thought that "none of us is ever going to work out 'what it all meant' (apart from the third-rate scholars who knew the answer before they started)." I have been mulling over his message ever since, my mental synapses also triggering vague recollections of Eric Hobsbawm's warning that "historians as an occupation are the primary producers of the raw material that is turned into propaganda and mythology. We must be aware that this is so."[1]

This study has been infinitely more conjectural than anything I have done in the past. Writing about the Cultural Revolution was easy, because so much received wisdom on the subject was in the public domain already and could be debated at length with individuals with firsthand experience of what it had been like. In this last respect, even talking to myself made sense: after all, I had been there. Doing research on agent work in Mao's China proved harder by an order of magnitude. Initially, as I have already hinted (in the Acknowledgments), I did not even know what the Chinese term *teqing* (agent) meant. History as a practice thrives on the exchange of ideas, but the number of historians who had studied agent work in Mao's China with whom I could have in-depth conversations turned out to be fewer than the number of fingers on Harold Lloyd's right hand. Therefore, this study, I fear, has only managed to throw a very faint beam

[1] Eric Hobsbawm, "The Historian Between the Quest for the Universal and the Quest for Identity," *Diogenes*, No. 168, Vol. 42, No. 4, Winter 1994, p. 61.

of light on an institution that is still shrouded in darkness and attended by a bodyguard of propaganda and mythology. My firm conclusions? Only one: that widespread – but not necessarily efficient – use of agents was made by the competent governmental authorities in the urban People's Republic up to 1967 in counterintelligence and in compliance-oriented surveillance of status offenders (that is to say, of "class enemies").

Agents are not history; Mao's China, on the other hand, is. Since 1973, when the line laid down at the 16th NPSC heralded its revival, the domestic use of agents in China has evolved ever further away from "spying for the people" toward simply spying on people. As once defined in opposition to non-people, "*the* people" no longer exist.[2] And at their disposal, the successors of Luo Ruiqing and Xie Fuzhi now have powerful operational tools that were not yet in existence – or even imagined – back in the 1950s and 1960s. But while it may be unprecedented technological innovation in digital biometrics, communication, and surveillance information storage and retrieval that increasingly undergirds the Harmonious Society in the PRC (and, in other parts of the world, sustains Secure Communities), this does not yet by any means render the human subject of this study "quaint." Where the rule of law ultimately prevails, it seems, states will always hesitate to dispense altogether with the service of the secret agent. In fact, the greater the regulation of what is now euphemistically referred to as "nonintrusive surveillance" – closed-circuit TV, mobile phone tracking, webtapping, and so on – the higher the value of the human source whose legal exploitation calls for no warrant at all.[3] Which brings me again to Eric Hobsbawm, this time to his compelling assertion that "paradoxically, the more we expect innovation, the more history becomes essential to discover what it will be like."[4] Many painful lessons from China's recent past have yet to be fully understood and appreciated, perhaps even more so by the rest of us than by the Chinese themselves.[5] When the time came, it was after all the leader of the CCP himself who was willing and prepared to "beat to a pulp" the domestic order of his own surveillance state: whether *our* political masters will ever agree to dismantle its global twenty-first-century equivalent remains to be seen.

---

[2] See Schoenhals, "Demonizing Discourse," pp. 466–67.
[3] This is a point also made in Hewitt, *Snitch!*, p. 148.
[4] Eric Hobsbawm, "The Social Function of the Past: Some Questions," *Past and Present*, No. 55, May 1972, p. 12.
[5] This is a point I have previously argued with reference to Mao Zedong's domestic war on revisionism after 1963. See Michael Schoenhals, "The Global War on Terrorism as Meta-Narrative: An Alternative Reading of Recent Chinese History," *Sungkyun Journal of East Asian Studies*, Vol. 8, No. 2, 2088, pp. 179–201.

Bibliography

Abliz. "Zai di liu ci quanguo gongan huiyi shang de fayan" (Statement at the 6th National Public Security Conference). *Gongan jianshe*, No. 102, October 12, 1954, pp. 18–21.

Aldrich, Richard J. *The Hidden Hand: Britain, America and Cold War Secret Intelligence*. London: John Murray, 2001.

Andrew, Christopher. "Intelligence, International Relations and 'Undertheorization,'" in L. V. Scott and Peter Jackson, eds., *Understanding Intelligence in the Twenty-First Century: Journeys in Shadows*. London: Routledge, 2004, pp. 29–41.

Andrew, Christopher, Richard J. Aldrich, and Wesley K. Wark, eds. *Secret Intelligence: A Reader*. London: Routledge, 2009.

Andrew, Christopher, and David Dilks, eds. *The Missing Dimension: Governments and Intelligence Communities in the Twentieth Century*. London: Macmillan, 1984.

Andrew, Christopher, and Vasili Mitrokhin, eds. *The Mitrokhin Archive II: The KGB and the World*. London: Penguin, 2006.

Anshan shi gonganju. "Zhenpo 'Zhongguo guomindang fangong jiuguotuan' an jingyan jieshao" (Presenting Experiences from Cracking the "China Guomindang Anti-Communist National Salvation Regiment"). *Jingji baowei gongzuo*, No. 9, April 1958, pp. 11–15.

Bai Jun. "Xiang dang qingzui" (Asking for Punishment from the Party for My Crimes). *Gongan jianshe*, No. 326, December 30, 1959, pp. 41–56.

"Baogao" (Report) [February 7, 1964]. Original handwritten six-page text from closed Beijing Bureau of Public Security 5th Office file on prisoner XXX. Purchased by the author in a Beijing flea market.

Baowei gongzuo jianshe (*Protection Work Construction*). Beijing: Protection Department of the PLA North China Military Region Political Department. Issues marked "Confidential."

Barnett, A. Doak. "Social Controls in Communist China." *Far Eastern Survey*, Vol. 22, No. 5, April 22, 1953, pp. 45–48.

Beijing dangshi ziliao tongxun (*Beijing Party History Materials Newsletter*). Beijing: Party History Materials Collection Committee of the Municipal CCP Committee.

Beijing shi gonganju. "Guanyu jiedao mingfang zhong qunzhong dui wo gongan bumen suo tide yijian de zhenggai qingkuang baogao" (Situation Report on Responses to Criticisms Voiced against Our Public Security Organs by the Urban Masses During the Airing of Views). *Gongan jianshe*, No. 238, May 20, 1958, pp. 4–6.

"Zhixing di si ci quanguo gongan huiyi jueyi jihua" (Plan for the Implementation of the Resolution of the 4th National Public Security Conference). *Renmin gongan zengkan*, No. 30, November 20, 1951, pp. 41–53.

ed. *Zhengzhi jiaocai* (*Political Teaching Materials*). Beijing, 1950.

Beijing shi gonganju Xisi fenju. "Guanyu guanche zhixing di liu ci quanguo gongan huiyi jueyi de shishi jihua" (Plan on How to Put into Effect the Implementation and Carrying Out of the Resolution of the 6th National Public Security Conference). *Shoudu gongan zengkan*, Vol. 6, No. 1, February 21, 1955, pp. 51–62.

Beijing shi shinei dianhuaju, ed. *Bufen dianhua haoma 1967* (*Beijing Telephone Directory 1967*). Beijing, 1967.

"Beijing shi 'wenhua dageming' dashiji" (Record of Major Events in the "Great Cultural Revolution" in Beijing). *Beijing dangshi ziliao tongxun*, supplement No. 18, June 1987, pp. 2–45.

Biligbaatar. "Guanyu canjia Baotou shi zhencha gongzuo huiyi he dui jige zhongdian gongchang baowei gongzuo de kaocha baogao" (Report on Participation in Baotou Municipality's Operational Work Conference and Survey of Protection Work in Some Key Factories). *Gongan jianshe*, No. 244, June 12, 1958, pp. 21–23.

Brook, Timothy. *Collaboration: Japanese Agents and Local Elites in Wartime China*. Cambridge, MA: Harvard University Press, 2005.

Brown, Jeremy. "Finding and Using Grassroots Historical Sources from the Mao Era." Dissertation Reviews, December 15, 2010, http://dissertationreviews.org/archives/310. Accessed February 2, 2012.

Brown, Jeremy, and Paul G. Pickowicz, eds. *Dilemmas of Victory: The Early Years of the People's Republic of China*. Cambridge, MA: Harvard University Press, 2007.

Byron, John, and Robert Pack. *The Claws of the Dragon: Kang Sheng – The Evil Genius Behind Mao – and His Legacy of Terror in People's China*. New York: Simon & Schuster, 1992.

"Chaling xian gonganju zhenpole yige ancang de fangeming jituan an" (The Chaling County Bureau of Public Security Has Broken up a Hidden Counterrevolutionary Clique). *Jingji baowei gongzuo*, No. 9, April 1958, pp. 4–5.

Changcheng (*The Great Wall*). Beijing: Chinese Academy of Sciences, Department of Philosophy and Social Sciences.

Chedi qingsuan Luo Ruiqing zai zhengfa gongzuo fangmian de taotian zuixing (*Throughly Eradicate the Heinous Crimes of Luo Ruiqing in the Field of Politics and Law*). Shanghai: Shanghai shi zhengfajie doupigai lianluozhan, 1967.

Chedi suqing Liu Deng Peng Luo zai Shanghai gongan bumen de liudu (*Throughly Eradicate the Poison That Liu Deng Peng and Luo Spread Throughout the Organs of Public Security in Shanghai*). Shanghai: Shanghai shi gonganju lianhe doupigai xiaozu, 1967.

Chen Yi. "Zai gonganbu di yi ci quanguo wenhua baowei gongzuo huiyi shang de baogao" (Report to the Ministry of Public Security's 1st National Conference on Cultural Protection Work) [November 29, 1954]. Original nineteen-page conference transcript. Purchased by the author in a Beijing flea market.

Chen Yun wenji 1935.10–1949.09 (*Chen Yun's Collected Writings, October 1935–September 1949*). 3 vols. Beijing: Zhongyang wenxian chubanshe, 2005.

Cheng Chao and Wei Haoben, eds. *Zhejiang "wenge" jishi (1966.5–1976.10)* (*Record of Events in Zhejiang's "Cultural Revolution"* [*May 1966–October 1976*]). [Hangzhou]: Zhejiang fangzhi bianjibu, 1989.

"*Chengqing jianli teqing pishi biao*" (Agent Opening Authorization Form) [n.d.]. Photograph of original document as seen on the PRC antqiuarian booksellers' network, http://auction.kongfz.com. Accessed January 15, 2011.

The China Quarterly. London: Contemporary China Institute, School of Oriental and African Studies.

Chongqing shi gonganju. "Guanyu jinian lai teqing gongzuo jianshe de jiben qingkuang ji jinhou gongzuo de yijian de baogao" (Report on the Basic Situation in Recent Years with Respect to Agent Work Development and Views on Future Work). *Gongan jianshe*, No. 132, July 16, 1955, pp. 12–15.

Clark, Gerald. *Impatient Giant: Red China Today.* New York: David McKay, 1959.

"Da duzhe wen" (Replies to Readers' Questions). *Renmin gongan*, No. 10, August 30, 1956, p. 17.

Da pipan ziliao (*Great Criticism Materials*). Beijing: Shoudu dazhuan yuanxiao hongdaihui zhengfa gongshe ziliaozu, 1967.

Dadao litong waiguode fangeming xiuzhengzhuyi fenzi Wang Jian (*Down with Counterrevolutionary Revisionist Element Wang Jian Who Maintains Illicit Links with Foreign Countries*). Shanghai: Shanghai shi gonganju bangongshi zhengzhibu nongbaochu geming zaofandui, 1967.

Dai Wendian, ed. *Zhongguo gongan tushu zongmu* (*General Index of Chinese Books on Public Security*). Beijing: Zhongguo renmin gongan daxue chubanshe, 2007.

Deriabin, Peter, and Frank Gibney. *The Secret World.* Garden City, NY: Doubleday, 1959.

"Di ba ci quanguo gongan huiyi guanyu 1956 nian gongan gongzuo zhuyao qingkuang he 1957 nian gongzuo de yijian" (Opinion of the 8th National Public Security Conference on the Major Circumstances of Public Security Work in 1956 and Work in 1957). *Gongan jianshe*, No. 184, March 5, 1957, pp. 3–13.

"Diguozhuyi, Jiang feibang he minzuzhuyi guojia zai woguo zhouwei jiaqiang tewu jigou" (Imperialist, Chiang Kai-shek Bandit Gang and Nationalist States Reinforcing *Tewu* Organs around Our Country). *Gongan qingbao*, No. 6, January 26, 1960, pp. 3–5.

"Di-Jiang tewu jiguan jiji xiang woqu paiqian tewu" (The *Tewu* Organs of the Imperialists and Chiang Kai-shek Actively Dispatch *Tewu* to Our Region). *Gongan qingbao*, No. 8, February 3, 1960, pp. 2–4.

Di jiu ci quanguo gongan huiyi shiwuge jueyi (The Fifteen Resolutions of the 9th National Public Security Conference). Guangzhou: Guangzhou sheng gonganting, 1958.

"Di liu ci quanguo gongan huiyi jueyi" (Resolution of the 6th National Public Security Conference). *Gongan jianshe*, No. 98, September 28, 1954, pp. 3–20.

"Di san ci quanguo jingji baowei gongzuo huiyi jueyi" (Resolution of the 3rd National Conference on Economic Protection Work). *Tielu gongan tongxun*, No. 13, December 8, 1952, pp. 5–9.

Dimmer, John P., Jr. "Observations on the Double Agent." In *Inside CIA's Private World: Declassified Articles from the Agency's Internal Journal, 1955–1992*, selected and edited by H. Bradford Westerfield. New Haven, CT: Yale University Press, 1995, pp. 437–39.

Diwei renyuan chazhao xiansuo huibian (Collected Leads in the Search for Enemy and Puppet Personnel). Jinzhou: Liaoning sheng Jinzhou shi geweihui qingcha diwei dang'an bangongshi, 1970.

Dongbei renmin zhengfu gonganbu. "Dui youdian jiancha de jige wenti" (Some Problems in Postal Examination). *Gongan baowei gongzuo*, Vol. 17, February 15, 1950, pp. 40–42.

"Gei Liaodong sheng gonganting de xin: guanyu teqing gongzuo de jige sixiang renshi wenti" (Letter to the Liaodong Provincial Bureau of Public Security: On Certain Matters of Ideology and Understanding Relating to Agent Work). *Gongan baowei gongzuo*, No. 19, September 15, 1950, pp. 55–58.

"Guanyu gaijin zhencha gongzuo wenti" (On the Problem of Improving Operational Work). *Gongan baowei gongzuo*, No. 20, November 25, 1950, pp. 19–24.

"Guanyu jiaqiang zhencha gongzuo de zhishi" (Instructions on Strengthening Operational Work). *Gongan baowei gongzuo*, No. 17, February 15, 1950, pp. 18–26.

"Guanyu jingji baowei gongzuo de zhishi" (Instructions on Economic Protection Work). *Gongan baowei gongzuo*, No. 17, February 15, 1950, pp. 27–32.

"Jiu shi yuefen gongzuo baogao" (Work Report for September and October). *Gongan baowei gongzuo*, No. 20, November 25, 1950, pp. 10–18.

"Wu liu liangge yue de gongzuo zonghe baogao" (Comprehensive Summary of Work in the Months of May and June). *Gongan baowei gongzuo*, No. 19, September 15, 1950, pp. 32–40.

Dongbei renmin zhengfu gonganbu zhengzhi baoweichu. "Guanyu muqian teqing renyuan de dongtai yu women shiyong duice" (On Current Trends among Agents and Our Utilization Responses). *Gongan baowei gongzuo*, Vol. 20, November 25, 1950, pp. 25–29.

Dongbei tielu gonganju. "Guanyu liangnian lai zhencha gongzuo de jiantao" (Self-Criticism for the Past Two Years of Operational Work). *Tielu gongan tongxun*, No. 13, December 8, 1952, pp. 15–16.

Donner, Frank J. *The Age of Surveillance: The Aims and Methods of America's Political Intelligence System*. New York: Vintage Books, 1981.

Dutton, Michael. *Policing and Punishment in China: From Patriarchy to "the People."* Cambridge: Cambridge University Press, 1992.

Policing Chinese Politics: A History. Durham, NC: Duke University Press, 2005.

"Duzhe laixin" (Letters from Readers). *Renmin gongan*, No. 11, September 30, 1956, p. 24.

Extracts from a work diary, copied by a member of the Beijing XX School Revolutionary Committee Political Work Group on June 2, 1972. Five pages in total, preserved in a Cultural Revolutionary case file purchased by the author in a Beijing flea market.

Faligot, Roger, and Remi Kauffer. *Kang Sheng et les services secrets chinois*. Paris: Robert Laffont, 1987.

"Fanying qingkuang" (Report on Circumstances) [March 15, 1957]. Handwritten one-page document from a closed Taiyuan Bureau of Public Security 4th Office file. Purchased in a flea market.

Fei Hsiao Tung. *Toward a People's Anthropology*. Beijing: New World Press, 1981.

Fei Yundong. *Zhonggong dang'an wenxian zhengji* (Collecting CCP Historical Archive Materials). Beijing: Zhongguo dang'an chubanshe, 2004.

Feng Jiping. "Jianjue guanche di liu ci quanguo gongan huiyi jueyi wei jinyibu jiaqiang shoudu gongan gongzuo er fendou" (Resolutely Implement the Resolution of the 6th National Public Security Conference and Struggle to Further Strengthen Public Security Work in the Capital). *Shoudu gongan zengkan*, Vol. 6, No. 1, February 21, 1955, pp. 1–50.

"Zai ganbu huiyi shang chuanda di wu ci quanguo gongan huiyi jueyi ji jian-cha zhenya fangeming gongzuo de baogao" (Report to a Meeting of Cadres Transmitting the Resolution of the 5th National Public Security Conference and Investigating the Work of Suppressing Counterrevolutionaries). *Shoudu gongan zengkan*, No. 38, December 2, 1952, pp. 1–38.

"Zai quanju ganbu huiyi shang guanyu Beijing zhenya fangeming gongzuo de zongjie baogao" (Summing Up Report at a Meeting of All Cadres in the Bureau on the Work of Suppressing Counterrevolutionaries in Beijing). *Renmin gongan zengkan*, No. 30, November 20, 1951, pp. 14–31.

"Zhi kaimuci" (Opening Remarks). *Renmin gongan zengkan*, No. 20, December 25, 1950, pp. 9–11.

"Fensui panluan fenzi de yinmou, nuli jianshe xin Xizang" (Smash the Plot of the Insurrectionist Elements and Strive to Build a New Tibet). *Renmin gongan*, No. 68, May 28, 1959, pp. 16–19.

Ferguson, Harry. *Spy: A Handbook*. London: Bloomsbury, 2004.

Fulbrook, Mary. *Anatomy of a Dictatorship: Inside the GDR 1949–1989*. Oxford: Oxford University Press, 1995.

"Ganbu jianlibiao" (Cadre CV Form) [January 30, 1953]. Original three-page form from a closed Beijing Bureau of Public Security 5th Office file on prisoner XXX. Purchased by the author in a Beijing flea market.

Gao Gang. "Zai dongbei di si jie gongan huiyi shang de jianghua" (Speech at the 4th Northeast Public Security Conference). *Tianjin gongan*, Vol. 1, No. 2, August 15, 1950, pp. 24–26.

*Gaoju geming de pipan daqi chedi dadao Shanghai shi gongan xitong de fange-
ming xiuzhengzhuyi fenzi Huang Chibo (Hold High the Big Banner of Revolutionary Criticism and Thoroughly Topple the Counterrevolutionary Revisionist Element in the Shanghai Public Security Sector Huang Chibo).* Shanghai:
Shanghai shi gonganju geming zaofan weiyuanhui, 1967.

"Gedi gongan xuanchuan gongzuo dongtai" (Trends in Public Security Propaganda Work). *Gongan jianshe,* No. 111, December 20, 1954, pp. 24–27.

Gieseke, Jens. *Die hauptamtlichen Mitarbeiter der Staatssicherheit: Personalstruktur und Lebenswelt 1950–1989/90.* Berlin: Christoph Links Verlag,
2000.

Gongan baowei gongzuo (Public Security and Protection Work). Shenyang: Ministry of Public Security of the Northeast People's Government. Issues marked
"Top Secret."

Gongan gongzuo jianbao (Public Security Work Bulletin). Beijing: Central Ministry of Public Security. Issues marked "Top Secret."

Gongan jianshe (Public Security Construction). Beijing: Central Ministry of Public
Security. Issues marked "Top Secret." For Lund University library holdings of
this rare serial, see http://libris.kb.se/bib/11813147.

Gongan jianshe hedingben (Collected Public Security Construction). Hong Kong.
An undated volume of unpaginated computer printouts of texts from the Top
Secret CMPS serial *Public Security Construction* in the library of the Universi-
ties Service Centre, Chinese University of Hong Kong.

Gongan qingbao (Public Security Intelligence). Beijing: Central Ministry of Public
Security. Issues marked "Top Secret."

Gongan shouce (Public Security Handbook). Beijing: Central Ministry of Public Security. Superseded by *Renmin gongan.* Issues marked "For Official Use
Only."

Gongan yewu xuexi cailiao (Public Security Vocational Study Material). Tianjin:
Tianjin tielu guanliju gonganchu, 1952.

Gonganbu. "Guanyu gaijin diaocha cailiao gongzuo de tongzhi" (Notification on
Improving Documentary Investigation). *Gongan jianshe,* No. 121, March 26,
1955, pp. 25–27.

Gonganbu Beijing shichazu. "Guanyu Beijing shi gonganju chuanda guanche di
liu ci quanguo gongan huiyi jueyi kaizhan piping yu ziwo piping qingkuang de
kaocha baogao" (Investigation Report on the Beijing Bureau of Public Security's Implementation of the Resolution of the 6th National Public Security
Conference and the Unfolding of Criticism and Self-Criticism). *Gongan jianshe,*
No. 112, December 31, 1954, pp. 1–5.

Gonganbu dangzu. "Guanyu guangbo diantai baowei baomi gongzuo qingkuang
de baogao" (Report on Situation with Respect to Protection and Secrecy Work
in Broadcasting Stations). *Gongan jianshe,* No. 414, March 10, 1961, pp. 1–4.

"Guanyu quanguo gongan tingjuzhang zuotanhui de qingkuang baogao" (Situation Report from a National Informal Conference of Directors of Bureaus of
Public Security). *Gongan jianshe,* No. 204, November 17, 1957, pp. 3–9.

"Muqian duidi douzheng qingkuang de huibao tigang" (Outline Report on the
Current Situation in the Struggle against the Enemy). *Gongan jianshe,* No. 420,
April 1, 1961, pp. 2–12.

Gonganbu erju. "Zhencha gongzuo qingkuang ji xiabannian de gongzuo jihua yaodian" (Operational Work Situation and Main Points of Work Plan for Second Half of [1956]). *Gongan jianshe*, No. 175, October 15, 1956, pp. 18–22.

Gonganbu erju bangongshi. "Nongcun zhencha poan zhong de yixie wenti" (Some Problems Affecting the Operational Cracking of Cases in Rural Villages). *Renmin gongan*, No. 13, November 20, 1956, p. 7.

Gonganbu erju sichu. "Jiexiu xian zhengdun teqing gongzuo jingyan" (Experiences from Overhaul and Consolidation of Agent Work in Jiexiu County). *Renmin gongan*, No. 9, August 10, 1956, pp. 21–22.

"Gonganbu fachu 1966 nian chunjie qijian kaizhan aiminyue huodong de tongzhi" (Ministry of Public Security Issues Notification Launching a Cherish-the-People Campaign during the Spring Festival). *Renmin gongan*, No. 216, December 4, 1965, pp. 3–4.

Gonganbu Jilin shichazu. "Guanyu changkuang zhineng keshi baowei gongzuo qingkuang de kaocha baogao" (Investigation Report Concerning Protection Work in Functional Offices of Factories and Mines). *Gongan jianshe*, No. 123, April 16, 1955, p. 8–13.

Gonganbu Liaoning shicha xiaozu. "Guanyu Anshan shi gonganju zhencha gongzuo de kaocha baogao" (Investigation Report Concerning Operational Work by the Anshan Municipal Bureau of Public Security). *Gongan jianshe*, No. 113, January 10, 1955, pp. 1–3.

Gonganbu Shanghai gongzuozu. "Shanghai shi duidi douzheng zhong de yixie wenti" (Some Problems in the Struggle against the Enemy in Shanghai). *Gongan gongzuo jianbao*, No. 166, November 26, 1960, pp. 6–8.

Gonganbu Shanxi shichazu. "Guanyu Shanxi sheng zhencha gongzuo 'guoguan' wenti de kaocha baogao" (Investigation Report into Whether Operational Work in Shanxi Is "Up to Scratch"). *Gongan jianshe*, No. 118, March 7, 1955, pp. 8–10.

Gonganbu Tianjin shichazu. "Guanyu Tianjin shi gonganju zhencha gongzuo de kaocha baogao" (Investigation Report Concerning the Tianjin Bureau of Public Security's Operational Work). *Gongan jianshe*, No. 118, March 7, 1955, pp. 1–5.

Gonganbu xibei gongzuozu. "Dui jiaqiang shaoshu minzu diqu gongan gongzuo de jige zhengce wenti de yijian" (Opinion in Certain Policy Matters Relating to the Strengthening of Public Security Work in National Minority Areas). *Gongan gongzuo jianbao*, No. 211, September 5, 1961, pp. 4–6.

"Gonganbu yiju tichu jinnian he mingnian dui Jiangbang de zhencha gongzuo guihua" (Ministry of Public Security 1st Bureau Puts Forth Plan for Operational Work Targeting Chiang Kai-shek Gang These Two Years). *Gongan gongzuo jianbao*, No. 77, October 20, 1959, pp. 2–5.

"Gongzuo renyuan dengjibiao" (Staff Registration Form) [1956]. Original one-page form, from a closed Beijing Bureau of Public Security 5th Office file on prisoner XXX. Purchased by the author in a Beijing flea market.

Guangdong sheng gonganting. "1957 nian gongan gongzuo jihua" (Plan for Public Security Work in 1957). *Gongan jianshe*, No. 186, April 15, 1957, pp. 14–23.

Guangdong sheng qingli youdian yaohai weiyuanhui. "Guanyu 1955 nian qingli youdian yaohai renyuan fucha panding gongzuo de bushu" (On Deployment of Work to Reinvestigate and Assess Personnel in Critical Positions in the Posts and Telecommunications Sector in 1955). *Gongan jianshe*, No. 123, April 16, 1955, pp. 1–7.

Guangzhou shi gonganju. "Guanyu XXX panbian toudi qingkuang baogao" (Situation Report on the Defection of XXX). *Gongan jianshe*, No. 236, May 8, 1958, p. 4.

"Guanyu zhencha gongzuo de jiancha" (Investigation into Operational Work). *Gongan jianshe*, No. 113, January 10, 1955, pp. 8–11.

"Guanyu fandong dangtuan tewu renyuan dengji chuli zongjie baogao" (Summing Up Report on the Registration and Disposal of Reactionary Party and Organization Tewu Personnel). *Tianjin gongan*, Vol. 2, No. 1, January 31, 1951, pp. 22–26.

"Guanyu jixu zhenya yi pi Mei-Jiang tewu, xianxing fangeming fenzi he xingshi fanzui fenzi de cailiao" (Documentation on the Continued Need to Suppress a Batch of American and Chiang Kai-shek *Tewu*, Active Counterrevolutionary Elements, and Criminal Elements) [Beijing, 1966]. Original four-page flier, purchased by the author in a Beijing flea market.

Guanyu Mao Zedong tongzhi wuchanjieji zhuanzheng xueshuo he sufan gongzuo fangzhen luxian de xuexi cailiao (*Materials for the Study of Comrade Mao Zedong's Doctrine on the Dictatorship of the Proletariat and Policy and Line in Elimination of Counterrevolution*). Beijing: Zhongyang zhengfa ganbu xuexiao zhengce falü jiaoyanshi, 1960.

Guo Yumin. "Zai huiyi shang guanyu Shijingshan fadianchang jianli anquan xiaozu gongzuo de dianxing baogao" (Pilot Conference Report on the Creation of Security Groups in the Shijingshan Power Plant). *Renmin gongan zengkan*, No. 20, December 25, 1950, pp. 18–23.

Guofang daxue dangshi dangjianshi, ed. *Zhonggong dangshi jiaoxue cankao ziliao* (*Reference Material for Teaching CCP History*). 27 vols. Beijing: Guofang daxue, 1986.

Guojia dang'anju bangongshi, ed. *Dang'an gongzuo wenjian huiji* (*Collected Documents on Archive Work*). Beijing: Dang'an chubanshe, 1986.

Guojia kewei jiguan dalianwei zhenggongzu dazibaozu, ed. *Wuchanjieji wenhua dageming dazibao xuanbian* (Selected Big Character Posters from the Great Proletarian Cultural Revolution). 14 vols. Beijing, 1968, 1969.

Guowuyuan jiguan shiwu guanliju dashiji 1950–1995 (*Record of Major Events in the State Council Department of Administraive Affairs 1950–1995*). Beijing: Guowuyuan bangongting mishuju, 1995.

Haidian fenju. "Guanyu baowei gongzuo jige wenti de zongjie" (Summary of Some Matters Relating to Protection Work). *Shoudu gongan zengkan*, No. 35, September 15, 1952, pp. 1–12.

Halebian, Olivia. "New Light on Old Spies: A Review of Recent Soviet Intelligence Revelations." Center for the Study of Intelligence, https://www.cia.gov/library/center-for-the-study-of-intelligence/kent-csi/vol9no4/html/v09i4a09p_0001.htm. Accessed February 2, 2012.

Hao Dianwen. "Renkou kapian guanli de fangfa haochu duo" (Numerous Things Good about Census Card File Management). *Renmin gongan*, No. 12, October 31, 1956, pp. 18–19.

Hao Zaijin. *Zhongguo mimi zhan (China's Secret Wars)*. Beijing: Zuojia chuban-she, 2007.

Hebei gongan tongbao (Hebei Public Security General Circular). Tianjin: Hebei provincial Bureau of Public Security. Issues marked "Secret."

Hewitt, Steve. *Snitch! A History of the Modern Intelligence Informer*. London: Continuum, 2010.

Hoare, J. E. *Embassies in the East: The Story of the British and Their Embassies in China, Japan and Korea from 1859 to the Present*. Richmond, VA: Curzon Press, 1999.

Hobsbawm, Eric. "The Historian Between the Quest for the Universal and the Quest for Identity." *Diogenes*, No. 168, Vol. 42, No. 4, Winter 1994, pp. 51–63.

"The Social Function of the Past: Some Questions." *Past and Present*, No. 55, May 1972, pp. 3–17.

Huabei junqu zhengzhibu baoweibu. "Guanyu xianyi cailiao zhuanyi deng wenti de jidian yidian" (Some Views on the Transmission of Suspects' Documentation and Other Matters). *Baowei gongzuo jianshe*, No. 7, January 15, 1951, pp. 12–14.

Huadong gonganju. "Guanyu zai Huadong qu qingli youdian xitong yaohai ren-yuan de qingkuang baogao" (Situation Report on the Weeding Out of Critically Positioned Persons in the Post and Telecommunications Sector in East China) [June 1954]. *Gongan jianshe hedingben*, pp. 31–34.

Huadongju. "Su-Tuo gongzuo zongjie" (Trotskyite Elimination Work Summary) [June 1954]. *Gongan jianshe hedingben*, pp. 15–24.

Huang Chibo zuixing lu (Huang Chibo's Criminal Record). Shanghai: Shanghai shi gonganju lianhe doupigai xiaozu, 1967.

Huang Yingke and Xie Yinhui. "Zhenpo 'Zhongweihui erzu' tewu XXX an" (Cracking the Case of the "Central Committee Group Two" *Tewu* XXX). *Renmin gongan*, No. 18, March 25, 1957, pp. 16–17.

Huges, R. Gerald, Peter Jackson, and Len Scott, eds. *Exploring Intelligence Archives: Enquiries into the Secret State*. London: Routledge, 2008.

Hunan sheng Xiangxi tujiazu miaozu zizhizhou gonganju. "Guanyu Yongshun, Longshan, Jishou deng di pohuo 'Zhongguo minzhudang renmin geming wei-yuanhui' fangeming anjian de zongjie baogao" (Summing Up Report on Crack-ing the Case of the Counterrevolutionary "China Democratic Party People's Revolutionary Committee" in Yongshun, Longshan, and Jishou). *Gongan jian-she*, No. 220, March 10, 1958, pp. 17–20.

"Jiangbang 'guojia anquanju' zuijin tichu dui woqu paiqian huodong de jixiang cuoshi" (Some Recent Measures by the "National Security Bureau" of the Chiang Kai-shek Gang Involving Dispatch to Regions We Control). *Gongan qingbao*, No. 108, November 9, 1960, pp. 4–5.

"Jiangbang tewu jiguan jiji souji wo guofang jianduan kexue qingbao" (Chiang Kai-shek Gang *Tewu* Organs Actively Collecting Intelligence on Our Most

Advanced National Defense Science). *Gongan qingbao*, No. 25, March 18, 1960, p. 3.

"Jiangbang tewu jiguan zuijin shiqi dui woqu de zhuyao yinmou huodong" (The Major Plots Targeting Our Region Presently Plotted by Chiang Kai-shek Gang *Tewu* Organs). *Gongan qingbao*, No. 75, August 5, 1960, pp. 3–5.

Jiangsu sheng gonganting. "Guanyu gongkuang qiye neibu diqing zonghe baogao" (Comprehensive Report on the Threat Level in Factories, Mines, and Corporations). *Gongan jianshe*, No. 111, December 20, 1954, pp. 14–16.

"Guanyu jingji baowei gongzuo de jiancha" (Examination of Economic Protection Work). *Gongan jianshe*, No. 111, December 20, 1954, pp. 9–13.

Jiangsu sheng gonganting di si chu. "Guanyu Nanjing shi ge dazhuan xuexiao guanche Zhongyang gonganbu wenhua baowei gongzuo zhishi de jiancha baogao" (Examination Report Concerening the Implementation of the Central Ministry of Public Security's Instructions on Cultural Protection Work in Institutions of Higher Learning in Nanjing) [February 1954]. *Gongan jianshe hedingben*, pp. 11–15.

Jiangsu sheng shengji jiguan geming zaofanpai dalianhe zongbu, ed. *Mao zhuxi dang zhongyang ji zhongyang shouzhang guanyu Jiangsu wuchanjieji wenhua dageming de zhongyao zhishi huibian* (*Collected Instructions from Chairman Mao, the Party Center, and Central Leaders Concerning the Great Proletarian Cultural Revolution in Jiangsu*). Nanjing, 1968.

"Jiangsu sheng wenhua baowei gongzuo qingkuang he 1955 nian gongzuo jihua" (The Situation in Cultural Protection Work in Jiangsu Province and Work Plan for 1955). *Gongan jianshe*, No. 131, June 25, 1955, pp. 4–9.

Jianguo yilai gongan gongzuo dashi yaolan (*Survey of Major Events in Public Security Work Since the Founding of the Nation*). Beijing: Qunzhong chubanshe, 2003.

"Jianjue xiang shimi xingwei zuo douzheng!" (Resolutely Fight Behavior Compromising Secrecy!). *Renmin gongan*, No. 19, April 10, 1957, p. 13.

"Jianxun" (News in Brief). *Gongan jianshe*, No. 107, November 23, 1954, pp. 29–31.

"Jianxun" (News in Brief). *Gongan jianshe*, No. 120, March 21, 1955, pp. 25–27.

"Jianxun" (News in Brief). *Gongan jianshe*, No. 148, December 29, 1955, pp. 27–29.

"Jianxun" (News in Brief). *Jingji baowei gongzuo*, No. 9, April 1958, pp. 20–21.

"Jiemi mimi qingbaozhan '208': jiejue Chuanxi 'lushang Taiwan'" (Uncovering the Secrets of Secret Intelligence Station No. 208: Resolving Western Sichuan's "Taiwan on Land"). Xinhua News Agency, http://news.xinhuanet.com/mil/2010-01/26/content_12875155.htm. Accessed February 2, 2012.

Jinggangshan bao (*Jinggangshan Report*). Beijing: Tsinghua University.

Jingji baowei gongzuo (*Economic Protection Work*). Beijing: 2nd Bureau of the Central Ministry of Public Security. Issues marked "Secret." Supersedes *Jingji baowei gongzuo huiji*.

Jingji baowei gongzuo huiji (*Collected Economic Protection Work*). Beijing: 2nd Bureau of the Central Ministry of Public Security. Issues marked "Confidential." Superseded by *Jingji baowei gongzuo*.

Jintie gongan (Tianjin Railroad Public Security). Tianjin: Public Security Office of the Tianjin Railroad Management Bureau. Issues marked "For Official Use Only."

The Journal of Intelligence History. Engen, Germany: International Intelligence History Association.

KGB Lexicon: The Soviet Intelligence Officer's Handbook, edited and introduced by Vasiliy Mitrokhin with a foreword by Peter Hennessy. London: Frank Cass, 2002.

Lanzhou junqu zhengzhibu zuzhibu, ed. *Zuzhi gongzuo wenjian huibian (Collected Organization Work Documents)*, 3 vols. Lanzhou, 1980.

Li Ping. "Women de zhencha gongzuo kaishi youle zhuanbian" (We Have Seen the Beginning of a Turnaround in Our Operational Work). *Gongan shouce*, No. 37, March 31, 1955, pp. 26–29.

Li Woru. "Zai di wu ci quanguo tielu gongan huiyi shang de zongjie" (Summary at the 5th National Railroad Public Security Conference). *Tielu gongan tongxun*, No. 12, September 17, 1952, pp. 10–16.

Li Zhao. "Jin yi bu guanche qunzhong luxian geng haode baowei gongye dayuejin" (Implement the Mass Line One Step Further and Do an Even Better Job of Protecting the Industrial Great Leap Forward). *Jingji baowei gongzuo*, No. 17, November 12, 1958, pp. 1–7, 30.

"Rang anquan hongqi chabian quanguo" (Plant Red Banners of Security Nationwide). *Jingji baowei gongzuo*, No. 12, September 1958, pp. 5–7.

"Ligong shuzui ziyuanshu" (Voluntary Offer of Meritorious Service to Atone for Crimes Committed) [May 8, 1952]. Photograph of original document as seen on PRC antiquarian booksellers' network, http://auction.kongfz.com. Accessed January 15, 2011.

Liaoning sheng gonganting dangzu. "Guanyu '1956 nian quansheng gongan gongzuo jiben zongjie he 1957 nian gongzuo renwu' de baogao" (Report on "Basic Summary of Province-Wide Public Security Work in 1956 and Tasks for 1957"). *Gongan jianshe*, No. 186, April 15, 1957, pp. 2–14.

Liaoning sheng renmin jianchayuan. "Guanyu Shenyang shi gonganju Jiaodong fenju weifa luanji bisi 'teqing' XXX shijian de baogao" (Report on the Incident of the Eastern Suburb Branch of the Shenyang Bureau of Public Security in Violation of Law and Discipline Hounding the "Agent" XXX to Death). *Gongan jianshe*, No. 122, April 12, 1955, pp. 23–26.

Lieberthal, Kenneth. *Governing China: From Revolution Through Reform*. New York: W. W. Norton, 1995.

Lin Deming de zuixing (Lin Deming's Crimes). Shanghai: Shanghai shi gonganju zhian huzheng chu dou-Lin xiaozu, 1967.

Ling Yun. "Jinyibu tigao douzheng yishu zhansheng yinbi diren" (Further Improve the Art of Struggle and Defeat the Hidden Enemies). *Renmin gongan*, No. 84, April 8, 1960, pp. 18–20.

"Zai di liu ci quanguo gongan huiyi shang de fayan" (Statement at the 6th National Public Security Conference). *Gongan jianshe*, No. 102, October 12, 1954, pp. 11–13.

"Lingxun" (Miscellaneous News). *Gongan gongzuo jianbao*, No. 83, December 14, 1959, pp. 12–14.

"Lingxun" (Miscellaneous News). *Gongan qingbao*, No. 46, April 29, 1960, p. 4.

Liu Deng Peng Luo zai Shanghai shi gonganju de dailiren – Huang Chibo (Huang Chibo – Proxy of Liu Deng Peng and Luo in the Shanghai Bureau of Public Security). Shanghai: Shanghai shi yuan gongan renyuan doupigai xiaozu, 1967.

Liu Guangren, Zhao Yimin, and Yu Xingqian. *Feng Jiping zhuan (Biography of Feng Jiping)*. Beijing: Qunzhong chubanshe, 1997.

68 jun zhengzhibu baoweibu. "Dui 53 fen kapian yanjiu de zongjie" (Summary of Research into 53 Card Files). *Baowei gongzuo jianshe*, No. 7, January 15, 1951, pp. 15–19.

Liu Xingyi. *Yang Qiqing zhuan (Biography of Yang Qiqing)*. Beijing: Qunzhong chubanshe, 2006.

"Lizheng wancheng 1957 nian gexiang yewu gongzuo de zhibiao" (Strive to Meet the Targets for Vocational Work in 1957). *Renmin gongan*, No. 16, February 15, 1957, pp. 12–13.

Lu Qian. "Zemyang faxian he peiyang jijifenzi" (How to Identify and Foster Activists). *Renmin gongan*, No. 9, June 25, 1950, pp. 89–97.

Lu Zheng zuixinglu (Record of Lu Zheng's Crimes). Shanghai: Shanghai shi gonganju zhengzhibu bangongshi nongbaochu geming zaofandui, 1967.

Luo Ruiqing. "Di liu ci quanguo gongan huiyi de zongjie" (Concluding Summary at the 6th National Public Security Conference). *Gongan jianshe*, No. 98, September 28, 1954, pp. 50–69.

  "Guanyu jiunian douzheng zongjie de jige wenti" (On How to Summarize Nine Years of Struggle). *Gongan jianshe*, No. 277, December 1, 1958, pp. 7–30.

  "Zai Beijing shiju xuexi di si ci quanguo gongan huiyi jueyi zongjie dahui shang de baogao" (Report to the Concluding Meeting of the Beijing Bureau of Public Security to Study the Resolution of the 4th National Public Security Conference). *Renmin gongan zengkan*, No. 30, November 20, 1951, pp. 32–40.

  "Zai di ba ci quanguo gongan huiyi shang de zongjie" (Concluding Summary at the 8th National Public Security Conference). *Gongan jianshe*, No. 184, March 5, 1957, pp. 13–22.

  "Zai di er ci quanguo gongan huiyi shang de baogao" (Report to the 2nd National Public Security Conference) [October 16, 1950]. Handwritten partial copy of original transcript preserved in an archive of compilers of official history of public security on North China railroads after 1945. Purchased by the author in a Beijing flea market.

  "Zai di liu ci quanguo gongan huiyi shang de baogao" (Report to the 6th National Public Security Conference). *Gongan jianshe*, No. 98, September 28, 1954, pp. 21–49.

  "Zai gonganbu quanti ganbu dahui shang de jianghua" (Speech at a Gathering of All Cadres in the Ministry of Public Security). *Renmin gongan*, No. 78, October 26, 1959, pp. 1–7.

  "Zai liang sheng yi shi huibao huiyi shang de zhishi" (Instructions at Report-Back Meeting for Two Provinces and One Municipality). *Gongan jianshe*, No. 245, June 16, 1958, pp. 2–8.

"Zai quanguo jingji baowei gongzuo huiyi shang de zongjie baogao" (Summing Up Report at the National Conference on Economic Protection Work). *Gongan baowei gongzuo*, No. 18, June 1, 1950, pp. 4–24.

"Zai quanjun di er ci baowei gongzuo huiyi shang de zongjie baogao" (Summing Up Report at the 2nd All-Army Conference on Protection Work). *Jingji baowei gongzuo huiji*, Vol. 5, July 1953, pp. 1–3.

Luo Ruiqing lun renmin gongan gongzuo (*Luo Ruiqing on People's Public Security Work*). Beijing, 1994.

Lü, Xiaobo, and Elizabeth J. Perry, eds. *Danwei: The Changing Chinese Workplace in Historical and Comparative Perspective*. Armonk, NY: M. E. Sharpe, 1997.

Lüdtke, Alf, ed. *The History of Everyday Life: Reconstructing Historical Experiences and Ways of Life*. Princeton, NJ: Princeton University Press, 1995.

MacFarquhar, Roderick, and Michael Schoenhals. *Mao's Last Revolution*. Cambridge, MA: Belknap Press of Harvard University Press, 2006.

Mao zhuxi Lin fuzhuxi guanyu baokan xuanchuan de zhishi (*Chairman Mao's and Vice-Chairman Lin's Instructions on Press and Propaganda*). Beijing, 1970.

Marcuse, Jacques. *The Peking Papers: Leaves from the Notebook of a China Correspondent*. New York: E. P. Dutton, 1967.

Marx, Gary T. "Thoughts on a Neglected Category of Social Movement Participant: The Agent Provocateur and the Informant." *American Journal of Sociology*, Vol. 80, No. 2, 1974, pp. 402–442.

"Meiguo tewu jiguan yong dianzi toutingqi lai kongzhi renmin" (American *Tewu* Organs Employ Electronic Eavesdropping Devices to Control the People). *Renmin gongan*, No. 22, June 12, 1957, p. 17.

"Mei-Jiang tewu jiguan gaibian zai huaqiao zhong wuse paiqian duixiang de zuofa" (American and Chiang Kai-shek *Tewu* Organs Are Changing Their Profiling for Targets to Dispatch among Overseas Chinese). *Gongan qingbao*, No. 16, February 27, 1961, p. 4.

"Mei-Jiang tewu zai Gang you neng shougou dao wo difang baokan" (American and Chiang Kai-shek *Tewu* Are Again Able to Obtain Our Local Newspapers in Hong Kong). *Gongan qingbao*, No. 108, November 9, 1960, p. 5.

Mu Xin. *Yinbi zhanxian tongshuai Zhou Enlai* (*Supreme Commander on the Covert Front Zhou Enlai*). Beijing: Zhongguo qingnian chubanshe, 2002.

Mu Yumin. *Beijing jingcha bainian* (*One Hundred Years of the Beijing Police*). Beijing: Zhongguo renmin gongan daxue chubanshe, 2004.

Nanjing junqu zhengzhibu baoweibu, ed. *Xianchang kancha yewu cankao ziliao* (*On-the-Scene Investigation Vocational Reference Materials*). Nanjing, 1955.

National Photographic Interpretation Center. *Probable Atomic Energy Complex Under Construction Near Chih-Chin-Hsia, China*. The National Security Archive, George Washington University, http://www.gwu.edu/~nsarchiv/NSAEBB/NSAEBB186/index.htm. Accessed October 19, 2011.

"Pingji dingxin gongzuo zongjie" (Summary of Rank and Salary Setting Work). *Tianjin gongan*, Vol. 1, No. 2, August 15, 1950, pp. 14–18.

"Pingshi bu xuexi kaoshi chu xiaohua" (Those Who Do Not Study Regularly Make Fools of Themselves When Taking Exams). *Renmin gongan*, No. 147, February 20, 1063, p. 12.

Pipan ziliao: Zhongguo Heluxiaofu Liu Shaoqi fangeming xiuzhengzhuyi yanlun ji (Denunciation Materials: Counterrevolutionary Revisionist Utterances by China's Khrushchev Liu Shaoqi). 3 vols. Beijing: Renmin chubanshe ziliaoshi, 1968.

"Piping yu jianyi" (Criticism and Suggestions). *Gongan shouce*, No. 31, December 10, 1954, pp. 43–44.

Preobrazhensky, Konstantin. "Russian Espionage on China." International Analyst Network, http://www.analyst-network.com/about.php. Accessed March 10, 2010.

Qi Baozhu. "Fuqin de 'qianfu' shengya" (My Father's Career "Under Deep Cover"). Zhongguo jingcha wang, http://www.cpd.com.cn/gb/newspaper/2010-01/19/content_1274057.htm. Accessed January 18, 2011.

Qinghai sheng gonganting. "1958 nian gongan gongzuo guihua (chugao)" (Plan for Public Security Work in 1958 [Draft]). *Gongan jianshe*, No. 266, August 5, 1958, pp. 2–6.

"Quanguo you duoshao fangeming he fangeming shehui jichu?" (How Many Counterrevolutionary Elements and Foundations of Counterrevolution Are there Altogether Nationwide?). *Gongan gongzuo jianbao*, No. 80, November 25, 1959, pp. 11–12.

Renmin gongan (People's Public Security). Beijing: Central Ministry of Public Security. Issues marked "For Official Use Only." Supersedes *Gongan shouce*. For Lund University library holdings of this rare serial, see http://libris.kb.se/bib/11810143.

"Renmin gongan weishenme you youju faxing?" (Why Is *People's Public Security* Distributed by the Post Office?). *Renmin gongan*, No. 19, April 10, 1957, p. 5.

Renmin gongan zengkan (People's Public Security: Supplement). Beijing: Beijing municipal Bureau of Public Security. Issues initially marked "For Official Use Only," later "Secret." Superseded by *Shoudu gongan zengkan*.

Renmin ribao (People's Daily). Beijing.

"Rucheng soubu gongzuo zongjie baogao" (Summary of Location and Detention Work Since Entering the City). *Tianjin gongan*, Vol. 2, No. 1, January 31, 1951, pp. 15–18.

Schoenhals, Michael. "The Central Case Examination Group, 1966–1979." *The China Quarterly*, No. 145, March 1996, pp. 89–111.

"Demonizing Discourse in Mao Zedong's China: People vs. Non-People." *Totalitarian Movements and Political Religions*, Vol. 8, Nos. 3–4, September–December 2007, pp. 464–82.

Doing Things with Words in Chinese Politics: Five Studies. Berkeley: University of California Institute of East Asian Studies, Center for Chinese Studies, 1992.

"The Global War on Terrorism as Meta-Narrative: An Alternative Reading of Recent Chinese History." *Sungkyun Journal of East Asian Studies*, Vol. 8, No. 2, 2088, pp. 179–201.

"Outsourcing the Inquisition: 'Mass Dictatorship' in China's Cultural Revolution." *Totalitarian Movements and Political Religions*, Vol. 9, No. 1, March 2008, pp. 3–19.

"Recruiting Agents in Industry and Trade: Lifting the Veil on Early People's Republic of China Operational Work." *Modern Asian Studies, FirstView* Article, pp. 1–25, published online November 25, 2011, http://dx.doi.org/10.1017/S0026749X11000734. Accessed December 13, 2011.

"'Why Don't We Arm the Left?' Mao's Culpability for the Cultural Revolution's 'Great Chaos' of 1967." *The China Quarterly*, No. 182, June 2005, pp. 277–300.

"Zhongguo gongchandang zhongyang diaochabu jianshi" (Brief History of the Central Investigation Department of the Chinese Communist Party), in Zhu Jiamu, ed., *Dangdai zhongguo yu tade fazhan daolu* (*Contemporary China and Its Development Road*). Beijing: Dangdai Zhongguo chubanshe, 2010, pp. 252–72.

ed. Mao's Great Inquisition: The Central Case Examination Group, 1966–1979. Published as *Chinese Law and Government: A Journal of Translations*, Vol. 29, No. 3, May–June 1996.

ed. and trans. Public Security in the People's Republic of China: A Selection of Mood Assessment Reports (1951–1962). Published as *Contemporary Chinese Thought: Translations and Studies*, Vol. 38, No. 3, Spring 2007.

Schram, Stuart, ed. *Mao Tse-tung Unrehearsed: Talks and Letters 1956–71*. Harmondsworth: Penguin Books, 1974.

Selected Works of Mao Zedong. 5 vols. Beijing: Foreign Languages Press, 1965–77.

Shandong sheng gonganting erchu. "Xiang Zhongyang gonganbu erju de baogao" (Report to the 2nd Bureau of the Central Ministry of Public Security). *Jingji baowei gongzuo huiji*, Vol. 5, July 1953, pp. 5–12.

"Shanghai cong dazi tengxieshe zhong chachu yi pi wulei fenzi" (Shanghai Discovers a Number of Five-Category Elements in Typing and Copying Shops). *Gongan gongzuo jianbao*, No. 138, July 27, 1960, pp. 7–8.

Shangqiu xingzhengqu gonganchu. "Guanyu pohuo fei 'Dixiajun Xuzhou di san fangmianjun Su-Lu-Yu-Wan jiaofei zongsilingbu' an de chubu zongjie" (Tentative Summary of Cracking the Case of the Bandit "Underground Army Xuzhou 3rd Front Army Jiangsu-Shandong-Henan-Anhui Bandit Extermination General Command"). *Tielu gongan tongxun*, No. 3, December 15, 1950, pp. 13–15.

Shanxi sheng gonganting. "Guanyu jiehe zhenggai jinxing baomi jiancha de zongjie" (Summary of a Rectification and Reform Investigation into the Maintenance of Secrecy). *Gongan jianshe*, No. 252, June 25, 1958, pp. 12–13.

"Shaoshu yu wo you maoyi wanglai de waishang Huashang de zhengzhi qingkuang jiwei fuza" (The Political Circumstances of a Small Number of Foreign and Overseas Chinese Firms That Trade with Us Are Extremely Complex). *Gongan gongzuo jianbao*, No. 236, March 21, 1962, pp. 3–5.

Shaw, Victor N. *Social Control in China: A Study of Chinese Work Units.* Westport, CT: Praeger, 1996.

"Shen Anna: Jiang Jieshi shenbian de hongse nüdie" (Anna Shen: The Red Female Spy by Chiang Kai-shek's Side). Xinhua News Agency, news.xinhuanet.com/theory/2008–12/19/content_10526532.htm. Accessed February 2, 2012.

Shen Zhihua. *Sulian zhuanjia zai Zhongguo* (1948–1960) (*Soviet Experts in China* [1948–1960]). Beijing: Zhongguo guoji guangbo chubanshe, 2003.

Shenyang shi gonganju di er chu. "XXX jiuhe fangeming yinmou an shi zemyang pohuode" (How the Case of XXX's Counterrevolutionary Networking Plot Was Cracked). *Jingji baowei gongzuo*, No. 9, April 1958, pp. 8–11.

"Shenyang shi gonganju yansu chuli bisi 'teqing' XXX shijian" (Shenyang Municipal Bureau of Public Security Deals Seriously with Incident of "Agent" XXX Being Hounded to Death). *Gongan jianshe*, No. 128, June 5, 1955, pp. 16–17.

Shenyang shi renmin zhengfu gonganju jingji baoweichu. "Guanyu jianli teqing gongzuo de fangfa" (Agent Work Initiation Procedures). *Gongan baowei gongzuo*, No. 20, November 25, 1950, pp. 30–40.

Shi Yizhi. *Wo zai gonganbu shi nian* (*My Ten Years in the Ministry of Public Security*). Beijing: privately printed, 2002.

"Shier hao zhuan'an huibao tigang" (Report Outline on Case No. 12) [October 20, 1963]. Photocopy of a handwritten forty-nine-page draft, preserved in an archive of compilers of official history of public security on North China railroads after 1945. Purchased by the author in a Beijing flea market.

Shijiazhuang shi gonganju dangzu. "Guanyu pohuo 'Huadi zongbu,' 'Guomindang Hebei sheng zhengfu,' 'Zhonghua chixindang' san qi fangeming baoluan anjian de baogao" (Report on Cracking Three Cases of Attempted Counterrevolutionary Riots by the "China Region General HQ," "Guomindang Hebei Provincial Government," and "China Scarlet Hearts Party"). *Hebei gongan tongbao*, No. 19, April 1961, pp. 2–4.

Shoudu gongan zengkan (*Capitol Public Security: Supplement*). Beijing: Beijing municipal Bureau of Public Security. Classified serial. Supersedes *Renmin gongan zengkan*.

Shue, Vivienne. *The Reach of the State: Sketches of the Chinese Body Politic*. Stanford, CA: Stanford University Press, 1988.

Sifa zhengce xuanbian (*Selected Judicial Policies*). Shanghai: Shanghai shi gaoji renmin fayuan and Shanghai shi sifaju, 1982.

Sun Mingshan, ed. *Lishi shunjian II* (*Moments in History II*). Beijing: Qunzhong chubanshe, 2001.

ed. *Lishi shunjian III* (*Moments in History III*). Beijing: Qunzhong chubanshe, 2004.

ed. *Lishi shunjian IV* (*Moments in History IV*). Beijing: Qunzhong chubanshe, 2006.

Suqing "Liu" du (*Eradicate "Residual"* [Liu] *Poison*). 2 vols. Shanghai: Shanghai shi gonganju bangongshi nongbaochu geming zaofandui, 1967.

Taiyuan shi gonganju di yi chu. Untitled one-page document [August 7, 1957]. From a closed Taiyuan Bureau of Public Security 4th Office file. Purchased in a flea market.

"Wei jiang XXX jian wei teqing you" (Motivating the Opening Up of XXX as Agent) [June 6, 1956]. Original one-page document, from a closed Taiyuan Bureau of Public Security 4th Office file. Purchased in a flea market.

"Wei tingzhi teqing XXX de cailiao" (On Terminating Agent XXX) [June 28, 1957]. Original two-page document from a closed Taiyuan Bureau of Public Security 4th Office file. Purchased in a flea market.

"Wei tingzhi teqing XXX de cailiao" (On Terminating Agent XXX) [July 9, 1957]. Original two-page document from a closed Taiyuan Bureau of Public Security 4th Office file. Purchased in a flea market.

Tao Siju, ed. *Gongan baowei gongzuo de zhuoyue lingdaoren Xu Zirong zhuan* (*Biography of the Outstanding Leader of Public Security and Protection Work Xu Zirong*). Beijing: Qunzhong chubanshe, 2002.

ed. *Xin Zhongguo di yi ren Gongan buzhang Luo Ruiqing* (*New China's First Minister of Public Security Luo Ruiqing*). Beijing: Qunzhong chubanshe, 2002.

"Tehu guanli yu teye guanli" (Management of Special Households and Special Trades). *Tianjin gongan*, Vol. 1, No. 4, September 30, 1950, p. 18.

"Teqing anjuan yijiaoshu" (Agent File Transfer Form) [n.d.]. Original one-page form from a closed Taiyuan Bureau of Public Security 4th Office file. Purchased in a flea market.

"Teqing gongzuo chengji jileibiao" (Agent Work Accumulated Achievements Form) [1956]. Photograph of original document as seen on the PRC antiquarian booksellers' network, http://auction.kongfz.com. Accessed July 18, 2008.

"Teqing gongzuo" jiangyi (*Lectures on the Subject of Agent Work*). Beijing: Zhongyang renmin gongan xueyuan, 1957.

"Teqing renyuan dengjibiao" (Agent Registration Form) [1956]. Photograph of original document as seen on the PRC antiquarian booksellers' network, http://auction.kongfz.com. Accessed July 18, 2008.

"Teqing renyuan dengjibiao" (Agent Registration Form) [June 15, 1956]. Original one-page form from a closed Taiyuan Bureau of Public Security 4th Office file. Purchased in a flea market.

"Tianjin deng shi zai lüdian zhong chahuo dapi weifa fanzui fenzi" (Large Numbers of Lawbreaking Criminal Elements Found in Hotels in Tianjin and Other Cities). *Gongan gongzuo jianbao*, No. 226, December 11, 1961, pp. 4–5.

Tianjin gongan (*Tianjin Public Security*). Tianjin: Tianjin municipal Bureau of Public Security. Issues marked "Confidential."

Tianjin shi renmin zhengfu gonganju. "Zhishi" (Directive). *Tianjin gongan*, Vol. 2, No. 1, January 31, 1951, pp. 22–24.

Tiedao gongan (*Railroad Public Security*). Beijing: Bureau of Public Security of the Central People's Government Ministry of Railroads. Issues marked "For Official Use Only."

Tiedaobu gonganju. "Guanyu tielu zhencha gongzuo de jianyao zongjie" (Brief Summary of Operational Work on the Railroads). *Tielu gongan tongxun*, No. 13, December 8, 1952, pp. 12–15.

Tielu gongan tongxun (*Railroad Public Security Newsletter*). Beijing: Bureau of Public Security of the Central People's Government Ministry of Railroads. Issues initially marked "For Official Use Only," later "Secret."

"Tigao jingti yanfang zichanjieji sixiang de qinshi" (Be More Vigilant and Firmly Guard against the Corrosive Power of Bourgeois Ideology). *Gongan shouce*, No. 37, March 31, 1955, p. 39.

Time magazine. New York: Time, Inc.

Vogel, Ezra F. "Preserving Order in the Cities," in John W. Lewis, ed., *The City in Communist China*. Stanford, CA: Stanford University Press, 1971, pp. 75–93.

Wakeman, Frederic, Jr. *Spymaster: Dai Li and the Chinese Secret Service.* Berkeley: University of California Press, 2003.

Wang Dinglie and Wen Xianmei, eds. *Bashu jiangshuai zhuan (Biographies of Generals and Commanders from Sichuan).* Chengdu: Bashu shushe, 1989.

Wang Dongning. "Zai Hebei quansheng zhencha gongzuo huiyi shang de zongjie baogao" (Summing Up Report at the Hebei Province-Wide Conference on Operational Work). *Gongan jianshe,* No. 132, July 16, 1955, pp. 9–12.

Wang Fan and Dong Ping. *Lingxiu shenbian teshu weidui (The Leadership's Special Bodyguard).* Beijing: Zhongguo wenshi chubanshe, 2009.

Wang Jinxiang. "Dongbei gongan baowei gongzuo qingkuang yu jinhou renwu" (Situation and Future Tasks of Public Security and Protection Work in the Northeast). *Gongan baowei gongzuo,* No. 17, February 15, 1950, pp. 2–17.

"Xin xingshi xia de jingji baowei gongzuo: zai di jiu ci quanguo gongan huiyi shang de fayan" (Economic Protection Work in New Circumstances: Speech at the 9th National Public Security Conference). *Jingji baowei gongzuo,* No. 23, February 15, 1959, pp. 8–14.

"Zai di qi ci quanguo tielu gongan baowei gongzuo huiyi shang de baogao" (Report to the 7th National Conference on Railroad Public Security and Protection Work) [March 18, 1955]. Draft text containing passages subsequently redacted from the report as ratified by the conference on April 9, 1955. Photocopy preserved in an archive of compilers of official history of public security on North China railroads after 1945. Purchased by the author in a Beijing flea market.

"Zai di yi ci quanguo caizheng maoyi baowei gongzuo huiyi shang de zongjie" (Summary at the End of the 1st National Conference on Protection Work in Finance and Trade). *Gongan jianshe,* No. 166, July 6, 1956, pp. 4–12.

"Zai dongbei zhengzhi jingji baowei chuzhang yewu gongzuo huiyi shang de baogao" (Report to Vocational Work Meeting of Political and Economic Protection Office Chiefs from the Northeast). *Gongan baowei gongzuo,* No. 19, September 15, 1950, pp. 18–28.

"Zai Sichuan, Yunnan, Guizhou sansheng gongan gongzuo zuotanhui shang de zonghe fayan" (Comprehensive Statement at Informal Meeting on Public Security Work in Sichuan, Yunnan, and Guizhou). *Gongan jianshe,* No. 260, July 1, 1958, pp. 6–16.

Wang Lin. "Zai huiyi shang de zongjie baogao" (Summing Up Report at the Conference). *Renmin gongan zengkan,* No. 20, December 25, 1950, pp. 23–36.

Wang Zhao. "Zai di yi ci gongan xuexiao jiaoyu gongzuo huiyi shang de zongjie" (Concluding Summary at the 1st National Conference on Educational Work in Public Security Schools). *Gongan jianshe,* No. 194, July 15, 1957, pp. 11–15.

Wang Zhongfang. *Lianyu (Purgatory).* Beijing: Qunzhong chubanshe, 2004.

Wang Zhongxing and Liu Liqin. *Di er yezhanjun – Liu Bocheng huixia de 10 ge jun 247 wei jiangjun (The 2nd Field Army – The 10 Corps and 247 Generals Under Liu Bocheng's Command).* Beijing: Guofang daxue chubanshe, 1996.

Wasserstrom, Jeffrey N., and Elizabeth J. Perry, eds., *Popular Protest & Political Culture in Modern China,* 2nd ed. Boulder, CO: Westview, 1994.

Wei Dianjiu. "Huimou mimi judian" (A Safe House Remembered). Zhonggong Liaoning sheng lao ganbu ju, http://www.lnlgb.gov.cn/lgb/website/informationShow.jsp?id=402880e425667d7001256d454be600b4&type=8a8080e911585fa80111159354f940007. Accessed February 2, 2012.

Wen Minsheng. "Dali jiaqiang yinbi douzheng zhong de zhencha gongzuo" (Strongly Reinforce Operational Work on the Covert Front). *Gongan jianshe*, No. 113, January 10, 1955, pp. 4–8.

Wu Tong. "Zai di liu ci quanguo gongan huiyi shang de fayan" (Statement at the 6th National Public Security Conference). *Gongan jianshe*, No. 102, October 12, 1954, pp. 14–17.

Xi Zhongxun. "Wei jiaqiang renmin de gongan gongzuo er douzheng" (Fight to Strengthen the People's Public Security Work). *Gongan baowei gongzuo*, No. 18, June 1, 1950, pp. 62–72.

"Xiang qu tepaiyuan, xiang zhian baowei weiyuanhui zhuren ji cheng, zhen paichusuo ganbu chuanda di liu ci quanguo gongan huiyi jueyi de baogao tigang" (Outline of Report Transmitting the Resolution of the 6th National Public Security Conference to District Specially Appointed Officers, Heads of Township Public Order Committees, and Officers in Urban and Market Town Police Stations). *Gongan shouce*, No. 26, September 3, 1954, pp. 3–31.

Xiang Yang. Work diary [June 25, 1967–August 29, 1968], kept by a young member of the staff of the Chinese Academy of Agricultural Sciences. Purchased by the author in a Beijing flea market.

"Xiangxiang shixian dang'anhua" (Each and Every Township Its Own Archive). *Renmin gongan*, No. 50, October 5, 1958, pp. 16–17.

Xibei ganxian gongchengju gonganchu. "Guanyu modi gongzuo qingkuang de baogao" (Situation Assessment Work Report). *Tielu gongan tongxun*, No. 13, December 8, 1952, pp. 17–19.

Xie Fuzhi. "Xuexi jiefangjun dalian guoying benling" (Learn from the Liberation Army and Train Hard to Perfect Your Skills). *Renmin gongan*, No. 184, October 15, 1964, pp. 2–3.

"Xiemi shimi shijian buduan fasheng" (Constant Leaks and Loss of Secrets). *Gongan gongzuo jianbao*, No. 18, March 1, 1960, pp. 11–13.

Xikang sheng gonganting. "Guanyu guanche di liu ci quanguo gongan huiyi jueyi jiaqiang jingji baowei gongzuo de jihua" (Plan for the Implementation of the Resolution of the 6th National Public Security Conference and Strengthening Economic Protection Work). *Gongan jianshe*, No. 111, December 20, 1954, pp. 6–8.

"Xi'nan ge shengshi zhengbao bumen diaocha yanjiu gongzuo de jidian jingyan" (Some Experiences Gained from Investigation and Research Work by Political Protection Departments in Southwest China). *Gongan jianshe*, No. 113, January 10, 1955, pp. 19–20.

"Xinde fangeming dou shi shenme ren?" (Who Are the New Counterrevolutionaries?). *Gongan gongzuo jianbao*, No. 93, January 27, 1960, pp. 7–10.

Xiu Lairong. *Chen Long zhuan* (*Biography of Chen Long*). Beijing: Qunzhong chubanshe, 1995.

"Xizang jingguan gaodeng zhuanke xuexiao jiben qingkuang" (Basic Introduction to the Tibet Police College). Tibet Police College, http://www.tpa.net.cn/show_gk.asp?id=5. Accessed February 2, 2012.

Xu Jianguo. "Zhengdun duiwu gaijin lingdao tigao zuzhi zhandouli" (Rectify Our Contingents, Improve Leadership, and Raise the Combat Power of Our Organization). *Tianjin gongan*, Vol. 1, No. 2, August 15, 1950, pp. 9–14.

Xue Guozheng and Jing Yongsheng. *Fangjian baomi gongzuo jianghua* (*Lectures on Antiespionage and Secrecy Work*). Beijing: Guofang daxue chubanshe, 1987.

Xuexi Mao zhuxi zhexue zhuzuo de fudao baogao (*Lectures to Guide the Study of Chairman Mao's Philosophical Works*). Nanjing: Nanjing junqu zhengzhibu, 1965.

Yan Dingchu. "Zai di yi ci quanguo caizheng maoyi baowei gongzuo huiyi shang de baogao" (Report to the 1st National Conference on Protection Work in Finance and Trade). *Gongan jianshe*, No. 166, July 6, 1956, pp. 13–23.

Yan Youmin. *Gongan zhanxian wushi nian: yi wei fubuzhang de zishu* (*Fifty Years on the Public Security Front: A Vice-Minister's Own Account*). Beijing: Qunzhong chubanshe, 2004.

Yang Qiqing. "Guanyu Anhui sheng dangqian gongan gongzuo de jige wenti xiang bu dangzu de baogao" (Report to the Ministry Party Group on Some Matters Concerning Public Security Work in Anhui Province at Present). *Gongan jianshe*, No. 259, July 1, 1958, pp. 2–8.

"Zhuan'an xiaozu zemyang jinxing gongzuo" (How Case Groups Carry Out Their Work). *Gongan jianshe*, No. 147, December 20, 1955, pp. 17–23.

Ye Jianying. "Zai di shiliu ci quanguo gongan huiyi shang de jianghua" (Speech at the 16th National Public Security Conference) [afternoon of May 5, 1973]. Handwritten fourteen-page transcript from an archive of Nankou Railroad Junction Police Station. Purchased by the author in a Beijing flea market.

Ye Song. "Zai di liu ci quanguo gongan huiyi shang de fayan" (Statement at the 6th National Public Security Conference). *Gongan jianshe*, No. 102, October 12, 1954, pp. 21–23.

Yi Bei. *Keyi baolie keyi wenrou: sifang yuedu nü jiandie* (*Fierce* and *Gentle: A Confidential Reading of the Female Spy*). Guilin: Guangxi shifan daxue chubanshe, 2011.

Yi chu junguan xiaozu 12 hao an zhuan'anzu, "Guanyu chongxin shencha di 12 hao an gongzuo baogao" (Report on the Reexamination of Case No. 12) [November 30, 1968]. Photocopy of a twelve-page report (stamped "Secret") preserved in an archive of compilers of official history of public security on North China railroads after 1945. Purchased by the author in a Beijing flea market.

"Yike yongyuan buhui yunluo de jiangxing – Zhang Minghe" (Zhang Minghe – A Never-Setting Star of a General). Xy-yanxin's blog, March 24, 2010, http://blog.sina.com.cn/s/blog_606dd3950100hsjb.html. Accessed December 13, 2011.

"1964 nian gongan gongzuo yaodian" (Main Points of Public Security Work in 1964). *Gongan jianshe*, No. 562, April 24, 1964, pp. 1–9.

"1949 nian xiabannian tehu guanli gongzuo zongjie" (Summary of Special Household Management Work in the Second Half of 1949). *Tianjin gongan*, Vol. 1, No. 4, September 30, 1950, pp. 12–15.

1956–2006 Qunzhong chubanshe chengli 50 zhounian (*1956–2006: Fifty Years of the Masses Publishing House*). Beijing: Qunzhong chubanshe, 2006.

1955 Renmin shouce (1955 People's Handbook). Tianjin: Dagongbao she, 1955.

"Yindu tewu jiajin zai Xizang diqu de huodong" (Indian *Tewu* Intensify Activities in Tibetan Region). *Gongan qingbao*, No. 35, April 11, 1960, p. 3.

"Yinian lai fandong dangtuante dengji gongzuo zongjie" (Summary of a Year's Registration of Reactionary Party and Organization Members and *Tewu*). *Renmin gongan zengkan*, No. 7, May 25, 1950, pp. 24–31.

"Yinian lai tehu guanli gongzuo de shouhuo ji jingyan jiaoxun" (Gains, Experiences, and Lessons Learned from a Year of Special Household Management). *Tianjin gongan*, Vol. 1, No. 4, September 30, 1950, pp. 15–17.

Ying Ruocheng and Claire Conceison. *Voices Carry: Behind Bars and Backstage during China's Cultural Revolution*. Lanham, MD: Rowman & Littlefield, 2009.

Yingkou shi gonganju. "Yingkou shi qi ba yue kaizhan gongchang qiye teqing gongzuo zongjie" (Summary of Work at Developing Agents in Factories and Enterprises in Yingkou Municipality during July and August). *Gongan baowei gongzuo*, No. 20, November 25, 1950, pp. 41–49.

Yu Jianping et al., eds. *Jianguo yilai fazhi jianshe jishi (Record of Events in Legal System Building since the Founding of the Nation)*. Shijiazhuang: Hebei renmin chubanshe, 1986.

Yu Maochun. *OSS in China: Prelude to Cold War*. New Haven, CT: Yale University Press, 1996.

Zhang Minghe. "Zai kuoda juwu huiyi de baogao" (Report to an Enlarged Bureau Affairs Meeting). *Renmin gongan zengkan*, No. 9, June 25, 1950, pp. 1–11.

Zhang Youyu. "Zai huiyi shang de jianghua" (Speech at the Conference). *Renmin gongan zengkan*, No. 20, December 25, 1950, pp. 12–16.

Zhang Yulin. "Yige xiang de gongan dang'an gongzuo" (A Township's Public Security Archive Work). *Renmin gongan*, No. 45, July 1, 1958, pp. 16–17.

Zhang Zhaojin and Ding Zhaojia. "Guanyu yuan 811 chang jianchang chuqi bufen qingkuang de huiyi" (Recalling the Early Years of Factory 811). Feiyang junshi blog, August 8, 2007, http://www.fyjs.cn/ bbs/read.php?tid=1050200. Accessed December 13, 2011.

Zhao Derun. "Jianli shiyong teqing yao shenzhong kaocha" (Careful Observation and Study Should Precede the Recruitment and Utilization of Agents). *Gongan shouce*, No. 21, May 10, 1954, pp. 27–28.

Zhao Jialiang and Zhang Xiaoji. *Banjie mubei xia de wangshi: Gao Gang zai Beijing (The Past Beneath a Broken Tombstone: Gao Gang in Beijing)*. Hong Kong: Dafeng chubanshe, 2008.

"Zhengzhou gonganchu pohuo wei 'Yu-E suijingqu dihou gongzuo weiyuanhui zanbian di yi lu di yi zongdui' an" (Zhengzhou Public Security Office Cracks Case of Puppet Henan-Hubei Regional Pacification and Enemy Rear Work Committee Temporary 1st Route 1st Column). *Tielu gongan tongxun*, No. 4, February 10, 1951, pp. 7–8.

Zhonggong Nanjing shiwei bangongting mishushi. "Guanyu jiaotong, shoufa gongzuo zhong liangge juti wenti de tongzhi" (Notification Concerning Two Concrete Problems in Communication and Dispatch Work) [December 22, 1954]. Original two-page document from the archive of a PLA Navy Cadre School in Nanjing. Purchased in a Nanjing flea market.

Zhonggong Nanjing shiwei baomi weiyuanhui. "Guanyu XXX XXX yanzhong xielu dang he guojia jimi shoudao kaichu dangji tuanji chufen bing song fayuan yifa chengchu de tongbao" (General Circular on XXX and XXX Being Expelled from the Party and League and Sent to the Court for Punishment According to Law for Having Seriously Leaked Party and State Secrets) [December 6, 1954]. Original three-page document from the archive of a PLA Navy Cadre School in Nanjing. Purchased in a Nanjing flea market.

Zhonggong zhongyang wenxian yanjiushi, ed. *Deng Xiaoping nianpu 1904–1974 (Deng Xiaoping Chronicle 1904–1974)*. 3 vols. Beijing: Zhongyang wenxian chubanshe, 2009.

ed. *Zhou Enlai nianpu 1949–1976 (Chronicle of the Life of Zhou Enlai 1949–1976)*. 3 vols. Beijing: Zhongyang wenxian chubanshe, 1997.

Zhonggong zhongyang wenxian yanjiushi and Zhongyang dang'anguan, eds. *Jianguo yilai Liu Shaoqi wengao (Liu Shaoqi's Manuscripts Since the Founding of the Nation)*. 7 vols. Beijing: Zhongyang wenxian chubanshe, 2005–8.

eds. *Jianguo yilai Zhou Enlai wengao (Zhou Enlai's Manuscripts Since the Founding of the Nation)*. 3 vols. Beijing: Zhongyang wenxian chubanshe, 2008.

Zhonggong zhongyang xuanchuanbu bangongting, ed. *Dang de xuanchuan gongzuo wenjian xuanbian (Selected Documents on the Party's Propaganda Work)*. 4 vols. Beijing: Zhonggong zhongyang danxiao chubanshe, 1994.

Zhonggong zhongyang zhengce yanjiushi, ed. *Zhengce huibian (Collected Policies)*. Beijing: Zhonggong zhongyang Huabeiju, 1949.

Zhonggong zhongyang zuzhibu bangongting, ed. *Zuzhi gongzuo wenjian xuanbian 1949 nian 10 yue–1952 nian (Selected Organization Work Documents: October 1949–1952)*. Beijing, 1980.

ed. *Zuzhi gongzuo wenjian xuanbian 1953 nian–1954 nian (Selected Organization Work Documents: 1953–1954)*. Beijing, 1980.

ed. *Zuzhi gongzuo wenjian xuanbian 1963 nian (Selected Organization Work Documents: 1963)*. Beijing, 1980.

Zhongguo gongchandang lun guoji xingshi he shehuizhuyi guojia duiwai zhengce (The Chinese Communist Party on the International Situation and the Foreign Policy of Socialist States) Beijing: Renmin chubanshe, 1964.

Zhongguo renmin gongan shigao (Draft History of the Chinese People's Public Security). Beijing: Jingguan jiaoyu chubanshe, 1997.

Zhongguo renmin jiefangjun baomi weiyuanhui bangongshi, ed. *Baomi gongzuo wenjian huibian (Collected Documents on Secrecy Work)*. Beijing, 1987.

Zhongguo renmin jiefangjun Beijing tielu fenju gongan fenchu junguanzu. "Guanyu ermu jianshe gongzuo de shixing yijian" (Tentative Views on How to Develop Eyes and Ears) [February 26, 1973]. Original five-page document from the archive of the Nankou Train Depot Police Station. Purchased by the author in a Beijing flea market.

Zhongguo renmin jiefangjun Beijing weishuqu qingcha diwei dang'an xiaozu, ed. *Fei Beiping juntong tewu ziliao (Material on Bandit Military Statistics Bureau Tewu in Beiping)*. 3 vols. Beijing, 1969.

ed. *Fei Beiping zhongtong tewu ziliao (Material on Bandit Central Statistics Bureau Tewu in Beiping)*. 3 vols. Beijing, 1969.

Zhongguo renmin jiefangjun ganbu lülishu (*Chinese People's Liberation Army Officer Curriculum Vitae Form*). [Beijing]: Zhongyang renmin zhengfu renmin geming junshi weiyuanhui zongganbubu, 1953.

Zhongguo renmin jiefangjun zong zhengzhibu baoweibu, ed. *Sufan yundong wenjian xuanbian* (*Selected Documents from the Campaign to Eliminate Counterrevolutionaries*). Beijing, 1959.

Zhonghua renmin gongheguo falü guifanxing jieshi jicheng (*Collected Normative Interpretations of Laws and Regulations of the People's Republic of China*). Changchun: Jilin renmin chubanshe, 1994.

Zhonghua renmin gongheguo neiwubu, ed. *Renminglu* (*List of Appointments*). Beijing, 1964.

Zhongyang gonganbu. "Guanyu daibu ji yushen gongzuo de zanxing tiaoli" (Arrest and Preliminary Hearing Work Temporary Statutes) [August 14, 1954]. Original thirty-four-page document (including numerous appendixes and a CMPS preamble) as issued by the secretariat of the CMPS General Office. Purchased by the author in a Beijing flea market.

"Guanyu jiaqiang yaohai bumen huwei de zhishi" (Instructions on Reinforcing the Safeguarding of Crucial Assets). *Tielu gongan tongxun*, No. 4, Feburary 10, 1951, p. 6.

"Guanyu quanguo youdian xitong qingli yaohai renyuan de qingkuang tongbao" (Situation General Circular on the Weeding Out of Critically Positioned Persons in the National Post and Telecommunications Sector) [1954]. *Gongan jianshe hedingben*, pp. 25–31.

"Guanyu zai shaoshu minzu diqu guanche di liu ci quanguo gongan huiyi jueyi de zhishi" (Instructions on the Implementation of the Resolution of the 6th National Public Security Conference in National Minority Areas). *Gongan jianshe*, No. 97, September 18, 1954, pp. 1–7.

"Liuyue zhi jiuyuefen gongzuo buzhi baogao" (Work Deployment Report for the Months of June through September). *Tielu gongan tongxun*, No. 11, August 12, 1952, pp. 1–3.

"1958 nian quanguo gongan gongzuo jihua yaodian" (Key Points of Plan for Public Security Work in 1958). *Gongan jianshe*, No. 212, January 13, 1958, pp. 2–7.

Zhongyang gonganbu and Dizhibu. "Guanyu zai dizhi xitong jixu guanche qingli duiwu gongzuo de zhishi" (Instructions on Continuing Purification of Workforce in Geological Sector). *Gongan jianshe*, No. 103, October 15, 1954, pp. 9–12.

Zhongyang gonganbu erju. "Jiguan fangdie baomi gongzuo tongze (caoan)" (General Rules for Counterespionage and Confidentiality Work in State Organs [Draft]). *Tielu gongan tongxun*, No. 3, December 15, 1950, pp. 6–8.

Zhongyang gonganbu jiaotong baoweiju. "Guanyu hangyun gongan baowei gongzuo xiang Zhongyang gonganbu he Zhongyang jiaotongbu dangzu de baogao" (Report to the Central Ministry of Public Security and the Party Group of the Ministry of Communications Concerning Public Security and Protection Work in the Shipping Sector). *Gongan jianshe*, No. 202, October 17, 1957, pp. 10–16.

Zhongyang gonganbu shijiuju. "Dangqian yushen gongzuo de qingkuang he jin-hou renwu" (On Present Preliminary Hearing Work and Future Tasks). *Gongan jianshe*, No. 227, April 1, 1958, pp. 2–11.

Zhongyang gonganbu yiju. "Guanyu jixiang jiguan fangdie baomi zhidu de gui-ding" (On Some Regulations Governing Counterespionage and Confidentiality Routines in State Organs). *Tielu gongan tongxun*, No. 3, December 15, 1950, pp. 8–10.

Zhongyang gonganbu zhengzhibu. "Guanyu gongan bumen mouxie reyuan zhong weifa luanji he wu zuzhi wu jilü qingkuang de tongbao" (General Cir-cular on the Situation in Public Security Departments with Respect to Certain People Violating the Law and Discipline and Flouting Organization and Dis-cipline). *Gongan jianshe*, No. 214, January 31, 1958, pp. 17–19.

"Guanyu tuihua bianzhi fenzi XXX suo fan cuowu de tongbao" (General Cir-cular on the Errors Committed by the Degenerate Element XXX). *Gongan jianshe*, No. 216, February 21, 1958, pp. 13–15.

Zhongyang guanyu chuli Neimeng wenti de youguan wenjian he zhongyang fuze tongzhi jianghua huibian (*Center's Decision on Resolving Matters in Inner Mongolia and Collected Central Leaders' Speeches*). 2 vols. Huhehot: Huhehaote geming zaofan lianluo zongbu, 1967.

Zhongyang renmin zhengfu renshibu, ed. *Zhongyang renmin zhengfu renminglu* (*List of Appointments by the Central People's Government*). Beijing, 1952.

Zhongyang renmin zhengfu renminglu (*List of Appointments by the Central People's Government*). Beijing, 1954.

Zhongyang renmin zhengfu zhengwuyuan. "Guanyu zai guojia caizheng jingji bumen zhong jianli baowei gongzuo de jueding (Decision to Launch Protection Work in State Financial and Economic Departments)." *Tielu gongan tongxun*, No. 3, December 15, 1950, p. 1.

Zhou Xing. "Zai di liu ci quanguo gongan huiyi shang de fayan" (Statement at the 6th National Public Security Conference). *Gongan jianshe*, No. 97, September 18, 1954, pp. 15–17.

"Zai quanguo xingshi zhencha gongzuo huiyi zongjie" (Summary at National Conference on Criminal Surveillance Work). *Gongan jianshe*, No. 130, June 18, 1955, pp. 1–19.

"Zhou zongli jiejian di shiwu ci quanguo gongan gongzuo [*sic*] huiyi quanti tongzhi de jianghua" (Premier Zhou's Address to All Comrades Attending the 15th National Public Security Conference) [5.30–7.30 pm, February 8, 1971]. Handwritten twenty-one-page transcript from the archive of the Tianjin Precision Casting Factory. Purchased by the author in a Beijing flea market.

Zhu Chunlin, ed. *Lishi shunjian I* (*Moments in History I*). Beijing: Qunzhong chubanshe, 1999.

Zhu Zhencai. *Jianguo chuqi Beijing fan jiandie daan jishi* (*True Record of Big Counterespionage Cases in Beijing Shortly After Liberation*). Beijing: Zhong-guo shehui kexue chubanshe, 2006.

Zuojia wenzhai (*Writer's Digest*). Beijing: Chinese Writer's Federation.

Index